Winning Revolutions

**Recent Titles in
Psychology, Religion, and Spirituality**
J. Harold Ellens, Series Editor

The Serpent and the Dove: Celibacy in Literature and Life
A.W. Richard Sipe

Radical Grace: How Belief in a Benevolent God Benefits Our Health
J. Harold Ellens

Understanding Religious Experiences: What the Bible Says about Spirituality
J. Harold Ellens

Miracles: God, Science, and Psychology in the Paranormal, 3 volumes
J. Harold Ellens

Speaking of Death: America's New Sense of Mortality
Michael K. Bartalos, editor

The Invisible Church: Finding Spirituality Where You Are
J. Pittman McGehee and Damon Thomas

The Spirituality of Sex
J. Harold Ellens

The Healing Power of Spirituality: How Faith Helps Humans Thrive, 3 volumes
J. Harold Ellens, editor

Families of the Bible: A New Perspective
Kamila Blessing

Explaining Evil, 3 volumes
J. Harold Ellens, editor

Cruel God, Kind God: How Images of God Shape Belief, Attitude, and Outlook
Zenon Lotufo, Jr.

100 Years of Happiness: Insights and Findings from the Experts
Nathan Carlin and Donald Capps

WINNING REVOLUTIONS

The Psychosocial Dynamics of Revolts for Freedom, Fairness, and Rights

**Volume I
Religious Revolts**

J. Harold Ellens, Editor

Psychology, Religion, and Spirituality
J. Harold Ellens, Series Editor

AN IMPRINT OF ABC-CLIO, LLC
Santa Barbara, California • Denver, Colorado • Oxford, England

Copyright 2014 by J. Harold Ellens

All rights reserved. No part of this publication may be reproduced, stored in a retrieval system, or transmitted, in any form or by any means, electronic, mechanical, photocopying, recording, or otherwise, except for the inclusion of brief quotations in a review, without prior permission in writing from the publisher.

Library of Congress Cataloging-in-Publication Data

Winning revolutions : the psychosocial dynamics of revolts for freedom, fairness, and rights / J. Harold Ellens, editor.
    volumes cm. —(Psychology, religion, and spirituality)
  Includes bibliographical references and index.
  ISBN 978-1-4408-0372-7 (hardback) — ISBN 978-1-4408-0373-4 (ebook)
1. Revolutions—Social aspects.   2. Revolutions—Religious aspects.
3. Liberty—History.   4. Equality—History.   I. Ellens, J. Harold, 1932–
   HM876.W56   2013
   303.6′4—dc23   2013009298

ISBN: 978-1-4408-0372-7
EISBN: 978-1-4408-0373-4

18 17 16 15 14   1 2 3 4 5

This book is also available on the World Wide Web as an eBook.
Visit www.abc-clio.com for details.

Praeger
An Imprint of ABC-CLIO, LLC

ABC-CLIO, LLC
130 Cremona Drive, P.O. Box 1911
Santa Barbara, California 93116-1911

This book is printed on acid-free paper ∞
Manufactured in the United States of America

"We Never Know"

We never know the baggage people carry,
The tragedies their eyes have seen
The loved ones they have lost,
Who will live now only in their memories;
The challenges they came across,
The battles they have won
The battles they have lost
The love they've felt for others
Or the hatred for themselves
We just never know.

Summit Dempster
Grade 7

Contents

Series Editor's Foreword		ix
Introduction by J. Harold Ellens		xiii
Chapter 1	*Behind the Sun:* A Dramatic Study on the Roots of Revolution *Patricia Nobre da Silva*	1
Chapter 2	A Model for Understanding the Psychology of Revolts and Revolutions *Steven A. Rogers and Hector F. De Los Santos*	15
Chapter 3	The Driving Forces in the Jewish Revolt of 66–73 CE *John T. Greene*	35
Chapter 4	The Dynamics and Dénouement of the Bar Kochba Revolt of 132–135 CE *John T. Greene*	53
Chapter 5	Imagine This: Jesus and the Kingdom of God *Gregory C. Jenks*	91
Chapter 6	Jewish Followers of Jesus and the Bar Kokhba Revolt: Reexamining the Christian Sources *Isaac W. Oliver*	109
Chapter 7	Jewish Apocalyptic Expectations During and After the Revolts against Rome *Isaac W. Oliver*	129

Chapter 8	The Pauline Revolution: Religion That Changed the World *J. Harold Ellens*	139
Chapter 9	The Protestant Reformation: A Failed Revolution *Raymond J. Lawrence*	147
Chapter 10	A Forgiveness Minirevolution: Reviewing a Historical and Scientific Movement *Everett L. Worthington Jr., Caroline Lavelock, Daryl R. Van Tongeren, Jeni L. Burnette, and Kayla Jordan*	163
Chapter 11	Revolution, the Sacred, and the Secular *Richard Fenn*	183
Chapter 12	Freud on Religion: Force of Oppression and Source of Resilience *Cassandra M. Klyman*	205
Chapter 13	Fundamentalist Revolutionary Ideology and Its Consequences *J. Harold Ellens*	221
Chapter 14	Fundamentalism in the Methodist Church, 1890–1930: Did the Failed Revolution Ultimately Succeed? *Jack T. Hanford*	253
Chapter 15	Doug Hall on the Death of the Imperial Church *J. Harold Ellens*	271
Chapter 16	Malcolm X and American Self-Understanding: On the Legacy of Islamic Leadership *Joseph M. Kramp*	289
Chapter 17	The Religious Ideology of Reform in Iran *Avideh Mayville*	301

Conclusion by J. Harold Ellens 317

Index 319

About the Series Editor and Advisors 329

About the Editor and Contributors 333

Series Editor's Foreword

J. Harold Ellens

The books in this series are written for the general reader, the local library, and the undergraduate university student. They are also of significant interest to informed professional persons, particularly in fields corollary to their primary interest. The volumes in this series have great value for the academic disciplines, informed lay readership, and public policy. Our series on *Psychology, Religion, and Spirituality* has gained extensive international attention and positive reader-response, prompted by the large number of notable publications in the series. *The Destructive Power of Religion: Violence in Judaism, Christianity and Islam* (4 vols.) appeared in 2004. Thereafter appeared approximately 50 volumes including *Where God and Science Meet, How Brain and Evolutionary Studies Alter Our Understanding of Religion* (3 vols., 2006) *Miracles: God, Science, and Psychology in the Paranormal* (3 vols., 2008), *Explaining Evil* (3 vols., 2011), *Understanding Religious Experience, What the Bible Says about Spirituality* (2008); *Speaking of Death, America's New Sense of Mortality* (2009), and numerous others.

These works and their authors represent a broad international spectrum of scholars. Most of them are noted for their scientific contributions over the last four decades. They are specialists in the fields of religion, psychology, sociology, biology, chemistry, public policy, military expertise, and numerous ancillary fields such as neurology and brain function. Many of them have spent their professional lives studying such specific aspects of their fields as the works and models of Freud or Jung, personality theory and character development, biology and neurology of the brain, the interface of biochemistry and psychological states, politics and economics in social process, and the like. These scholars have frequently been cited as reaching the top of their fields and being honored with singularly notable awards for their publications. In *Explaining Evil*, Dan Merkur has chapters in volume 2 and volume 3. The latter, *The Doubling of Conscience in Groups* recently won the William Alanson White Institute, Psychoanalytic Perspectives on Prejudice, First Annual Paper Prize. We congratulate him again for this special honor.

This series editor has spent his professional lifetime focused specifically upon research into the dynamics of religion, politics, and economics in social turbulence. This present work on *Winning Revolutions: The Psychosocial Dynamics of Revolts for Freedom, Fairness, and Rights* provides a careful analysis of some of the most shaping facets of the human struggle with the hopes and fears of the apparently inevitably turbulent nature of human existence. A large assembly of internationally notable scholars have joined me in preparing this comprehensive 3-volume work on the psychology of religious, political, and economic revolutions during the last 6000 years.

These three volumes, *Winning Revolutions: The Dynamics of Successful Revolts for Freedom, Fairness, and Rights*, are focused on specific revolutions, historical situations, government actions, religious dynamics, and economic forces that have driven major social disruptions and cultural changes throughout history. The primary goal at play here is to recognize and understand what motives and objectives empower people over the long run to sacrifice short-term life and comfort for ideologies and end goals sought in revolts. Contributors have examined the thinking that both led up to revolutions and sustained them through to victory or drove them to failure.

How did leaders of those ultimately victorious ones come to be the leaders, what motivated them, and how did they translate that dedication to enflame, inspire, and draw significant dedication from the masses? Did the figureheads and frontline leaders tightly plan their battles, both literal and psychological, or were they experts at adapting to developments so as to make them work for the cause? How did they use their minds to change their world and history?

In these volumes we have endeavored to explain the very thoughts that changed, and are still changing, our world in the name of freedom, fairness, and rights. This is a look at revolutions across time, cultural historical situations, systems of government, and religious establishments, setting forth the factors that fuel, drive, play into, and motivate people to revolution instead of societal evolution. What works and why? What fails? Why do they fail?

Revolution, as addressed in this set of volumes, is defined as a systemic interruption of the cultural, political, and economic evolution of a society by forces driven by conscious and intentional objectives for radically changing the *status quo* and producing a new mode for operating that society. These volumes attempt to understand and explicate what those driving forces were in a variety of historic cases from pre-history 4000 BCE, ancient Rome in 131 BCE, to the 21st-century Arab Spring. These forces are assessed in terms of historical, psychological, spiritual, socio-political, and economic dynamics. The language we use, the images we conjure, and the goals we set are capable of inducing surprisingly revolutionary change in our modes of daily life and our hopes for a usable future.

Introduction

J. Harold Ellens

Few factors are as characteristic of religions throughout history as their tendency to incite revolutionary violence. This is particularly true of the religions of the Western world, the Abrahamic faith communities, which are all accurately described as action religions. The authenticity of that contention is amply illustrated by Judaism, Christianity, and Islam throughout their histories. Nevertheless, although the Eastern religions tend to be more passive, interiorizing within the individual, the histories of Jainism, Hinduism, Sihkism, and the like are also fraught with the frequent rise of radical groups that have revolted against traditional norms and perpetrated violent rebellions.

As in all communities with dearly held and hotly defended dogmas, ethical codes, sacred scriptures, and modes of worship, challenges to traditions are usually felt to be life and death issues. Indeed, such cherished values and behaviors are embraced as defining the community's and individual's identity, and perhaps eternal security. Such precious "communal jewels" are never taken lightly by the community because of the deep character-forming and life-shaping import of spiritual and religious values.

In this volume, eighteen scholars have joined to describe the ways and reasons cherished spiritual values that form the drivers of religious behavior readily become the forces moving humans to revolution and destructive mayhem. Patricia Nobre de Silva dramatically illustrates how the language we employ reflects our spiritual character and sets patterns that are not to be challenged or modified with impunity. Unconsciously it forms our individual and communal natures and modes of relating, idealizing, and setting the boundaries for how much we can tolerate ambiguity in our spiritual sense of ourselves. Rogers and De Los Santos pick up that thread and explicate the psychodynamic powers inherent in human personality that move us from the sense of spiritual danger to revolutionary defensive-aggressive behavior.

This volume illustrates in detail the large number and variety of historic explosions of violent revolt that have been caused and empowered by religious motives. These range from ancient warfare, to the bloody Protestant–Catholic battles of the Reformation era, to modern-day ecclesiastical fights and heresy trials. Not all of these revolutions have been physically violent, but ideological revolutions that have changed or destroyed communities, religions, or seriously distorted historic faith-traditions are psychologically and spiritually violent even when no red blood is shed. Violation of the spirit is as real a violence and a revolution as the physical violence of brawls and warfare. Which, for example, is more comprehensively destructive in the chronic conflict in Northern Ireland? Is it the actual blood that is shed, or the horrid hatreds and denigration of spirit that are inflicted generation after generation upon the children of that lovely country?

The pain and spiritual perplexity produced by religious revolts probably do as much damage to the character and style, tone of life and tranquility of spirit, creative energy and confident productivity in a human social culture as do physical violence and overt warfare. It is our concern in this volume to offer examples that ferret out the causes and consequences of that reality and offer humans a readable religious self-critique.

CHAPTER 1

BEHIND THE SUN: A DRAMATIC STUDY ON THE ROOTS OF REVOLUTION

Patricia Nobre da Silva

INTRODUCTION

Revolutions are a thing of the heart. They hatch in the depth-psychology of the human person. Much later, if at all, they become a matter of the head, of thought, or an action plan. A startling film has recently awakened us to the unexpected awareness that the unconscious sources of revolution are always with and within us. They are inherent to the structure and dynamics of human nature and society. The very things that give us comfortable structure, security, and direction in our communal life are the forces that make us vulnerable to or capable of revolution.

Behind the Sun is a Brazilian film by Walter Salles. It is a work of the highest caliber of human social analysis and commentary and describes human existence as a revolutionary metaphor. Human life is mainly about growth and development, both of which imply inevitable change. Change brings loss of the past and the sense of loss inherent in the threat of the unknown of the future. This inevitable loss brings grief and pain. We naturally resist this progress into grief and pain. Humans try to protect ourselves against it by establishing an ordered and regulated society in which values, goals, and methods are standardized. The language for describing these security-affording aspects of society takes on a stereotypical pattern in which our values, goals, and methods are enshrined. In this process alternative ways of thinking about life are subtly closed out. The consequence is that community formation inherently violates the core needs of individual humans for free thought and action, independence, and creativity of all kinds. As that process drives the central forces of human nature "underground," it induces a repressed gestation that can turn those core needs into forces of resistance and revolution in people who are restive about the constraints of tradition.

The cornerstone of the film is its quest to unravel the threads of discourse that weave a cloak concealing the impact our social context has on persons. The film is designed to reveal the way human discourse shapes the subjective self-perception we acquire in living life in society. It undertakes the arduous, frustrating task of critical analysis of that discourse. *Behind the Sun* reverberates with the echo of our defining words, the *Logos*, that runs through the constructions of society, the language of the cocreators of community, the shared communications of the participants of social discourse, and our multiple social creations.

Behind the Sun is the cry of the mad prophet who expresses the inconvenient, subversive complaints that the revolutionary thinker may raise against society. The film presents this revolutionary dynamic in a metaphoric narrative of the insulting harangues that the authorities dump on prisoners incarcerated and handcuffed in the Tagore prison. These authorities and the prisoners are the residents and cocreators of the society expressed in *Behind the Sun*. Salles offers this narrative picture as a metaphor of human society in general, in which the creators and enforcers of social tradition tend the general population that may or may not like the values imposed by tradition, though they contribute to the creation of their closed society by their compliance or resistance.

EXPOSITION

This chapter raises these issues through reflective dialogue between differing ideas and concepts that when taken seriously produce a vertigo of doubt about the ethical legitimacy of human discourse. Such discourse is defined as any reflections or verbal and nonverbal expressions, together with their social context. The key issues are the production, constructions, perceptions, and beliefs that are reproduced or shaped by speech. These are all taken as instances of the expressed power that is involved in and shapes human society and destiny.

Far from offering any kind of intellectual chimera or modern panacea, it is the purpose of this chapter to simply raise honest doubt about the ethics of standard social discourse, in terms of its constructive and destructive impact on human life and destiny. Salles's film urges the notion that standard social discourse, which produces secure society, inherently creates the conditions for revolution, which must manifest themselves as the community matures.

Behind the Sun raises issues about the power in the discourse that shapes human personality, literally producing the subjects or characters that inhabit the social process. What is it about a society's discourse that, by the production of knowledge, actually develops both the individual characters and their society? The knowledge exchange in social discourse forms the arcs and rings that intricately forge the individual and society, either entangling or freeing them.

The film suggests that the power of the implied ideals, expressed in the ordinary sociocultural knowledge exchange from generation to generation, forms and sustains the shackles in society that bind us to traditional social conformity. This is evident, for example, in the power postures assumed for marriage, employment contracts and relationships, professional roles, regulations of law, and obligations to institutions. These rubrics of discourse determine language, shape persons and their understanding, and impact society.

It is important to understand and clarify the epistemological foundations of social discourse for persons and society. In the maze that constitutes the film, the roles of animals and humans are confused in their relationships to each other. Both animals and humans are submerged in the film's alienating treadmill of constant labor that is spinning and spinning at an accelerating rate. It is a dizzying cycle. The order—the authority—is governed and maintained at all costs by tradition, imposed by the authoritative traditional discourse.

Order is maintained, grounded in tradition, by the authority of the structural customs and their specific thought patterns. These are legitimized by the higher power of a social aura that transcends each person. In *Behind the Sun* the characters fall into a confused distancing of the social self, motivated to social conformity, from the person's primal being itself, which probes for individuation and freedom. Each person is submerged in the depths of the dialectic of this inevitably conflictual and unresolvable tension. The inner world of each person is set over-against the outer world of the community, creating a universe of paradoxes.

This paradoxical universe produces a hierarchical system, a pragmatic *modus vivendi*, in which persons are artifacts. The main focus of this chapter is the revolutionary nature of the person who is affected by the social discourse, formed, shaped, and validated by individuals of the past, living or dead, who are not part of the current interaction of the present social reality. This inherited social structure is nearly impervious to change and drains the present living bodies and souls of their creative energy and imagination. Thus the current inhabitants of a society become incarnations of the given standards. They become, in turn, the main discursive coproducers and maintainers: the new creators of the authoritative social system in each unfolding new generation.

Why do we perpetuate this constraining, "imprisoning" system? No one knows. We only know that it must be so! This is the way we have always done it.

While the fulfillment of the action ordered by our "communal-speak" violates "me and the other" in the drama of raw life, the thoughtless action perpetrated from generation to generation reinforces the discursive "truth." It must be the unquestioned authoritative speech, fundamentalism, a producer of absolute truth, made absolute by the emblem of the sacred, the divine *mysterium tremendum* that is the voice of "the way we always do it."

The constant "prophetic harangue" in *Behind the Sun* urges that dedication to the social order requires sacrifice. Humans must conform, body and soul. The film depicts people as caught in the last gasps of "life and death," begging for a little more of the same life ordeal. Social rituals, terminated only by the pain of death, drowning reason, limit the possibility of a real meeting of the self with the other. The discursive tradition supported and perpetrated by the citizens of *Behind the Sun* raises the issue of the basic legality of the system. Revolutions are made of the subversive discourse produced in lives that are taxed by the authority and power of the unchallenged social order. This rebellion against the system is often silenced by violence.

Freedom of relationships, love, and life itself is subjugated to the rule of tradition, until the exhaustion of death. The traditional logic urges the idea that there is nothing beyond conformity, compliance with tradition, or the law. Any subversive idea about trying to get away from this condition leads to summary social excommunication: shunning or worse. Revolution is the resort to rejection of the system and hence of the honored memory of the past and action taken to move outside the tradition and its constraints.

THE STORY

Behind the Sun is about Pacu. His narrative is the counter-story in the film. It is a fairy tale or mythic fable treated as though it happened historically. It relates to and sounds like reality. The story narrated by Pacu wears the mantle of *Alethia* (truth). It reveals something unnameable, unrepresentable, and revolutionary in Pacu's society. This mythical story is about the essence of universal and inviolable principles inherent in our humanness. The story opens the viewer to the authentic inner core of human personhood. The qualities of freedom, independence, and creativity found there are ahistorical and timeless. They are the aspects of the human condition that are not subject to imprisonment in the determinism of a specific social tradition in a historical time and place. This awareness is Pacu's revolutionary idea and his revelation.

In Pacu's speech the social system's depersonalization of the core nature of authentic persons is revealed. Pacu is an only child with no name, no identity. He is referred to as "the echo of a Child." However, he is a revolutionary herald who denounces that verdict placed on him. He launches two brothers,

Ignatius and Tonho, who are even more subversive and disruptive to the traditional social fabric than Pacu himself. In one scene Pacu is caught up in trying to balance himself between the old tradition and his new revolutionary ideas. He is aware of and embraces the risk of death and of losing his revolutionary vision in the "dreams of a lost soul."

The reality and myth in his vision mingle, like an emulsified mixture. Pacu speaks of Tonho, who is imprisoned and facing an irrevocable sentence of death. Tonho is the undead dead. The narrative speaks to those who are simply part of the social system, who have to do their daily work to succeed and thus survive at any cost. They are the pragmatic and utilitarian traditionalists. They are another kind of undead dead, locked into the social patterns. In the story line they are bound in servitude to the survival of a large royal estate. They are sustained by sacrificing their lives for the sake of the estate's name and place in the social order. When Tonho dares to dream, he is able to flee. He escapes metaphorically under the wings of Pacu.

Without this myth, with its creativity and dream, life becomes unbearable in the face of the irrational rationality that holds the traditional social structure in place. The irony and tragedy of that enigma lie in the fact that "the jailer is always making his or her own prison." Tradition derives from a kind of automatic trance, Salles claims. It is a macabre dance of ghouls, impenetrable, preserved, and perpetuated generation after generation, demanding compliance for the sake of "honor." Pacu and Salles think it a kind of madness.

The supreme sacrifice of revolution is always the poured out blood. Pacu takes on the role of the sacrificial messianic martyr. To subvert the order, he offers his soul. He breaks with tradition and honor and gulps the fresh air of real vitality. While the land drinks innocent blood, Tonho escapes the "safety" of his cage, seeking the infinite potential of human freedom, away from imprisoning tradition.

Pacu sees himself as "a shirt in the wind." Is this the voice of a mad prophet, introducing the social importance of thought, exposing the powers of convention that constrain the implicit and explicit relationships of humankind? For Walter Salles, speech reveals that faithful subjects of the system find tradition a sanctuary, as it is for Tevya in *The Fiddler on the Roof*. However, Salles believes it is exactly this facilitator of community entrenchment that exposes the necrosis latent in all community traditions. The word, the Logos, becomes incarnate, and hence imprisoned, by our communal security needs, in our language, our social discourse, and hence that which is unique to creative human nature and destiny is set aside.

Hence, *Behind the Sun* creates the image of human community as a climate of discontent. Its spirit, values, and goals are filled with tensions that are resolved only by what Thomas Jefferson described as "the spilling of patriot blood," the burnt offerings of human sacrifice. This is the Platonic dichotomy between the transcendent ideal on the one hand and the pragmatic social imperative on the other. Exactly this impasse seems now to prevail in American politics, in which the government expands to intricate control of social norms and functions, but is incapable of accomplishing any constructive action for the commonweal: massive and detailed constraint on all citizens and stalled government action to rid the body politic of its dysfunctional members or aspects. Not surprisingly, one hears again from public media commentators echoes of Jefferson about the blood of patriots in our streets if things do not change.

Salles's film takes place in an early twentieth-century rural backland. The narrative unfolds as Pacu's stream of consciousness. He envisions metaphorically that "The brook dried up. Humanity seemed like disembodied souls." On the face of the earth two traditionally rural families maintain their estates by the *Lex Talionis*. This regimented tooth and claw rivalry is an inherited state: "This is the way it always was." The knowledge of that law of the jungle is the living tradition. It is adhered to as a sacred commandment. Maintaining it is seen by both adversarial families as a necessary commitment to their ancestors. The societies are honor bound, and this preserves their sense of continuity with their past and the platform for their future. So the rural estates hold in their wombs the dead souls of the living dead. The implied, but unspoken questions, are: "Is the system capable of growth or change? Is revolution possible and necessary?" These are exactly the questions Americans and the whole world seem to face today.

Based on the literary work of Ismail Kadare, *Behind the Sun* the novel chronicles the events in the Albanian Kanuma, purportedly the code name for the forces that regulate violent crime in that country. This gives a sense of anguished finitude and the seal of death to the dialectical tensions between humans facing the inevitable conflicts. In the film the dialectical conflict revolves around the lives of the two families intertwined over initiatives about control of land. In the past this control forged the esteemed name and glory of their large estates.

Progressively the families became overwhelmed by their preoccupation with honor and the family name. The traditional language for the individual was, "You are brief," and for the family, "You are eternal." This language expressed the paternal law that legitimized the ethics of the preservation of these large estates. It symbolized the maintenance of the society's forces of self-preservation. Tonho is the firstborn of one of the families and is assigned the arduous task of avenging the death of his brother, Ignatius, killed by Fabiano Ferreira, the firstborn of the other family. This a compulsory retaliation driven by no pragmatic need except maintenance of the social tradition.

THE MEANING IN THIS METAPHOR

In *Behind the Sun* life is metaphorically like living in the gears of a big wheel that rotates constantly, driven by forces beyond human control. Like dumb animals, humans continue in the routine movement. This paternal structural reality embraces husbands, wives, and children. They are all living out the inevitability of the traditions, breathing in their own sweat and breathing out their own blood. They are connected only to their work in perpetuating the routines, a posture inherently at odds with their own existence.

We are reminded here of Hannah Arendt's *The Human Condition* and her three defining human activities: labor, work, and action. A brilliant philosopher of the twentieth century, she makes a further distinction: "*Work* is considered here as the 'activity that corresponds to the biological process of the human body, whose spontaneous growth, metabolism, and eventual decline are linked to vital needs for the work produced to feed the process of life. . . . *Labor* is life itself'" (Arendt 2010).

Arendt further states that *work* is the production of individual human existence, which is not inherent in the life cycle of the species, and whose demise is not compensated for by that cycle. *Action* is activity exerted directly between humans for achieving a shared goal.

Walter Salles moves around in the two-family environment, entering the rooms of their houses with his cameras and challenging the zeal of their entrenched traditional discourse. On the wall of the two houses are macabre altars commemorating the dead and jaunty photographs of the volunteers who gave their lives to maintain the power system. The Tower of Babel erected in the land demarcated with blood is the monument dedicated in honor of a name, a name that transcends Pacu's own. Salles, in his work as skilled craftsman, carves universal features of humans applicable to any society. The emotions manifested in the skillful camera shots help us penetrate the window of the soul of each character. We look, we see, we understand. The vision is the look of death by ambush.

THEOLOGY: HUMAN OR DIVINE REVELATION?

Is humankind an image and likeness of God, or is God an image and likeness of people? "God is the name the humans give everything that touches them in an unconditional and final way. That is the name of what is absolute, being above all values, not determined by historical or social conditioning. So there are many initiatives by God and humans that are to be desired. Because there are many high quality human creations of the absolute, unconditional and the a-historical" (Tillich 2007).

Behind the Sun raises the point that theology, the study of things having to do with God, has always acted to legitimize societal norms and reinforce the imprisoning capacity of tradition. It has more to do than any other force with the certification of tradition and so with the constraints on human creativity, freedom, and independence. It is therefore responsible in part for those who decide to sacrifice their lives for the social system and for "the women of the world mourning their dead." This is inevitably a repressed but gestating force for revolution. Thus religion also becomes inversely responsible for those who give their lives to the revolutionary vision of freedom and independence. These two contradictory aspects of religious motivation seem particularly well illustrated today by the confusion in Muslim world terrorism and in the "Arab Spring," in both of which traditional religious structures are giving rise to revolutionary innovations, and these innovations in turn are pressing for a return to an authentic form of religious traditionalism.

Fustel de Coulanges, in *Old Town*, intimates that revolutionary thinking was necessary to develop civilization's innovative creativity. A revolutionary thought in ancient times set in motion the founding of cities and the change in lifestyles they required. People who wanted more than primitive rural existence heroically forged the new way of being in the world so as to create a better future for their children. Family values, set in a new context, then gave birth to the duties and obligations of their progeny for keeping the new system operational and safe. Thus the initial creativity of the new model initiated a new cycle of constraint and tradition. Coulange's model is ancient Rome, moving from creative initiative to established society, and on to the safety-oriented constraints of law, regulation, and confining traditions.

Every culture develops a method to face the inevitable ossification of its own lively creativity. This generates an increase in the helplessness and hopelessness of the common life, making a new revolution urgently necessary but increasingly feared. The revolution is then warded off by the stereotyping of refined manners, imposition of formalized routines, and pressures of shame and guilt to compel uniformity of thought, language, and values. Salles's point is that this self-deception is present in everyday life in the construction of the real and explicit, as opposed to the revolutionary veiled truths of philosophy and art, an indispensable resource of a society's self-critique.

A society's security lies first of all in the way it verbally images, that is, languages things, and secondarily in the way it graphically images things. So language moves a society toward preservation of its conservative security needs. Graphic imaging often challenges the way things are traditionally languaged and urges revolutionary alternatives. Sigmund Freud saw this as a perpetual source of tension and the inevitable sense of helpless hopelessness of civilized human communities.

Hannah Arendt was quite sure that this perceived helplessness is considerably more dangerous than the unorganized impotence of those who are controlled, for example, by a dictator. Tension and helpless hopelessness in a society threaten to devastate the world as we know it—a world that everywhere seems to have come to an end—before beginning a new emerging order that has had time to establish itself. Societies need and fear revolutionary thinking and action, but the dynamics of revolution are inherent in the very nature of all human community, latent in the core tension between needs for security and stability, on the one hand, and for creative new vitality, on the other.

What is surprising from the perspective of the camera angles in *Behind the Sun* is the tension between darkness and light, beautifully expressed in the scene in which Tonho walks through the night with a weak, sputtering candle, to the shrine for his brother Ignatius. Metaphorically, Pacu and Tonho walk blindly in the darkening twilight of a society that dares not remit their sentences and restore their lives, while it also hesitates to execute them. The ambivalence of the society and the intensity of their desire to resist that society are reflected in the bloody retaliatory quality of their death sentences. The word has been given, the Logos has been incarnated for the society, and cannot be altered.

Arendt (2010) quoted Augustine in her comment that every end in history necessarily contains a new beginning. This new beginning is the promise, the only "message," that the end can produce. That new beginning marks the potential dimension of human freedom. *Initium ut homo esset creatus est*—"so that there was a beginning, man was created," said Augustine (City of God, Book 12, ch. 20). This beginning is guaranteed by each new birth, is in fact inherent in every human. "I tell you the truth, unless a grain of wheat falls to the ground and dies it remains alone. But if it dies, it produces many seeds" St. John, ch. 12, vs 24, trans. NIV). Pacu's vision will in the end be irrepressible. Life always bears the seeds of revolution.

THE CONCEPT OF LIFE AS REVOLUTION IN *BEHIND THE SUN*

The questions in theology, philosophy, sociology, cosmology, art, ethics, bioethics, and the empirical sciences all give rise to the revolutionary potential in all social and scientific quests and communities. Woven through them all, driving each of them, is the question about the nature of life in time and space. Societies and systems move toward the formulation of universals. Life is formed of the particulars in each person's situation, need, and desire. Each concept emerges from one or more points of view, each representative of an aspect of a resurgent human experience. Thus are the threads formed that weave the complex and dynamic existential mesh of communal life, from general to particular and from the particular to the general. Thus is formed the tangle of paradoxes, summaries of grand and simple events in the world of paradoxes.

Each sociohistorical community conceives its life according to its communal interests, values, beliefs, worldviews, and behaviors. *Behind the Sun* is about listening first and foremost to the variety of dissonances this process creates, rather than to the harmonies it seeks. The refined artist hears the cry of the world of the disparate voice within the harmonic line of social orthodoxy. Metaphorically Pacu and Tonho live out the life of this inevitability and pay the price of heroic revolution. There is no judgment here about whether the revolutionary spirit and action are right or wrong, moral or immoral, necessary or destructive. There is only the ordeal of the existential inevitability of revolution in the essence of human existence.

Life in *Behind the Sun* goes back to the Greek tragedies, the lyrical Greek of Homer, the absolute immanence of this ordeal in life. The authoritative command of the living word is subversive to routinized life in the temporal world. It is the story of the entrenched past always threatening to devour the children of the present by repressing their creativity, so as to ensure that in their future they do not unseat the authority of tradition. This sets the stage for the tragic fate of the Greek hero, who must lose himself in conformity or in revolution. In either case he is consigned to the loneliness of which Georg Lukács (2009) speaks in declaring that the tragedy of history is always the failure of trust.

Behind the Sun describes, in poetic story, the state as a god on the throne of tyranny, traveling the roads of indifference, holding in his right hand the banner of repression and retaliation. But as in Zeus's world order, the unpredictability, the inconvenient, the inherently revolutionary escapes the authoritative control. The nameless boy, Pacu the Contrary, must be taken account of. He is the potential for creative change and freedom. He plumbs the human process for those dynamics of our depth-psychology that unite us more than divide us in our individual quests for freedom and creativity. His quest leads him symbolically to find the forbidden love, Clara, with whom he consummates the impermissible, revolutionary acts of love. In one fell swoop the entire issue of society's quest for conformity and security, in the tension with its inherent dynamics of resistance, creativity, and revolution, is caught up in the exotic, erotic paradox of the consummation of forbidden love: the violation of the lawful by the revolutionary acts of the creative and loving unlawful. This act of love is the devotion to a new ideal that revolutionizes the social order for better or for worse, an ideal that is inherent to human existence.

Columns creak, temples are overthrown, sacred cows are slaughtered, the unpredictable happens. Mummified gods are thrown to the ground by the explosive discourse of apparently new truths. In *Behind the Sun* the failure of the gods is pervasively evident in the chaos of destruction lying raw and uncovered upon the face of the earth. In the chaos Tonho redeems himself as he champions the quest for the illumining knowledge that drives humans to our ethereal reach beyond our grasp.

CONCLUSION

In *Behind the Sun* life is lived under the weight of an authoritative discourse that dictates a MODUS VIVENDI. The society that owns that discourse is unaware of the destructive forces inherent in the potentially alienating structures of thought that move toward corrosive power, in the admirable human quest for a safe and secure society. Is this about legislation and popular opinion that promotes wiretapping and gun control to protect us against the alien, while slowly eroding citizen freedom and creativity? Eventually and inevitably this trajectory of social conformity and control leads to blood in the streets. Revolution is inherent in the healthy human heart.

Behind the Sun depicts the human condition darkly. Is this the nature and the fate of contemporary men and women? In the most tranquil of all communities, the irrepressible forces of curiosity flip the coin of social order, revealing the nakedness of life, demonstrating the normally unrepresented aspects of our humanness that are not represented in our societal condition. What that is common to our contemporary world can be learned from *Behind the Sun*? What are the bars of the cages that bind us? What are the kinds of materials we have used to forge our chains of discourse? Who forged these? What does this insight contribute to these volumes about winning revolution?

Are these legitimate or useful questions? Are we the watchmen of our own prisons? Does *Behind the Sun* reveal what is common and familiar, though hidden under the robes of the agreed-upon speech of our Western society? What images echo from our pulpits? What structures of thought are we purveying? Backed with which flags? What interests, and whose? How many necessary creative ideas have been covered with the mantle of "undisputed fact," made absolute, divine, legitimized, and legalized by generations and attributed to time immemorial? How many of these supposed truths, concepts, and ideologies are circulating in our social codes and clothing? How many creative and thoughtful souls have been allowed to die and be forgotten? How many mutilated utopias, shattered dreams, imaginative minds, empathetic hearts, and vigorous bodies have been buried in the epilogue of the authoritarian power of our communal speech?

Wire to wire, wall to wall, *Behind the Sun* breaks the mosaic of *apparent* realities, revealing hidden realities, forgotten by the subject of history, exiled from the core of existence, and close to extinction. The film exposes the great contemporary anguish, the guilty, misty gray of the blinded views that struggle between the ideal and mere trivializing ideologies. What is the game of our discourse? Is it the one we intended to play?

Salles is sure that the Logos breeds revolution. That is, the words of social discourse, incarnated in a culture, stereotype and repress freedom of thought, independent values, and creative action. This limitation of possible or permissible new ways of thinking inherently breeds resistance. Eventually a society must provide a channel for this resistance to develop creative new possibilities for that community, or the inherent fact becomes the inevitable fact that the pressure will grow until explosion.

The rise of al Qaeda over the last couple of decades is a classic example. Osama bin Laden and his extended family were esteemed citizens of Saudi Arabia. However, that restrictive society was characterized by three constraints on individual thought that were offensive to bin Laden. First, the country was too ethically and culturally liberal in its financially motivated political and economic enmeshment with the Western world, particularly the United States. Second, the form of Islam promoted by that liberally disposed government did not meet the conservative religious standards of bin Laden. This was probably because he saw its religious disposition as reinforcing the politico-economic liberalism, and not because bin Laden was actually a conservative or devoted Muslim. Third, bin Laden's leadership in promoting a way of thinking that constituted an alternative to that championed by the government was not accepted by either the Saudi government or people.

This ferment in the Saudi community, induced by bin Laden's resistance to the prescribed policy and social discourse, resulted in bin Laden's expulsion from Saudi society. The revolution then broke out on a broader scale in international Islam. Had the Saudi government been less prescriptive and less proscriptive in what it allowed in its national discourse, and had it provided more room for pluralism, the dialogue could have continued within that community and need not have broken out in the form of armed revolution throughout Islam.

What one is permitted to say limits what it is possible to think and to conceptualize and translate into language. What one is permitted to translate into new language for a society becomes the source of growth in an open society and the aegis of revolution in a closed society. Perhaps Salles is correct in *Behind the Sun* in his claim that the incarnated Logos always inherently has the potential for inciting revolution, either because it forms a fundamentalist orthodoxy that is resistive of growth and change, or because it resists such fundamentalism and entrenched dogma. Salles suggests that the Western world, particularly, should listen and take heed. Constraints on constitutionally guaranteed individual and institutional freedom will eventually and inevitably bring about blood in our streets. Revolution is an inherent drive that functions chronically just below the surface of our placid social realities.

REFERENCES

Arendt, Hannah. (2010). *The Human Condition*. Rio de Janeiro: Forensic University.
Becker, Ernest. (2007). *The Denial of Death: A Psychological Approach of Human Finitude*. Rio de Janeiro: Record.
Bultmann, Rudolf. (2005). *Jesus Christ and Mythology*. New York: New Century.
Campbell, Joseph. (2003). *The Masks of God: Primitive Mythology*. London: Pallas Athena.
Champlin, R. N. (2007). *Encyclopedia of Bible, Theology and Philosophy*. New York: CPAD.
Coulanges, de Fustel. (1966). *The Ancient City*. New York: Edameris.
Gouvéa, Ricardo Q. (2006). *The Perverted Mercy—An Anti-Fundamentalist Manifesto in the Name of a Theology of Transformation*. New York: Graph Press.
Josephus Flavius. (2001). *History of the Hebrews: Complete Works*. Rio de Janeiro: CPAD.
Kierkegaard, Soren. (2007). *The Concept of Anxiety*. New York: Hemus.
Lacan, Jacques. (1998). *Writings*. Rio de Janeiro: Zahar.
Lacan, Jacques. (2008). *The Seminar: Book Eleven, Four Fundamental Concepts of Psychoanalysis*. Rio de Janeiro: Zahar.
Lowy, Michael. (2000). *The War of the Gods: Religion and Politics in Latin America*. Rio de Janeiro: Voices.
Lukács, Georg. (2009). *The Theory of the Novel: A Historico-philosophical Essay on the Ways of the Great Epic*. New York: Two Cities, 34 Ed.
Nietzsche, Friedrich Wilhelm. (1988). *The Curse of the Antichrist Christianity*. Rio de Janeiro: Integral.
Nietzsche, Friedrich Wilhelm. (2010). *Twilight of the Idols*. London: L & PM.
Otto, Rudolf. (1985). *The Sacred*. New York: Methodist Press.
Ramachandra, Vinoth. (2000). *The Failure of the Gods: Modern Idolatry and Christian Mission*. New York: ABU.
Sartre, Jean Paul. (2009). *Being and Nothingness: Essay Phenomenological Ontology*. Petropolis: Voices.
Scala, Angelo. (2004). *The Man and His Destiny*. Sao Paulo: Latin Publisher Network.
Sousa, Ricardo B. *The Way of the Heart: Essays on the Trinity and Christian Spirituality*. Curitiba: Meeting Publications.
Sousa, Ricardo B. (2004). *The Way of the Heart: Essays on the Trinity and Christian Spirituality*. Curitiba: Meeting Publications.
Tillich, Paul. (2007). *History of Christian Thought*. New York: Aste.

CHAPTER 2

A Model for Understanding the Psychology of Revolts and Revolutions

Steven A. Rogers and Hector F. De Los Santos

Revolutions defy most laws of society and both individual and group behavior. Newtonian principles contend that objects at rest seek to remain inert, physiological psychology attests that the human nervous system is ornately orchestrated to maintain homeostasis, and even social psychology suggests that the minds of individuals in a group oscillate until centering on conformity rather than divergence or autonomy. Revolutions, therefore, may represent an anomaly, an uncommon variation on the laws of nature and social behavior. Be they social, religious, or even individual, revolutions represent a fundamental change, modification, or departure from a prior way or state of being. This defiance of the norm may account for the mutual fascination and discomfort that revolutions often cultivate. It also fosters much of the interest in better understanding the ingredients that constitute a revolution.

Granted, any attempt to dissect revolts or revolutions into their constituent parts will fall short in scope and comprehensiveness, particularly considering their multidimensional nature, with interacting spheres of political, social, psychological, and religious influences. However, because revolts are often linked to group behavior and therefore become the purview of sociologists and political scientists, little attention or appreciation may be devoted to the sphere of psychology, to those internal, psychological dynamics occurring within those participating in revolutions. Arguably, most cultural, political, and religious revolts either commence with or necessitate an internal revolution within individuals. Therefore, understanding some of the elements and stages involved in internal, psychological revolution or change may illuminate some of the processes critical to social, political, and religious revolutions. What follows is an attempt to use a leading model of psychological change, the transtheoretical model, to explore the stages and processes involved in change and to harness some of these insights for application to larger revolts and revolutions, with a focus on the civil rights movement and the Protestant Reformation.

INTERNAL REVOLUTIONS: THE TRANSTHEORETICAL MODEL

Among the most empirically supported and validated models for understanding psychological change or revolution is the transtheoretical model (TTM). This model, which was advanced by Prochaska and DiClemente (1984), is an empirically derived, multistage, sequential approach for framing and identifying the processes and stages of change that occur in individuals and groups. One of the givens in this model is that change is dynamic and a process. There are occasions of instantaneous internal change, such as a religious conversion or someone electing to spontaneously quit smoking, but even in these cases, there were probably gradual and insidious processes involved in cultivating the moment of departure from homeostasis. There were likely false starts, failed attempts, and periods of mild movement that preceded the overt action of change (DiClemente 2007). In their studies of change, Goldfried and Davila (2005) found that "it is the rare situation where a single experience can bring about the needed therapeutic change. More often, a number of such experiences are needed, with each further enhancing an increasing awareness that the difficulties experienced in the past need not continue in the present" (427). Consequently, change is a process and a journey for individuals, groups, and institutions alike.

So what is this journey or process of change? According to the TTM, change unfolds in five stages. Each stage represents a distinct task that has to be accomplished for change to be initiated and consolidated, and the tasks build on each other so that the end product is a new pattern or outcome that is supported by accomplishment of the preceding tasks. In each stage, the active ingredients are distinct cognitive, behavioral, and experiential processes of change. It is these processes, focusing on how individuals experience, think, and act, that energize and drive the movement through the five stages. These processes are implemented and applied so that individuals can progress from stage to stage. Put differently, if the stages represent *when* people change, the processes entail *how* people change and *how* the stages can be accomplished (Norcross, Krebs, and Prochaska 2011).

Precontemplation

The first stage, precontemplation, is essentially status quo. The individual or institution is not particularly thinking about performing the new behavior or aware of the implications of the current or new behavior. There is no intention of change in the immediate future. This lack of interest in change may be secondary to defensiveness, a want of concern, or an absent awareness of the need for change, such as ignorance that one's diet can have deleterious physical and psychological effects. The climate may also be one in which the hope for change has been cast aside because of former failures or a lack of hope or belief in oneself. As a result, those in this stage are not likely to experience, and may even offer resistance to, change, perhaps evaluating the advantages of their problem behaviors as outweighing the disadvantages. However, as the precontemplator experiences concern, interest in change, and a vision for this change, he or she can transition to the next stage, contemplation.

Contemplation

During the contemplation stage there is an arousal of concern about the status quo and an emerging interest in a new behavior or state. The idea of change begins to take hold because of an awareness of the need for change in response to a problem or conflict, and though change is still not imminent, the resistance to change is lessened. Greater thought is given to the potential need for making the change, and there is growing confidence in one's ability to change, although no commitment to change has been made. Those in this stage typically undergo a risk/reward analysis of the current status quo and the new behavior or decision. They begin to weigh the positive and negative consequences of their behavior by considering problems, causes, and cures, but they remain trapped in ambivalence about making change. Because of this cost-benefit analysis, "individuals in the Contemplation stage are more likely to recognize the benefits of changing. However, Contemplators continue to overestimate the costs of changing and therefore are ambivalent and not ready to take action" (Prochaska et al. 2006, 1104). Put simply, they are aware of the problems related to their behaviors and think about changing, but they often evaluate the benefits of their behavior as equal to its limitations, which keeps the norm in place (Prochaska and Prochaska 1999). If this analysis tips toward a more favorable view of the desired behavior, however, it can lead to a decision to make change (DiClemente 2007).

To complete these precontemplation and contemplation tasks, Prochaska and DiClemente (1984) identified three necessary affective and cognitive processes that need to occur. First, it is important to engage in consciousness-raising for the group or individual. This involves increasing insight about the problem, its processes and consequences, and the steps necessary to support the change (Madsen 2003). Another important process in this stage is endorsing and encouraging precontemplators to engage in environmental reevaluation. This entails a cognitive and affective assessment of how the problem or status quo affects one's environment. The final process is dramatic relief, which involves experiencing and expressing emotions about the problem and its solutions. This process is critical, because strong emotional arousal, like anticipatory grieving, can incite change. It can also foster an appreciation of the direct connection between positive emotions and action toward change.

Preparation

The fostering of these three processes can facilitate transition into the next stage, preparation. In this stage individuals are increasing their commitment to change, intend to take action in a definitive time frame, and have even begun to make behavioral or mental steps toward larger, ostensible change, such as formulating a plan for change to occur. They have not yet reached effective action, but the pros of change clearly outweigh the costs, so they are preparing themselves and their social worlds for change.

To accomplish this, Prochaska and DiClemente (1984) identified the most important and productive process as self-reevaluation. During this evaluative process, preparers assess their feelings and emotions about themselves and the behavior or issue to be changed (Madsen 2003). This includes exploring their values, personal goals, and the reasons for the desired changes, all in the name of reappraising their self-image and their ability to succeed against the issue that needs to be remedied. It also involves finding self-meaning within the change, such as realizing that one's values are in conflict with certain behaviors or summoning up positive images about how one might feel if change is enacted. When this self-reevaluation has occurred, the opportunity for intentional, apparent change arises.

Action

It is in the action stage that individuals have successfully and consistently performed the desired behavior. It is here that people modify their behavior, experiences, and/or environment to overcome their particular problem (Norcross, Krebs, and Prochaska 2011). This is where the most overt behavioral change occurs, and it is this stage that requires the most time and energy. The action of change can manifest itself institutionally as an alteration in legislation, individually as liberation from a vice or the conquering of a fear, or organizationally as a new focus on emotional intelligence or the connection between employee happiness and productivity. It is in this stage that individuals have begun engaging in new behaviors, and the change plan is implemented, revised, and formulated to commence a new pattern that can remain stable over time.

The important process in the action stage is self-liberation. During this existential process, actors experience emancipation of the self by believing they can successfully change and possess the ability to choose their behavior or lives. They become aware of new alternatives, realize they can create these alternatives, and recognize that they can be effective in making success happen (Madsen 2003). This acceptance of responsibility for one's change and behavior may foster some mild anxiety, but seeing the positive consequence of change strengthens belief and self-esteem, reinforcing the commitment to change.

Maintenance

The final stage is maintenance, in which the change has already occurred for a substantial period of time and become the new normative behavior. Those in this stage have been consistently acting on a change over a period of time, so the new behavior has become habitual and integrated into their lifestyles. As a result, the goal of this stage is to sustain growth and consolidate the gains achieved in action so as to prevent relapse into old behavioral or psychological patterns. If relapse occurs, it is construed as a normal part of change and utilized as an opportunity for learning. Rarely does anyone go through a journey of change or revolution without obstacles and setbacks, so these are not depicted as a failure or inability to change. Instead, they are used to understand how to better complete each of the processes and stages. This means relapse may be part of the process of change, making it a form of successive approximation learning, wherein individuals arrive closer to the desired change by learning how to better master all of the processes (DiClemente 2007).

To progress from the action stage to the maintenance stage, it often helps if the individual engages in the humanistic process of participating in helping relationships and the behavioral processes of contingency management, counterconditioning, and stimulus control (Prochaska, Redding, and Evers 1997). The first entails relying on social support to enhance behavioral change, whereas the second means changing the contingencies or consequences that govern the behavior, preferably using rewards rather than punishment. In counterconditioning, more useful responses are substituted for certain problem behaviors, such as replacing anxiety with relaxation, so there is a change in the way individuals experience or respond to stimuli. In stimulus control, the environment is restructured by removing cues for unwanted habits or instilling prompts for desired behaviors or responses. These processes are integral to discouraging relapse and further consolidation of the change that has been achieved.

CLINICAL EXAMPLE

To cast this model in the context of an example, imagine that a husband is coming to see a psychologist about marital concerns. According to the client, most of his friends, biological family members, and even his wife's relatives are encouraging him to leave the marriage because of his wife's mistreatment. She has engaged in six extramarital affairs despite rebuffing his approaches for sex, refuses to work either outside or inside the home, leaves most of the child-rearing responsibilities to her husband, and shows dangerous unpredictability by vacillating between transitory periods of affection and long periods of criticism and threatening behavior. This includes sending him acerbic text messages throughout the day while he is working and accusing him of physical and emotional abuse, despite his passive demeanor and the suggestions from police officers that *he* could file for domestic violence in light of her physical attacks. According to the client's wife, she is not interested in remaining in the marriage or getting a divorce, nor is she willing to participate in marital therapy.

When the client first comes to psychotherapy, he is in the precontemplation stage, not particularly thinking about or interested in the relational changes suggested by his friends and family. There is no intention of change in the immediate future, predominantly because he assumes his wife's behavior is merited and because he does not believe he can find better companionship. Gradually, and owing to some of the cognitive and affective activities of the psychologist, he gains consciousness about his relational problems; engages in environmental reevaluation by examining the effects of these problems on himself and his children; and experiences emotional arousal by processing his disappointment, anger, grief, and fear. These processes foster his transition into the contemplation stage, in which he kindles concern about his marriage and home environment, as well as a nascent interest in divorce. However, the financial, emotional, and familial costs of this change are perceived to outweigh the benefits of relational reconfiguration, keeping him in ambivalence until he engages in greater self-reevaluation.

As he realistically examines his emotions and self-worth, as well as his goals for being a father and spouse, he connects more positive emotions to the possibility of a life apart from his wife and accepts that the advantages of leaving his wife eclipse the benefits of remaining in their marriage. This places him in preparation for change, and he begins to make behavioral or mental steps toward divorce. If he comes to believe he can change, recognizes his agency in creating new alternatives, and accepts the positive consequences of his ability to create a life for himself and his children after a divorce, he has achieved the self-liberation that can move him into the action stage of pursuing the divorce and new patterns of relationship with himself and others. As the new behavior persists, he should exhibit actions of maintenance aimed at consolidating his gains and preventing relapse. These will be most successful if he can accept assistance from helping relationships, including his psychologist and friends; rely on counterconditioning to change any self-defeating behaviors or thoughts, such as developing a new way of responding to texts from his ex-wife; and implement stimulus control to reward himself for self-enhancing behaviors. This entire process may take well over a year, but if engaged in, it will have resulted in a personal revolution that will probably stimulate expanding spheres of revolt within the larger areas of his life.

These same stages and processes seem to occur in most areas of change and may have direct application to larger revolts and revolutions.

APPLICATIONS OF THE TTM TO REVOLTS AND REVOLUTIONS

Relying on these stages and their corresponding processes, the TTM has been empirically supported as an effective model for understanding, explaining, and potentiating the change journey for individuals, groups, and institutions. Although the preponderance of this research has focused on individual health-related change, ranging from stopping negative behaviors (e.g., addictions, depressive symptomatology) to commencing positive habits (e.g., exercise, using sunscreen), it has recently been used to capture the dynamics of group and institutional change. This includes reflecting the stages and processes involved in the changes that occur in group therapy (Alexander et al. 2010), family service agencies (Prochaska 2000), and various aspects of the workplace, including getting physicians to recommend preventive services (Madsen 2003). The TTM has been recommended as an essential tool for business coaches to cultivate organizational change (Stober 2008), and it has been used to create a revolution in the advancement of female psychologists to offset the dearth of female scientists (Prochaska et al. 2006). Moreover, in a comprehensive review, Prochaska, Prochaska, and Levesque (2001) demonstrated how the TTM explains organizational change in areas as varied as merger/acquisition, readiness to purchase software, and preparedness for quality improvement, within settings ranging from the Veterans Administration hospital administration to university and even food brokerage employees. This review also illustrated how the TTM can be applied by leaders to reduce resistance, increase participation, reduce dropout, and increase change progress among employees and group members.

At first glance, it might be easy to protest that these types of organizational change share few commonalities with individual behavior change. However, many organizational change theories recognize that the core of group change is change in the individual member (Prochaska et al. 2001). As articulated by Stober (2008), organizational change is "made up of many, many individual change efforts by different people at different times all directed at meeting a group goal" (75). This may account for why many organizational change theories borrow from theories of individual psychotherapy. When this is paired with the empirical support for the validity of applying the TTM to group behavior, the TTM not only serves as an empirically verified model for explaining many of the dynamics involved in individual change, but also offers a useful and validated lens for understanding the stages and processes involved in larger group and social change. This suggests that it may be a useful way to understand revolts and revolutions. Perhaps this can be most clearly demonstrated by viewing two historical revolts, the civil rights movement in the United States and the Protestant Reformation, through the lens of TTM.

Civil Rights Movement

The civil rights movement in the United States was invariably subserved by many factors and represents a long journey toward change, which likely began during the inception of the African slave trade. However, one of the particular areas of change and revolt that most dramatically revolutionized the livelihood of African Americans was the repudiation of "separate, but equal," a rule instituted by the Jim Crow laws. These laws, beginning in 1890, instigated the acceptability of racial segregation and racial denigration of African Americans. The process of abrogating these laws may gain new organization and perspective when viewed against the backdrop of the TTM's stages and processes of change.

Precontemplation

Until the 1950s, the Jim Crow laws were used to perpetuate racial inferiority and served as a "new form of white domination, which insured that Blacks would remain oppressed well into the twentieth century" (Morris 1999, 517). Socially, politically, and economically, African Americans were psychologically denigrated and debilitated in the areas of voting, education, and occupation. Essentially they were oppressed to the point of inaction (McClellan 1964). Under this Jim Crow regime, African Americans were collectively suspended in a state of precontemplation, where change was not something to be grasped, nor hope entertained. "Racial realities suggested that the color line was not likely to undergo substantial change during the twentieth century" (Morris 1999, 518). In this climate, African Americans appeared unready to fight for change.

However, the catalytic processes of change necessary at this stage, namely consciousness-raising, environmental reevaluation, and dramatic relief, were occurring. Increased awareness of the issue of racial segregation was being disseminated through the spread of ideas such as, "Don't work where you can't buy." The proliferation of black protest literature began to encourage hope, just as the Garvey movement promulgated black nationalism and pride, helping to encourage black America to see itself as smart and beautiful. The National Association for the Advancement of Colored People shed light on the oppression and helped African Americans better assess the effects of the current laws. These actions and endeavors allowed for the emotional expression of previously constrained grief and anger, as well as a better understanding of how change might occur. Through consciousness-raising, environmental reevaluation, and dramatic relief, African Americans began to understand that segregation and denigration could be remedied.

Contemplation

Two events were integral to the increased arousal of concern and interest in change that characterize the contemplation stage. The first, the U.S. Supreme Court ruling in *Brown v. Board of Education* (1954), was monumental because it challenged and defeated the unconstitutional segregation of schools. There had been previous attempts to overthrow segregation in education, but this ruling severed the legal power that had enabled the segregation. This began to dismantle the grip of the Jim Crow laws, provide legal ground for continued reappraisal, and enliven African Americans with hope and confidence in their ability to enact change. In the years leading up to the *Brown* verdict, there had been recurrent though isolated acts of resistance by African Americans seeking to energize a lethargic community against segregation (Weisbrot 1990). After this verdict, however, the black community attained a new symbol of legitimacy, thereby reducing its uncertainty and the perceived costs of change.

The gruesome lynching of Emmitt Till served as a second event galvanizing the contemplation of African Americans. This lynching of a fourteen-year-old boy for whistling at a white woman, paired with the subsequent exoneration of the murderers by an all-Caucasian jury, sparked an awareness of the need for change and the value of fighting against injustice and prejudice. There was some ambivalence about this fight because of the severe backlash from Caucasians in the South and the terrible pain and even death endured by African American leaders, but many in this movement began recognizing the profound meaning in Martin Luther King Jr.'s arguments related to "why we can't wait" (King 1964).

Preparation

Throughout the late 1950s and early 1960s, black America began to quickly prepare and increase its commitment to change. The black church became a unifying and stabilizing organization for the civil rights movement, as it was "capable of generating, sustaining, and culturally energizing large volumes of protest. Its music and form of worship connected the masses to its protest tradition stemming back to the days of slavery" (Morris 1999, 523). Similarly, the sit-ins of February 1960 were small steps toward larger change, just as the yearlong bus boycott from 1955 to 1956, led by Dr. Martin Luther King Jr., imbued the black community with confidence in its own ability to effectively end the reign of the Jim Crow laws (Gordon 2000).

Forces and events like these facilitated the self-reevaluation requisite for this stage. African Americans began consolidating their values and the reasons for pursuing equality, reappraising their ability and power, and cultivating optimism about their possible lives following change. Because some of their protests were highly publicized and the sit-ins were successful in crippling unsympathetic white businesses, the assessments of African Americans clearly began favoring the value of change over its perceived costs. They were becoming prepared to commit themselves to enacting positive change.

Action

Ultimately, the tasks and processes from the previous three stages propelled the civil rights movement to success in achieving equality and freedom from the Jim Crow laws. With Martin Luther King Jr. as its charismatic and unifying leader, the black community implemented its change plan through mass nonviolent action in the form of sit-ins, freedom rides, large marches and jailings, and consistent challenges to the prevailing laws. These persistent actions demonstrated African Americans' awareness of new alternatives and their responsibility in effecting these desired outcomes. The success of these behaviors culminated in the institution of the Civil Rights Act in 1964 and the Voting Rights Act in 1965. With these two legal actions, Jim Crow's demise was completed, and the phrase "separate but equal" lost credibility and validity. A new pattern was established that would persist and remain stable. Moreover, because there were no longer any legal grounds for subjugation, self- and collective liberation of the black community had been attained, with freedom and equality in voting, education, and employment.

Maintenance

Following the implementation of the Civil Rights and Voting Rights Acts, equality became more of the habitual and normative ethos and behavior. Gone was the legal rationalization of racism and segregation that had been enforced by the Jim Crow laws, although much was required to acclimate to equality and prevent relapse. Racism and disparity in pay and educational opportunity continued as obstacles, but consolidation of the gains, counterconditioning, and contingency management were all accomplished through affirmative action in education and some business arenas. The deaths of Malcolm X and Martin Luther King Jr. were not seen as failures, but rather as incidents to galvanize change, rely on social support, and demonstrate effective stimulus control. Through implementation of these processes, civil rights became standard and expected, forming new legal, psychological, and social patterns.

As this example demonstrates, the TTM provides one way of framing and appreciating the stages and processes of change that characterized one of the monumental revolts in human history.

Protestant Reformation

The Protestant Reformation may represent a different type of revolt or revolution illustrating the TTM's utility in understanding and appreciating the dynamics involved in revolutionary change. Although the processes involved in any aspect of religion and spirituality may seem beyond reduction to psychological explanations, stage-based models have been increasingly applied to varieties of religious experience (Hay 2001), including religious conversion. As Bockian, Glenwick, and Bernstein (2005) suggest, the stages of an individual's conversion process are accurately captured and described by the TTM. This includes those in the precontemplation stage who have thought about conversion but lack intention, those in the contemplation stage who intend to convert in the near future, those in the preparation stage who have taken steps toward conversion, those in the action stage who learn new beliefs and implement new behaviors, and those in the maintenance stage who sustain conversion change. In the same way, perhaps the TTM describes the conversion of several individuals, including the formation of new religions and theologies, as well as departures from old ones. This is particularly apparent when examining the application of the TTM to the Protestant Reformation of the sixteenth century.

Precontemplation

Immediately prior to the Protestant Reformation, the primacy of authority in the Catholic faith belonged to the Catholic Church. The Church alone was God's instrument and ambassador, with the pope serving as the personal representative of Christ. It was only through membership in the Church and the discretion and intervention of Church leaders that salvation could be achieved. By the sixteenth century the Church had even expounded on the steps outlined by scripture as necessary for salvation. The first step was an act of contrition involving the confession of sin, which was to be followed by some form of sacramental penance to purify one's soul for entry into heaven. And replacement penances in the form of indulgences could be purchased from the Church, suggesting that the Church could be involved in selling salvation.

In this climate, and perhaps out of the assumed authority of the pope and Church, many believers did not experience awareness of a need for change. For those who did recognize the value of change, there was no immediate intention, perhaps because of the threat of excommunication for those who did not adhere to the primacy of the Church. The risk in suggesting or advancing change seemed to outweigh any perceived benefits of change.

Contemplation

Gradually, however, dissatisfaction with this status quo increased and interest in questioning the authority of the Church emerged. Among the events critical to elevating this awareness were the activities of Albrecht of Brandenberg and the Dominican friar Johan Tetzel. To pay the Vatican for the privilege of serving as the archbishop of two dioceses, which had been previously forbidden by the Council of Nicaea, Albrecht collected revenue from indulgences, which he suggested would not only absolve the purchaser from the need to make penance, but also forgive one's sins. In a similar maneuver, Johan Tetzel raised funding to construct St. Peter's Basilica by commissioning wholesale retailing of indulgences and allegedly suggesting that these would serve penance for sins not yet committed.

Even with the restlessness incurred by these events, many believers probably would have remained in precontemplation had they not experienced the consciousness-raising, environmental reevaluation, and dramatic relief provided by Martin Luther's *Ninety-Five Theses* in 1517. In this letter, Luther condemned the Church for commercializing repentance and suggesting that the absolution of sin could be purchased or sold. Starkly opposing the Church, Luther contended that forgiveness was a free gift from God's mercy and purchased solely through the sacrifice of Christ. Salvation and justification therefore occurred by faith alone, not through payments to the Church or obedience to the pope.

The theses that articulated this reformed theology spread throughout Germany and voiced many of the questions and concerns that believers had previously been afraid to utter. Was the pope truly infallible, or was his power determined by the authority of God? Does not scripture serve as the primary and critical source of Christian theology? Is everyone equally capable of achieving the remission of sin and guilt because it is freely given by God's mercy alone? Is it not more important to help the poor and needy than to purchase pardons? Due to Luther's writings and the perceived egregiousness of some of the activities of the Church, believers gained insight into the problem and its consequences, as well as courage to express previously contained emotions and reactions. Resistance to change decreased and a risk/reward analysis of inciting theological reform began.

Preparation

As Luther's writings became more widely disseminated, believers increased their commitment to change and even started to take steps toward larger, ostensible change. Statues and images were being torn down, and some priests, particularly those at the university in Wittenberg, began to lead services without vestments and violate the Catholic customs of communion by serving both bread and wine, rather than wine alone, to the congregation as part of the Eucharist. In 1526, the First Diet of Spyer edict allowed every German province the right to live, govern, and believe according to its own standards, which enabled princes to advance the protest for reform. Moreover, in support of the idea that all believers were priests and that the Bible superseded the authority of the Church, the New Testament was translated into the vernacular language of German. Within two months, five thousand copies had been sold, which was impressive considering that only one-third of city inhabitants and one-twentieth of rural residents could read (Hill 2006). Clearly, many believers were engaging in self-reevaluation, exploring their values and feelings about the theological issues raised by the proponents of the Reformation. The benefits of revolution were beginning to outweigh the disadvantages, believers were feeling that success was likely, and a vision of positive emotion and lifestyle was formed if change were enacted.

Action

Gradually the anchor of Reformation took hold, and theological revolution began to spread. In 1527, King Gustavus Vasa declared Lutheranism the official state religion, and in Denmark one of Luther's followers was invited to crown the king and appoint new bishops. In Switzerland, Ulrich Zwingli's protests against Church offenses, which included the use of iconic images and the practice of priests taking mistresses, led to the abolition of indulgences, pilgrimages, and confession. At Zwingli's instigation, clerical celibacy and even the Catholic mass were abolished, replaced with clerical marriage and a liturgy for communion. With the passing of the Act of Supremacy in 1534, the English Parliament challenged papal supremacy over religious matters and conferred authority over the Church of England, including its finances and appointments, on the king of England. Monasteries loyal to the pope were destroyed, and a new Church of England, the Anglican Church, was erected. The *Book of Common Prayer*, which was used in English churches, was written in English rather than the expected Latin and lacked many features of Catholicism, such as representing the Eucharist as sacrifice. There were even several martyrs for the Protestant faith, including the three hundred individuals who were executed by the queen, Mary Tudor, when they refused to renounce Protestantism.

Even within the Catholic Church there were efforts to investigate abuses and make recommendations for reform. The Council of Trent strengthened and upheld many of the theological positions of the Catholic Church, but it also resulted in some reform in the trading of indulgences and the prevention of one person serving as bishop in multiple areas (Hill 2006). As each of these changes suggests, reformation had successfully and consistently occurred. Believers had modified their behavior and environment to overcome the perceived theological problems and to promote stability in a new pattern of theology and church organization. There was self- and collective liberation, with individuals assuming responsibility for change and experiencing the positive consequences of this change.

Maintenance

As the Reformation succeeded and became the new normative theology for its followers, several events sustained this growth and consolidated the gains achieved. Among these was the signing of the Peace of Augsburg in 1555, which officially ended the religious struggles in Germany and allowed each prince to permanently select the religious affiliation of his domain. However, there is probably no better example of this maintenance than John Calvin's influence in Geneva. Under the direction of Calvin, Geneva was transformed into something akin to a Protestant theocracy (Hill 2006), where the ideologies and behaviors of the Reformation became habitual and integrated into the fabric of followers' lifestyles. Calvin instituted a new church order that not only focused on the spiritual independence of the church from state interference, but also reorganized the governance of the church. In particular, pastors in Geneva were to meet for administration and mutual encouragement and discipline. This structure served as a forerunner of Scotland's disestablishment of the Roman Church and subsequent institution of a Reformed Church that relied on a system of elders rather than bishops.

Martin Luther also founded the Geneva Academy, which spotlighted international Reformed scholarship, with a focus on the sole authority of the Bible and the sufficiency of faith alone. Because this academy was free, even to Catholics, it became a way to propagate the Protestant ideal and suggested that authority does not belong to the Church alone. In a sense, both the new church in Geneva and the academy reflect all the processes critical to this stage, including the use of social support to enhance behavioral change, the changing of consequences to reward behavior, and the instillation of prompts to promote the new theology.

This is not to suggest an absence of resistance to these maintenance behaviors. On the contrary, more than a hundred years elapsed before religious tolerance and reconciliation could exist between Catholics and Protestants.

But this resistance was used as an opportunity for learning to successively accomplish the desired theological reform. By the middle of the 1600s, the Catholic Church had lost its claim to control all religious affairs, and Christian theology had become grounded in the authority of scripture and the conviction that salvation and justification occurred by faith alone.

As with the civil rights movement, it is likely that other historical events factored into each of these stages and that some of the mentioned historical events could be placed in different stages. However, as this review intimates, the TTM may offer a viable model for capturing the stages and processes involved in the Protestant Reformation. Perhaps the TTM reflects many forms of change, individual and collective, cultural and religious.

ADVISEMENTS AND IMPLICATIONS

This use of the TTM to explicate the processes involved in religious, cultural, and political revolts is not without its liabilities and limitations. Central to these is acknowledgment that the problems that originate a majority of revolts are multidimensional and composed of various spheres, ranging from social to political and even theological. However, most of the application of the TTM has been to individual problem behaviors, such as smoking cessation, one person's religious conversion, or preparing organizations for merger or implementation of new software. Revolts might not so easily be broken into such unique and discrete areas of dissatisfaction. Rather, there are probably multiple problems involved in revolts.

This argues for some caution before unequivocally using a model for individual behavioral change to explain the multilayered and multidimensional problems that accompany revolts. Even if the TTM clearly captures the process for change in one dimension of a revolt, such as revolutionizing the theological idea of baptism, there are competing problems, environmental impingements, and system challenges that may interfere with the principles that normally dictate change in one problem area (DiClemente 2007).

Nevertheless, even if revolts and revolutions constitute multiple areas for change, this does exclude the possibility of a common and isomorphic process of change. Even individual problem behaviors have broad and multifaceted contexts, such as the social and environmental surroundings of those attempting to cease an addiction, and the TTM has been validated across these individual behaviors and larger contexts. Revolts focusing on a particular area, such as civil rights, may therefore be a macrocosm of the change that occurs in individual problem behaviors and their contexts. Moreover, accounting for these contexts is inherent to the TTM, as evident in the processes of environmental reevaluation, contingency management, and stimulus control. Because of the complexity of revolt behavior, there may be multiple areas in which the stages of change are occurring, and it may be necessary to apply the TTM to each problem area associated with the revolt, but this is not unlike using the TTM with each contextual problem to promote change in individual behavior. Put simply, the TTM may be a general model for change that characterizes both the overall nature of revolts and the multiple problem areas within the revolt that require change for the success of the larger revolt or revolution.

Another caveat is that it may be more accurate to conceptualize revolts and revolutions as unfolding in phases rather than stages. Even in the TTM, the precontemplation, contemplation, and preparation stages appear to be distinctly different from the action and maintenance stages. This suggests that any form of change may be more accurately depicted by a two-phase model (Armitage 2009), with a motivational phase summarizing all the motivation required to engage in a particular action, and a volitional phase that translates motivation into action. Such a two-phase model streamlines the process of change into a degree of intentionality and implementation of this intention, which might make the transitions between phases more clear.

However, despite the appeal of this two-phase model to parsimony and elegance, it may collapse across some of the important complexities of change that occur in revolutions. One of the advantages of the TTM is an appreciation of the nuances of change and the capacity to identify a revolution's location in the stage model, which could lead to a greater understanding of the exact processes that the revolt or revolution requires to facilitate success. If a religious group that is trying to stage a revolt is in the contemplation stage, but is misidentified as simply being somewhere in a broad motivational phase, its promoters may inadvertently focus on simply cultivating self-reevaluation within the movement. As the TTM model shows, this may unduly curb the growth of the revolt, because the group truly needs consciousness-raising or dramatic relief rather than self-reevaluation. Blurring these distinctions may lose the multifaceted evolution of a revolt and frustrate the work of those attempting to either facilitate or quell the movement.

Moreover, the TTM is a model for intentional and volitional change. Prochaska and Prochaska (1999) caution that it cannot be used to explain changes that occur outside of voluntary control, like imprisoning pedophiliacs and converting them into convicts. This change is necessarily coercive and not volitional, but instead relies on factors outside the individual to modify behavior. In the same way, the TTM is unlikely to explain forced or unintentional revolts, such as a religious movement spearheaded by one leader who demands certain rituals or ideologies that may not fit the values of individual members. Although the originators of these forms of revolt may follow the stages and processes of the TTM, the movement or revolt itself may not adhere to the principles of TTM because of the nonvolitional elements. For the TTM to match a revolution or revolt, the revolutionary movement has to be freely chosen by the constituent members. In the absence of this freedom of choice and responsibility, other processes will likely be involved and other models will probably offer a better description.

These limitations notwithstanding, the use of the TTM to understand and explain revolts and revolutions has some distinct conceptual and practical implications. Overall, it suggests that a revolt or revolution should not be expected to occur quickly or discretely. It will probably be gradual and dynamic, with some changes visible and others imperceptible. It will also most likely unfold through some distinct stages and processes, although the time in each stage can vary. This is distinctly different from an action-oriented model that only equates a revolution or revolt to overt actions, like the tearing down of statues and walls, the adoption of new legislation, or other symbols that have come to demarcate the success of a revolution. It is tempting to focus exclusively on these symbolic and important moments, but the TTM reminds us that these are only singular events in a series of events that promote and sustain the revolutionary movement.

Restriction of one's lenses to these action behaviors neglects those activities, emotions, and processes scaffolding these moments and maintaining the continued success of the movement. Moreover, using a purely action-oriented model may decrease participation and minimize the likelihood of the desired action occurring, because those who are contemplating change or at risk for recidivism will likely be overlooked, whereas a stage-based model allows for inclusivity for all individuals to participate in the revolution, even those in precontemplation and maintenance stages. By appreciating variability in levels of readiness and preparation, the TTM is facilitative rather than imposed and integrates the when, why, and how of change, thereby maximizing the impact of change (Prochaska 2000).

Adoption or application of the TTM also allows identifying where a revolutionary movement is located in the change process, including where it might be getting stuck, and implementing the most appropriate interventions to successfully accomplish that stage. According to the TTM, each stage or task has to be accomplished well enough to support action and maintenance. Otherwise, the change, be it individual behavior or a revolt, will fail and demand a recycling through the tasks. Accomplishment of each stage, though, requires completion of the motivational processes commensurate with the respective stage. This means that strategies aimed at increasing motivation for the revolt or revolution should be stage-specific and tailored to the readiness and needs of the revolution's members at each stage.

For example, if a client who is attempting to lose weight is in the preparation stage, a psychologist assisting the client will experience greater success if he or she implements cognitive or emotional therapies that focus on self-reevaluation than if he or she relies exclusively on the behavioral strategies of stimulus control or contingency management that are most effective in the maintenance stages. In the absence of this matching, there will be resistance to change because of a want of fit between change action and the movement's stage of change. Without this congruence, defensiveness, elevated stress, and delayed movement will likely emerge.

In the same way, interventions aimed at fostering a revolt or revolution should be tailored to the movement's stage of change and the needs of the individuals in the revolution. Raising consciousness, providing dramatic relief, or engaging in self-reevaluation are appropriate for earlier stages of revolt, but they may deflate, inhibit, or even reverse the progression of those revolts that are already in the action or maintenance stages. Like any type of change, revolts and revolutions will therefore be most effectively promoted if the implemented interventions are stage-matched.

As this suggests, leaders of revolts may have personally accomplished each of the stages and arrived at action and maintenance regarding the change issue in question, but it may behoove them to suspend their frustration with followers' lack of action and instead understand the tasks and processes necessary for the followers' stage, such as patiently helping them assess the costs and liabilities of change. This avoids the risk that followers will perceive the leader as attempting to impose or coerce change. Similarly, followers of revolts or revolutions may benefit from considering the stage of the leader so as to best support the leader's actions and prevent relapse. Therefore, adopting the TTM may make progression to a revolt or revolution quicker, more efficient, and less painful for those in the revolt process.

CONCLUSION

There are multiple lenses through which to view revolts and revolutions, and none alone will capture all the dynamics involved. However, an examination of the TTM's utility in describing the stages and processes involved in group change, the civil rights movement, and the Protestant Reformation suggests that this stage-based model may be a viable method for understanding revolts and revolutions. To be sure, there is room for greater empirical analysis of the TTM's application to these larger movements, but it removes revolts and revolutions from the realm of the extraordinary and suggests that they may not be significantly different from other types of change. Like a change in someone's habits or a group's approach to a problem, revolts and revolutions may be mediated through relatively ordinary change mechanisms. They may be organized into the stages of precontemplation, contemplation, preparation, action, and maintenance, with corresponding cognitive, affective, and existential processes energizing and mobilizing movement through each stage. This does not eliminate or dilute any of the impact or power of revolts and revolutions, but it may make the ingredients more accessible and malleable to those on either side of the revolutionary movement.

REFERENCES

Alexander, P. C., E. Morris, A. Tracy, and A. Frye. (2010). "Stages of Change and the Group Treatment of Batterers: A Randomized Clinical Trial." *Violence and Victims* 25: 571–87.

Armitage, C. J. (2009). "Is There Utility in the Trans-theoretical Model?" *British Journal of Health Psychology* 14: 195–210.

Babcock, J. C., B. E. Canady, A. Senior, and C. I. Eckhardt. (2005). "Applying the Trans-theoretical Model to Female and Male Perpetrators of Intimate Partner Violence: Gender Differences in Stages and Processes of Change." *Violence and Victims* 20: 235–50.

Bockian, M. J., D. S. Glenwick, and D. P. Bernstein. (2005). "The Applicability of the Stages of Change Model to Jewish Conversion." *The International Journal for the Psychology of Religion* 15: 35–50.

DiClemente, C. C. (2007). "The Trans-theoretical Model of Intentional Behavior Change." *Drugs and Alcohol Today* 7: 29–33.

Goldfried, M. R., and J. Davila. (2005). "The Role of Relationship and Technique in Therapeutic Change." *Psychotherapy: Theory, Research, Practice, Training* 42: 421–30.

Gordon, J. (2000). "The African American Male in American Life and Thought." *Annals of the American Academy of Political and Social Science* 569: 42–55.

Hall, S. (2007). "Civil Rights Activism in 1960s Virginia." *Journal of Black Studies* 38: 251–67.

Hay, D. (2001). "The Cultural Context of Stage Models of Religious Experience." *The International Journal for the Psychology of Religion* 11: 241–46.

Hill, J. (2006). *Handbook to the History of Christianity.* Grand Rapids, MI: Zondervan.

King, M. L., Jr. (1964). *Why We Can't Wait.* New York: Harper & Row.

Madsen, S. R. (2003). "A Model for Individual Change: Exploring Its Application to Human Resource Development." *Human Resource Development Review* 2: 229–51.

McClellan, G. S. (1964). *Civil Rights.* New York: H. W. Wilson.

Morris, A. D. (1999). "A Retrospective on the Civil Rights Movement: Political and Intellectual Landmarks." *Annual Review of Sociology* 25: 517–39.

Norcross, J. C., P. M. Krebs, and J. O. Prochaska. (2011). "Stages of Change." *Journal of Clinical Psychology* 67: 143–54.

Prochaska, J. M. (2000). "A Trans-theoretical Model for Assessing Organizational Change: A Study of Family Service Agencies' Movement to Time-limited Therapy." *Families in Society* 81: 76–84.

Prochaska, J. M., L. M. Mauriello, K. Sherman, L. Harlow, B. Silver, and J. Trubatch. (2006). "Assessing Readiness for Advancing Women Scientists Using the Trans-theoretical Model." *Sex Roles* 54: 869–80.

Prochaska, J. M., J. O. Prochaska, and D. A. Levesque. (2001). "A Trans-theoretical Approach to Changing Organizations." *Administration and Policy in Mental Health* 28: 247–61.

Prochaska, J. O., and C. C. DiClemente. (1984). *The Trans-theoretical Approach: Crossing the Traditional Boundaries of Therapy.* Malabar, FL: Krieger.

Prochaska, J. O., C. DiClemente, and J. Norcross. (1992). "In Search of How People Change: Applications to Addictive Behavior." *American Psychologist* 47: 1102–14.

Prochaska, J. O., and J. M. Prochaska. (1999). "Why Don't Continents Move? Why Don't People Change?" *Journal of Psychotherapy Integration* 9: 83–102.

Prochaska, J. O., C. A. Redding, and K. E. Evers. (1997). "The Trans-theoretical Model and Stages of Change." In *Health Behavior and Health Education*, edited by K. Glanz, F. M. Lewis, and B. K. Rimer, 60-84. San Francisco: Jossey-Bass.

Stober, D. R. (2008). "Making It Stick: Coaching as a Tool for Organizational Change." *Coaching: An International Journal of Theory, Research, and Practice* 1: 71–80.

Weisbrot, R. (1990). *Freedom Bound: A History of America's Civil Rights Movement.* New York: Norton.

CHAPTER 3

THE DRIVING FORCES IN THE JEWISH REVOLT OF 66–73 CE

John T. Greene

What happened to the inhabitants of Julias during the first Jewish revolt (Loftus, 1977/1978)? Did they belong to the rebels; were they to be counted among the "innovators"; or were they hellenizers, loyal to Herod Agrippa II and by extension to Roman overlordship? Bethsaida-Julias and the summit of Gamla, farther up on the Golan plateau, remained within unaided sight of each other, and stood as border cities within Agrippa's kingdom (*Jewish Wars* [JW] 4:1.1). What relationship, if any, did they have during this conflict? Aside from archaeological remains, evidence of a cultural and period connection, whatever else we know about the two locales must be gleaned from the evidence provided by the writings of Josephus Flavius (1958–1965; Whiston 1752/1999), as well as from further evidence of a material culture nature yielded by results from continued excavations, especially at et-Tell-Bethsaida (Arav and Freund 1995–2009), but also at Gamla (Gutmann 1994; Syon and Yavor 2010). Had not Josephus written about this first Jewish rebellion against Roman overlordship (66–73 CE), we would have learned about at least its aftermath from the writings of Pliny the Elder, governor of Bithynia (Rackham, Jones, and Eichholz, 1938–1962). He discusses the postwar colonization practices of the Romans in his *Natural History*, written between 77 and 79 CE (Pliny 5.69). We reference him here because his encyclopedic knowledge is personally tied to the fortunes of the imperial family that would—while two (later) Caesars, Vespasian and his son and successor, Titus, were Roman generals prosecuting the war in the Galilee(s)—change the future of the inhabitants of both Gamla and Bethsaida/Julias (Feldman 1981). Yet our major source for knowledge and development of this conflict remains the copious writings of the "historian" and apologist and contemporaneous biographer of the imperial Flavian family, the Jewish priest, scholar, and soldier, Josephus Flavius (Yosef ben Mattiyahu). His major works concerning the Jewish wars of the revolt of 66–73 CE, *Life* (V), *Jewish Wars* (JW), and *Antiquities* (A), though fraught with difficulties for the analytical scholar/(text) historian, are valuable assets in studying the progress of that revolution (Linder 1992). This chapter argues that there is evidence to suggest a plausible relationship between Bethsaida-Julias and Gamla during the first Jewish revolt. We comb Josephus's works to see if he can be of assistance in producing a clearer picture of the developments and that relationship.

One might argue that this conflict was made inevitable the moment Rome came to impose its will on the ancient Middle East in general, and over the Jews of greater Syro-Palestine in particular. Here we discuss briefly its general, then specific, causes to determine why Bethsaida and Gamla, the foci of the present study, became involved. Only then may we seek any direct connection between the two cities.

When studying the earliest roots of the eventual encounter between the Jews of ancient Syro-Palestine and the Romans (and their supporters both foreign and domestic), most begin with Gnaeus Pompeius Magnus's (i.e., Pompey's [106–48 BCE]) annexation of the small Jewish kingdom to the province of Syria after (or even ending) the bloody civil war involving John Hyrcanus II and his brother Aristobulus II (ca. 67 BCE). Few, however, begin with the reason why Pompey on behalf of Rome was in the area, or why some Jews enlisted his aid in adjudicating their civil war.

Mention the "Manilian Law," and few outside of classicists will have heard of it. Yet it was this law, offered to the Roman Assembly by Manilius and defended on the floor of the Roman Senate by the brilliant orator Marcus Tullius Cicero (1939), the then recently elected praetor for the year 66 BCE, that delivered into Pompey's hands full authority over all armies and lands then under Lucullus. Immediately thereafter, Pompey, Crassus, and Caesar led the three most powerful and successful armies of Rome. Cicero's eloquence is worth noting:

> The whole system of finance which is carried on here at Rome is inextricably bound up with the revenues of the Asiatic provinces. If these revenues are destroyed, our system of credit will crash. . . . If some lose their entire fortunes they will drag many more down with them. Save the state Prosecute with all your strength the war against Mithridates, by which the glory of the Roman name, the safety of our allies, our most valuable revenues, and the fortunes of innumerable citizens will be effectively preserved. (Cicero 1939; Durant 1944, 140)

Enter Mithridates VI (132–63 BCE), king of Pontus (now Armenia), who dreamed of crafting a Hellenistic empire in and around Asia Minor. In essence, he desired to revive and emulate the glory of the former Achaemenid (Persian) Empire. Taking the surname Eupator (the Great), he also had himself proclaimed the "New Dionysus." When he expanded his kingdom to Bithynia, he made the mistake of challenging an ally of Rome. Spurred on by both Manilius's law and the eloquent rhetoric of Cicero, Rome came to its ally's aid militarily. Thereafter, three main engagements were fought between 88 and 63 BCE. They are known as the First (88–84), Second (83–81), and Third (74–63) Mithridatic Wars. The period of the third war corresponds to that during which the Jewish civil war involving the pro-Hyrcanus II and pro-Aristobulus II factions raged. Pompey eventually replaced Lucullus, who had prosecuted the third war. It was he who finally and decisively ended the war. Thus, the outcome of the encounter between Eupator (the Great) and Magnus (the Great) settled the issue of who was the superlative! After defeating Mithridates, Pompey went on to subject almost the entire Middle East to Rome.

THE MAJOR DEVELOPMENTS IN OUTLINE

The main developments leading up to the revolt of 66 CE may be traced in outline. Those immediately relevant to the present discussion are in boldface print.

A. Pompey and Mithridates
B. Pompey and Hyrcanus II versus Aristobulus II
C. Antipater and Antigonos
D. Antony and Antipater/Herod
E. Augustus and Herod
F. Herod receives the Perea (won by the Hasmoneans after Simon [143 BCE])
G. Syria and Egypt almost given to Herod by Augustus
H. Palestine under Herod to 4 BCE
I. Developments after 4 BCE
   1. Archelaus (Judea, Samaria, Idumea)
   2. Antipas (Galilee and the Perea)
   3. Philip (Batanea, Bethsaida, Capitolias, Gerasa, Philadelphia, and Bostra)
J. The activities and subsequent banishment of Archelaus to Gaul
K. The introduction of the procuratorship and the second-class province status of Judea
L. Simultaneous developments in the Galilee, the Perea, and Batanea (significance of three separate governments)

M. Caesarea, now the capital of the procuratorship (more non-Jews than Jews lived in the cities of the coastal plain), becomes the administrative center for the likes of Felix, Festus, Pilate, and most important, Florus.
N. Florus robs the Temple, Jewish unrest responds through rebellion. The rebels acquire a majority of support; the "peaceniks" become a minority voice of persuasion.
O. Jerusalem becomes the capital of the rebellion and sends Yosef ben Mattitiyahu to "organize" the rebellion in the (two) Galilee(s).
P. The roles and importance of the cities of Sepphoris, Tiberias, Jotapata, and Bethsaida-Julias
Q. Bethsaida: location, importance (Jewish, Roman)
R. The Golan: location, importance (Jewish, Roman)
S. Roman versus Jewish engagement(s) at Julias
T. Roman versus Jewish engagement(s) at Gamla
U. Gamla/Bethsaida-Julias/Jerusalem/Masada: a perspective

To save space, when discussing below any of these issues, I refer to them by the letter used in the outline.

The First Issue: The Problem of Josephus (and His Sources) as a Research Source

Since Josephus is the author and/or compiler of our main literary source, we may approach both problems in one section. Concerning many literary-critical/text-critical problems one encounters in Josephus's accounts, there are many who have essayed competently (Smith 1971, 182, 188; Cohen 1979; Bilde 1988; Sievers and Lembi 2005; Parente and Sievers 1994; Jossa 1994; Feldman 1984; Feldman and Hata 1987). They are well-known and well-documented. Were there many other, and competing, accounts of the events he narrates, one would be tempted to relegate his works to a peripheral or secondary status. Alas, his accounts are central, but fraught with apparent contradictions. We therefore address (1) relevant Josephan texts that discuss (2) Josephus's role in the Galilee(s) during the rebellion as we focus on the Jewish war efforts at Bethsaida-Julias and at Gamla, and the relationship, if indeed any, between the two cities.

The various documentary hypotheses that attempt to secure authorship/editorship for the so-called Pentateuch all maintain that there are visible in the texts at least two accounts of many stories/episodes. One learns that there are two names for the deity of Israel: Yahweh and Elohim. There are two different stories of creation: one at Genesis 1:1-2:4a and a second at Genesis 2:4b ff. Two stories of Noah compete in terms of not only how many and which kinds of animals were brought aboard an arc, but how long the arc floated before dry land was signaled and by which kind of winged signal. Moreover, there are at least two accounts of (different) Ten Commandments that differ as to whether the name of the "mountain of the commandments" was Sinai or Horeb. It was the discovery of the Yahweh/Elohim difference in a consistent manner within literary environments that precipitated the search by critical scholars of the Old Testament/Hebrew Scriptures for this binary/bifurcation phenomenon and its meaning/significance.

O. Those who study Josephus Flavius's copious writings encounter this dual account phenomenon also. Of importance for the present topic—specifically how he came to command Jewish forces in the Galilee(s)—the account contained in the *Life* (V) and that in *Jewish Wars* (JW) do not accord well with each other. In the latter he states that he was sent to command the two Galilees (Armenti 1981) and that he was also given command of the strongest city in the region, Gamala (JW 2:568). In the former he stresses his peaceful intentions in carrying out his mission of calling for restraint (*Life* 30–53 = **V** 4–8). As with biblical dual accounts, there are those who would engineer harmony rather than acknowledge multiple accounts that seek reasons therefor. I cast my lot with the latter. The duality reveals a Josephan tendency noticed throughout his writings: a pro-Jewish stance, as well as a pro-Flavian one. For the scholar it comes down to this. Either the accounts are irreconcilable and must be studied separately for what they may still yield of importance, or because there are two, they are de facto unable to be of much use in attempting to assign specific reliable meaning to the actions in which he relates having engaged. Because of the numerous problems presented by the writings of Josephus, new translations of his work(s) are accompanied by new reconstructions of certain key events. One such event is his mission to the Galilee.

The scholarly extremes of attitudes toward this problem are exemplified by, and may be studied in the works of, Shaye J. D. Cohen (1979) and Parente and Sievers (1994). On the one hand, concerning the territory over which Josephus exercised some form of leadership, and focusing on his treatment of Gamla, for instance, Cohen concludes, "We cannot hope to recover . . . what transpired in Gamala in 66–67" (1979, 168). And again: "What actually occurred in Gamala is nearly irretrievable" (135). On the other hand, Giorgio Jossa (1994), one of the contributing scholars to the Morton Smith festschrift, in an article entitled "Josephus' Action in Galilee during the Jewish War," writes: "As it is known, Josephus gave us two versions of his mission in Galilee" (267). Jossa goes on to develop a thesis that the two accounts are not contradictory, but point to two developments growing out of the same mission. Thus he writes: "Therefore it is not true that Josephus put himself at the head of the brigands (i.e., radical revolutionaries), as Laqueur (1920, 108–16) writes, and that having broken all relations with the government in Jerusalem, he became a thorough 'rebel.' He put himself, instead, at the leadership of the

Galileans (i.e., 'innovators,' moderate revolutionaries, the defenders of culture and tradition and who feared the brigands who accepted 'protection money' from the Galileans) adopting the tactics of waiting and trying to still keep open the possibility of a mutual understanding with the Romans" (277). Wisdom and knowledge of the nature of our sources dictate, therefore, that we steer a cautious path between these two extremes of viewpoint.

When considering the connection between Bethsaida-Julias and Gamla, several preliminary issues must be addressed that serve to place these two cities in important relief for the efforts of excavators and the importance of the cities themselves in historical and geographical contexts.

One gleans from the Josephan accounts that address events leading up to the rebellion in Jerusalem that the final procurator, Gessius Florus, engaged in acts that so insulted and infuriated Jewish sensibilities that those Jewish elements who did not have to sublimate their outrage through contemporaneous "political correctness" made it known (N.). Florus, convinced of that outrage and concomitant actions toward gaining redress, contacted the Syrian legate, Cestius Gallus, who responded by beefing up the Roman presence in Jerusalem and ultimately engaging rebellious elements, which had, by this time, become well-organized. Surprisingly, after several days of fierce fighting the Romans—of all combatants—under Gallus had to withdraw, having been roundly trounced! Having been routed somewhere near the present Ben Gurion international airport, they were last seen scurrying toward present-day Tel Aviv in order to scurry further northward up the Mediterranean coast in the direction of Caesarea Maritima and beyond. Rebelling Jewish elements found it prudent to not pursue them further. One of the political results of these actions was the creation of a provisional government in the spiritual (for certainly not the political) capital of contemporaneous Jewry, Jerusalem. Disaffected Jews within the other region (formerly this had been two regions [I. 2 & 3]) revolted also, and attacked local targets known to be pro-Roman centers and potential staging areas for Roman countermilitary measures. The cities of Sepphoris and Tiberias were typical but not exclusive of such targets in the former Galilee, while Gamala was certainly indicative of the latter in Batanea.

While the provisional Jerusalem leadership consolidated its power/responsibilities there in face of this military windfall, sympathetic elements in the now directly Roman ruled areas of the former tetrarchies of Antipas and Philip (now ruled by the Roman-appointed King Herod Agrippa II) were in need of leadership and someone to coordinate their prospective and demonstrated activities from the spiritual—and now rebel—center, Jerusalem. It is at this point that Josephus becomes relevant for us. It is also at this point that he attempts to write himself in as a necessary point of confluence for all in Jewish history that preceded him, as well as that which subsequently occurred until the final punctuation mark of the writings he produced/recorded.

These developments bring us to the point of necessarily reviewing the two Josephan accounts mentioned previously and subjecting them to close scrutiny. The first account (JW 2.xx.3–5) states:

> But as to those who had pursued after Cestius when they returned back to Jerusalem ... got together in great numbers in the temple, and appointed a great many generals for the war ... John, the son of Mattathias, was made governor ... as was Josephus, the son of Mattathias, of both the Galilees. Gamala also, which was the strongest city in those parts, was put under his command.

The second (**V** 4–8) shows Josephus counseling the Jerusalem leadership against revolt almost immediately after his return from Rome. This attitude he maintains in **V** 7–8 when he writes: "So when Gessius had been beaten ... the principle men of Jerusalem ... sent me and two others of the priests ... in order to persuade the ill men there to lay down their arms" In JW Josephus has himself brandish the weapons of war; in **V** he intimates that he brandished nothing more than reason and an olive branch in the face of Galilean hotheadedness.

In either instance, Seth Schwartz, writing of the "cottage industry" of detecting Josephus's biases, dutifully reminds the researcher that whatever Josephus writes about the Galilee/Golan campaign, his major interest, and therefore the greater percentage of his writings, is devoted to accounts of Judaea. Instead of "Jewish Wars," Schwartz suggests renaming it "Judaean Wars" because of the glaring "Judahcentrism" of his works. (Schwartz in Parente and Sievers 1994, 290). "Nevertheless," he writes, "this Galilean episode is important because Josephus' reports of it mark his only major departures from his urban and Judaean biases—at least one can say that here their influence on his account is more subtle than usual" (291). Nevertheless, this leaves one who would essay to provide needed details in reconstructing this history with numerous lacunae in data.

Gamla and Bethsaida-Julias

Both Bethsaida-Julias and Gamla are mentioned in Josephus not as the foci of any of his accounts concerning them, but as incidentals on the periphery of detailed stories that throw a considerable spotlight on a specific person (himself, Vespasian, Titus, Philip son of Jacimus, etc.). The military engagement at Julias (V 72) is related in autobiographical accounts. It lacks the necessary detail germane to intentional accounts about wars, battles, and skirmishes. Gamla is mentioned by him indirectly when writing of Agrippa II's minister/procurator/officer, Philip son of Jacimus. In fact, Schwartz is unique in that he discusses the revolt at Gamla in terms of a landlord's (Herod Agrippa II's) loss of control over a section of his population. This loss he examines within what he argues are patronal networks (in Parente and Sievers 1994, 295). One of Philip's responsibilities was to recover the patron's lands and populations. Because they are more detailed, let us unpack the Gamla references first.

Gamla

Josephan references to Gamla (T.) may be divided into two groups for purposes of analysis: (1) those which, although providing information about the city, are useless in determining just how and why the revolution against King Herod Agrippa II occurred there; and (2) those which, when properly gleaned, provide a sufficient glimpse into the attitude of those who defended it against both the king's besiegers and against the legions and cohorts of Vespasian. Both literarily and archaeologically, the latter will prove more rewarding than the former.

Book IV of JW initially describes Gamla as

> situated upon a rough ridge of a high mountain, with a kind of neck in the middle: where it begins to ascend, it lengthens itself, and declines as much downward before as behind, insomuch that it is like a camel in figure from whence it is so named, although the people of the country do not pronounce it accurately. (Whiston 1752, 1999, 522)

On the one hand, Josephus focuses on Philip son of Jacimus—around whom the account concerning the introduction to Gamla is arranged—and a cavalry officer, Darius the hipparch (Master of Horse). Both, it seems, were sent at the head of about two thousand cavalry troops in Agrippa's response to the priest Eleazar ben Ananias's instigating the Jerusalem priests (some of whom hearkened to his plea!) to refuse the sacrifices of local, but Temple active, non-Jews. This is according to JW's version. V, on the other hand, has him in Jerusalem at the surrender of Herod's Jerusalem-posted troops to the rebel faction there. Philip apparently escaped (both execution and the city) and fled (in V's account) to an unnamed village near Gamla. After a brief meeting with Agrippa, Cestius, and his council, the former sent him to Gamla (which was by that time in revolt) to pacify it. Jacimus's conduct in Gamla, like his conduct in Jerusalem (two cities in revolt and dominated by revolutionaries), fell under suspicion. V claims that Philip succeeded in pacifying Gamala (V 59–60). He is at least depicted as having engaged in pacific activity there in V 183–84. JW maintains that the revolt of Gamla began on 24 Gorpiaios, which refers to either 66 or 67 CE. (Cohen 1979, 163, n. 194). If 66 is the correct year, Gamla revolted before the defeat of Cestius and two weeks after Philip departed Jerusalem (according to V). Gorpiaios 24 of the year 67 seems to be a better date, however, for it refers to the beginning of the revolt against Vespasian. When the city refused to surrender to the Roman commander, his siege of it began. Cohen admits: "No matter which account (JW or V) we follow, the actions of Philip must be understood in conjunction with the history of Gamala" (164). I would merely add that this is true even though Josephus's focus is on Philip and only incidentally on Gamla here.

In Batanea as well, as everywhere on the eastern Mediterranean littoral and adjacent lands where they lived together, there were conflicts between Jews and Jews as well as between Jews and "Greeks." These conflicts served to determine much of the course and conduct of the war wherever it was fought. Between Jews and Greeks there the conflict led ultimately to the Babylonian Jews who had settled in Ecbatana having to seek refuge in Gamla after they had been victimized by one Varus, a royal family member and pretender to Agrippa II's throne. This had occurred, no doubt, before Josephus's embassy to the Galilee(s). "Gamala and its Babylonian immigrants evinced sentiments hostile to Agrippa's lieutenant who had to be replaced" (Cohen 1979, 165).

V 114 holds that the lieutenant, Aequus Modius, besieged Gamla. The text is not clear on the chronology of the war, however. It also mentions another Josephus (Not our source! Let us refer to him as Josephus 2.) who revolted against Modius (also called Noarus) in Gamla. This reference, at V 179–87, also fails to provide a chronological context, thus leaving it possible for this revolt to have taken place before the one mentioned in V 114.

Returning to Philip, V 180–83 has Agrippa send him to Gamla and instruct him to take the emigrating Babylonian Jews who had taken refuge there from Varus's wrath and machinations back to Ecbatana and to guard the peace (Cohen 1979, 166). There are statements to the effect that after Philip's departure the men of Gamla, fighting with the Babylonians, killed relatives of Philip and of Justus of Tiberias (V 177), and that this was done when Gamla, under the leadership of Josephus 2, revolted against the king (V 185–87).

Even at feuding Gamla, it was unclear whether the *staseis*, that is, feuding parties, were the Gamlaites and the Babylonians (as mentioned in V 177) or the revolutionaries and the aristocrats of the city (as told in V 185). At any rate, the revolution at Gamla was a success. Modius (V 114) laid a seven-month siege to the city (JW 4.10). From this time (the year 67 CE) until Vespasian captured the city later that same year in November, Gamla remained in revolt (JW 4.11–53, 62–83). Thus Gamla's stripes as a revolution center kept company with those of Jotapata, Jerusalem, and Masada. Yet Cohen repeats that "we cannot hope to recover . . . what transpired in Gamla in 66-67" (1979, 135) and that "what actually occurred in Gamala is nearly irretrievable" (135).

This situation forces the researcher into a narrower trajectory of approaches to Gamla. Since the issue of just how the revolution at Gamla occurred, and specifically by whom is not immediately forthcoming, we shall resort to an "end run" and approach the city's place and importance for the overall revolt from other Josephan texts. These should prove more helpful.

Gamla

There is slowly emerging a body of critical research focusing on the numerous geographical excurses that appear in Josephus. JW's 4.2–10, concerning Gamla (R./T.), is merely one of these (Parente and Sievers 1994, 248–49). Specifically, in JW 4.2–8, Josephus provides:

> A parenthetical, integrated description of the cities of Gaulanitis. First, the general geographical situation and affiliation of Gamala, Sogane and Seleucia . . . a detailed description of the characteristic natural conditions of Gamala clinging to the camel-like mountain-top surrounded by inaccessible ravines except from the north-eastern side. (Parente and Sievers 1994, 254)

See the discussion of just what constitutes such excurses on pages 252–57 in Parente and Sievers (1994).

Josephus's description of what happened during Vespasian's two attacks within the breached walls of Gamla provides the most specific and detailed information about any aspect of Gamla's history. Yet even here an argument may be made that this is merely one of numerous places where the reader is vouchsafed another mini-biographical sketch of the soon-to-be emperor of Rome. On this very point, in fact, ample discussion of certain pro-Flavian elements in Josephus's accounts is the focus of Harold W. Attridge in "Josephus and His Works" (in Stone 1984, 185–232). The pro-Flavian elements are discussed on pages 200–203. Attridge warns, however, that the Flavians who receive more attention are the sons of Vespasian rather than the emperor himself. Returning to Vespasian, however, clustered about his figure are constellations of information about his prosecution of the battles that eventuated in the fall of Gamla. The Gamla account, remember, begins when the activities of Philip son of Jacimus are introduced. Appropriately, in JW the account of Gamla ends on a note involving him as well:

> [W]hile the Romans slew but four thousand, whereas the number of those that had thrown themselves down was found to be five thousand: nor did any one escape except two women, who were the daughters of Philip, and

Philip himself, who was the son of a certain eminent man called Jacimus, who had been general of King Agrippa's army; ... And thus was Gamala taken on the three-and-twentieth day of the month Hyperberetaeus [Tishri] whereas the city had first revolted on the four-and-twentieth day of the month Gorpiaeus [Elul]. (Whiston 1752, 1999, 525)

Knowing now the fate of its inhabitants in November 66 CE, what remains is to address briefly the issue of the people who inhabited Gamla, when, and why (R./T.). The place appears to have provided an ideal home for people as early as the Early Bronze period (3200–2400 BCE), and their remains have been discovered. These remains are of a walled city mentioned in the Talmud and that refer also to a city dating to the time of Joshua. Even then, however, the evidence points to it lying in ruins like contemporaneous Ai, a word itself meaning "ruin." It appears to have remained uninhabited until Hellenistic times, when it was resettled by Babylonian Jews returning to their ancestral homeland. Evidence also suggests that the Hasmonean priest-king Alexander Jannaeus captured the city from Hellenistic rulers during his frequent wars against territories surrounding the ever-growing Kingdom of the Jews (103–76 BCE). Still later, and now a part of the northeastern frontier of his considerable kingdom, Herod the Great (38–4 BCE) settled Jews at Gamla in frontier American, pioneer fashion to repopulate the region and make it fruitful. It was therefore a defensive outpost. The descendants of these people raised the standard of revolt against Herod's descendant, King Herod Agrippa II, and thereby against Rome itself, in the year 66 CE. They appear to have been adamantly and equally opposed to both antagonists, but not for exactly the same reasons. We now know their fate and some of the circumstances, albeit through a plethora of data provided in a less than adroit manner by Josephus, that sealed that fate. The heroic tragedy has survived in Jewish legend and lore, referred to as having occurred in the "Masada of the North."

Bethsaida-Julias (Q./S.)

Allied to Gamla and its fate, as I shall demonstrate plausibly, is the city Julias on the banks of the Jordan. An important critical note by Morton Smith in *Palestinian Parties and Politics Which Shaped the Old Testament*, concerning the "foundation" of a *polis*, reads: "Foundation might mean the creation of an entirely new city on a site formerly empty or occupied only by a village.... It seems that no Palestinian city of the first importance was founded in this way before the Herodian period" (1971, 65). The reference to "a village" certainly is apropos when tracing the fortunes of the former fishing village, Bethsaida, which was transformed into a new city, Julias. Moreover, it was still during the Herodian period when this honor was bestowed on it, for it was the tetrarch Philip, son of Herod the Great, who brought about the transformation. Smith informs further that "'Foundation' was often no more than a legal and financial transaction: the city, for a price, got the right to call itself after some member of the royal family, to revive its constitution along Greek lines, and to govern itself by its own representatives, elected according to the revised system" (65). Yet a "royal military commander, treasury officials, and the like remained" (65).

While Smith's description is certainly true of Greek policies in Hellenistic cities and during Hellenistic times (57–81), our gaze should remain fixed on the Herodian period, and we should look for these applications there also. When this is undertaken with respect to Bethsaida-Julias, a curious piece of knowledge emerges. Renamings in honor of specific Romans-royal indeed become evident. However, they form a particular pattern. Specific members of the Herodian family named specific locales in honor of specific royal members in a manner that was most personal. Stated differently, these honorific naming practices occurred not for political reasons primarily, but as a result of genuine mutual respect. Other relationships and perspectives will no doubt be brought out in studies on emperor cults, but evidence still remains for pursuing a most personal trajectory of honorific naming practices by the Herodian family. I have discussed elsewhere the specific issue of how Bethsaida became honorifically renamed and in honor of which specific Julia of the Julio-Claudian family, and need not repeat that here (Greene 1998). What should be pointed out here is that with respect to Bethsaida, all such references are of this personal nature. This appears to point to a strong connection between Bethsaida-Julias and the Herodian family, which further suggests a strong trajectory of positive sentiments of citizenry toward the royal Jewish family and imperial Roman family as well.

THE ARCHAEOLOGICAL EVIDENCE

Were David Goren (2010, 111–48), an Israeli archaeologist, my coauthor he would no doubt prosecute similarities of material culture between Gamla and Bethsaida. Like me, he has on-site, excavation experience at the sites of both ancient Gamla and ancient Bethsaida-Julias. In fact, we worked together with Shemarya Gutmann (1981) at Gamla in 1985, and at Bethsaida in 1994 with Rami Arav (Arav and Freund 1995–2009). Goren has spent more time at the former, I at the latter. To employ one category of material cultural remains in investigating the question of possible Bethsaida-Gamla connections, we may utilize the *objects militaires* found at both sites.

Josephus informs us that much activity of a military nature occurred at Gamla in Book IV of JW. In his somewhat autobiographical **V,** he describes an engagement between his military forces and those of Agrippa II just outside Bethsaida-Julias. Excavating both sets of ruins, therefore, the researcher focusing on military history and concomitant artifacts would tend to count and assign great importance to the number of ballistas, arrowheads, and spearheads; breached walls; military campsites arranged in a siege pattern (dictated by the immediate terrain); evidence of (earthen) ramps; and fairly thick layers of ash mixed with the debris of sudden destruction and chaos. That is, the apparent telltale signs of a military engagement having occurred and its aftermath. However, one would exercise care in differentiating between destruction and debris caused by war and that occasioned by natural catastrophe such as an earthquake. The Jordan Valley rock slides between the Hulah Valley and the Sea of Galilee (studied recently by Professors John Shroder and Michael Bishop), the ruins of Beth Shean, and the steps leading to one of the cisterns-immersion pools at Qumran demonstrate evidence of destruction by the latter, more natural method.

The Golan Archaeological Museum, located at modern Kazrin on the Golan Heights, contains numerous artifacts from the military engagement at Gamla. Among them are Roman arrowheads and spearheads, as well as assorted non-Roman arrowheads found both inside and outside the massive defensive wall. Ballista stones used by Roman siege machines have been found in abundance also. With them the Romans were able to breach the wall in at least three places.

On the site itself, the area where the terraced residences were located shows signs of houses having collapsed. Under the debris were found numerous entire cooking vessels and storage jars in situ. The position of the debris supports Josephus's account of collapsed houses being due to Roman attackers inside the city pursuing the Jewish defenders while they slowly backed up toward the summit of the city. Stepping onto the flat, beaten earth roofs of the houses in full armor, they proved too heavy for the wooden beams of these roofs to support them. The roofs therefore collapsed, preserving the pots, jars, and other material culture that has subsequently been recovered.

Material culture evidence that usually points to a military engagement at Bethsaida-Julias is, in a word, lacking. Granted, there is the Josephan account of a military engagement in the area, and to this account we will eventually turn. At present, however, we remain focused on what the site itself has yielded. Some years ago, Dr. Arav sent me a drawing in actual dimensions of a spearhead discovered in Area C (the northernmost area). One! Uncovered from time to time in each of the three areas of the summit have also been large, round(ed) stones. I hasten to add, however, that one spearhead and a few round stones bespeak neither a military engagement nor ballistas any more than one Springfield rifle and a piece of a tread are proof positive that a major infantry engagement supported by armored units occurred during the First World War was fought where those objects were discovered.

Concerning ballistas, for instance, they were not only round; they weighed a certain, specific amount. Morphological similarity is an insufficient criterion. Lacking also are walls of a defensive nature around the Hellenistic occupation area of et-Tell and thick layers of ash had there been some conflagration there. While granting that the absence of walls and ash do not a priori prove that no military engagement occurred at Julias, the ground has to date yielded nothing that supports such a claim, either.

THE LITERARY EVIDENCE

Turning now squarely to the Josephan account found in **V** 71, he juxtaposes what action he took at Sepphoris with that taken at Julias. Both cities have in common that they appear to have been pro-Roman at the time of the engagements recounted. Both were located at extreme opposite ends of Roman-policed territory: Sepphoris on the extreme western side on the border of the province of Syria and Julias on the eastern banks of the Jordan on the Galilee–Gaulanitis border. According to Josephus (**V** 71), when war between Jews and Romans broke out in the Galilee:

> [T]he people of Sepphoris ... sent to Cestius Gallus, and desired him to come to them immediately, and take possession of their city, or else to send forces sufficient to repress their enemies' incursions upon them; and at the last they did prevail with Gallus to send them a considerable army, both of horse and foot, which came in the night-time, and which they admitted into the city.

Not foolish enough to take on this Roman force now at Rome-loyal Sepphoris, Josephus decided to challenge Roman patrols around the area and to engage them. Julias, like the city of Garisme mentioned in connection with Sepphoris, was the locus for a bank Josephus threw up in preparation for an attack on the city by night and on Rome-loyal, Jewish troops near Julias by day. Indeed, Josephus's military initiatives at Sepphoris, at an (unspecified) plain also in the immediate vicinity (where he suffered a defeat by Roman cavalry) and at Julias are related/connected. In fact, while in retreat from the ill-fated "plain" engagement, contingents of his forces were pursued by infantry and cavalry units of Herod Agrippa II (fighting in conjunction with those of the Romans), at the head of which was Sylla, captain of his guard. Near Julias, Sylla pitched his camp, probably because he had nothing to fear from the city's inhabitants. He then set up a road block that was able to control all traffic moving from Julias-at-the-Jordan either toward Gamla and other Gaulanitis cities in the east, or toward Cana-near-Nazareth and Sepphoris in the west, including those cities located on the northern shore of the Sea of Galilee. Julias's location appears to have been pivotal in the Syllan strategy.

Phase 1

This development was strategically critical enough to prompt Josephus to engage Sylla with (eventually) five thousand troops. Josephus's commander, Jeremiah, who had thrown up a long bank near Julias, was in charge of two thousand. These skirmished with Sylla's troops until Josephus presently arrived with the remaining three thousand. He contrived to draw Sylla away from Julias in the direction of the Jordan to its west and the Beteha Plain to the south, southwest, by devising an ambush stratagem that made it appear that his forces were retreating in those directions. Initially it succeeded, and Sylla was drawn in to think that Josephus's five thousand were in flight. Suddenly they wheeled around and sandwiched Sylla between those who appeared to flee and those who had lain in ambush the entire time. All went well for Josephus until he fell from his mount and sustained a debilitating wrist injury, requiring that he be evacuated from the field of battle to Capernaum on the lake shore to receive medical attention. His forces, upon hearing what had happened, failed to decimate Sylla's fleeing troops, but returned to check on their fallen leader. His wound was worse than originally thought; his physicians advised that he be evacuated to Taricheae (Magdala). Phase 1 of the on-Julias-centered military engagement was over by nightfall (**V** 72).

Phase 2

Phase 2 commenced when Sylla learned that Josephus had been injured and evacuated. He then devised a similar stratagem to that employed by Josephus against him, placing cavalrymen in concealed places east of the Jordan during the night. The early morning witnessed Josephus's men being taunted from their camp to what appeared to be an infantry engagement on the plain (before Julias?). After drawing Josephus onto this plain, Sylla then commanded his concealed cavalry-in-ambush to attack. Several of Josephus's footmen were killed during this engagement. One may conclude that rather than resulting in a defeat or victory for either side, the two-phased engagement before Julias resulted in a draw. Mention of Julias as a locale near an extended engagement between Jewish and Jewish and between Jewish and Roman forces is found nowhere else in Josephus's military accounts. All other mentions occur in material discussing honorific renamings of Bethsaida.

The Sepphoris-Julias episode is employed by Josephus to introduce Vespasian's arrival in Tyre to take command of the Syrian Province. He was accompanied by King Herod Agrippa II, who came almost immediately under verbal attack by Tyrian enemies, who attempted to smear him before Vespasian. At issue was the king's allegedly having chosen Philip son of Jacimus to betray the Herodian royal palace and the Roman soldiers stationed in Jerusalem to guard it and other Roman concerns to the rebels there. This Philip, who appears at the beginning and ending of accounts introducing Gamla and its fall in **JW**, shows up here in **V** like a bad penny. Indubitably, Philip was the nucleus around which Josephus arranged a constellation of historiographical data in his "Hellenistic" genre of history writing.

TOWARD A DENOUEMENT

Let us consolidate what we (think we) know relevant to Gamla. We know that Gamla revolted and remained anti-Roman as well as anti-Herodian. We know that Philip and Josephus 2 led and sustained the revolt. We know that in early 67 Agrippa's officer, Modius, laid siege to Gamla for seven months without success before Vespasian laid a subsequent and successful siege in November of the same year. In addition, we know that from a staging area in Beth Shean in late 66 or extremely early 67, Vespasian, now joined by Titus and his forces, campaigned successfully to retrieve and secure under Roman authority all the cities located along the western coast of the Sea of Galilee before turning eastward along the northern shore en route to Gamla and its now known fate.

It falls to us at this juncture to ask two questions: (1) Where was Julias in all this development? (2) What relationship, if any, did it have with Gamla? Let's review and consolidate the evidence provided thus far.

Sepphoris and Julias belonged to geographical (then) extremes of Rome-loyal territory in the Galilee-Golan, with several revolting locales in between. We know that cities along the northern and northwestern coasts of the Sea of Galilee during Josephus's campaigns there were positively disposed toward the rebels, that is, toward our understanding of what were "innovators." After his wrist wound, for example, it would not have been thought impractical for Josephus to have received medical care at Capernaum or to have been evacuated from there further to Taricheae. We know from the success of Vespasian's west and north seacoast campaign, however, that loyalty status of a given city or village could change overnight. We can demonstrate that this was the case for cities and villages from the southern coast up to Taricheae, where a naval/water battle was also fought. Accordingly Capernaum, once Vespasian turned eastward along the coast, could not have been allowed to remain rebel-loyal; no Roman commander with the stature and experience of a Vespasian would have allowed an enemy with the ability to strike retaliatorily to exist on his (and his legions'!) flanks. After all, when one considers Vespasian's whole military strategy in pacifying revolting Palestine, he campaigned in the Galilee and Golan first and secured them before moving methodically southward toward Jerusalem. Looking even further southward, to Masada, that campaign under another member of the same Flavian, ruling family, the procurator Flavius Silva, was merely a campaign afterthought and directional extension (Cohen 1992). Though good Roman propaganda, perhaps, it was totally unnecessary militarily speaking.

Returning to the Capernaum area and Vespasian's push eastward to assist Agrippa's forces in recouping cities, towns, and villages in his realm (thus further securing his own rear), only Chorazim and Julias deserved any serious consideration. Chorazim, though located in the area, is not mentioned in Josephus. Evidence only hints strongly, and then only at the time before Vespasian arrived in Tyre and later Galilee, that Julias was securely in pro-Roman hands. This forces the investigator into one of two theoretical camps: (1) Either Julias remained Rome-loyal and was bypassed by Vespasian after crossing the Jordan on his way to Gamla, or (2) Julias joined the revolt of the "innovators"; realized that it would suffer the same fate as Tiberias, Taricheae, and Capernaum; and decided to evacuate the city, with many of its more staunch citizens seeking refuge in Gamla, the major beacon of revolt in the region. By foot Gamla is located 10.2 kilometers from Julias.

EPILOGUE

While we have raised fair, impartial, and important questions, and pursued numerous trajectories attempting to address them, the accurate answer to which will contribute to filling one of the many existing lacunae in the writing of a comprehensive history of the Galilee-Golan during this period, we have nevertheless arrived at a state of informed speculation. At this point in our investigations, neither the archaeological evidence produced to date (2011) nor the literary evidence suffice to answer the most important of the questions posed above: What was the relationship between Julias and Gamla during the first Jewish revolt? At least now, however, we know why we don't know. That, too, is knowledge. Further evidence from future excavations at et-Tell may alter this paucity of knowledge.

REFERENCES

Arav, Rami, and Richard Freund, eds. (1995–2009). *Bethsaida: A City by the North Shore of the Sea of Galilee*. Vols. 1–4. Kirksville, MO: Thomas Jefferson University Press/Truman State University Press.

Armenti, Joseph R. (1981). "On the Use of the Term 'Galileans' in the Writings of Josephus Flavius: A Brief Note." *Jewish Quarterly Review* 72 (1): 45–49.

Bilde, Per. (1988). *Flavius Josephus Between Jerusalem and Rome: His Life, His Works and Their Importance*. Sheffield, UK: Sheffield Press.

Cicero, Marcus Tullius. (1939). *Cicero's Manillian Law*. New York: Fordham University Press.

Cohen, Shaye J. D. (1979). *Josephus in Galilee and Rome. His Vita and Development as a Historian*. Columbia Studies in the Classical Tradition, no. 8. Leiden: Brill.

Cohen, Shaye J. D. (1992). "Masada: Literary Tradition, Archaeological Remains, and the Credibility of Josephus." *Journal of Jewish Studies* 33: 385–405.

Durant, Will. (1944). *The Story of Civilization. Caesar and Christ.* Vol. 3, *A History of Roman Civilization and of Christianity from Their Beginnings to A.D. 325.* New York: Simon & Schuster, Inc.

Feldman, L., and Gohei Hata, eds. (1987). *Josephus, Judaism, and Christianity.* Leiden: Brill.

Feldman, Louis. (1981). "The Term 'Galileans' in Josephus." *Jewish Quarterly Review* 72 (1): 50–52.

Feldman, Louis. (1984). "Flavius Josephus Revisited. The Man, His Writings, and His Significance." In *Aufstieg und Niedergang der Roemischen Welt*, 21.2.

Goren, David. (2010). "The Architecture and Stratigraphy of the Hasmonean Quarter (Areas D and B) and Area B77." In *Gamla II: The Architecture: The Shmarya Gutmann Excavations, 1976–1989*, edited by Danny Syon and Zvi Yavor. IAA Reports no. 44. Jerusalem: Publications of the Israel Antiquities Authority.

Greene, John T. (1998). "The Honorific Naming of Bethsaida-Julias." In *Bethsaida: A City by the North Shore of the Sea of Galilee*, edited by Rami Arav and Richard Freund, vol. 2. Kirksville, MO: The Thomas Jefferson University Press.

Gutmann, Shemarya. (1981). *Gamla: The Excavations of the First Eight Seasons.* Israel: Kibbutz Meuhad Publications.

Josephus, Flavius. (1958–1965). *[Works, English and Greek, 1958–]*. Loeb Classical Library. 9 vols. Cambridge, MA: Harvard University Press; London: W. Heinemann.

Jossa, G. (1994). "Josephus's Action in the Galilee During the Jewish War." In *Josephus and the History of the Greco-Roman Period*, edited by F. Parente and J. Sievers. Leiden: Brill.

Laqueur, Richard. *The Jewish Historian Flavius Josephus: A Biographical Investigation Based on New Critical Sources.* Giessen: Muenchow'sche Verlagsbuchhandlung, 1920.

Linder, Helgo. (1992). *Die Geschichtsauffassung des Flavius Josephus im Bellum Judaicum.* Gleichzeitig ein Beitrag zur Quellenfrage. Leiden: Brill.

Loftus, Franci. (1977/1978). "The Anti-Roman Revolt of the Jews and the Galileans." JQR 68.

Parente, F., and J. Sievers, eds. (1994). *Josephus and the History of the Greco-Roman Period: Essays in Honor of Morton Smith.* Leiden: Brill.

Rackham, H., W. H. S. Jones, and D. E. Eichholz, trans. (1938–1962). *Pliny: Natural History.* 10 vols. Loeb Classical Library. Cambridge, MA: Harvard University Press.

Sievers, Joseph, and Gaia Lembi, eds. (2005). *Josephus and Jewish History in Flavian Rome and Beyond.* Leiden: Brill.

Smith, Morton. (1971). *Palestinian Parties and Politics That Shaped the Old Testament.* New York and London: Columbia University Press.

Stone, Michael E., ed. (1984). *Jewish Writings of the Second Temple Period.* Vol. 2. Philadelphia: Van Gorcum, Assen, Fortress Press.

Syon, Danny, and Zvi Yavor. (2010). *Gamla II: The Architecture: The Shmarya Gutmann Excavations, 1976–1989.* IAA Reports no. 44. Jerusalem: Publications of the Israel Antiquities Authority.

Whiston, William, trans. (1752, 1999). *The (New) Complete Works of Josephus.* Grand Rapids, MI: Kregel Publications.

CHAPTER 4

THE DYNAMICS AND DÉNOUEMENT OF THE BAR KOCHBA REVOLT OF 132–135 CE

John T. Greene

INTRODUCTION

In Wars 6:329 Josephus (1960/1981, 434–35) describes the Jewish attitude toward Rome in Palestine thus: "Ever since Pompey reduced you by force [you] never ceased from revolution." Pompey's "reduction" came in the year 63 BCE. When one traces the litany of (especially Palestinian) Jewish protests against Rome, the Great War, the Great Jewish Revolts in Egypt, Cyrene, on Cyprus, and in Babylonia (and possibly to a lesser extent in Palestine also), and the Bar Kokhba Rebellion/War were not only assured, they occurred within due course, were natural, and should have been expected.

More recent studies have revisited the entire era of the Bar Kokhba Rebellion, and some revision of thought from earlier studies is quite evident. Because there is a paucity of contemporaneous literary witnesses, archaeology has contributed more recent evidence. Yet even these findings, when combined with earlier archaeological evidence, has not resulted in the desired comprehensive or coherent picture sought by researchers. The available information has made it possible to challenge old results and reconsider other aspects of this rebellion that had not received much attention (such as evidence produced from studies of caves of refuge).

To focus on just one issue, it remains unknown how much of Judea "Simeon Prince of Israel" ruled. An accurate map of his "realm" has heretofore not been available. It is likewise impossible to know the extent of his physical influence. On the other hand, it is quite clear from the literature ascribed to him that he was indubitably in charge, the de facto leader. And his influence was apparent from the evidence in Jerusalem and areas to the south and southwest more than anywhere else. South of Jerusalem, the Judean Desert (south, central, and east) seems to have been the area reflecting his most direct and efficient control. But his influence was felt in areas north and northeast of Jerusalem (near Michmash and Jericho, respectively) as well. Bethar/Battir, five or six miles southwest of Jerusalem, was the locus of his final stand against his Roman opponents, and there his influence—and fall!—was felt most acutely.

To reassess the geographical limits of this southern "princedom" and its influence, importance, and strategies for survival, this chapter blends a revisit of earlier literary/historical materials with a survey of new information produced by archaeologists from, but not limited to, the caves that appear to have been used by Bar Kokhba's associates in a strategic manner.

JERUSALEM: A HISTORY GAME

Consider the following quotation and attempt to locate it within Jerusalem's history: "The[y] ... were expelled from Jerusalem, for two years sacrifices were renewed on the Temple altar, and an independent state was created that went so far as to issue its own currency" (Schweitzer 1971, 37). This passage describes—either ideally or (nearly) factually—several occurrences in Jerusalem's most turbulent history. The description may recall the events surrounding Judah the Maccabee's victory in 165 BCE (I Macc. 3:23–4:36) (Goodspeed 1938/1959, 385–90). But that prima facie recollection would be erroneous. Sacrifices, although indeed renewed, were offered for a lot longer than two years. And though it was another victory in a concomitant series of them against Syrian-Greek tyranny, the independent state did not emerge until the time of Judah's brother Simon. The Hasmoneans issued coins in an independent Jewish state during the time of Alexander Jannaeus, 103–76 BCE.[1]

During the Great Jewish Revolt of 66–70 CE, the legions led by Cestius Gallus, Roman legate of Syria, were indeed expelled from Jerusalem by Jewish rebels. Spurred on by this victory, the latter then pursued them, nipping guerrilla style at their retreating flanks, down the mountains and lower hill country as far as Lydda. Rather than being renewed, however, sacrifices at the still-standing Temple were certainly altered to omit those on behalf of Caesar. Coins had been issued by the various Herods prior to this period (Strickert 1995, 165–89; 1998, 144–49). The overall purpose of the rebellion had been a coordinated effort to create an independent state. Those attempts ended in the debacles of 70 and 73/74 CE.

If we thus replace the ellipsis in the quotation above with "Syrian-Greeks," our identification would be far too inaccurate. Considering the First Jewish

Rebellion against Roman overlordship, we would be more accurate. Yet, the two events—(1) restriction on sacrifices and (2) the issuance of currency—do not fit either period. Neither, therefore, does "Romans" correctly "fill in the blank" here.

But before we abandon "Romans" as a possibility, let us consider yet another encounter between Romans and Jews rebelling against them in (primarily) Judea. "Romans" is indeed correct, but only as it refers to the period 132–135 CE, that is, during what is now known as either the Second Jewish Revolt or the Bar-Kochba Revolt/Rebellion (Yadin 1971). Historians disagree when sequencing the Jewish revolts against Roman overlordship.

Since their Great Revolt of 66–70 CE had been crushed, what had been Jewish Jerusalem, capital of a hoped-for, independent, Jewish state, had remained a charred ruin. The palaces and three towers built by Herod the Great, all located on the western side of the city, had been untouched by Titus's strategy. Jerusalem as locus had since 70 CE been home to a Roman military unit posted on a hill southwest of the city Titus had otherwise destroyed thoroughly and systematically. Whatever symbolism the site held for Jews living and eking out a living in its shadow, its memory and significance had not faded for many who had nevertheless been prone to take no action to restore it! There would be one eager to rebuild Jerusalem, but for reasons other than those of the indigenous people who loved and venerated her as a city. The interest in restoring the city was nevertheless genuine. And therein crouches an interesting oddity.

LEADING PERSONALITIES, BOTH JEWISH AND ROMAN

When wars are analyzed, the focus is usually on the generals, their strategies, and their tactics. Numerous, often brilliant pairs of opponents come readily to mind (Lee versus Grant, Rommel versus Montgomery, Patton versus Rommel, Schwartzkopf versus Sadam Hussein, Alexander versus Darius III, Constantine versus Maxentius, and Octavian versus Antony/Cleopatra, to name but a few). It has also been fashionable to study opposing monarchs or other political leaders during a conflict; thus the illuminating study of President Lincoln versus President Davis during the American Civil War.[2] It is extremely unusual, however, to approach a famous conflict taking into account the role played by intellectual luminaries on both sides, generally because we tend to eschew thinking of intellectuals as being associated with an activity as brutal as war. But this is merely an illusion, and in the present study, would be a gross omission.

A review of the most important figures active during the final, Great Jewish Revolt centered on Jerusalem between 132 and 135 CE reveals an interesting fact. Four (possibly five) figures dominate the stage of this era. Two, Rabbi Aqiva and Emperor Hadrian, were among the greatest intellectuals their respective people could claim. Two others, Sim(e)on Bar-Kocheba (Yadin 1971) and Julius Severus, were the best and most able contemporaneous military leaders their respective people had on whom to call in trying to resolve their differences militarily. One may even argue that minimum study cannot proceed unless the roles played by these personalities are at least acknowledged. It was one of those rare times in late classical antiquity when two opposing peoples were very evenly matched and committed on both levels! The Bar Kochba Rebellion cannot be studied sufficiently without at least a brief and honorable minibiography of five personalities: a rabbi, an emperor, and three generals—two Roman and one Jewish, proclaimed by at least one person Messiah. Precious little seems to have been known about the general who defeated Bar Kohba. Apparently he and his skill were as known to Hadrian as the skills of Vespasian had been known to Nero, for their roles and goals were uncannily similar.

Rabbi Aqiva: A Mosaic of a Minibiography

Rabbi Aqiva ben Yosef, head of the Beth Din HaGadol (Great Court) and a leading figure at the Yavneh Academy—and because of this the bridge between Pharisee-led Jews and the authorities of the Roman Empire—was of necessity a statesman/politician. A brief discussion of this and the office of Av Beth Din (the [Friendly] Opposition Head) found in Ellis Rivkin's *The Shaping of Jewish History* is well worth the read (1971, 88–90). Aqiva was a late-blooming scholar who became one of the most famous *torah* academy masters and shapers of rabbinical Judaism. Yet like what we know of Bar-Kocheba, much of a biography that may be cobbled together comes from his obvious detractors (who apparently also admired and respected him, grudgingly). Much of what we learn about Aqiva comes from a negative critique of him as he is being associated with others who share his critical fate. He—along with Bar-Cocheba (who is reputed to have demanded extraordinary demonstrations of bravery and fidelity of men who wanted to be counted among his corevolutionaries),[3] the suspect, if not hated, Samaritan sect, and mention of Hadrian—is referenced in the *Talmud Yerushalmi* in what may be described as legendary material. Typical of such material is the following from *Tractate Berachot*, IX, $7, f. 14b., line 59:

> When Akiba was being tortured, the hour for saying the Shema arrived. He said it and smiled. The Roman officer called out, "Old man, art thou a sorcerer, or dost thou mock at thy sufferings. That thou smilest in the midst of thy pains?" "Neither," replied Akiba, "but all my life, when I said the words, 'Thou shalt love the Lord thy God with all thy heart and soul and might,'

I was saddened, for I thought, when shall I be able to fulfil the command? I have loved God with all my heart and with all my possessions [might], but how to love Him with all my soul [i.e., life] was not assured to me. Now that I am giving my life, and that the hour for saying the Shema has come, and my resolution remains firm, should I not laugh?" And as he spoke, his soul departed. (Montefiore and Loewe 1960/1963, 269–70)

Fortunately, as for many teachers, we may add to our knowledge of Aqiva indirectly by examining the circumstances concerning one of his most illustrious students, Rabbi Shimeon Bar Yochai. Rashbi, as he has become known affectionately, was one of the alleged 24,000 students of Aqiva. Because he was understood to be Bar Kokhba's "arms bearer," much as David was to Saul—and as is said also of Elijah the prophet in 2 Kings 13:14 ("The chariots of Israel and its horsemen!")—Rabbi Aqiva, as seen by the account that so many of his students/disciples died during the Bar Kokhba Rebellion, should be considered (like his intellectual adversary Hadrian) a scholar soldier! He, like Bar Kokhba, whom he supported, fell in battle, in that he languished in prison for several years before being tortured and then executed. He died as a prisoner of war. More than his teacher, Rashbi exhibited the characteristics of a Jewish scholar/soldier. Even after 135, as one of Aqiva's remaining students he continued to let it be known that he despised and opposed Roman overlordship, even at his own continuing great peril. Like his master, his rebellion in the face of imminent and constant danger from Roman power forced him and his son, Elazar, to go "underground" for some thirteen years. An example of his spirit is seen in *Tractate Shabbat*, 33 of the *Mishna*, where the reader is told:

Once Rabbi Yehuda said, "How fine are the works of this nation (Rome). They have made streets, they have built bridges, they have erected baths." Rabbi Yossi remained silent (from fear). Rabbi Shimon Bar Yochai answered and said, "All that they have made they have made for themselves; they built market places to put harlots in them; baths to rejuvenate themselves; bridges to levy tolls for themselves."

We see the spirit of the teacher in the student, and thereby get a glimpse of him. Rabbi Aqiva hailed Bar Kokhba as the Messiah. But we do not know the extent to which this was acknowledged by other rabbis, his numerous disciples, or the general public. For all we know, he was expressing only his own opinion. As we learn from *Berachot* of the *Talmud Yerushalmi* above, the Romans held him fully responsible for his belief. Yet even if he stood alone in this view (which appears highly unlikely), others became infected with his effortless blending of militant nationalism and zeal for Torah as his brand of

Pharisaism understood that concept generally. He would spend most of the period of the rebellion incarcerated, until his eventual execution.

Publius Aelius Hadrianus (76–138 CE): A Working Minibiography

Aqiva's intellectual equal, for purposes of this inquiry, was the one person who planned to rebuild, if not restore, Jerusalem. He was a Roman born in Spain in 76 CE and orphaned soon after. And not just any Roman. He became the ward of Trajan, who served as emperor from 98 to 117 CE. Publius Aelius Hadrianus (117–138 CE) had been both a distinguished commander in Dacia, as well as a competent administrator, and was as good and skillful a soldier as any who served him in any of his thirty legions. He visited them often, marched with them carrying his own seventy-five-pound pack, and lived and ate with them in the field on their movements and maneuvers. A soldier's emperor, Hadrian is linked with the final military blow that caused the devastation of contemporaneous Palestinian Jews. On his orders the (almost) final national death knell was delivered to them in 135 CE. When refracted through the prism of Jewish vicissitudes and opinions, he holds for them a place of dishonor and deserved vilification equal to that of Haman, Antiochus IV Epiphanes, Titus, and Josephus Flavius. Much Jewish literature about persecution may be arranged thematically around the intentions of these and other characters toward Jews at crucial periods in their associations with Persians, Greeks, and Romans/Jewish Hellenists.

Let us regard him more closely. Hadrian enjoyed many distinctions. Titus Flavius Sabinus Vespasianus (who ruled as Emperor of Rome from 69 to 79 CE), while commander of legions, pacified the Galilee and portions of Judea during the Great Jewish Revolt of 66–70/(73/74) CE (*Jewish Wars* [JW], 4) before being called to Rome to assume the throne. Once there, he remained there. In contrast, Hadrian (like the American president William Jefferson Clinton, who had the distinction of visiting each of the states at least once during his term of office) visited all parts of his empire. In some regions he initiated renovation or rebuilding campaigns. Such, for example, was the case when he visited historic Athens. He essentially rebuilt this city (an example is the Arch of Hadrian), the history and significance of which tremendously impressed the scholar, artist (designer of statues and writer and performer of music), intellectual/poet, and philosopher within him. In Rome he enlarged the Forum, rebuilt the Pantheon, and erected a mausoleum. In a similar manner, and for similar reasons, he planned to have the "phoenix" rise out of the ashes of Jerusalem's long-standing ruins. Durant describes Hadrian's visit there in 130 CE thus:

> The Holy City was still in ruins, almost as Titus had left it sixty years before; a handful of destitute Jews lived in lairs and hovels amid the rocks.

Hadrian's heart was touched by the desolation; and his imagination was moved by the empty site . . . he dreamed of transforming Zion itself into a pagan citadel. He ordered that Jerusalem should be rebuilt as a Roman colony and renamed Aelia Capitolina in memory of Hadrian's gens and Jupiter's Capitol in Rome. (Durant 1944, 419; Eshel 1997, 46–48/73)

It was another five years before this project actually got under way, however. His decision in 130 is described by Durant as "an astonishing error of psychology and statesmanship in one of the wisest statesmen in history" (1944, 419). The proposed rebuilding would be truly a case of the road to hell being paved with good intentions and their attending consequences!

Immersed in paradoxes, Hadrian, though linked with the final, military blow that caused great devastation of Jews and delivered the (almost) death knell to Palestinian Judaism(s) in 135 CE, was a ruler devoted primarily to peace. His reign was characterized by the greatest period of peace. Commenting on this, Michael Grant observes that "although wars were few, no emperor was closer to his soldiers than Hadrian. . . . Hadrian devoted numerous years to traveling around his empire. . . . [H]e viewed the provinces as integral portions of the empire with their own particular regional characteristics" (1974, 237). This helps explain Durant's reference to an "astonishing error of psychology."

Hadrian enjoyed his sixty-fifth through sixty-ninth birth years between 132 and 135 CE. Although he is thought of as prosecuting a most bloody and devastating war against the Jews of Syria Minora, he is actually credited with withdrawing Roman troops from Parthia, Mesopotamia, Assyria, and Armenia; the latter he promoted to a client kingdom (Durant 1944, 414). Thus, his eastern border in the Middle East was the Euphrates River. He commanded thirty legions, and the period of his reign was essentially peaceful, and "the Roman army was never in better condition than in his reign" (Durant 1944, 417).

Such was the ambiguity both Rabbi Aqiva and Emperor Hadrian generated in those who would attempt to chronicle them and their activities.

General Julius Severus: A Wisp of a Minibiography

Equally ambiguous is the Roman commander Julius Severus, who defeated the Final Jewish Revolt's combatants. Precious little seems to have been known about the general who defeated Bar Kokhba. Apparently he and his skill were known to Hadrian as the skills of Vespasian had been known to Nero, for their roles and goals were uncannily similar. Severus, brought from Britain—where as governor he had been engaged in similar "brushfire extinguishing" activities—to Judea, had under his command the 2nd, 3rd, 4th, 5th, 6th, the renewed 10th, and the 11th Legions. This was a much larger force than that which had been at the disposal of and commanded by

Tinneius Rufus.[4] Yet only a paucity of biographical information exists concerning this famous commander and his accomplishments. He was one of Hadrian's most able generals. We must examine the results of his work to produce a mosaic-like glimpse of him, and then only as a commander and strategist. How long he remained after quelling the rebellion, and whether he proved to be an able administrator in Palestine as he had been in Britain, we do not know.

Sim(e)on Bar-Cocheba: An In-Process Minibiography (?–135 CE)

The person most opposed to Hadrian's urban renewal plans, especially for the Jerusalem ruins, was another in a long series of Jewish men who could be located in the Messianic tradition:[5] Sim(e)on Bar-Cocheba.[6] He would emerge, being proclaimed as a messiah/savior; raise a formidable Jewish fighting and supportive force imbued with almost superhuman zeal; challenge, successfully for a time, Rome's local might; defeat the Roman governor/commander Rufus and his army; capture Jerusalem and a number of strongholds and villages; acquire two sobriquets, Bar-Kochba (Son of a Star) while alive and Bar-Koziba (Son of Lies) posthumously; and die doing what most (thought as or proclaimed) messiahs did for a living (Horsley 1985). He would perish defending the city of Bethar/Battir in August 135 CE. He would fortunately also leave behind some of his correspondence, ostensibly to some of his commanders (Schaefer 1981; Mildenberg 1980, 311–35; Lewis 1996). Discovered in 1960, the contents of seventeen communications from him help dispel some of the enigma and ambiguity surrounding him. Concerning the messianic title ascribed to him, he shares with another in that long list, Jesus the Galilean, the characteristic of being unable to have a complete and reliable biography written about him. Research concerning both these men, and numerous others designated as messiahs, is ongoing (Vermes 1973/1981; Horsely and Hanson 1985). Scholars are still divided over what the title meant after 587/586 BCE, when Zedekiah/Mattaniah enjoyed it.

Concerning family ties, Bar-Cocheba is referred to as the nephew of a Rabbi Eleazar of Modi'im. This is also stated in the *Talmud Yerushalmi*, *Tractate Ta'anit* IV, 8, f. 68d., line 43 (Montifiore and Loewe 1960/1963, 264). This, if reliable information, is all the more amazing because he is said to have trampled his uncle to death, thinking he had betrayed him and the city of Bethar to Severus's forces (264). It should be remembered, however, that the biographical "glimpses" afforded us by the Talmud serve the postrebellion, Monday morning quarterbacking critique of the rabbis, now disappointed by Bar-Cocheba's failure to deliver Judea from Roman control. Thus, allegations that he had men cut off fingers to show boldness, or that he accepted the counterproposal of the Sages and accepted men who could uproot a cedar tree, are more than likely spurious. Close examination reveals the text to have numerous goals: it is anti-Samaritan, anti-Hadrian, and anti-Bar-Cocheba. By a slight stretch of the imagination, the text could also be considered a negative critique of Rabbi Aqiva. The Talmudic text relating this refers to the time of Rabbi Judah the Patriarch (ca. 200 CE). Referring to the Hadrianic persecutions, he and fellow Sages are recorded as commenting:

> "The voice is the voice of Jacob, but the hands are the hands of Esau" (Gen. 27:22) thus: Hark! The voice of Jacob, crying out for what Esau's hands have wrought in Bethar. R. Simeon b. Yohai said, "My teacher Akiba used to expound Num. 24:17 ('A star has gone forth from Jacob') as 'A liar has gone forth from Jacob'." Nevertheless, when R. Akiba [first] saw Bar Koziba [liar, i.e., Bar Kokba], he said, "This is King *Messiah*." Johanan b. Torta said to him, "Akiba, grass will sprout through your cheeks [i.e., you will be dead] ere the son of David comes."
>
> R. Johanan said: "Hark! The voice of Hadrian Caesar slaying eighty thousand myriads in Bethar!" . . . And there was Bar Koziba, with two hundred thousand men who had cut off their fingers . . . When Bar Kokba set out to fight he said: "Sovereign of the Universe! Neither aid us nor destroy us." "Who will lead me into Edom? Wilt not thou, O God, who has cast us off, and thou, O God, who didst not go out with our armies?" (Ps. 60: 9, 10). (Montifiore and Loewe 1960/1963, 262)

From Talmudic sources, therefore, one gains the oblique knowledge that Bar-Cocheba must have been, as should be expected, a controversial figure. He may have had personal characteristics of an abrasive nature, but he appears also to have had a charisma like that of, say, David, Judah the Maccabee, Herod the Great, Jesus the Galilean, Judas the Galilean, and Josephus Flavius. Sifting through the scattered pearls of rare factual data, all may conclude that he was an effective leader, a skilled tactician, architect of a temporarily free Jewish state, and administrator and defender to the death of that state and its dreams of independence. Not bad mosaic pieces!

It should be borne in mind that the *Yerushalmi*'s description of Bar Cocheba was written after his rebellion had been crushed. Losers are not treated well by their biographers and chroniclers. No doubt there are exaggerations about him contained therein. To be sure, however, a more reliable picture of him lies somewhere between the hailing of him as the Messiah (in the spirit of Num. 24:17–19) by Rabbi Aqiva, and the acrimonious statement embedded in the *Talmud Yerushalmi, Ta'anith*, IV. F. 68a (which may be compared to *Midrash Echa Rabba*, II, 2), attributed to Rabbi Johannan ben Torta: "O Aqiva, grass will sprout between your jaws sooner than the Son of David will appear."

The literary sources that allow one to cobble together an outline of Bar-Cocheba's life or his activities are understandably meager. Like many people destined for notoriety or even greatness, no ready scribe imbued with prophetic foresight was present at his birth to record this event, not even as an apocryphal event. Likewise, there is no chronicle of his entering puberty or displaying precocious wisdom and understanding. Instead, in the tradition of most messiahs, Bar-Cocheba bursts upon the stage of conflict fully grown, like Pallas Athena from the forehead of Zeus. It is as an adult that the sources speak of him. This is backed up by the *Talmud*, Dio Cassius (1925, [I] xix. 12–14), and Eusebius Pamphili (1965, 157). And it is as an adult that the correspondence ascribed to him (Yadin 1971; Schaefer 1981; Mildenberg 1980, 311–35; Lewis 1996) was written. Still, precious little about him and the course and conduct of the war can be harvested from them. We know more of what he did than about the man who did those deeds.

Summary

The aims and worldviews of these four (to five) men may serve as the ideational and personalities "framework" within which a study of their points of confluence—either ideologically/politically or militarily—may be undertaken. This chapter examines the military strategies employed by the generals, with the overarching aims of the scholars in mind. Something of the Roman strategies—for there were two different commanders, Rufus and later Severus—and the strategies of the rebels and the method of urban and guerrilla warfare they prosecuted against these Roman adversaries is discussed in the section "Coins Found in Caves of Refuge from the Bar Kokhba Period," below.

SELECTED JEWISH LITERARY EVIDENCE CONTRIBUTING TO A "STATE OF REVOLUTIONARY MIND" DURING THE BAR KOKHBA ERA

The era of Bar Kokhba was charged with a flurry of literature, which when consolidated and studied provides clues to the general contemporaneous Jewish state of mind (both nationalist/traditionalist and progressive/Hellenist). J. J. Collins, for example, holds that within the well-known *Oracula Sibyllina* (written over a 700-year period!) Books 3, 4, 5, and 11 are from the period immediately before Bar Kokhba, and that "Books 1–2 preserve substantial portions of an underlying Jewish oracle from about the same time" (Collins 1984, 357–58).

Of the genre known as testaments, Collins also states that before the time of Bar Kokhba there were "a number of testaments imbedded in other Jewish works of the period" (1984, 329). He cites *Tobit* 14; *1 Macc.* 2:49–70; the *Book of Jubilees*' testaments of Abraham (Ch. 21) and Isaac (Ch. 36); the *Book of Biblical Antiquities* (testaments of Moses, Ch. 33); *2 Enoch* (Chs. 14–18); and *2 Apocalypse of Baruch* (Chs. 43–47). Although these are certainly not all, their contents point to dissatisfaction with the status quo and the inability since the First Revolt to attain national self-determination. Failure to gain national independence remained for many an embarrassment, as well as work unfinished. There had been many potential "Bar Cochebas."

SOME EXTRA-JEWISH LITERARY EVIDENCE

There are ancient and oft-quoted literary witnesses to Aqiva, Bar-Cocheba, Hadrian, and Severus. This section examines them carefully with the assistance of modern, scholarly commentary. Having already mined the Talmudic sources for our in-process and working minibiographies of Bar-Cocheba and Aqiva, we turn now to the extra-Jewish sources to provide ancillary background data and/or reactions. We seek the assistance of a Roman writer, a Church father/historian, and literary evidence produced through the efforts of modern archaeologists within the last four decades.

Dion Cassius Cocceianus (155–240? CE)

Known as Dio Cassius, the Roman historian summarizes the Second Jewish Revolt thus:

> [F]ifty of their most important outposts and nine hundred and eighty-five of their most famous villages were razed to the ground. Five hundred and eighty thousand men were slain in the various raids and battles, and the number of those that perished by famine, disease and fire was past finding out. Thus nearly the whole of Judea was made desolate. (Cassius 1925, [I] xix. 12–14)

Dio(n)'s view recalls the earlier description provided by Josephus Flavius following the defeat of the First Jewish Revolt (66–70[74] CE). Concerning the destruction of Jerusalem by Titus he wrote:

> Now as soon as the army had no more people to slay ... Caesar gave orders that they should now demolish the entire city and temple, but should leave as many of the towers standing as were of the greatest eminency ... and so much of the wall as enclosed the city on the west side. This wall was spared, in order to afford a camp for such as were to lie in garrison ... This was the end which Jerusalem came to by the madness of those that were for

innovations; a city otherwise of great magnificence, and of mighty fame among all mankind. (Josephus 1960/1981, VII, I. I, 589)

The aftermath of this destruction is what greeted the Emperor Hadrian some sixty years later in 130 CE.

Eusebius Pamphili, Bishop of Caesarea (260–340? AD/CE)

Between the Great (66–70 [73/74] CE) and the Bar-Cocheba Revolts (132–135 CE), the nascent estrangement between the Jewish-Christians (J-Cs) and the nationalistic, Jewish revolutionists in Judea grew exponentially. The gulf widened during the First Revolt when the J-Cs removed to, and resettled in, the Transjordanian city of Pella. After Titus had crushed this revolt, however, and had stationed the 10th Legion west of the ruins of Jerusalem, some J-Cs returned to what was now a more Gentile-populated area. Nationalistic Jews would have resented their presence on both political and theological grounds. By the time of the outbreak led by Bar-Cocheba, Judean Christianity was essentially—but not exclusively—Gentile Christianity. During this period even the interstitial Ebionites, the uniates, had all but disappeared also. The chief bone of contention between the two groups was their countermessianic claims: Jesus the Messiah versus Simeon Bar Kochba the Messiah to the extent that both "played this card."

Reading between the lines of the legendary accounts about Bar-Cocheba, as well as non-Jewish accounts about him, it is clear that the "Prince of Israel" would have wasted no sympathy on any of the Gentiles (especially Christians) located in the area comprising the short-lived state he carved out.

The bishop of the Gentile city of Caesarea Maritima, Eusebius Pamphili, has provided one later account. In his work *Historia Ecclesiastica* (Pamphili 1965, 157) the bishop reacts to the period of persecution under Bar-Cocheba. He references him twice. The first mention, in Book IV, vi, I ff., reads in part:

> When the Jewish revolt again grew to formidable dimensions, Rufus, governor of Judaea, . . . took merciless advantage of their crazy folly and marched against them. . . . The Jews . . . were under the command of a man called Bar Cochba, . . . a bloodthirsty bandit who . . . paraded himself as a luminary come down from heaven.

He continues:

> The climax of the war came in Hadrian's eighteenth year, in Betthera . . . not far from Jerusalem. The blockade from without lasted so long that hunger and thirst brought the revolutionaries to complete destruction, and the instigator of their crazy folly paid the penalty he deserved. (157)

Highlighted, then, are certainly the differences between Christians and Jewish nationalists. Other references provide little assistance in determining how long Bethar was under siege or why the "last stand" occurred there.

Pamphili's second mention, also in Book IV, viii, I ff., refers to "those who do battle for her," that is, Church scholars and defenders. He quotes Justin Martyr: "In the recent Jewish war, Bar Cochba, leader of the Jewish insurrection, ordered the Christians alone to be sentenced to terrible punishments if they did not deny Jesus Christ and blaspheme Him" (1965, 161).

Earlier Archaeological Evidence: The Documents from the "Cave of the Letters"

True to one of its primary purposes, archaeology and its production of material culture have helped flesh out the sketchy outline of the Second Jewish Revolt. Some four decades ago Israeli researchers discovered one of several caves of refuge used by associates of Sim(e)on Bar-Cocheba. One, which produced a cache of correspondence (and other material culture as well) ostensibly from Sim(e)on to one of his commanders at Ein Gedi on the Dead Sea, has subsequently been named the Cave of the Letters (Cotton and Yardeni 1997; Isaac 1992, 62–75).

The correspondence shows that Bar-Cocheba was indeed a real person. This may be surprising until one remembers that all other written material mentioning his name was produced after the period of the Second Jewish Rebellion, and then by enemies, critics, and detractors of that rebellion. The appearance of the name—itself often a detraction—recalls the use of Chrestos and others in the literature mined to prove the existence of Jesus outside the earliest Christian confessional literature.[7]

Rather than depicting Bar-Cocheba as a tactician, the concatenation of cave correspondence presents him as an administrator of a state. Similar in purpose to the undisputed Pauline correspondence of the New Testament, the scrolls are "business letters" (Stowers 1986). As such, this correspondence belongs to what P. S. Alexander terms nonliterary letters, which have a "more specific, everyday purpose: they issue orders, make requests ... and are normally meant for a very limited and precise audience" (1984, 583). They were written in Hebrew, Aramaic, and Greek.

Summary

From our brief, but necessary, review of the available ancient literary witness, we understand now why any study may be framed by the five principal Jewish and Roman personalities and the historical backdrop they share. We understand the motivations of Emperor Hadrian and how this statesman/

soldier/scholar/intellectual made a critical misjudgment. We know further why the misjudgment was addressed in an adroit and immediate way by Bar-Cocheba and his conationalists. One may view him as the point of confluence of regional Jewish, nationalistic frustrations. The picture of the rabbi that history has captured and promoted is a postrebellion portrait (Neusner 1975/1982). Disarmed and misled by that portrait, many may find Rabbi Aqiva's support and actions anachronistic. It forces us to explore more deeply the pre-*Mishna* period and look more closely at the numerous and understandable interpretive battles engaged in by the rabbis themselves that are mirrored in that *Mishna*. During the rebellion the "interpretive dust" could hardly have been settled. The promessianic stance of Aqiva has as much to support it as does the dissenting stance of Rabbi Yohannan ben Torta who criticized his colleague (*Talmud Yerushalmi, Ta'anith*, IV. f. 68a; *Midrash Echa Rabba*, II, 2). Equally understandable are the critiques of Eusebius and Justin Martyr. Caught up in the equally unsettled issue of reliable messianism, the tendency toward nationalism included viewing competing messianisms and those who promoted such views as hostile and dangerous opponents. Finally, the dispassionate reportage of Dio Cassius appears to have taken no stance for or against the rebellion. His account vies in manner with that of any contemporary foreign correspondent of the World Service of the BBC or CNN's *World Report*.

Because the literary evidence is both sparse and of uneven reliability, it is necessary to turn to archaeological research to appreciate other aspects of Bar-Cocheba's rebellion and Roman reaction to it. Minted coins, especially those discovered in context—but those discovered out of context as well!—and caves, many used for refuge and/or storage, are two more means by which information about the rebellion may be gleaned. Even better is when the two are combined, that is, when specific coins minted by Bar Cocheba are discovered in specific caves of refuge and/or storage. We turn first to accounts of general uses of caves, then to accounts of them employed strategically. This prepares us to assess cave usage during the Final Jewish Revolt and their strategic significance.

GENERAL USE OF CAVES IN ANCIENT ISRAEL

There never seems to have been adequate housing in ancient Israel. When one looks at the results of archaeological excavations in a particular area (e.g., at Et-Tell/Bethsaida), one notices that the dwellings apparent there from floor plans would not have been adequate to house all of the people who made such a town (at any period) work. An ancient example of the modern-day "street person" begins to loom large.

When archaeological survey teams fan out and systematically study the countryside surrounding a city or large town being excavated, one of their goals is to help determine the extent and kind of relationship that existed between those who resided in the urban area and those outside of its boundaries, a sort of socioeconomic symbiosis. It is generally found that many "residents" of city/town X actually lived in grottoes nearby. Those who died were also buried in other selected nearby grottoes.

Cities (towns/villages), tent camps, and grottos were the marketable and/or preferred "real estate" choices in ancient Israel, and it was always known to the local inhabitants where such "real estate" was located, as well as when it was available. When it became extremely hazardous to live openly in urban areas, grottos, channels, tunnels, and even large cisterns beneath the city, unknown to those threatening it, became important as places of refuge, storage, staging areas for urban guerrilla warfare, and sources of water and other provisions, to name but a few standard uses.

When it proved too dangerous to remain hidden in areas "under" the city, its defenders, aware of other sanctuaries, apparently withdrew to other residential and staging areas outside of but near to the city. Here they were near enough to their supply lines and sources, yet in no immediate danger of being either discovered or overrun by their (foreign) adversaries.

Depending on the power and determination of an adversary, it may have become necessary for defending combatants to make yet another phased retreat to natural sanctuaries located still farther from the city, yet close enough for them to be able to remain relevant as a fighting force and protect not only family, but important national treasures and symbols as well. This usually involves leaving the region or country.

There is such a thing as flight from before the enemy. In what we shall see from the goals of the Second Jewish Revolt and its participants, this was never their intention. Caves and significant other cavities appear to have been employed as part of a phased plan by those who knew when it was prudent to withdraw, but not flee, from the enemy. We shall put this view and strategic use of cavities and caves into perspective and see how similar that use was to the children's game of hide and seek.

Simon Prince of Israel communicated with, and received correspondence in writing from, "his lieutenants and various headmen in regions bordering on the desert of Judah by the northwest of the Dead Sea" (Gray 1969, 188–93). One learns from the preceding survey that the literature, even the most recent from (or about) the Cave of the Letters, is of important, but limited, worth in illuminating important aspects of the Second Jewish Rebellion. The discovery of that cave itself invites another trajectory of inquiry. Why, in essence, a cave and not some other contemporaneous locus of concealment and/or temporary refuge? This section and the next one study in some detail the strategic use of caves and other cavities of the earth, the Bar Kokhba era coins discovered in several of them, and how these natural structures were utilized by Jewish defenders (even against other Jews).

Several *ma'arot* (plural of *me'ara'*, cave) located in the Judean Desert and areas bordering on it were utilized by various militants against one power or another, both Jewish and non-Jewish, in the region, for as long as locals could remember. The caves near Adullum and the caves near Ein Gedi are two famous examples involving, for example, the outlaw David. King Saul (Ein Gedi) and the Tyrant of Gath, Achish (Adullum), were the pursuing powers during the tenth century BCE. No doubt each time Jerusalem was besieged, numerous caves in the vicinity became a refuge until that crisis had passed and it was once again safe to return to the city. At the end of the Second Jewish Revolt, return was impossible; Jerusalem languished as a set of scorched ruins until it was rebuilt by Hadrian.

Selected Examples of Cave Usage in the Hebrew Scriptures/Old Testament

Let us consider six references that illustrate strategic use of caves and caves as loci of refuge:

1. Out of fear, Lot left the city of Zo'ar and sought and found refuge in the hills nearby (Gen. 19:30).
2. Five Canaanite kings, having formed a coalition, fled from Joshua's forces and found refuge in a cave at Makkedah near Beth-horon. The kings were trapped therein, sentenced to death, and executed as examples, and their corpses were buried in the cave that was sealed by great stones (Josh. 10:6–27).
3. David (the outlaw) sought refuge from both Saul and Achish, king of Gath, in the cave of Adullum. Later, in the Wilderness of Ein Gedi, near a place called Wildgoat's Rocks, David and his band used certain caves as a stronghold. Unknowingly Saul, pursuing him, happened to enter his headquarters cave and could have been taken prisoner. David spared his life, but cut off a piece of his garment to let him know he had meant him no harm (1 Sam. 24:1–22). He employed this cave as a stronghold on a second occasion as seen in 2 Sam. 23:13.
4. Concerning warfare of a different kind, when Queen Jezebel attempted to wipe out Yahwistic opposition to her cult of Melkart, some one hundred prophets of Israel were hidden in caves by Obadiah, overseer of the royal household (1 Kings 18:4; 13).
5. The prophet Elijah also sought refuge in a cave on Mt. Horeb. But he was ejected from it swiftly by the god of Israel and was sent back to continue his struggle against Jezebel (1 Kings 19:9; 13).
6. The account in 1 Chronicles 11: 15, like those of 1 Sam. 22:1 and 2 Samuel 23:13, has David situated at the cave of Adullum mentioned in number 3 above.

David, then, was not the only combatant on whom it dawned to employ caves strategically as places of refuge. Records indicate that on several subsequent occasions refuge outside of cities, towns, and villages was deemed both necessary and desirable by Jewish freedom fighters against one or another perceived tyrant or tyranny. In that vein, it could also be that King Zedekiah, with his retinue, was escaping Jerusalem to seek refuge in either former "royal vacation cities" or known caves near the Dead Sea (2 Kings 25:4–7) where goods and supplies had already been stored.

There would have been numerous opportunities for those courageous fighters against Antiochus IV and his successors, the Maccabees and their coreligionist associates, to also seek refuge in caves of the Judean mountains and foothills during their guerrilla warfare phase to regain religious independence. These considerations bring us to the ninth century BCE.

Cave Usage in Selected Writings of Josephus and Through Archaeological Exploration: A Geographico-Taxonomy

Still later in the ancient chronology, the writings of Josephus Flavius illuminate the cave as a place of refuge in Jewish struggles against Roman overlordship—either directly or indirectly through its client-kings.

In 1947—and during the years immediately following—a systematic search of numerous caves in the desert bordering on the western shore of the Dead Sea and in a number of *wadis* (*Wadis Qumran*, *Murabba'at*, and *Daliyyeh*, etc.) brought to light numerous writings that helped researchers flesh out the role(s) more caves in the region had played. The post-1947 explorations contributed data helpful especially to research on the era after the Old Testament/Hebrew Scriptures. One of the most comprehensive and recent anthologies on cave research relevant to this inquiry is by Hanan Eshel and David Amit (Eshel et al. 1998). The cave as storage locus of a nation's or group's literary and sacred treasures is evident here.

Caves and other orifices were employed for both refuge and storage. Let us explore this use of places of refuge to see whether a specific pattern emerges in their use by Jewish defenders in the Galilee and Judea. Here, rather than take a chronological approach, we shall begin in the north and progress, through examples in selected literature, to the most recent evidence supplied by the places of refuge in the Judean Desert (south). It is therefore a geographico-taxonomic approach we shall pursue, including eleven examples.

Galilee/Golan—Sepphoris Taken by Herod: The Case of Robbers in Caves of Refuge

After Herod had taken the Galilean capital Sepphoris with great ease during a snowy period, he pursued "robbers" holed up in caves near the village of Arbela, which overlooks the Sea of Galilee on its western side. Josephus says that "their skill was that of warriors, but their boldness was that of robbers" (Josephus 1960/1981, Wars, Bk. I: XVI: 2, 3, 4, 447). Accordingly, these almost matched in might and skill of arms those troops led by Herod. Only his strategic superiority enabled the tide of battle to turn in his favor. Those who were not defeated sought refuge in Arbela's caves. Mounting a campaign specifically against these men, Josephus describes Herod's challenge thus:

> Now these caves were in the precipices of craggy mountains, and could not be come at from any side, since they had only some winding pathways, very narrow, by which they got up to them; but the rock that lay on their front had beneath it valleys of a vast depth, and of an almost perpendicular declivity; . . . that the king was doubtful for a long time what to do. (446)

Herod finally resolved to have soldiers lowered in baskets to the mouths of the caves, where they slew those defenders who challenged them. The remainder they attempted to force out of the caves by throwing in containers of fire. Many, however, decided to slay their families and themselves rather than submit. Herod left one Ptolemy in charge of a garrison stationed there and retired to Samaria. In the annals of military tactics, this "basket maneuver" is considered brilliant.

Bogs and Places Not Easily Discovered: The Case of More Galilean Marauders after Herod's Arbela Episode (Josephus 1960/1981, Wars, V, 447)

Herod removed to Samaria after having subdued the rebels of Arbela. Shortly after he departed, other adversaries (termed brigands) took up a similar cause. They fell upon Herod's commander of Arbela's garrison, Ptolemy, and killed him. When this news reached Herod, he returned and fought with them. When his attacks and successes proved too strong for them, they "retired to the bogs, and to places not easily to be found; . . ." (447)

Ditches and Mines: The Case of the Gamla Underground (Josephus 1960/1981, Wars, IV: 1:2, 522)

Josephus, describing the defenses of Gamla in preparation for the inevitable and dreaded Roman siege, writes: "As this city was naturally hard to be taken, so had Josephus, by building a wall about it, made it still stronger, as also by ditches and mines underground" (522).

Urban Caves and Caverns: Jerusalem/Jebus's Caves and Tunnels

From its very beginnings Jerusalem/Jebus has relied upon a cave and the lifeblood of the city, the Spring Gihon located within it, for its existence. Without this secret water source, there would have been no city.

During the sixth century BCE King Hezekiah of Jerusalem had a tunnel dug from the Spring Gihon, located on the eastern side of the city (outside the wall), to the Pool of Siloam, located on the western side of the Ophel (the southward-extending geographical "finger" on which the city was developed, also located outside the city wall). This was to protect the city's water supply still further.

In portions of this same tunneling system is a channel leading directly southward. In the ninth century BCE King Solomon had gardens on the southern terraces of the Ophel protrusion. These gardens were probably watered through this channel from the Spring Gihon. Hezekiah, however, had it blocked when he decided to dig the tunnel that now bears his name from the Assyrians under Sennacherib I who were besieging the city. The first sixty-five feet of this tunnel follow the original course of an old tunnel that had been dug and used by the Jebusites. At the end of this span, after one makes a sharp right turn followed by an almost immediate ninety-degree left turn, Hezekiah's tunnel begins. At this juncture is a shaft through which David and his men may have gained entry into the Jebusite stronghold and captured the city in ca. 1000 BCE.

The Case of Simon Bar-Giora(s) in Jerusalem (Josephus 1960/1981, Bk. VII: 2:1, 495, 541, 590, 954; Bk. IV: 9)

According to Josephus, a rebel named Simeon Bar-Giora(s), shortly before the start of the Roman siege of Jerusalem in 70 CE, "enlarged many caves, many of which he found to be suited for his needs, and he made them into depositories for his treasures and a place to collect his loot." It is most probable that these same caves were reused for similar purposes between 132 and 135 CE.

Simeon Bar-Giora was considered by Rome (incorrectly; there were several factions of rebels, some fighting each other) to be the leader of the Great Revolt of 66–70/(74) CE He was eventually captured, taken to Rome, and executed there.

Urban Caves (Subterranean Galleries) and Cisterns: The Case of Warfare within Jerusalem (Gray 1969, 186)

Regarding the Jerusalem-based rebels during the First Jewish Revolt, historian John Gray writes:

> The rebels retired to the Upper City . . . the Romans had cleared the Lower City, setting everything on fire as far as Siloam. The extremists were even

then prepared to resist. . . . The whole city was taken. The rebels were hunted down mercilessly. John and Simon were captured; starved out of the cisterns and subterranean galleries where they had taken refuge. (186)

"John" refers to John of Gishala in the Galilee; "Simon" refers to Simon Bar-Giora(s). Both were leaders of rebel factions.

Taking Refuge in the Judean Mountains: The Case of Mattathias Hasmon and Judas Maccabaeus Against the Seleucids (Josephus 1960/1981, Bk. I: 1:3, 61)

Succinctly yet poignantly, Josephus described Mattathias's strategy of refuge and engagement:

> Bacchides with daggers; and thereupon, out of the fear of the many garrisons [of the enemy] he fled to the mountains; and so many of the people followed him, and he was encouraged to come down from the mountains, and to give battle to Antiochus' generals, when he beat them, and drove them out of Judea.

1 Maccabees 2:28 confirms Josephus's statement that the followers of Mattathias indeed sought refuge initially in the mountains. 1 Maccabees 2:32 adds that his followers removed from their cities and towns to *"hiding-places in the wilderness."* And 2 Maccabees 2:41 states that *"our brothers died in the hiding-places."* Because of the success of the Maccabees and their demonstrated military prowess, their fighting forces did not have to occupy caves of refuge for very long.

The Maccabees texts demonstrate the hide-and-seek strategy of the use of caves, as well as that the enemy often discovered them and slew their occupants from time to time.

The Copper Scroll from the Caves of Qumran: Found in a Place of Both Storage and Refuge (Josephus 1960/1981, 61)

The Copper Scroll, the metal scroll found during excavations at Qumran, lists sixty-four hiding places in the desert areas around Jerusalem where gold, silver, Temple gifts, and manuscripts were deposited. The sixth column of the scroll reads:

> In the Cave of the Pillar, with two openings that look toward the east, Dig in the northern opening, three cubits, for there is a ritual vessel there. In it a scroll, under it twenty-two talents.

This important scroll refers to the cave's function as a secret storage center. Some are prepared to argue that it is the Cave of the Letters.

Methods of Evading a Conquering Army in Underground Caverns: The Case of Simeon Bar-Gioras (Josephus 1960/1981, Bk. VII: 495, 541, 590, and 594)

There is another Josephan account that describes the hide-and-seek tactics of Simeon Bar-Gioras. After Jerusalem had been taken by Titus, he garrisoned the 10th Legion there and then retired to Caesarea Maritima for feasting and resting. He later visited Caesarea Philipi and exhibited bloody shows there. During one such visit there, he was informed of the capture of Simeon Bar-Gioras. When Jerusalem was besieged, Simeon and many of his trusted followers secreted themselves in several tunnels under the city that had been dug many years before. Their plan was to escape the city. Many of his party were either experienced miners or stonecutters. Armed with their tools and adequate provisions, at first they made considerable headway, but then encountered difficulties in progressing further underground. Although they had been prudent in eating their provisions sparingly, they eventually ran out. Simeon devised the stratagem of donning a white gown and a purple cloak. Being at this time in a secret tunnel below the former Temple, he decided to emerge from this cavern in an attempt to so startle the Roman guard posted there that he and his party might effect an escape. His "apparition" or "resurrection" had only a momentary success, for he was then captured and taken to Tertius Rufus, commander of the legion. It was Rufus who then informed Titus of Simeon's capture. When Titus returned to Caesarea Maritima, Rufus sent Simeon to him in chains. He was taken by Titus to Rome when he returned there with numerous other Jewish captives and other trophies of war. There he was made a spectacle, then was executed.

Underground Conduit: The Case of Survivors at Masada (Josephus 1960/1981, Bk. IV)

Two old women and five children crawled out from an underground conduit to relate the last stand of the Zealot defenders of Masada. According to Josephus (1960/1981, Wars, Bk. IV: 9:1):

> So these people died [who had agreed to the death pact at Masada] with this intention, that they would not have so much as one soul among them all alive to be subject to the Romans. Yet was there an ancient woman, and another who was of kin to Eleazar, and superior to most women in prudence and learning, with five children, who had concealed themselves in caverns under

ground, and had carried water thither for their drink, and were hidden there when the rest were intent upon the slaughter of one another.

In this account (if verifiable!) one reads of people using caves to protect themselves from members of their own group who had made a death pact.

Qumran's Cemetery: The Possibility of Cave Usage in the Wadi Qumran

According to Devorah Dimant, the graves of Qumran "contained skeletons of men, women and children, and are oriented with their heads toward the south. Later remains attest to the presence of a small Roman garrison until around 90 CE and a short sojourn of Bar-Kokhba fighters" (1984, 484). With the immediate area honeycombed with caves, this suggests that associates of Bar Kokhba may have made use of these caves and of the structures whose remains are at Qumran itself as places of refuge.

Summary

Following this brief survey, it becomes clear that caves and other cavities were employed frequently in ancient Israel for purposes of strategy, storage, and refuge, especially by rebel forces against majority aggressor forces. Whether in the northern portion of the country, dotted with many large urban areas, or in the sparsely populated Judean Desert and adjacent areas of the south, caves, channels, and tunnels within cities such as Jerusalem and known caves, caverns, cisterns, and other cavities in rural areas were employed frequently as places of refuge and/or storage. By the time of the Bar Kokhba Rebellion, this would have been both a known and commonly employed practice in their tactics. In light of the paucity of contemporaneous descriptive-tactical literature, we shall assume that activities similar to those described in these eleven examples were often repeated by the co-combatants of Bar Cocheba during the Final Rebellion.

COINS FOUND IN CAVES OF REFUGE FROM THE BAR KOKHBA PERIOD: THE POSSIBILITY OF CONSTRUCTING "BOUNDARY MARKERS" FOR A STATE

The historian Dio Cassius wrote that 50 of the rebels' important outposts and 985 of their most famous villages had been razed to the ground (1925, I xix, 12–14). Though this may provide important general information about Jewish losses of loci of support, supply, and possible refuge, Cassius provides no information to help us establish the geographical extent of the area affected or wherein these outposts and villages were located, nor does he provide the specific place-names in his account. This greatly impedes our ability to craft an accurate or reliable map of the area of Bar Kokhba's influence and control, that is, the physical "kingdom" over which he ruled as "Prince of Israel." To establish a probable boundary for Bar Kocheba's political entity, we must resort to other means.

More helpful in approaching this problem is the numismatic evidence provided by Bar Kokhba's participation in the well-established practice of minting coins as symbols of an established political entity. Their modern-day equivalent would be a political ad on television or radio, in the newspaper or weekly news magazine, or on a public billboard. The "messages" inscribed upon them addressed simultaneously those within the political entity and those who were considered its enemies and/or detractors. The studies by Amit and Eshel (1990/1991, 33–35), Barag (1980, 30–33), Mildenberg (1984), and Strickert (2001), to name but four the last three decades, enable the researcher to generate a more reliable general boundary and map of the area of Bar Kokhba's princedom, while appreciating the science of numismatics in general. However, any map generated by where coins have been discovered, while contributing valuable data, is only a map of where Bar Kokhba coins have been found; one cannot be sure that the picture presented is any more reliable than what Dio's information already provides. Yet coins found in caves surrounding Jerusalem allow a tentative reconstruction of their use as refuge loci, as strategic outposts by various associates of Bar Kokhba, and as possible boundary markers of the rebel state (princedom). These loci were for a time under the control of the rebels. We examine the results of coins discovered in three areas near Jerusalem: one north, one northeast, and the desert wilderness area south and southeast of the city.

Cave Coins Discovered North of Jerusalem

Three cave areas north of Jerusalem have yielded significant coins. First, an impressive hoard or treasure of some seventeen silver coins was discovered in the northernmost cave complex of 'Araq En-Na'saneh (Eshel 1997, 78–82). Nine are from the reign of Trajan, seven are from the period of Hadrian's rule, and one is a provincial tridrachm. A tridrachm, like a tetradrachm, was a silver coin issued by various Greek mints from 600 BCE to 200 CE. It was the equivalent of three (four) drachmas. Second, among the finds of the Wadi Makuck, also north of Jerusalem, were two coins: one silver of Hadrian, the other bronze with a palm tree on the obverse side and a vine on the reverse side. This second one was from Bar Kokhba (Eshel et al. 1998, 90). Third, in the Cave El Jiy of the Wadi Michmash (also north of the city), sixteen coins were harvested from the days of both Hadrian and Bar Kokhba. Ten were bronze and six were silver (Eshel, 98–103, 213–219).

Ketef Yericho (Jericho Rim), Northeast of Jerusalem

In Ketef Yericho some twenty-six coins were discovered. They were studied in three groups: (1) Group A contained six coins, (2) Group B, seven coins; and (3) Group C, thirteen coins. Of these, no coins of the first group were from Hadrian's/Bar Kokhba's era. Of the second group (nos. 7–13), two were from Hadrian. In the largest group (Group C), numbers 19, 20, 24, 25, and 26 bore the image of Hadrian (Eshel 1997, 128–136).

South and Southeast of Jerusalem

South of Jerusalem and southeast of Hebron is located the Tetradrachm Cave (Eshel 1997, 185–209). In it was discovered the famous coin known as the Tetradrachm of Bar Kokhba (Eshel, 200). This famous coin has an image of the Temple flanked on either side by two columns. Between them is an ark. Above the structure is a star. On the right side of the coin on the obverse side are written (in ancient Aramaic script) the letters shin and mem. These signify nw [msh] Shim'on or Simeon.

Prior to Eshel and others (1998), who document twenty-three Bar Kokhba-minted coins harvested from the caves of refuge used during the Bar Kokhba Rebellion (213–219), there had been no return to the Cave of the Letters. Since the summer campaigns of 1999 (preliminary) and 2000 (the three-week expedition in which the writer participated and excavated), more important coins have been discovered and processed. At the 2001 Society of Biblical Literature International Conference held in Rome, Italy, Professor Fred Strickert presented evidence of these newest finds and placed them in the context of the known numismatic evidence from the Bar Kokhba period.

Although the latter finds allow no alteration of the basic map outline, when all "dots" of the coin locations are connected, they do provide expansive evidence of greater Bar Kokhba activity in the eastern sector of Nahal Hever. Numismatists, like any other historians, can never have too much (physical) evidence!

Geographical Distribution and Location of the Caves Containing the Numismatic Evidence: A Summary

According to Eshel and colleagues (1998), caves of refuge employed by Bar Kokhba's associates were located north of Jerusalem (Cave of Araq En-Na'saneh in the Wadi ed-Daliyeh; a cave in Wadi el-Makuck; and two caves in Wadi Suweinit); in Ketef Jericho (Abi'or Cave); and in the Judean Desert (numerous sites including Nahal Hever). On page 15 of their work, the authors provide an excellent map of the distribution of the caves of refuge. In all, they identify twenty-seven caves located in thirteen separate areas. The most numerous were located in the Judean Desert (nineteen). Only one (or a series in one location) was located east of the Dead Sea (in Zarqa' Ma'in).

The most numerous (nineteen in the Judean Desert) were located southeast of Jerusalem near the western shore of the Dead Sea. Four of these are in Nahal Hever (Hever [Band or Company] Canyon). The northernmost cave discovered to the time of Eshel and colleagues' writing is called Ma'arath 'Araq en-Na'asaneh (Cave of Desertion/Run Away) in the Wadi Daliyeh (1998, 71). The southernmost was the Yahal Cave west of Noah-Zahar near the Dead Sea.

Interpreting Some Numismatic Evidence

From the total concatenation of coins, one may construct the hazy outline of the (probable) parameters of Bar Kokhba's "princedom." Activities during the rebellion and strategies are approachable either within these parameters, or as forays against "legitimate" targets (e.g., Samaritans, Christians [the messianic opposition], supporters of pro-Roman rule, and non-Jews in general, in Emmaus and Nablus and other colonies or protocolonies).

Although we have intimated, if not stated outright, that desired details of this rebellion are not forthcoming due to a paucity of contemporaneous documentation, three coins minted during the Bar Kokhba era appear to tell the entire story of the goals of the rebellion. Through them and their enshrined message, one may again "connect the ideational dots."

One, the Tetradrachm, with its Temple columns, ark, star, and name "S[I]m[eon]," symbolizes the hope and goal of a restored and free Jewish state at the center of which would be the Temple (destroyed by fire in 70 CE) cult with its priest-king/messiah (the "Son of David") as its and the state's legitimate head. This coin is the numismatic equivalent of the *Mishna*'s literary interpretation of the significance of the (also nonexisting and middle-Platonic-presented) Temple and its significance. Thus the Tetradrachm and the *Mishna*'s maintenance of the significance of the Temple are two sides of the same "coin"! This (restored) state would once again be the place where God and humankind, led by the legitimate entrepreneurs between Heaven and Earth, with the Messiah at their head, would once again reestablish all of the abiding dreams of Israel-the-Jewish-People. Paramount in the platform of the new government would be sanctification after the plank of salvation had been laid into place as a result of necessary and ruthless military means.

A second coin, bearing two trumpets side by side, with mouthpieces at the bottom, symbolizes the announcement/proclamation that the God of Israel and his covenanted community have been reestablished and will continue their relationship toward the telos of divinely ordained and guided history.

Its theme is communication. The symbol of the trumpet is well chosen. Of the fifty-one occurrences of the word trumpet (*hatzotzrah* in Hebrew) in the Hebrew Scriptures, three texts appear to have captured the spirit of these trumpets: Zechariah 9:11–17; Joel 2:1–2; and Zephaniah 1:14–17. Their theme is both offensive and defensive military aggression within the suggested framework of holy war. One trumpet signals Israel, the other her God, and together a covenant reestablished. The Zechariah text reads:

> As for you also, because of the blood of my covenant with you, I will set your captives free from the waterless pit. Return to your stronghold, O prisoners of hope; today I declare that I will restore to you double. For I have bent Judah as my bow; I have made Ephriam its arrow. I will brandish your sons, O Zion, over your sons, O Greece (read Rome!) and wield you like a warrior's sword. Then the Lord will appear over them, and his arrow go forth like lightning; The Lord will sound the trumpet, and march forth in the whirlwinds of the south.

Likewise, Joel 2:1–2, employing *parallelismus membrorum*, captures the same spirit of this coin: "Blow the trumpet in Zion; sound the alarm on my holy mountain! Let all the inhabitants of the land tremble, for the day of the Lord is coming, it is near, a day of darkness and gloom, a day of clouds and thick darkness!" So, too, Zephaniah 1:14–17 states:

> The great day of the Lord is near, near and hastening fast; the sound of the day of the Lord is bitter, the mighty man cries aloud there. A day of wrath is that day, a day of distress and anguish, a day of ruin and devastation, a day of clouds and thick darkness, a day of trumpet blast and battle cry against the fortified cities and against the lofty battlements. I will bring distress on men, so that they shall walk like the blind, because they have sinned against the Lord; their blood shall be poured out like dust, and their flesh like dung.

All three citations reflect varying aspects of the importance of the trumpet in the life and thought of ancient Israel, and they send powerful messages. Israel's God may take the initiative and blow the trumpet himself. This signals the possibility of divine intervention and assistance (the Divine Warrior imagery; Zechariah). The trumpet's blast is to be a signal to Israel's enemies that they have much to fear and that their threat will be short lived (Joel). It also signals the actual attack against all of the inhabitants of cities that thought to oppress the people of Bar Kokhba (Zephaniah).

The third coin minted by Bar Kokhba displays a *qinor* (a harp) prominently in the center. It represents both David (the first Messiah and "Sweet Singer of Israel") and the joy of the restored Israel at being able to communicate sweetly (through liturgical music) with her God. It signals the festivals that allow a people to celebrate their uniqueness and praise their God. 1 Maccabees 3:43–45 has captured the spirit of the significance of the *qinor* and the situation that may have inspired this symbol for the "Prince of Israel": "Jerusalem was uninhabited like a wilderness; there was not one of her children who came in or went out, the sanctuary was trodden down, the sons of aliens were in the citadel, it was a stopping-place for heathens. Joy vanished from Jacob, and the flute and the harp ceased to play." This coin was a call to strike up the harp once again and all that the harp symbolized in the life of Israel.

When viewed closely, these three symbols tell the story of *tiqvah*, hope, in Bar Kokhba's and Rabbi Aqiva's machinations and anticipated goals. Three important and necessary leadership and propaganda ingredients are evident in the symbolism of these three coins: (1) the Messiah (not necessarily Bar Cocheba!), the priest-king in whose person are contained the "Son of God"/ David and the Highest Priest who sanctifies his people and maintains a ritual connection between Heaven and Earth through his high-priest-led priesthood; (2) a call to action and an announcement (through communication praxis), both between members of Israel and between Israel and her God (ergo two trumpets!) (Both human and heavenly guidance [through the fates], necessary for the maintenance of any state, are deemed as being in place by this symbol); and (3) the *qinor*, which suggests national communication, song, and celebration. It urges one to recall the liturgical festivals that connect the major events of the national year of a people, those celebrations that make a people unique in the world and within the family of humankind. Thus whatever the goal of Bar Kokhba and his associates, they were to stand on and be supported by the three "pillars" of messiah, communication/call, and celebration. These symbols on the coins in the hands of Bar Kokhba supporters proved for a time to be as effective as today's saturation advertising, and they help us understand something of why these particular symbols were chosen.

THE BAR COCHEBA REBELLION: A PHASED STRATEGIC OUTLINE

When one focuses on any war, the question arises of how it was either won or lost. This is the pragmatic "bottom line." Thus, the question of strategies comes immediately under the light of close scrutiny. Let us now address the strategies of both commanders.

Although there are neither accounts like those contained in 1 and 2 Maccabees, nor a Josephus-like account (as in Wars, Bk. IV) concerning how the Final Jewish Revolt was conducted, the meager available evidence

(*Yerushalmi*; Cassius 1925; Eusebius 1926–1932; and Eshel et al. 1998; on both caves of refuge and coins, as well as physical evidence from the most recent explorations in the Cave of the Letters) suggests that there were several discernible strategic stages/phases through which Bar Cocheba led the revolt, and ways that either Rufus or Severus reacted to them. Because detailed evidence is impossible to recover at this point, these phases are outlined, with commentary.

An Active, Engaging Phase

First, we may assume that Bar Cocheba took the initiative and attacked Roman forces. Whether this initial attack was on the force quartered on Zion Hill or elsewhere we are unable to say. From staging areas near Jerusalem, a well-coordinated attack on the garrison inaugurated a guerrilla warfare phase, engaging the forces of the Roman governor Tinneius Rufus in the open, then withdrawing in small groups to the rough countryside around Jerusalem, which was honeycombed with numerous limestone caves. The attack from several directions would have been designed to separate the concentrated force of the legions. This tactic had been utilized with great success by various groups of Jewish combatants since the Maccabean Revolt and perhaps beyond. It had been particularly successful during the early months of the First Jewish Revolt against the forces of the legate Cestius Gallus in 66 CE and was equally successful during this final revolt also. These tactics succeeded in defeating the army of Tinneius Rufus, putting him on the defensive and forcing him to relocate away from Jerusalem. Afterward, Jerusalem was occupied by "Bar Kokhba," and his government was centered on this city. He would have begun to secure the boundaries of his state. This would have involved establishing armed outposts and early warning posts. For these, known caves, generally unknown to the enemy, would have been designated and occupied. The storage of weapons and supplies also would have been initiated during this stage/phase.

After having been pushed from his camp on Zion Hill, and reacting to the stratagem described above, Rufus withdrew his forces from Jerusalem to keep them from becoming encircled when the rebels attacked (probably in several waves). Though forced into a defensive posture, this withdrawal maneuver enabled him to take advantage of the broken lines of communication, with so many Jewish rebel cells now having been established in so many places. As discussed in the first three subsections of "Coins Found in Caves of Refuge from the Bar Kokhba Period" above, Eshel and others provide loci of caves near Jerusalem on three sides that were probably utilized by the rebels. Thus Rufus, too, would have employed small, mobile (i.e., cavalry) units in a flexible and secretive way to match the strategy of Bar Cocheba and his forces and develop a sense of their tactics and the lay of their terrain, supply and escape routes, and availability of water and food. Rufus would have only strategized for a police action. That an all-out war had been declared on Rome would not have dawned upon him or his legions. The game of hide-and-seek was on!

A Sedentary Phase

With the former Roman force on Zion Hill no longer a threat, the site of the leveled and prepared area awaiting the building of the future Aelia Capitolina (the Temple Mount area of Jerusalem the Ruin) was next occupied and fortified by a major body of Jewish forces. Because of the importance of the sacred area for the ideology of the revolt, it was imperative that this area be controlled by the Bar-Kokhba government in the making. It would serve as the center of the rebellion and of the Jewish government. Archaeologically considered, the so-called Mayer-Sukenik wall (consisting of a mixture of hewn blocks and ill-fitting, squared stones, themselves often leveled by small stones) may have been constructed by Rufus's engineers to help isolate the Jewish defenders of this fortified area (Gray 1969, 190). Without further physical or literary evidence, however, we cannot be certain who built it or for what specific purpose. We know from Josephus's account of the previous war that a portion of the western side of Jerusalem had been spared. Titus had left standing the three pillars/towers that had been built by Herod the Great: Phasael, Hippicus, and Miriamne (Josephus 1960/1981, Wars, IV: IX: 1). The capital of Bar Kokhba would have been a large tent city with three well-built towers on its western side, as usual since the days of Herod, a prominent, well-graded square area on the eastern side of the city where the former Temple had stood. For some time the area of the Temple Mount was used by Jews in renewed sacrificial and other cultic activities. It is difficult to imagine other masonry edifices standing during the early first year of Bar Kokhba's occupation. Once they felt secure from Roman attack, the inhabitants probably once again erected buildings. At the same time, either the old underground caverns and tunnels would have been reassessed or new ones would have been dug for safety and storage. The appearance of this makeshift Jerusalem would have been simultaneously as discouraging as the Second Temple was described as appearing to those who remembered the splendor of Solomon's edifice and as marvelous as anything for which others had wished for so long, almost to the point of desperation. But walls keep some out and others in!

The Hateful/Hurtful Phase

In preparation for reoccupying their former garrison on Zion Hill and the taking of "makeshift reoccupied Jerusalem," during what may be termed a *milhemet 'atashah* (war of attrition) of sorts, Rufus's legionaries and auxiliaries were often ordered to kill the wives and children of the rebels when they discovered their abodes in villages and towns, in an attempt to reclaim the outlying areas surrounding Jerusalem. They also sought out their hiding places, such as underground tunnels, conduits, caves, and galleries, but often failed to make contact with the rebel fighting men themselves, who had withdrawn to many surrounding caves located further afield. Many of these are discussed above in my survey of Eshel's work. These people viewed the Romans as butchers of noncombatants. In retaliation for these acts, non-Jews living in (now) unfortified settlements and towns were identified and summarily slaughtered mercilessly. The Roman colony at Emmaus (also known as Colonia), for example, was so singled out by Bar Cocheba and subjected to his nationalistic zealous response. We learn of this town and its fate from the Christian writer and leader Justin Martyr (Barnard/Justin 1996, I, 31, 6). Justin, himself from another such Roman colony, Nablus (Neapolis, New City) had reason to note this, for he belonged to a contemporaneous movement with competing messianic claims: those of Jesus the Messiah and his church. Bar Cocheba had reasons to both suspect the Jesus party of collaborating with the Romans (of whom they were also suspicious!) and to hate them. It was ideologically and militarily expedient for Bar Cocheba to issue orders to exterminate them. Yet how he is described in the *Talmud Yerushalmi* plays no relevant role in understanding why he would have reached this decision. These actions were, at any rate, more than simple *lex talionis*. Many lives on both sides were squandered during this phase.

A Change of Commanders: The New Strategy Phase of Julius Severus

In an otherwise unusually peaceful empire, Hadrian received disturbing reports from Rufus in Judea. Hadrian perceived that Rufus was no match for his Jewish adversary. He ordered his most able general to the area to restore order. Presently Julius Severus arrived in Judea (it had not yet become a part of Roman-ruled Syria Palestina) from Britain (where he had served as governor) in 133 CE as the new commander. Engagements on both sides intensified. As in the cases of Cestius Gallus and Gessius Florus during the First Jewish Rebellion, the rebels had learned how to outfox and either defeat or neutralize the local Roman forces and their commander(s), Tinneius Rufus and his officers, in the field. Vespasian, and later his son Titus, had turned the tide in favor of Rome in 66–70 CE. It was now hoped that Julius Severus would perform a similar "turn of the tables" after he arrived in 133 CE. He and Bar Kokhba would have ample time to test each other as strategists/adversaries. All of Hadrian's reasons for choosing him are as unknown as were the reasons Emperor Nero had chosen Titus Flavius Vespasianus (who had served as a senator) during the previous Jewish rebellion. We merely acknowledge that from the position of hindsight each decision was the best choice to have been made at that time and under those circumstances. Under Severus's leadership the Romans systematically destroyed the support base(s) of the rebels. The outposts under rebel control (reputed to have been 50 in number) and a reported 985 villages were razed to the ground on his orders. Because there is such a paucity of information on specific Roman tactics, we are uncertain whether these proved to be successful stratagems. Severus was repeating in the "princedom" what he had practiced in Britain. At any rate, when Severus knew of extensive cave use as a place of refuge and strategy by the rebels, he garrisoned troops in fortress camps nearby (such as above Nahal Hever) in an attempt to contain rebel activities and hinder their strategies in rural areas. It appears also that in Herod-like tactical fashion, at the Caves of Arbela, Severus's legionnaires may have descended into some of the better-situated caves of refuge (e.g., at the Cave of Horrors and the Cave of the Letters) and executed many who were hiding therein. This strategy having proven successful for Severus, the rebel government was ejected from Jerusalem (once again dispossessed as the Jewish capital).The course of military engagements on both sides (ever-increasing numbers of rebel hiding places and supplies were discovered and appropriated and defenders killed) progressed to the point that the main body of the rebels further fortified itself and took a final stand (Alamo-like) at Battir/Bethar, a stronghold some five or six miles southwest of Jerusalem (Eusebius 1926–1932, IV. Vi. 3) As happens in most sieges, the defenders were starved, their sources of water were expended, and their attempts at relief were thwarted. The last stand of the rebels and the commander who was with them there was finally crushed. Dion Cassius (1925, I. vix. 14) writes that more than 580,000 Jews were killed, in addition to others who had died of hunger and disease or who had been reported as missing. As a postscript to this phase, Durant reminds the reader: "The markets at Hebron and Gaza had so many Jewish prisoners that they sold as cheaply as horses! There were also survivors. These hid underground in channels. Most died, however, for the Romans surrounded them. Although some practiced cannibalism, most died of hunger" (1944, 548).

The Post-Bethar/Battir Consolidation Phase

The Romans had destroyed Jewish strongholds, denied the rebels access to the formerly fortified areas within Jerusalem, blocked them from their most important caves of refuge and storage, and ended their final stand at Bethar in slaughter and Roman victory. The defeated rebels languished in captivity while Severus's forces engaged in mopping up activities and operations.

But Rufus's and Severus's troops had paid a heavy price for this victory. The 22nd Legion (Deiotariana) was decimated. It has been rumored that poison wine may have contributed to its undoing, but this is unsubstantiated. At any rate, that year (135 CE), while addressing the Senate, Emperor Hadrian was unable to add in his report that the army was well! This had been a tradition, and it had been formerly true. That it now was not was oblique proof of the generalship, statesmanship, administrative ability and tactical ability of the emperor's formidable opponent, Simeon Bar Cocheba.

However brief it was, and regardless of how tragic its eventual demise was, Bar-Cocheba's government could count some successes. As Schweitzer points out: "The Romans were expelled from Jerusalem, for two years sacrifices were renewed on the Temple altar, and an independent state was created that went so far as to issue its own currency" (1971, 37). We have come full circle with our study.

CONCLUSION

There are numerous similarities among the Maccabean Revolution (167 BCE) (MR), the First (i.e., Great) Jewish Revolution (66–[70]73/74 CE) (GJR), and the Final Jewish Revolution (132–135 CE) (FJR). Certain scenarios were repeated in all three. Messianic overtones were noticeable in each (but do not eclipse the main cause or goal of any of them). Quite naturally Jerusalem was the ultimate focal point of each; it was for a time taken over and controlled by adversaries of all three groups of rebels. The city was subsequently wrenched from each adversary and (for a period of time at least) was restored as the capital of a free Jewish state. In the first case (the MR) the Temple and its sacrificial cultus were restored. In the second (GJR) the Temple was destroyed (by Titus) and its cultus denied. In the third (FJR) the (nonexistent) Temple was established in middle Platonic fashion (comparable to that in the *Mishna*) in the hearts and minds of those who hoped, worked, and fought for its restoration, and its image was held before all through the specific coinage of the Tetradrachm. Two other coins, one bearing twin trumpets and one bearing the *qinor*, completed the tripartite imagery, which provided inspiration and hope for the execution and sustenance of the FJR and its telos. The propaganda value of just these three coins proved invaluable. Madison Avenue advertising agencies and political spin doctors should sit at the feet of such genius!

In typical fashion, Josephus touts himself as the major Jewish intellectual, scholar, and soldier who attempted to prevail during the GJR. Yet he submitted to Vespasian, became his prophet and then biographer, and presented himself as a righteous adversary against most (if not all) other Jewish leaders of that revolt. Names such as John of Gishala, Menachem-the-priest, Simeon bar Gioras, and Eleazar ben Ya'ir (all important leaders of factions during the GJR) swirl around Josephus in his accounts like planets around the sun and like moons around planets (or even asteroids in an asteroid belt)! They are penned to appear equally as lifeless as all but the earth.

Although precious little detail is recoverable from the FJR, more chief players on both sides emerge upon the stage of this revolt/conflict, and in each case that role is quite clear and significant. Unlike in Josephus, where there emerged only one significant player (himself; even Vespasian and Titus are his twin moons), here there were five such players. We have been able to provide the barest raisons d'être for each in the minibiographies to demonstrate that this conflict was driven equally by the highest intellectual, as well as by the most skillful military, motivations and goals on both sides.

Additional literary evidence discussed in this chapter falls into three groups: (1) that which pointed in general toward a Jewish state of revolutionary mind; (2) that which provided later and extra-Jewish commentary on Bar Kokhba's Revolt; and (3) Jewish-written documents discovered by archaeologists in the Cave of the Letters. Under the first grouping we mined the Sibylline Oracles, Tobit, 1 Maccabees, Jubilees, the Book of Biblical Antiquities, 2 Enoch, and the Second Apocalypse of Baruch. Under the second, we examined relevant writings of Dio Cassius (Roman history) and Eusebius (Church history) and the latter's reliance on Justin Martyr. And the third group, the Bar Kokhba correspondence (and the Babatha Archive), produced letters in Hebrew, Aramaic, and Greek. These addressed contemporaneous practical, ideational, legal, cultic, and military matters.

Turning our attention squarely to caves and other cavities as places of refuge and for strategic use, we first conducted a study of this use of them as recorded in the Hebrew Scriptures/Old Testament, in Josephus (Wars), and in 1 Maccabees. We supplemented this evidence with what modern archaeology had to contribute. The work of the late Israeli professor Hanan Eshel and his colleagues was of paramount importance here.

We addressed the extent of Bar Kokhba's geographical "princedom." This was necessary to draw a provisional map, as it were, of that geographical entity and to be able to plot within its boundaries the significant course of the military engagements between Bar Kokhba's forces and those of their adversaries. Josephus spoiled us by providing an almost blow-by-blow account (whether truly reliable or not!) of the prosecution of the conflict on both sides during the GJR. The documentation of Bar Kokhba coins discovered in specific caves located north, northeast, south, and southeast of Jerusalem from the studies of Eshel and collegaues allowed us to construct a serviceable makeshift map of the area under the influence of the "Prince of Israel," thereby adding space, as it were, to our study. (The newest contributions to this study were presented by Professsor Strickert in his numismatic study at the 2001 conference in Rome). Only the issue of "time" (i.e., 132–135 CE) had presented us with no formidable challenge.

With these studies in place, we were able to combine their data to produce a probable phased outline of how the Bar Kokhba Rebellion was prosecuted; how his two main adversaries (Generals Rufus and Severus) reacted; and how caves, channels, and other cavities (for refuge and other purposes) were utilized in a Jewish strategy. Thereby, we detected an active, initial engaging phase between both parties, which was followed by Jerusalem being regained, repopulated, and resettled for a time by victorious Jewish forces. It became once more the capital of a free Jewish state. These two phases were followed by what this writer calls a *milhemet 'atashah*, or war of attrition phase, during which both sides attempted to whittle down through "body count" the number and kind of combatants and their support populations. This hateful/hurtful phase ushered in an intensification of efforts by the Romans in which Hadrian replaced Rufus with his best general, Julius Severus. We compared this with Nero having replaced Cestius Gallus and Gessius Florus with Vespasian and Titus, who then achieved similar results. This phase, lasting almost two years, resulted in Bar Kokhba's defeat at Bethar/Battir. In what was a fifth and final phase, the Romans consolidated their victories and continued mopping up operations. Those rebels fortunate enough not to have been at Bethar or to have been captured during any of the Roman raids would have continued to employ their caves and other loci of refuge until it was safe to emerge, after Roman bloodlust and acts of revenge had subsided.

An accurate map of the geographical area under Bar Kokhba's influence still needs to be drawn so that the limits of his efforts and of the revolutionary attempts he led may be known, appreciated, and studied archaeologically as a unit. Caves and Bar Kokhba–minted coins found in them make one contribution to helping scholars produce such a map. Once such a map is produced with accuracy, researchers can with more precision study the contemporaneous geographical areas that did not come under Bar Kokhba's control, as well as those that did, contributing to a more precise religio-political history (intellectual, social, cultural, and economic factors included) of the peoples of the eastern Mediterranean littoral under Rome's direct influence between 132 and 135 CE. For some this period (and the loss of this war and independent "princedom") marks the end of Jewish independence in Judea and the beginning of foreign rule until modern times. For others it marks the beginning of a more subtle form of Jewish self-rule and politics unbounded by the physical restraints of occupying foreign armies, Jewish sectarian politics, the loss of physical Jerusalem, the ignominy of having been denied the "navel of the earth" (the Temple) and its active cultus, and even historical Judah itself. But we have now made the transition into the era of the transformation of the Pharisaic movement. Its literary fruits, known as the *Mishna*, and its active exponents, known as Tanna'im, are the natural offspring of the failed rebellion led by Simeon Bar-Cocheba.

The Bar Kokhba Rebellion may have been the final attempt to return to the highest ideals of the pre-Herodian Second Temple Judaism period, or it may have been an attempt to eradicate all that was thought to have been gained by Antipater the Idumean and held by his descendants as (over) zealous supporters, "friends," and client agents whose pleasure it was to guard and defend the southeastern borders of the Roman Empire from ca. 65 BCE until well into the second century of the present era. On these two interpretations interpretive battle continues to be waged.

CRITICAL NOTES

1. While excavating the ruins of Gamla in 1985, this author discovered almost daily coins from the period of Alexander's rule there, so plentiful were they. Consult further Meshorer (1982 and 1967). On specifically Hasmonean coinage, see Rappaport (1976).

2. Cf. *Theory and Practice in Historical Study: A Report of the Committee on Historiography*, The Social Science Research Council, Bulletin 54 (New York: Social Science Research Council, 1946); on Davis, see 59–62, 68–69, 75, 95; and Hamilton J. Eckenrode, *Jefferson Davis, President of the South* (1923). On Lincoln, see the same work, 57–58, 60–61, 64–65, 67–68, 74–77, 79–83, 87, 89, and 123.

3. Reference the famous account in the *Talmud Yerushalmi, Masechet Ta'anit*, IV, $ 8, f. 68d., line 43, quoted in Montefiore and Loewe (1960/1963,, 261–64).

4. Equally little is known of his predecessor, the governor Tenneius Rufus. He had commanded four legions, several cohorts, and the Syrian fleet, which he employed along the eastern Mediterranean coast. Cf. Gray (1969, 19 and fn. on that page).

5. See Vermes (1973/1981) for just how little can be stated factually about Jesus. For a more broad treatment of messiahs and allied figures, consult Horsely and Hanson (1985).

6. There are reasons that the reader encounters several renderings of this and similar names. Many texts list this leader's name as Bar-Cocheba (such as the *Encyclopedia Britannica*). An alternate rendering is Bar-Kosiba. These may be considered transcriptional synonyms (although only the latter renders the more accurate gens in the Aramaic language). Bar Kokhba is a messianic title bestowed upon Simeon by at least Rabbi Akiva ben Joseph (but following him, by several others). Bar Kozib(v)a is designed as a derisive play of words by his would-be detractors and critics after Simeon had been captured and slain by General Severus's forces after the fall of Bethar/Battir in 135 CE.

7. Letter number XCVII to the Emperor Trajan reads: "Esteemed as almost the only genuine monument of ecclesiastical antiquity relating to the times immediately succeeding the Apostles." Written some forty years after the death of the Apostle Paul, Pliny the governor informed the emperor about "those who profess Christianity" and "the nature of their crimes." The emperor assured him that his course was correct "in investigating the charges against the Christians" and if "the crime is proved, they must be punished" in letter number XCVIII in William Melmoth, trans., *Letters of Gaius Plinius Caecilius Secundus*, The Harvard Classics, ed. Charles W. Eliot (New York: Collier & Son, 1909), 425–28.

REFERENCES

Alexander, P. S. (1984) "Epistolary Literature." In *Jewish Writings of the Second Temple Period*, edited by Michael Stone. Philadelphia: Fortress Press.

Amit, David, and Hanan Eshel. (1990/1991). "A Tetradrachm of Bar Kokhba from a Cave in Nahal Hever." *Israel Numismatic Journal* 11: 33–35.

Barag, D. (1980). "A Note on the Geographical Distribution of Bar Kokhba Coins." *Israel Numismatic Journal* 4: 30–33.

Barnard, Leslie W. (1996). *St. Justin Martyr: The First and Second Apologies*. Ancient Christian Writers. Mahwah, NJ: Paulist Press.

Cassius, Dion Cocceianus [Dio Cassius]. (1925). *Roman History*. Translated by Earnest Cary. Loeb Classical Library, vol. 8. Cambridge, MA: Harvard University Press.

Cohen, S. J. D. (1987). *From the Maccabees to the Mishna*. Philadelphia: Westminster.

Collins, J. J. (1984). "The Sibylline Oracles." In *Jewish Writings of the Second Temple Period*, edited by Michael Stone. Philadelphia: Fortress Press.

Cotton, H. M., and A. Yardeni. (1997). *Aramaic, Hebrew and Greek Documentary Texts from Nahal Hever and Other Sites*. Discoveries in the Judean Desert, no. 27. Oxford.

Dimant, Devorah. (1984). "Qumran Sectarian Literature." In *Jewish Writings of the Second Temple Period*, edited by Michael Stone.. Philadelphia: Fortress Press.

Durant, Will. (1944). *Caesar and Christ: A History of Roman Civilization and of Christianity from their Beginnings to A.D. 325*. New York: Simon & Schuster.

Eshel, Hanan. (1997). "Aelia Capitolina, Jerusalem No More." *Biblical Archaeology Review* 22 (6): 48–8/73.

Eshel, Hanan, et al., eds. (1998). *Ma'arot HaMiflat Mittuqufath Marad Bar-Kokhva [Caves of Refuge from the Period of the Rebellion of Bar Kokhba]*. Tel Aviv: The Israel Exploration Society.

Eusebius. (1926–1932). *Church History. Ecclesiastical History*. Edited and translated by K. Lake and J. E. L. Oulton. Loeb Classical Library. Cambridge, MA: Harvard University Press.

Freyne, S. (1980). *Galilee from Alexander the Great to Hadrian, 323 BCE to 135 CE: A Study of Second Temple Judaism*. Wilmington: Glazier.

Goodman, M. (1987). *The Ruling Class of Judea: The Origins of the Jewish Revolt against Rome A.D. 66–70*. Cambridge, UK: Cambridge University Press.

Goodspeed, Edgar J. (1938/1959). *The Apocrypha: An American Translation*. New York: Random House.

Grant, Michael. (1974). *The Army of the Caesars*. New York: M. Evans & Company.

Gray, John. (1969). *A History of Jerusalem*. New York: Frederick A. Praeger.

Horsely, Richard A., and John S. Hanson. (1985). *Bandits, Prophets, and Messiahs: Popular Movements in the Time of Jesus*. New York: Winston-Seabury.

Isaac, B. (1990). *The Limits of Empire: The Roman Army in the East*. Oxford, UK: Clarendon.

Isaac, B. (1992). "The Babatha Archive: A Review Article." *Israel Exploration Journal* 42: 62–75.

Jones, A. H. M. (1937). *The Cities of the Eastern Roman Provinces*. Oxford, UK: Clarendon.

Josephus, Flavius. (1960/1981). *Complete Works.* Translated by William Whiston. Grand Rapids, MI: Kregel Publications.

Josephus, Flavius. (1926–1981). *Josephus.* Edited and translated by H. S. Thackeray, R. Marcus, and L. H. Feldman. Loeb Classical Library. Cambridge, MA: Harvard University Press.

Lewis, N. (1996). *The Documents from the Bar Kokhba Period in the Cave of Letters: Greek Papyri.* Jerusalem: Israel Exploration Society.

Mare, W. (1987). *The Archaeology of the Jerusalem Area.* Grand Rapids, MI: Baker Books.

Meshorer, Ya'akov. (1967). *Jewish Coins of the Second Temple Period.* Jerusalem: 'Am Hassefer.

Meshorer, Ya'akov. (1982). *Ancient Jewish Coinage.* Dix Hills, NJ: Amphora Books.

Mildenberg, L. (1980). "Bar Kokhba Coins and Documents." *Harvard Studies in Classical Philology* 84: 311–335.

Mildenberg, L. (1984). *The Coinage of the Bar Kokhba War.* Frankfurt: Verlag Sauerlander.

Milik, J. T. (1959). *Ten Years of Discovery in the Wilderness of Judea.* London: SCM.

Montefiore, C. G., and H. Loewe, eds. (1960/1963). *A Rabbinic Anthology.* Philadelphia: The Jewish Publication Society of America.

Neusner, Jacob. (1973). *From Politics to Piety: The Emergence of Pharisaic Judaism.* Englewood Cliffs, NJ: Prentice-Hall.

Neusner, Jacob. (1975/1982). *First Century Judaism in Crisis.* Augmented ed. New York: Abingdon Press/KATAV Publishing House.

Pamphili, Eusebius. (1965). *Historica Ecclesiastica [Church History].* Translated by G. A. Williamson. The History of the Church. New York: Penguin Books.

Rappaport, U. (1976). "The Emergence of Hasmonean Coinage." *AJS Review* 1: 171–186.

Richardson, Peter. (1996). *Herod: King of the Jews and Friend of the Romans.* Columbia: University of South Carolina Press.

Richardson, Peter, et al. (1991). *Law in Religious Communities in the Roman Period: The Debate over Torah and Nomos in Post-Biblical Judaism and Early Christianity.* Waterloo, ON: Wilfrid Laurier University Press.

Rivkin, Ellis. (1971). *The Shaping of Jewish History: A Radical New Interpretation.* New York: Charles Scribner's Sons.

Rutgers, L. V. (1994). "Roman Policy towards the Jews." *Classical World* 13/1: 56–74.

Schaefer, P. (1981). *Der Bar Kokhba-Aufstand.* Texte und Studien zum antiken Judentum, 1. Tuebingen: J.C.B. Mohr (P. Siebeck).

Schweitzer, Frederick M. (1971). *A History of the Jews since the First Century A.D.* New York: Macmillan.

Smallwood, E. M. (1976). *The Jews under Roman Rule.* Leiden: Brill.

Smith, G. A. (1902). *The Historical Geography of the Holy Land.* London: Hodder and Stoughton.

Stowers, Stanley. (1986). *Letter Writing in Greco-Roman Antiquity.* Library of Early Christianity, vol. 5. Edited by Wayne Meeks. Philadelphia/San Francisco: Westminster/Knox.

Strickert, Fred. (1995) "The Coins of Philip." In *Bethsaida: A City by the North Shore of the Sea of Galilee*, edited by Rami Arav and Richard Freund, vol. 1. Kirksville, MO: Thomas Jefferson University Press.

Strickert, Fred. (1998). *Bethsaida: Home of the Apostles.* Collegeville, MN: The Liturgical Press.

Strickert, Fred. (2001). "The Bar Kokhba Coins from the Cave of Letters." Paper presented at the Annual International Meeting of the Society of Bibical Literature in Rome.

Vermes, Geza. (1973/1981). *Jesus the Jew: A Historian's Reading of the Gospels.* Philadelphia: Fortress Press.

Yadin, Yigael. (1971). *Bar Kokhba.* London: Weidenfeld and Nicholson.

Zeitlin, Solomon. (1962). *The Rise and Fall of the Judean State.* Philadelphia: Jewish Publication Society of America.

CHAPTER 5

IMAGINE THIS: JESUS AND THE KINGDOM OF GOD

Gregory C. Jenks

The significance of "the kingdom of God" in the original practice of Jesus as well as in the earliest Christian accounts of his activity is widely accepted. The following quotation from David Aune (1992, 600) represents this consensus and nicely captures the dilemma faced by any modern attempt to investigate the precise meaning of this theme:

> The kingdom of God, which is the focus of the teaching of Jesus in the Synoptic Gospels, was also central in the proclamation of the historical Jesus. Jesus proclaimed the kingdom, explained it through parables, enlisted disciples to help in its proclamation, was involved in disputes with Jewish religious leaders about its meaning, and very probably died as a consequence of the controversy which the proclamation of the kingdom of God generated. Despite this emphasis on the kingdom, the Gospels preserve no sayings in which Jesus explains precisely what he meant by it.

As a contribution to this current volume on revolutions in the human spirit that have transformed, or at least challenged, conventional assumptions about the human experience, this chapter revisits the earliest Jesus traditions that preserve—or perhaps represent—his concept of the kingdom of God.

PRELIMINARY REFLECTIONS

This is well-trodden academic territory, with a vast body of technical literature. The significance of the kingdom of God for understanding Jesus, and debates about the nature of this kingdom, have been central to New Testament studies for more than a century. Giants in the field—from Schweitzer (1925) to Dodd (1936), Bultmann (1958), Perrin (1963), and Schnackenburg (1963)—have shaped the debate. For a helpful overview of this debate and its current status, see the excellent essay by Dennis Duling (1992a) in the *Anchor Yale Dictionary of the Bible*.

This study focuses on the theme of the kingdom of God in the earliest Jesus traditions, giving particular priority to those traditions that have some claim to represent the original teaching and practice of Jesus. This is itself a problematic and highly contested assumption, but the gift that I bring to the table of this collection of wisdom is derived largely from my personal involvement in the work of the Jesus Seminar and more recently my continuing work with the Jesus Database project.

For the purposes of this discussion, I am not especially interested in what others in antiquity thought Jesus meant by this phrase. This is not a study of the history of the idea of the kingdom of God in early Christianity, but an investigation of the kingdom of God *in the teaching and practice of Jesus of Nazareth*. I focus on what Jesus is remembered as having said and done about the kingdom. Realistically, not every memory of Jesus having said this or done that is historically accurate. However, it is interesting to observe whether a coherent and engaging perspective on "the kingdom" is transmitted by this ancient witness to the legacy of Jesus.

Historical questions of this sort are not the only intelligent questions for modern people to ask about biblical traditions. They may be ultimately unanswerable questions, because the methodological challenges are immense. There are also other questions, some of which may be more relevant to the nature of the biblical texts and certainly more reflective of the ways in which contemporary readers engage with the sacred documents.

Nonetheless, historical questions have a certain fascination for me even if that means I engage in a quixotic charge at the windmills from time to time. Without imagining that a resolution of the quest for the historical Jesus is either probable or authoritative for contemporary Christian practice, I believe that asking questions about the historical Jesus is a healthy corrective to many traditional forms of Christian belief and practice, not least the simplistic What Would Jesus Do (WWJD) paradigm, with its individualistic and moralizing dynamic.

I am seriously interested in what Jesus may have done about certain issues we face as humans. I doubt that we can answer such a question with precision and certainty, but I am convinced that applying our best efforts to such a project is one way to grasp that deep wisdom needed if we are to shape lives that are "holy" and "true." This is not because we will discover exactly what Jesus might have thought or done about some issue. Rather, it is because—in the process of reflecting deeply on the problem—we may just discover what *we* need to do about that issue. And that, I suspect, is what Jesus wants most of all—not imitation, but a sustained effort to practice the kind of faith he seems to have found, to live with the kind of wisdom that he seems to have embodied, and in the end to die with the kind of integrity that he seems to have demonstrated.

Central to the faith of Jesus, to the wisdom of Jesus, and to the integrity of the crucified One, is the concept of the kingdom of God. So it is to that topic that I now turn.

THE JESUS DATABASE

During the initial phase of the Jesus Seminar the fellows worked with an inventory of historical Jesus materials prepared by John Dominic Crossan (1986). Given the seminar's initial focus on the sayings of Jesus, that collection was an inventory of the sayings material, although some narrative elements were included. Items such as the miraculous conception of Jesus (item 26), the birth of Jesus (item 367), his baptism by John (item 58), a leper healed (item 110), and the crucifixion of Jesus (item 5) all occur in the inventory of traditions about Jesus.

More recently the Crossan inventory has been developed as an annotated online resource, the Jesus Database (www.jesusdatabase.org). There are 522 items in the Crossan inventory, which serve as the basis for the Jesus Database project. That set of items encompasses a larger data set comprising more than 1,500 extant versions of various sayings (some with multiple attestation, but 342 items with just a single witness), as well as another 387 reports of 176 separate events.

The material in the database comprises all extant texts prior to the fourth century CE that cite the sayings or deeds of Jesus. This sample covers the first 300 years after Jesus and reflects the vagaries of historical circumstances during the three centuries between his execution by the Roman occupying powers in first-century Palestine and the adoption of Christianity by Constantine in 312 CE.

For the purposes of the Jesus Database, the material is initially grouped on the basis of the date of its earliest extant witness. Documents are assigned to one of four strata: 30–60, 60–80, 80–120, and 120–150 CE. Interestingly, though all the extant texts created prior to 300 CE are included, none has an initial witness later than the middle of the second century CE. This reflects the "thick" data for Jesus traditions during the first one hundred years of their development.

Within each historical stratum the extant texts are then ranked according to level of independent attestation. Items with multiple attestations are ranked higher within the stratum to which their earliest witness is assigned, whereas those with just a single witness are ranked lower in the relevant stratum.

The result is a series of cascading strata, with the 522 items being distributed over a series of historical periods and then ranked by attestation (see table 5.1). Within those items are 30, represented across at least 80 different versions, that refer explicitly to the kingdom of God/kingdom of heaven (see table 5.2).

Table 5.1. The Jesus Database by Date and Attestation

Stratum	Date	Total Items	Extent of Independent Attestation			
			Multiple	Triple	Double	Single
1	30–60	186	29	36	66	55
2	60–80	178	3	5	18	152
3	80–120	123	1	1	21	100
4	120–150	35	0	0	0	35

Table 5.2. Kingdom Sayings in the Jesus Database

Jesus Database	Jesus Seminar
Stratum One (30–60 CE)	
1+. *Mission and Message* (1a) 1 Cor. 9:14; (1b) 1 Cor. 10:27; (2) *Gos. Thom.* 14:2; (3) 1Q: Luke 10:(1), 4–11 = Matt. 10:7,10b,12–14; (4) Mark 6:7–13 = Matt. 10:1, 8–10a,11 = Luke 9:1–6; (5) *Dial. Sav.* 20 [53b, or 139:9–10]; (6) *Did.* 11–13 [see 11:4–6 & 13:1–2]; (7) 1 Tim. 5:18b.	At the Town Luke 10:9, 11.
8+. *When and Where* (1a) *Gos. Thom.* 3:1 & P. Oxy. 654.3:1; (1b) *Gos. Thom.* 51; (1c) *Gos. Thom.* 113; (2) 2Q: Luke 17:23 = Matt. 24:26; (3) Mark 13:21–23 = Matt. 24:23–25; (4?) *Dial. Sav.* 16; (5) 1Q?: Luke 17:20–21.	When and Where Luke 7:20b–21; POxy654 3:1; GThom 3:1; 113:2.
16–. *Supper and Eucharist* (1a) 1 Cor. 10:14–22; (1b) 1 Cor. 11:23–25; (2) Mark 14:22–25 = Matt. 26:26–29 = Luke 22:15–19a[19b–20]; (3) *Did.* 9:1–4; (4) John 6:51b–58.	Supper and Eucharist Matt. 26:29; Mark 14:25; Luke 22:16, 18; Did 9:4.
20+. *Kingdom and Children* (1) *Gos. Thom.* 22:1–2; (2) Mark 10:13–16 = Matt. 19:13–15 = Luke 18:15–17; (3) Matt. 18:3; (4) John 3:1–5,9–10.	Kingdom and Children Matt. 18:3; 19:14; Mark 10:14b, 15; Luke 18:16b, 17; John 3:3, 5; GThom 22.
35+. *The Mustard Seed* (1) *Gos. Thom.* 20:1–2; (2) 1 or 2?Q: Luke 13:18–19 = Matt. 13:31–32; (3) Mark 4:30–32 = Matt. 13:31–32.	The Mustard Seed Matt. 13:31b–32; Mark 4:30–32; Luke 13:18–1; GThom 20:1–2.
43+. *Blessed the Poor* (1) *Gos. Thom.* 54; (2a) 1Q: Luke 6:20 = Matt. 5:3; (2b) Pol. *Phil.* 2:3e; (3) Jas 2:5.	Blessed the Poor Matt. 5:3; Luke 6:20b; GThom 54; Pol *Phil* 2:3b.

Jesus Database	Jesus Seminar
75+. *The Harvest Time* (1) *Gos. Thom.* 21:4; (2) Mark 4:26–29.	The Harvest Time Mark 4:26b–29; GThom 21:4.
85+. *Greater than John* (1) *Gos. Thom.* 46; (2) 2Q: Luke 7:28 = Matt. 11:11.	Greater Than John Matt. 11:11; Luke 7:28; GThom 46.
90+. *The Planted Weeds* (1) *Gos. Thom.* 57; (2) Matt. 13:24–30.	The Planted Weeds GThom 57; Matt. 13:24b–30.
92–. *Knowing the Mystery* (1) *Gos. Thom.* 62:1; (2a) *Secret Mark* f2r10; (2b) Mark 4:10–12 = Matt. 13:10–11,13–15 = Luke 8:9–10.	Knowing the Mystery Matt. 13:11; Mark 4:11; Luke 8:109; GThom 62:1.
98+. *The Pearl* (1) *Gos. Thom.* 76:1; (2) Matt. 13:45–46	The Pearl GThom 76; Matt. 13:45–46.
104+. *The Leaven* (1) *Gos. Thom.* 96:1; (2) 1 or 2?Q: Luke 13:20–21 = Matt. 13:33.	The Leaven Matt. 13:33b; Luke 13:20b–21; GThom 96:1.
105+. *Jesus' True Family* (1) *Gos. Thom.* 99; (2a) Mark 3:19b–21,31–35 = Matt. 12:46–50 = Luke 8:19–21; (2b) *2 Clem.* 9:11; (2c) *Gos. Eb.* 5.	Jesus' True Family GThom 99.
107+. *The Lost Sheep* (1) *Gos. Thom.* 107; (2) 1 or 2?Q: Luke 15:3–7 = Matt. 18:12–14.	The Lost Sheep GThom 107.
108+. *The Treasure* (1) *Gos. Thom.* 109; (2) Matt. 13:44.	The Treasure Matt. 13:44; GThom 109.
120–. *The Lord's Prayer* (1a) 1Q: Luke 11:(1) 2–4 =(!) Matt. 6:9–13; (1b) *Gos. Naz.* 5; (1c) Pol. *Phil.* 7:2a; (2) *Did.* 8:2b.	The Lord's Prayer Matt. 6:10; Luke 11:2.
150+. *By Whose Power* (1) 2Q: Luke 11:19–20 = Matt. 12:27–28.	By Whose Power Matt. 12:27–28; Luke 11:19–20.
166–. *Patriarchs and Gentiles* (1) 2Q: Luke 13:28–29 = Matt. 8:11–12.	Patriarchs and Gentiles Matt. 8:11–12; Luke 13:28–29.
168+. *Kingdom and Violence* (1a) 1 or 2? Q: Luke 16:16 = Matt. 11:12–14, (1b) *Gos. Naz.* 8.	Kingdom and Violence Matt. 11:12–13; Luke 16:16; GNaz 8.

(continued)

Table 5.2. *Continued*

Jesus Database	Jesus Seminar
Stratum Two (60–80 CE)	
199+. *Kingdom and Riches* (1a) Mark 10:23–27 = Matt. 19:23–26 = Luke 18:24–27, (1b) *Gos. Naz.* 16b, (2) *Herm. Sim.* 9. 20:1–4	Kingdom and Riches Matt. 19:23, 24; Mark 10:23, 24, 25; Luke 18:24, 25; GNaz 16; Herm *Sim* 9.20:1–4.
201–. *The Chief Commandment* (1) Mark 12:28–34 = Matt. 22:34–40,46b = Luke 10:25–28, (2) *Did.* 1:2a;	Chief Commandment Mark 12:28–34.
214–. *Kingdom and Repentance* (1a) Mark 1:14–15 = Matt. 4:12,17 = Luke 4:14–15 =(?) John 4:1–3,(1b) Matt. 3:2	Kingdom and Repentance Matt. 3:2; 4.17b; Mark 1:15.
243–. *Some Standing Here* (1) Mark 9:1 = Matt. 16:28 = Luke 9:27;	Some Standing Here Matt. 16:289; Mark 9:1; Luke 9:27.
248–. *Hand, Foot, Eye* (1a) Mark 9:43–48 = Matt. 18:8–9, (1b) Matt. 5:29–30	Hand, Foot, Eye Matt. 5:29–30; 18:8–9; Mark 9:43, 45, 47.
291–. *Fasting and Sabbath* (1) *Gos. Thom.* 27 & P. Oxy. 1. 27	Fasting and Sabbath POxy1 27; GThom 27.
299–. *Solitary and Elect* (1) *Gos. Thom.* 49	Solitary and Elect GThom 49.
313–. *Near the Fire* (1) *Gos. Thom.* 82	Near the Fire GThom 82.
320+. *The Empty Jar* (1) *Gos. Thom.* 97	The Empty Jar GThom 97.
321+. *The Assassin* (1) *Gos. Thom.* 98	The Assassin GThom 98.
327–. *Peter and Mary* (1) *Gos. Thom.* 114	Peter and Mary GThom 114.
Stratum Three (80–120 CE)	
(no items)	(no items)
Stratum Four (120–150 CE)	
(no items)	(no items)

Table 5.3. Kingdom Sayings: Independent Attestation

Strata	Total	Multiple	Triple	Double	Single
1	19	4	2	10	3
2	11	0	0	2	9
3	0	0	0	0	0
4	0	0	0	0	0

The Jesus Seminar considered 80 extant sayings when it voted on the kingdom sayings at its meeting at the University of Notre Dame in fall 1986 (Butts 1987). In the Jesus Database inventory the number of individual texts is a little higher, but the two lists effectively match.

These 30 items enjoy varying degrees of attestation, as can be seen in table 5.3. That table also demonstrates that none of the kingdom sayings is assigned to strata three or four. These strata mostly comprise material from outside the New Testament, so the lack of reference to the kingdom in the noncanonical sources suggests that this theme was more typical of the earliest phases of the Jesus tradition. As time passed, the Jesus movement lost interest in the kingdom of God as a core theme and focused more on individual salvation through personal faith or the acquisition of secret knowledge (gnosis).

The distribution of these kingdom sayings across the biblical and extracanonical texts can be mapped (see table 5.4) to reveal patterns in our data. The data represented here have been identified independently in my own investigations, but are also published in Duling (1992a, 56–62).

It is important to note that texts relevant to Jesus's understanding of the kingdom of God are not limited to those that explicitly use the phrase *basileia tou theou* or its cognates. Classic parables such as the Samaritan (Luke 10:29–37) or the Prodigal (Luke 15:11–32) are surely relevant to any investigation of the kingdom of God in the teachings and the practice of Jesus, even though they do not use the term. The same is true for the many anecdotes in which Jesus is celebrated as extending God's compassion to outcasts (Mark 2:13-17a), foreigners (Matt 15:13–28), and blatant sinners (John 7:53–8:11). Even the death of Jesus has to be understood as a key element of his understanding of the kingdom and its claim upon his own self.

For the purposes of this study, it must suffice to note the relevance of an even larger body of materials in which the term *kingdom* is not found, but which are essential for a complete description of the kingdom of God in the Jesus tradition. Although we focus on the explicit kingdom texts, it is important to look for the fit of that material in the wider Jesus tradition.

Table 5.4. Kingdom Sayings: Distribution

Ancient Document	Kingdom Sayings	
Sayings Gospel Q	13	Duling allocates 10 to the earlier 'wisdom speeches' stratum, and 3 to the later prophetic judgment stratum.
Mark	20	Duling notes 14 sayings about the kingdom of God, and another 6 references to Jesus as a king.
Matthew	54	38 of these refer to the kingdom of heaven/God.
Luke	32	Duling notes that 10 of the Lukan examples parallel Markan texts, 8 are from Q, and 17 have no other parallel.
Acts	6	
John	2	Both in the Nicodemus discourse (John 3:3,5).
Thomas	22	As Duling observes, the Thomas material represents a consistently non-apocalyptic understanding of the kingdom.

Before examining the explicit kingdom sayings attributed to Jesus, it is helpful to note the limited occurrence of this phrase elsewhere. As table 5.5 indicates, there are very few occurrences of the phrase "kingdom of God" (including its related forms, "kingdom of heaven" and "kingdom of YHWH") in the Jewish scriptures or other Jewish writings from the Second Temple period. The idea that God exercised ultimate authority over creation, over God's people, and over the nations is well attested in all these texts, and especially in the Tanakh and the apocalyptic literature of the time. For the most part, however, this central affirmation of ancient Israel was not expressed in the phrase the "kingdom of God."

Although it is clear that "kingdom of God" (*basileia tou theou*) was not unique to Jesus of Nazareth, it is also clear that his use of the expression is both characteristic and (potentially) distinctive. Unlike terms such as "messiah," "prophet," "servant (of YHWH)," or even "son of man," this is not an expression that Jesus could have derived from the Jewish scriptures, as it virtually never

Table 5.5. Kingdom of God in Jewish & Christian Texts

Texts	Kingdom of God Texts	
Tanakh/Old Testament	[2]	Numerous biblical references to YHWH as king. The 'kingdom of YHWH' occurs in 1 Chron 28:5 & 2 Chron 13:8.
OT Apocrypha	1	"she showed him the kingdom of God" (WisSol 10:10).
OT Pseudepigrapha	1	"And the Kingdom of God is forever over the nations in judgment" (PsSol 17:3).
Dead Sea Scrolls	0	Despite numerous texts that deal with God as a king, the precise term does not occur in the Dead Sea Scrolls.
Philo	0	Although Philo uses 'kingdom' in both its literal meaning and also as metaphor, he never uses the phrase 'kingdom of God.'
Paul	6	Rom 14:17–18; 1 Cor 4:18–20; 6:9–10; 15:23–25, 50; Gal 5:19–21.
Josephus	0	"the surviving writings of Josephus contain no explicit Kingdom of God sayings in relation to revolutionary movement" (Duling, 1992b).
Deutero-Paulines	4	Eph 5:5; Col 1:11–20; 4:10–11; 2 Thess 1:5–10.
Pastorals	2	2 Tim 4:1–2, 18.
Other NT Epistles	3	Heb 12:28–29; Jas 2:5; 2 Pet 1:11.
Revelation to John	8	Rev 1:56, 9; 5:8–10; 11:15–17; 12:10; 19:6; 20:4–6; 22:3–5.

occurs in the Tanakh. Although the term occurs occasionally in nonbiblical texts from the Second Temple period, it seems hardly to have been a feature of contemporary Jewish thought in the time of Jesus.

Further, in continuing Christian use after Jesus the idea quickly transformed into a rather static concept, centered around the idea of Jesus as the king of a future apocalyptic order in which the righteous would be rewarded for their virtue and sinners be punished. In such a form, the "kingdom of God" is no longer a template for life choices here and now (as we shall see it was for Jesus). It is no longer a way of life, but a future goal.

The Kaddish prayer from the Jewish synagogue liturgy may offer a parallel to the kingdom of God in the teaching of Jesus, and especially to the petition "your kingdom come" in the Lord's Prayer:

> Magnified and sanctified be his great name in the world that he has created according to his will.
>
> May he establish his Kingdom in your lifetime and in your days and in your lifetime of all the house of Israel, even speedily and at a near time.

However, as Duling (1992b) notes, the earliest explicit reference to this prayer is from the sixth century CE. Though the prayer seems to reflect a much earlier context (there is no reference to the destruction of Jerusalem and its Temple), we cannot be sure that this kind of prayer was common in synagogue liturgies in the Galilee in the time of Jesus. Indeed, there is considerable debate about the presence of synagogues in the Galilee in the time of Jesus.

Even assuming the earliest possible date for the Kaddish tradition, it seems reasonable to observe that both the idea and the expression played a much larger role in the teachings of Jesus than in those of any of his Jewish contemporaries. The theme is consistent with biblical and postbiblical Jewish writings and particularly resonated with Jewish apocalyptic thought, but it is especially typical of Jesus—who was thoroughly Jewish, even if innovative, in developing this theme in this way.

It may also be important to interpret the sayings and actions of Jesus within the context of Jewish resistance to the Roman occupation. As Horsley (2003) and Crossan (1991) have demonstrated so extensively, the hundred years before and after Jesus were marked by a series of prophetic and messianic resistance movements, culminating in several violent uprisings, of which the Jewish Wars of 66–73 and 132–135 are the most notable examples.

Below "the tip of the iceberg of popular resistance to Roman rule" (Horsley 2003, 53) lay a deeper and more extensive refusal to accept what Crossan calls the "normalcy of civilization" (2007). Horsley (2003, 53) cites the work of anthropologist and political scientist James C. Scott, who developed a distinction between the "official transcript" of the open interaction between the powerful and the oppressed and the "hidden transcript" by which the oppressed collude to deny legitimacy to the powers that be. "[E]very subordinate group creates, out of its ordeal, a 'hidden transcript' that represents a critique of power spoken behind the back of the dominant" (cited in Horsley 2003, 53).

This suggests a way to locate Jesus and his proclamation of the divine *basileia* within the broader grassroots tradition of resistance to Rome. While naturally having echoes of the more direct action seen in "popular prophetic movements" and "popular messianic movements," Jesus might be understood as an example of the "hidden transcript" within Second Temple Jewish life. Jesus articulated the peasant antipathy to Rome and its aristocratic Jewish collaborators in fresh and vivid ways. More troubling still for the authorities, whether imperial or provincial, Jesus seems to have begun to implement this fresh expression of long-standing Jewish resistance to self-serving corrupt power with a program of healing and open commensality.

The authorities were perhaps not mistaken in believing that this kind of development could quickly turn into a messianic resistance movement, even if it had not reached that stage by the time Jesus was arrested. His presence in Jerusalem at Passover, and the apparent enthusiastic response of the crowds to this "Galilean prophet," would certainly have provided the Roman and Temple authorities with good reasons to take steps against him.

At this point it may be relevant to mention the enigmatic saying of Jesus about the "sign of the prophet Jonah" (Matt. 12:39–41/Luke 11:29–32, as well as a shorter version of the saying in Matt. 16:4). As I have observed in several studies of this motif in early Christianity (2011, 2013a, 2013b), Jesus seems to have been identifying himself and his mission with the popular view of Jonah as an Israelite prophet of resistance to foreign empire. Jonathan Reed (1996) makes a strong case for such a view of Jesus's reference to Jonah during his public activity in the Galilee, while Naim Ateek (2008) argues that Jonah was the first Palestinian liberation theologian! All of this is entirely consistent with an approach that locates Jesus within the broader historical resistance to Roman power in ancient Palestine.

JESUS AND THE KINGDOM OF GOD

Having identified the material that serves as data for our investigation and placed Jesus within the context of popular resistance to Roman power in ancient Palestine, it is now possible to address some key questions about his understanding of the "kingdom of God." In seeking to systematize his view of the *basileia tou theou*, we are cutting against the grain of his own preferred way of proclaiming the kingdom. Jesus seems to have chosen to tease his audience with poetic speech and provocative acts, so that those with eyes could see, and those with ears might hear.

To Whom Does the Kingdom Belong?

This was a controversial question to ask within the context of first-century Palestine. Rome itself had not long emerged from a civil war. In their turn, both Augustus and Tiberius were quite clear to whom the *basileia* belonged: it belonged to them. The would-be heirs of Herod the Great were more vexed by this question. Jesus was not taking sides between Antipas and Phillip, but imagining that the kingdom of God belonged to those least likely to enjoy power and privilege in this world.

This was not an escape from a harsh reality in this life into a utopian dream of reversal and reward in the world to come. Jesus was not promising his disciples thrones in the afterlife, but a share of power in the present. He was not counseling submission to the tyrant in the hope of divine vindication in the next life, but inviting people to live here and now as if they were sons and daughters of their "father in heaven." Ultimately, this alternative vision of reality cost Jesus his own life. No utopian escapism there.

In the teaching and practice of Jesus, the kingdom of God belongs to the little ones: the poor, the children, women, fishermen, peasants, householders, the diseased, the blind, the outcast, the blatant sinners, the demon-possessed, and the outcasts. Even collaborators with Rome—the tax collectors—find a place at the table. So do the daughter of a Canaanite woman and the child of a Roman centurion. The leprous Samaritan and the deceased son of the widow from Nain each finds a place in this kingdom. There seemed to be no limit to the circle of humanity that Jesus imagined as beneficiaries of the *basileia tou theou*.

This radical inclusiveness survived in the first generation of Jesus communities outside Palestine, even if it is not typical of so-called Christian churches in our own time. Around the year 50 we find Paul of Tarsus celebrating the inclusive gospel of Jesus in a letter to his converts in Galatia:

> There is no longer Jew or Greek,
> there is no longer slave or free,
> there is no longer male and female;
> for all of you are one in Christ Jesus. (Gal. 3:28 NRSV)

In the earlier practice and proclamation of Jesus, this was far more than a theory about some future state of blessing, or even a "community of equals" as sketched by Elizabeth Schüssler Fiorenza (1993). This was a real-world community of transformation in which debts were canceled, and the hungry provided with food. The Q version of the Lord's Prayer echoes this practical transformation in the lines, "Give us each day our daily bread, and forgive us our sins, for we ourselves forgive everyone indebted to us" (Luke 11:3–4 NRSV).

What Does This Kingdom Look Like?

Like Andreas, the fictional character in Gerd Theissen's classic narrative (2007) about the quest for the historical Jesus, we find ourselves never quite encountering him. Instead, we rely on the mixed band of people who found themselves touched by his words and actions and were then drawn into the company of people with whom they may never have imagined themselves sharing life.

This motley band of misfits was a community of repentance. But this was no guilt-ridden association of ascetics. Jesus and his ragtag band of penitents were not so much fixated on their past sins as engaged by the possibility that the reign of God was already breaking into their experience. Repentance was a constructive and hopeful turn toward a better future, rather than remorse over past misdeeds. Sins were swept away by a mere scintilla of trust in God's own intrinsic generosity and without the need to engage in religious rituals for purification and restoration.

In this emergent community of fresh practice, sins were understood to have been forgiven, and disease was healed. Physical and social impairment ceased to mark off one person from another. In this fictive kinship system, people found new brothers and sisters and a shared affiliation with a "father in heaven" that supplanted traditional obligations to natural mothers and fathers.

Such trashing of traditional kinship obligations was offensive to those with privilege and status in the dominant purity system constructed around Temple and table. The open table practices of Jesus challenged these traditional boundaries and invited people to imagine—and to experience—the messianic age right now. It seems likely that his own family and village neither understood nor embraced his radical vision of the *basileia tou theou*. His spiritual cousins among the Pharisees, with whom he shared far more than traditional Christian stereotypes could ever admit, were offended by his failure to maintain a kosher table or take minimal precautions to maintain ritual purity.

Where (and When) Is This Kingdom to Be Found?

Interestingly, the question "when and where?" is the second highest scoring of the 30 kingdom sayings in the Jesus Database. Only *001 Mission and Message* rates more highly, as it enjoys even more extensive multiple attestation than *008 When and Where*. These are, of course, vital questions in response to the sayings and actions of Jesus. Where can we find this kingdom? When will it be part of our experience? Like the woman at the well in John 4, we find ourselves pleading, "Lord, give me this water!"

Though Jesus clearly shared the wider Jewish anticipation of a future day of judgment and the full inauguration of the messianic age, he seems to have had a distinctive take on the question of its immediacy. The kingdom is coming, it is already here, it is among us, and it is within us. At the same time its coming is to be requested in the prayer that Jesus teaches his disciples: "your kingdom come."

The future dimension of the kingdom is unremarkable given Jesus's context in Second Temple Judaism. He seems not to have been especially interested in elaborating on the apocalyptic scenarios often entertained by his peers when contemplating the divine reversal of life's current imbalances at the end of time. This did not prevent the tradition from attributing to him more common descriptions of cosmic disturbances and massive human suffering prior to the coming of the Son of Man.

On the contrary, Jesus seems to have been far more interested in celebrating and multiplying the miraculous signs of the kingdom's immediate presence among those who shared his mission and message. When the demons are cast out, when the blind have their sight restored, when the lepers are cured, when the lame walk, when the dead are raised, and when the poor have the good news proclaimed to them—then the kingdom has indeed come near (cf. Luke 4:17–21, 7:22).

In the spirit of Jesus, then, the answer to the question when and where is: Why not here? Why not right now? The ultimate fulfillment of the kingdom may not be experienced until the coming of the Son of Man, but the kingdom is already here, among, between, and within us. Grasp the moment. Release each others' debts. Heal each others' infirmities. Pass the bread and wine! We are the children of the generous Father, so let's live that deep truth here and now rather than wait one day longer.

Both the ultimate arrival of the kingdom and its present availability to those with eyes to see and ears to hear was deeply disturbing news to the powers that be. Men of power (and they mostly were/are males) in public life and in religion had no interest in hastening the coming of God's kingdom. Where possible its arrival was to be rescheduled until the distant future, and the little people were to return to their assigned roles in the wealth production system that benefited the privileged few. Jesus glimpsed the imminence of the kingdom and the possibility of living the blessing here and now. For that he had to be eliminated.

What Is the Role of Jesus in This Kingdom?

The final question to be considered in this short study concerns the role of Jesus in the kingdom that is coming and is already here. Though the post-Easter Jesus movement quickly attributed to him a decisive role in the future fulfillment of the kingdom, Jesus himself seems not to have been especially interested in such questions.

In the earliest stages of the Jesus tradition, Jesus is concerned to proclaim and to live the kingdom of God. While promising twelve thrones to his leading disciples (Q = Luke 22:28–30; Matt. 19:28), he says nothing of his own place in the kingdom that is already here and yet still to arrive. While "some standing here" (Mark 9:1; Matt. 16:28; Luke 9:27) will not taste death until they see the kingdom come with power, it is only in Matthew that "Son of Man" replaces "kingdom of God."

As a prophet within the broad Israelite traditions that seem still to have been preserved and celebrated by the poor of Galilee and Judaea, Jesus may well have had some sense of a special destiny—albeit more of a vocation than a privileged position—related to the coming of the long-awaited kingdom. At the very least, he would have known that crucifixion was the probable fate of anyone who challenged the Roman power system. In the spirit of Jonah—that local prophetic hero in the Galilee—Jesus may even have imagined that such a fate was no worse than being swallowed alive by a giant fish, and that after three days God would rescue him and restore him to his task of proclaiming and delivering the kingdom.

Certainly, in the post-Easter imagination of the Christian Church Jesus was thought to have contemplated both his death and his rising "after three days" (Mark 8:31 and parallels). The Johannine Jesus anticipates his crucifixion as a moment of epiphany and glorification (John 8:28; 12:32) and claims the power to lay his own life down and also to take it up again (John 10:18). The historical Jesus was probably more circumspect about his prospects, but willing to die a martyr like so many of the prophets before him (Luke 13:34).

In any event, it seems certain that Jesus's death by crucifixion was a direct result of his mission and message about the kingdom of God. From the perspective of the Roman authorities and their Temple collaborators, this prophet of the kingdom simply had to be eliminated. The more his program turned to implementation of the message, the more pressing his destruction. From the perspective of Jesus, his trust in the irreversible generosity of the Father made it impossible for him to do anything but follow the logic of his own message. He was not so much charging windmills as resting peacefully in the bottom of the ship while storms raged about him. His death was consistent with his life, his words, and his own actions. The cross became the ultimate symbol of his personal integrity within the fellowship of the kingdom.

CONCLUSION

Jesus invited people to imagine a world where God reigns, then to act accordingly. He lived the message that he proclaimed. He died in a way that demonstrated personal fidelity to the message of the kingdom and a deep confidence that even in a cruel and untimely death, the kingdom could be present.

So far as we can tell, Jesus did not denounce sinners or threaten divine wrath upon those who failed to believe. He was clearly critical of those with power and privilege, with his actions speaking even more loudly than his words. The renewal and reform movement that he triggered within Second

Temple Judaism would eventually break the banks of its own cultural stream and flood across a much broader swath of humanity.

His was a revolution of the human spirit, and it continues to evoke similar revolutions wherever people have eyes to see and ears to hear. The kingdom is indeed among us, between us, within us, and beyond us.

REFERENCES

Ateek, N. (2008). "Jonah, the First Palestinian Liberation Theologian." In *A Palestinian Christian Cry for Reconciliation*, 67–77. Maryknoll, NY: Orbis.

Aune, D. E. (1992). "Early Christian Eschatology." In *Anchor Yale Bible Dictionary*, edited by D. N. Freedman, 2: 594–609. New York: Doubleday.

Bultmann, R. K. (1958). *Jesus and the Word*. London: Collins.

Butts, J. R. (1987). "Probing the Polling: Jesus Seminar Results on the Kingdom Sayings." *Forum* 3 (1): 98–128.

Crossan, J. D. (1986). *Sayings Parallels: A Workbook for the Jesus Tradition*. Philadelphia: Fortress.

Crossan, J. D. (1991). *The Historical Jesus: The Life of a Mediterranean Jewish Peasant*. San Francisco: HarperSanFrancisco.

Crossan, J. D. (2007). *God and Empire: Jesus against Rome, Then and Now*. San Francisco: HarperSanFrancisco.

Dodd, C. H. (1936). *The Parables of the Kingdom*. Rev. ed. London: Nisbet.

Duling, D. C. (1992a). "Kingdom of God, Kingdom of Heaven: New Testament and Early Christian Literature." In *Anchor Yale Bible Dictionary*, edited by D. N. Freedman, 4: 56–69. New York: Doubleday.

Duling, D. C. (1992b). "Kingdom of God, Kingdom of Heaven: OT, Early Judaism, and Hellenistic Usage." In *Anchor Yale Bible Dictionary*, edited by D. N. Freedman, 4: 49–56. New York: Doubleday.

Horsley, R. A. (2003). *Jesus and Empire: The kingdom of God and the New World Disorder*. Minneapolis, MN: Augsburg.

Jenks, G. C. (2011). "The Sign of the Prophet Jonah: Tracing the Tradition History of a Biblical Character in Ancient Judaism and Early Christianity." In *How Jonah Is Interpreted in Judaism, Christianity, and Islam: Essays on the Authenticity and Influence of the Biblical Prophet*, edited by M. M. Caspi and J. T. Greene, 11–51. North Richland Hills, TX: Mellen Press.

Jenks, G. C. (2013a). "The Sign of Jonah: Re-reading the Jonah Tradition for Signs of God's Generosity." In *Pieces of Ease and Grace*, edited by A. Cadwallader. p. 71–84. Adelaide, Australia: ATF Press.

Jenks, G. C. (2013b). "The Sign of Jonah: Reading Jonah on the Boundaries and from the Boundaries." In *Bible, Borders, Belongings: Engaged Readings from Oceania*, edited by J. Havea, D. Neville, and E. Wainwright. Atlanta, GA: Society of Biblical Literature.

Perrin, N. (1963). *The Kingdom of God in the Teaching of Jesus*. London: SCM Press.

Reed, J. L. (1996). "The Sign of Jonah (Q 11:29–32) and Other Epic Traditions in Q." In *Reimagining Christian Origins: A Colloquium Honoring Burton L. Mack*, edited by E. A. Castelli and H. Taussig, 130–143). Valley Forge, PA: Trinity Press International.

Schnackenburg, R. (1963). *God's Rule and Kingdom*. Edinburgh: Nelson.
Schüssler Fiorenza, E. (1993). *Discipleship of Equals: A Critical Feminist Ekklesialogy of Liberation*. New York: Crossroad.
Schweitzer, A. (1925). *The Mystery of the Kingdom of God: The Secret of Jesus' Messiahship and Passion* London: Adam & Charles Black. (First published in 1901; first English ed. 1914)
Theissen, G. (2007). *The Shadow of the Galilean: The Quest of the Historical Jesus in Narrative Form*. Philadelphia, PA: Fortress Press.

CHAPTER 6

JEWISH FOLLOWERS OF JESUS AND THE BAR KOKHBA REVOLT: REEXAMINING THE CHRISTIAN SOURCES

Isaac W. Oliver

This chapter explores the relationship of "Jewish followers of Jesus" to Bar Kokhba and the Second Jewish Revolt by examining several ancient Christian sources on this topic.[1] By employing the phrase "Jewish followers of Jesus," I am following the lead of Boyarin (2009), who urges abandoning the use of the problematic term "Jewish Christians." With this rather pedantic nomenclature I am referring primarily to individuals of ancestral Jewish heritage (the ethnic criterion), still residing in Palestine, who observe the Torah in its so-called ritual dimension (the criterion of praxis), like many of their contemporary Jewish compatriots. In this chapter I am more interested in addressing the issue of Jewish (rather than Gentile) followers of Jesus and their responses to the Bar Kokhba Revolt, because the patristic sources (assessed below) assume the existence of an ethnically Jewish and Torah observant *ekklesia* (church) established in Palestine up until the Bar Kokhba Revolt. Evidence for the presence of Jewish followers of Jesus in Galilee also appears in the rabbinic sources (e.g., *t. Hull.* 2:24). I prefer using the term "follower" rather than "believer." Skarsaune (2007a, 3–21) currently employs the latter label, but its use risks overlooking other important factors for assessing the Jewish identity of followers of Jesus, particularly the significance of Torah observance.

According to many scholars, there was and only could have been one reaction on the part of the Jewish disciples of Jesus to the Bar Kokhba Revolt: to withdraw and not support such an endeavor at all. Jewish followers of Jesus, in conspicuous contradiction to many of their Jewish compatriots in Palestine, could respond to this political affair only negatively, because of a messianic dilemma they faced: they already had their messiah, Jesus, and could not dishonor that allegiance by submitting to another messianic claimant, Bar Kokhba (Dunn 2006, 317–18). Upon this stream of thought flows a wider metanarrative, substantially critiqued in recent times, which posits that the Second Jewish Revolt marked the immediate end of any real Jewish–Christian engagement, sealing the so-called "parting of the ways" between Judaism and Christianity. Dunn's words on this issue are well known by now among scholars of early Christianity and Judaism:

> *The period between the two Jewish revolts (66–70 and 132–135) was decisive for the parting of the ways.* After the first revolt it could be said that all was still to play for. But after the second revolt the separation of the main bodies of Christianity and Judaism was clear-cut and final, whatever interaction there continued to be at the margins. (2006, 312)

It is becoming clearer, however, that we should not exaggerate the immediate import and impact of the two Jewish revolts as watershed moments for all Jews and Christians from this period (Schwartz and Weiss 2012). Even Dunn subsequently recognized the complexity of this matter, in the preface to the second edition of his book (2006, xxii–xxiv). The question of the "parting of the ways" has often been analyzed with a disproportionate attention given to doctrinal disputes, to the detriment of appreciating social, political, and economic factors (Tomson 2003, 5). It comes as no surprise, then, that many scholars still make sweeping statements about the parting of the ways, positing an early date for a definitive and final separation between Judaism and Christianity by the first century. Thus, one prominent New Testament scholar roundly states in a commentary on the Book of Acts: "Judaism and Christianity began to emerge as clearly distinct entities c. 90 CE. A generation later, Luke was engaged in retrojecting this separation to the 'primitive' period" (Pervo 2009, 685). Quite tellingly, Mor, in his analysis of the Bar Kokhba Revolt, presupposes that the "Jewish Christians" formed part of the non-Jewish population during the revolt (1991, 187–90; 2002, 108).

But social factors and political events from those times as well as human experience teach us that the reality on the ground must have been far more complicated during and immediately after the revolt. Undoubtedly the two Jewish revolts marked and even destroyed the lives of thousands of Jews and many followers of Jesus living in Palestine. Nevertheless, Jewish memory could always recall the previous destruction of the First Temple and its successful reconstruction in order to cope with such trauma. Moreover, it would not have been entirely clear in the immediate aftermath of such wars in which direction events would turn, enabling some Jews to hope for eschatological liberation or at least to envision a pragmatic reconciliation with Rome that would allow for a return to a former state of events. Only with the passing of time, as it became increasingly clear that the Temple would not be restored in the immediate future and that the Judeans, prohibited from entering Jerusalem, would not gain independence from Rome, did Christian authors especially use the Bar Kokhba event as a means for polemically theologizing Jewish history and constructing Christian identity vis-à-vis a reified Judaism, contributing in this way to the general impression ever since that the Second Revolt represented a watershed moment and a final turning point in Jewish–Christian relations.

Unfortunately, given the state and provenance of the evidence available thus far, we are often forced to speculate on certain matters, especially the role, if any, that Jewish followers may have played during such turmoil. Nonetheless, I strive to point to social, political, and military considerations that have been neglected in many inquiries on this topic, to provide better avenues for examining the extant literary sources. Because the relevant material stems predominantly from patristic sources composed a couple of centuries or more after the reported events (save for Justin Martyr), it is important to highlight the patristic musings about the Bar Kokhba Revolt, how this event was refurbished by the church fathers in their attempt to shape the form of Jewish–Christian engagement in their own day and milieu. In other words, while seeking precious historical kernels that may shed light on the events of circa 132–135 CE, I have become especially aware of the ideological motives of various church fathers in rewriting the Bar Kokhba event. This phenomenon can in turn inform us about the ongoing process of separation between Judaism and Christianity throughout Late antiquity.

BAR KOKHBA'S MESSIANIC STATUS

In one of his numerous publications, Oppenheimer (1984) ponders whether Bar Kokhba was viewed as a messianic deliverer in a divine or supernatural sense, or his messianic status was understood in a more realistic manner, in other words, in a national, political, and military sense. The key rabbinic text, explicitly identifying Bar Kokhba as a messianic figure, appears in the Jerusalem Talmud (*y. Ta'an.* 4:6 68d):

> R. Shimon bar Yohai taught: "Akiva, my teacher, expounded [the verse from Num. 24:7] 'a star [*Kokhav*] shall come forth from Jacob' [to mean] 'Kozeva [meaning, "falsehood"] shall come forth." When R. Akiva saw Bar Kozeva he said: "This one is the king messiah." R. Yohanan ben Torta said to him: "Akiva, grass shall grow on your cheeks and still the son of David shall not come!" (author's translation)

According to this passage, R. Akiva, citing Num. 24:7, a biblical verse with messianic overtones for many ancient Jews, allegedly proclaimed Bar Kokhba "king messiah." R. Yohanan ben Torta reportedly rebuked R. Akiva for holding such views. Both rabbinic figures were contemporaries of Bar Kokhba. A rabbinic play on names occurs here between the word "star," which appears in Num. 24:7 and from which Bar Kokhba derives his messianized name, and "Kozeva," meaning falsehood. This pun conceals the largely negative portrait ascribed by later rabbinic sages to the figure of Bar Kokhba. Nevertheless, the Jerusalem Talmud portrays a central rabbinic figure, R. Akiva, as sympathetic to the Jewish leader.

Oppenheimer, like many other scholars, assumes that the historical R. Akiva actually supported Bar Kokhba. Peter Schäfer (2002) questions this assumption. Settling this matter is not essential for this inquiry. More significant is Oppenheimer's argument about the rabbinic perception in this passage of Bar Kokhba's messianic character and function. He maintains that we should put special stress on the word "king," rather than "messiah," which would emphasize the political and worldly expectations R. Akiva allegedly had of Bar Kokhba (1984, 154). In other words, Bar Kokhba should be viewed as a leader embodying earthly, military functions, much like the biblical figure David. Remarkably, the Bar Kokhba letters do not provide any evidence that Shimon ben Kosiva viewed himself as a superhuman or heavenly messiah, the savior of the end of days, one who would raise the dead or perform other similar fantastic miracles. Shimon ben Kosiva's administration of the revolt, as presented in his own letters, reflects pragmatic concerns and is devoid of mystical elements (Oppenheimer 1984, 161; Mildenberg 1984, 76; Jaffé 2006).

It also seems that extensive preparation and organization for the revolt were set in motion before confrontations erupted, with the banner of war being sagaciously raised only after Hadrian had left Palestine. Such indicators do not fit well with an eschatological messianic revolt, which by its very nature is characterized by spontaneous eruption (Oppenheimer 1984, 162).

Oppenheimer finds it more useful to compare Shimon ben Kosiva with Rabbi Judah the Patriarch, as both characters bore the same title, "Nasi," sometimes translated as "prince" or "patriarch" (see Goodblatt 1984). In his own letters and on coins from the period, Bar Kokhba is referred to as "Nasi," not "messiah." The essential difference between the two, however, according to Oppenheimer, lies in their divergent strategies in bringing redemption to the people of Israel. One employed military means, seeking to deliver a swift blow to the Roman Empire; the other used diplomacy and gradually restored some of Israel's former glory. But in the end, both sought to bring restoration to Israel through realistic and earthly means.

We have briefly rehearsed some of Oppenheimer's findings to emphasize how the Jewish perception of Bar Kokhba's messiahship during the revolt would not have necessarily complied with the polemically charged portrait we are about to discover in the patristic sources that portray him as an anti-Christ, the false counterpart of Jesus. As Bourgel notes: "It seems to us very unlikely that Bar-Kokhba was seen as a supernatural being by his contemporaries. Undoubtedly, at some points in the war, he was recognized as a messianic deliverer but it would be misleading to consider that his supposed messianism derived from a reflection on his very nature in the manner of Jesus-Christ" (2009, 270).

This suggests that the Jewish populace, including possibly even some Jewish followers of Jesus, could have viewed Bar Kokhba's messianic role in various ways and interpreted his movement in a manner that complied with their own ideology and expectations. Those positing a messianic dilemma allegedly confronting the Jewish followers of Jesus of that time should at least consider Oppenheimer's thesis. Though impossible to prove, it could be that *some* Jewish followers of Jesus did not view the roles and ideologies associated with the figures of Jesus and Bar Kokhba as mutually exclusive and irreconcilable.

JEWISH FOLLOWERS OF JESUS AND BAR KOKHBA IN THE CHRISTIAN SOURCES

Two works written in modern Hebrew are beneficial for assessing the question of the Christian descriptions of the Bar Kokhba Revolt. Yeivin's dated work (1957) is useful because it contains a large sampling of passages from Christian sources, but it only provides some preliminary comments on each passage. Duker-Fishman brings the majority of the texts into the conversation and concludes that generally the patristic authors blame the Jews for instigating the revolt, claim that the construction of Aelia Capitolina came only in response to the uprising of the Jews, and view the defeat and the ensuing sanctions against the Jews as proof of God's punishment (1984). Although Duker-Fishman does not deal with the issue of Jewish followers of Jesus proper, nor fully appreciate how her findings could address the question of Jewish–Christian *Auseinandersetzung*, her discussion of some of the ideological features in the Christian sources is worthwhile to consider as we take a closer look at some of the statements made by Justin Martyr, Eusebius, and other Christian writers.

Justin Martyr

Justin Martyr remains one of our most important literary sources on the Jewish revolt, because his writings are the nearest in time to the events and he explicitly refers to the revolt. Justin Martyr was also originally from Neapolis, Samaria, a region within the geographical scope of the revolt, although he was not present in the area at that time (see Justin Martyr, *1 Apology* 1; *Dialogue with Trypho* 28.2). Unfortunately, he provides us with virtually no information about the political and social causes for the revolt. His interest in Bar Kokhba lay more within the theological sphere.

In his *First Apology*, Justin Martyr asserts that Bar Kokhba commanded that *only* Christians should suffer persecution unless they would deny Jesus Christ and utter blasphemy (*1 Apol.* 31.6): "For in the Jewish war which now occurred, Bar Kokhba, the leader of the revolt of the Jews, ordered that Christians alone should be led to terrible punishments unless they would deny Jesus, the Christ, and blaspheme."

In this passage Justin Martyr describes the Bar Kokhba Revolt as an event that occurred recently in his own day. The fact that he already refers to Shimon ben Kosiva by his "nickname," Bar Kokhba, is indicative of how rapidly the image of the Jewish warrior became wrapped in a messianic aura. This observation does not go against the argument presented in the previous section, because I do not deny that Bar Kokhba was perceived as a messianic leader, though certainly not in the super-divine sense Christians view(ed) their own Christ. Mildenberg states:

> Even though this messianic pun may have been current during the war, the Jewish fighters and partisans should not be pictured as having actually believed that Shim'on ben Kosiba was the Messiah; the Judaean Desert documents make clear that the Jews knew their leader was a man like themselves. The creative pun on the leader's name in Aramaic would simply have given the Jews a popular rallying cry for their cause. (1984, 76)

Justin's declaration that Christians *alone* were persecuted by Bar Kokhba should lead us to question the authenticity of such a statement as well as the ideological motivations that may be lurking behind it. It is impossible to believe that Jewish followers of Jesus living in Palestine would have been the *only* group singled out by Bar Kokhba for persecution, because of clear evidence indicating otherwise. For example, the Bar Kokhba letters reveal that strong measures were applied against people who refused to participate in the war. Thus, in one interesting letter, Bar Kokhba threatens to put a certain Yeshua ben Galgoula in fetters for refusing to follow orders. The letter reads: "From Shimeon ben Kosiba [Bar Kochba] to Yeshua ben Galgoula and to the men of the fort, peace. I take heaven to witness against me that unless you mobilise [destroy?] the Galileans who are with you every man I will put in fetters on your feet as I did to ben Aphlul" (trans. from Yadin 1971, 137–38).

Yadin rightly rejects the suggestion that the reference to the Galileans alludes to Christians, since there is no further qualification of the term, which in any case could refer to a variety of people living in Galilee. Other attestations about Shimon ben Kosiva's attempts to punish those who did not support his revolt or follow his instructions could be easily multiplied (see Benoit, Milik, and de Vaux 1961; Yadin 2002). Quite significantly, we never come across the messianic criterion as the reason for meting out punishment against nonconformers and nonparticipants. Some Jewish disciples of Jesus, therefore, may have experienced persecution along with *other* non-Christian groups who refused to support the uprising, but the focus by Justin on an exclusive persecution against Christians cannot be trusted.

We should also pay careful attention to the wider literary context in which Justin Martyr's passage appears. In the thirty-first chapter of his *First Apology*, Justin also affirms that the Jews are Christians' foes and enemies, killing and punishing Christians *whenever* they have the power (*1 Apol.* 31.5). To bolster his theological claims about the supposed Jewish propensity toward persecuting Christians, he immediately describes briefly the Bar Kokhba Revolt.. Later in his *First Apology* (47.1–6), he even interprets the defeat of the Jews and their subsequent ban from Jerusalem as fulfillment of scripture. Citing Isaiah 64:10-12, 1:7 as well as Jeremiah 27:3, Justin asserts that it was God's will that Judea should be laid waste and that Jews should be prohibited from entering Jerusalem—a decree he claims was enforced up to his own day, some twenty-five years or so after the war (see Skarsaune 1987, 160–62, 288–95).

The reason for their expulsion, according to Justin, is their alleged slaying of the "Just One" and persecution of his followers (cf. *1 Apol.* 48.4; *Dial.* 16.4; 108:2; 133; 136). This polemical portrayal would fit perfectly with Justin's wider program of "formal" appeal to the Roman emperors and officials to recognize the legitimacy of Christianity. Let us not forget that Justin's *Apology* is nominally addressed to none other than the emperor Antoninus, his son Caesar Verissimus (i.e., Marcus Aurelius), Lucius Verus (also Caesar, an adopted son of Hadrian), and the Roman Senate (*1 Apol.* 1.1).

In harmony with his opening address, Justin seeks to demonstrate that Christians are not enemies of the state (e.g., *1 Apol.* chs. 11 and 12), but respect its official and recognized authorities (e.g., *1 Apol.* 17). Justin contrasts this Christian attitude toward the Roman Empire with the rebellious behavior of the Jews toward Romans and Christians alike (similarly, Bourgel 2009, 245–46; Flusser 1988, 636–37).

Justin's other work, *The Dialogue with Trypho*, was written in the shadow of the Second Revolt (Skarsaune 2007b, 384). Indirect references and allusions to the revolt appear in the background several times throughout this work. Thus, already at the beginning of the *Dialogue*, Justin presents Trypho as "a Hebrew of the circumcision" who had recently escaped from the war and found refuge in Greece (*Dial.* 1.3). This passage suggests that refugees from the war had left Judea and managed to find a safe haven elsewhere around the Mediterranean basin. Justin may have gathered some information about the revolt from such people. Obviously this does not mean that he transmitted what he had learned without theological bias and interest. Justin integrates the Bar Kokhba event into his wider ideological scheme, in which he seeks to highlight Christian abstinence from this anti-Roman affair and to announce the supposed eclipse of Judaism. Thus he transforms the traditional, positive symbolism ascribed by Jews to physical circumcision of the flesh into a sign that separated the Jews from all nations and Christians, so that the former might be singled out to incur their current suffering, that is, their banishment under the decree of Hadrian from going up to Jerusalem (*Dial*.16.2). Later in the *Dialogue* Justin draws again from the motif of circumcision in conjunction with the decrees issued against the Jews, reiterating that circumcision was given to the Jews as a distinguishing sign so that they alone could now suffer what they justly deserve. Because of their defeat, the Jews can no longer lay hands on Christians as they supposedly had in the past (92.2).

Of course Jews were not the only people who practiced circumcision in antiquity, although "for Greek and Latin writers the Jews were the circumcised *par excellence*" (Stern 1984, 1:444). But Justin is hardly interested in reporting accurate facts about history and ethnic practices. Just as he presents the Christians as the only victims persecuted by Bar Kokhba, so he also singles out Jewish circumcision as a sign of divine punishment.

In hindsight, of course, few would wish to be associated with a failed campaign, and it is understandable that some would seek ways to distance themselves from such events in the aftermath of failure. Thus, in a late rabbinic text from the Babylonian Talmud (*b. Sanh.* 93b), Bar Kokhba appears before the rabbinic sages and claims to be the messiah, but the rabbis actually find him to be an imposter and have him killed! Obviously there is no authentic historical recollection regarding Bar Kokhba in this anecdote. Instead, as the Babylonian rabbis looked back at Bar Kokhba, who from their angle was a false messiah and leader of a failed and misguided revolt, they wrestled with the issue of how one of their greatest rabbinic sages (R. Akiva) had offered his support for this "messianic pretender." As a result, the Babylonian sages polished their heritage by claiming that their rabbinic predecessors actually killed Bar Kokhba, thereby putting an end to a revolt they felt uneasy being associated with (Oppenheimer 1984, 156–57).

All of the aforementioned passages from the *Apology* and *Dialogue with Trypho* illustrate how Justin theologically interpreted and appropriated the Bar Kokhba event. While Ben Kosiva may indeed have persecuted Christians, he may have been indifferent about whether they wanted to continue believing in their messiah, provided they showed support for the war. As a pragmatic military leader, it would have been in his interest to recruit as many volunteers as possible for the war, and this could have led him to overlook some of the theological differences, magnified by Justin, in order to unite his front against the incoming Roman enemies. Dio Cassius (*Roman History*, 59.12–14) claims that even non-Jews participated in the war. This claim may be confirmed in part by some of the material data, such as papyrus Yadin 51 (Mor 1991, 182–87). If this was the case, then participation in the revolt did not require recognizing Bar Kokhba as the messiah, making the complete withdrawal of followers of Jesus even more conspicuous.

Nevertheless, the evidence from Justin Martyr, despite the theological issues highlighted above, suggests that some Jewish followers of Jesus could not negotiate and embrace a simultaneous allegiance to their Christ, Jesus, and the political messianism ascribed to Bar Kokhba and his movement. Bauckham (1998, 228) rightly claims that "it is unlikely that Justin should have cited this single instance of Jewish persecution of Christians unless he knew it to be true" (similarly Wilson 1995, 6). For whatever theological and social-political reasons, some Jewish followers of Jesus refused to participate in the revolt, and Bar Kokhba sought to punish them, as he did other non-Christian Jews, not necessarily because such people did not recognize his messiahship, which he apparently never openly confessed, but simply because they did not actively support and participate in his campaign against Rome.

Eusebius

As we turn to Eusebius, much of the preliminary comments applied to Justin's works seems equally appropriate to those penned by the church historian from Caesarea, whose apologetics lie on the same trajectory as his predecessor. Accordingly, Eusebius draws directly from Justin, repeating verbatim the latter's assertion that Bar Kokhba exclusively persecuted the Christians if they refused to blaspheme their Christ (*Hist. eccl.* 4.8). Moreover, for Eusebius, Bar Kokhba was nothing more than "a man inclined to murder and robbery," who built on the reputation of his name to mislead others into thinking that he was "like a starlight descended from heaven" who could perform wonders for the benefit of those suffering from misfortunes (*Hist. eccl.* 4.8). This tendency to highlight the false messianic credentials of Bar Kokhba continued to develop in the patristic tradition. Jerome, for example, portrays Bar Kokhba as a deceiving character, claiming that the "famed Bar Chocabas, the instigator of the Jewish uprising, kept fanning a lighted blade of straw in his mouth with puffs of breath so as to give the impression that he was spewing out flames" (*The Apology against the Books of Rufinus* 3.31, in Hritzu 1965).

On the other hand, Eusebius records an alternative tradition that merely states: "Cochebas, duke of the Jewish sect, killed the Christians with all kinds of persecutions, [when] they refused to help him against the Roman troops" (Latin version of Eusebius's *Chronicle* in Yadin 1971, 258). As Bourgel notes, the incentive for the persecution in the latter passage differs from the former: no mention is made of religious beliefs. Eusebius may have drawn here from a tradition he knew or had access to in Palestine. The reliability of this tradition seems stronger than Justin Martyr's idealized persecution, because it is not as apologetic and conforms to the military agenda advocated by Bar Kokhba (2009, 247–49). On the other hand, we must note that Eusebius's explicit claim that Christians were persecuted for their refusal to fight against the *Romans* signals more strongly than his predecessor, Justin Martyr did, Christian fidelity to the Roman Empire in an age when Rome was officially undergoing a process of Christianization. Thus, Eusebius portrays the Jews, as embodied by their notorious leader Bar Kokhba, as bitter enemies of the Roman state, persecuting the Christians who remain unwilling to fight against Rome.

Like his predecessor Justin Martyr, Eusebius interprets the defeat of the Jews as fulfillment of divine prophecy. In his work *Theophania*, Eusebius comments extensively on the prophecies ascribed to Jesus in the canonical gospels regarding the destruction of Jerusalem in 70 CE. After asserting the fulfillment of Jesus's prophecies on the destruction of the Temple during the First Jewish Revolt, Eusebius provides a new twist to the "prediction" appearing in the gospel of Luke that "Jerusalem will be trampled on by the Gentiles" (Luke 21:24), interpreting it in light of the Second Jewish Revolt:

> He says after this, that the city [Jerusalem] shall be inhabited, not by the Jews, but by the Gentiles, when speaking thus, *"And Jerusalem shall be trampled on by the Gentiles."* It was known therefore to Him, that it should be inhabited by the Gentiles. . . . And, how these things have been fulfilled, many words are not wanted (to shew); because, we can easily see with our own eyes, how the Jews are dispersed into all nations; and, how the inhabitants of that which was formerly Jerusalem—but is now named Aelia by Aelius Hadrian—are foreigners, and the descendants of another race. (in Lee 1843)

Eusebius applies a new reading to Luke's phrase, "Jerusalem will be trampled on by the Gentiles," never foreseen by the author of the third gospel. Whereas Luke could bemoan the fact that Gentiles would *trample* upon the city of Jerusalem and its Temple, Eusebius transforms this lamentation to state that divine will intended for non-Jews to *inhabit* the city. This understanding of prophecy complies with Eusebius's abrupt claim of an immediate reconfiguration of the Jewish *ekklesia* of Jerusalem, which existed until the Bar Kokhba Revolt. In his *Historia ecclesiastica* (4.5–6), Eusebius relates that until the Second Revolt all bishops in Jerusalem were of Hebrew descent:

> This much from things written have I ascertained, that until the siege of the Jews, during the time of Hadrian, there were in number fifteen

successions of bishops, whom they say were all by origin Hebrews, and purely received the knowledge of Christ, with the result that they were also in fact deemed worthy of the service of bishops among those able to judge such matters. For at that time the whole church was composed by them of Hebrew believers, from the time of the apostles up until the siege they endured at that time, during which the Jews, having rebelled again against the Romans, were conquered after not a few battles (*Hist. eccl.* 4.5.2). (author's translation)

For Eusebius, the Hebrew "church" of the circumcision existed in Jerusalem from the time of the apostles all the way to the Second Revolt. He emphasizes that this "dynasty" of Hebrew "bishops" ceased at that time and then enumerates the names of fifteen Hebrew bishops from James, the brother of Jesus, to Judas, the fifteenth and last bishop. Regardless of the question of the historical authenticity of this list (see Irshai 1993, 1:22–24; Bauckham 1990, 73–78), what is significant is Eusebius's claim that these Hebrew bishops were perfectly "orthodox": not only could they boast of an apostolic succession going back to James, a relative of Jesus, but they received the knowledge of Christianity *in purity*. In addition, Eusebius uses the term "Hebrews" instead of "Jews" to denote the church of Jerusalem that existed up until the Bar Kokhba Revolt.

Scholars have often noted that in Eusebius's writings the term "Hebrews" carries rather positive connotations, in contradistinction to the more polemically loaded label "Jews" (Ulrich 1999, 57–132). According to Eusebius, this Hebrew church of Jerusalem was replenished right after the Second Revolt by a Gentile populace, whose first bishop was a certain non-Jew by the name of Marcus (*Hist. eccl.* 4.6.4). Thus, for Eusebius, the Bar Kokhba Revolt marks the end of a legitimate ethnic Hebrew episcopate in Jerusalem and its immediate replacement by a Gentile church.

Some have rightly questioned Eusebius's simplistic portrayal of an immediate, smooth transition from a Jewish church to a Gentile one. Such a simplistic historiographical description of the change in the church of Jerusalem during the days of Hadrian seems rather mechanical and simply ignores the complex social reality left behind by an entirely uprooted community, a vacuum that certainly would have only gradually been filled (Irshai 1993, 1:25–26). Equally significant is Eusebius's belief that after the Second Revolt the *legitimate* ethnic Jewish segment of the Christian church vanished: that is, those of Hebrew descent who had *truly* received the knowledge of Christ.

This positive portrait of the Jewish *ekklesia* of Jerusalem in the era before Bar Kokhba stands in stark contrast to Eusebius's description of the so-called heretical "Christian Jewish" sect known as the Ebionites (*Hist. eccl.* 3.27.1–6). By claiming that the legitimate Jewish form of expressing allegiance to Jesus had ceased by the time of Bar Kokhba, Eusebius indirectly denies any historical continuity between the Jewish *ekklesia* of Jerusalem and surviving "Jewish Christian heretics" from his own day. Whatever one makes of this tentative thesis, the surge in fourth- and fifth-century patristic references to both the Bar Kokhba Revolt and "Jewish Christian" sects in general is quite remarkable (cf. Boyarin 2004, 207–11).

Sulpicius Severus

Sulpicius Severus, a Christian writer from the West who lived during the fourth to fifth centuries, interprets the expulsion of the Jewish followers of Jesus from Jerusalem in even more explicit providential terms than did Eusebius:

> And because the Christians were thought principally to consist of Jews (for the church at Jerusalem did not then have a priest except of the circumcision), he [Hadrian] ordered a cohort of soldiers to keep constant guard in order to prevent all Jews from approaching to Jerusalem. This, however, rather benefited the Christian faith, because almost all then believed in Christ as God while continuing in the observance of the law. Undoubtedly that was arranged by the over-ruling care of the Lord, in order that the slavery of the law might be taken away from the liberty of the faith and of the church. In this way, Mark from among the Gentiles was then, first of all, bishop at Jerusalem (*Chron.* 2.31.3–6, in Roberts 1991).

For Sulpicius Severus, the outcome of the war allowed Christianity to free itself completely from the yoke of the Law, which Jewish followers of Jesus so stubbornly held onto. There is no lament on Severus's part over the loss of a distinctive Torah-observant Jewish wing within the *ekklesia*. Rather, he openly welcomes such an outcome as a result of divine providence. Like Eusebius, he obviously knows that Christianity originally sprang from a group of ethnic Jews who were Torah observant, much like some of the pockets of so-called Ebionites and Nazoreans surviving well into the fourth and fifth centuries. Eusebius, however, speaks in positive terms of the primitive Hebrew church in Jerusalem, whereas Severus views the church at this stage as imprisoned in its blind devotion to the Mosaic Torah, requiring divine intervention to be liberated from this Jewish "yoke."

Theological biases notwithstanding, if we seriously consider Eusebius's and Severus's assertions about the extinction of a Jewish *ekklesia* in Jerusalem in the aftermath of the Second Revolt, this would imply that the Romans applied no special policy in discriminating between Christian and non-Christian Jews during or immediately after the war. In this instance, Jewish followers of Jesus qualified as "Jewish" in the eyes of the Roman outsiders. Although the Roman authorities would occasionally discriminate between Jews and Christians (e.g., the localized persecution of Nero in Rome), and Roman policies even played a role in accelerating the process of the parting of the ways (Heemstra 2010), in this instance the same policy of discrimination was applied across the board to all Jews, whether sympathizers of Jesus or of Bar Kokhba. In the immediate aftermath of the Bar Kokhba Revolt, one could even speak of a momentary "converging of the ways" between Jewish disciples of Jesus and their Jewish compatriots: both types of Jews were led out of Jerusalem and Judea into exile and the slave markets (Jerome, *On Jeremiah* 6:31), where they suffered the same fate. Such are the effects of war, when individuals from different groups and strands of society are brought together, often against their own will and regardless of their previous associations and protocols.

The Apocalypse of Peter

The Apocalypse of Peter (*Apoc. Pet.*) is most pertinent for our study because of Richard Bauckham's claim that this work is a "Jewish Christian" book written *during* the Bar Kokhba Revolt (1998, 288). Most scholars agree that it was composed sometime in the first half of the second century (see Bauckham 1998, 4712–50). Schäfer, on the other hand, dismisses reading the *Apoc. Pet.* in light of the Bar Kokhba Revolt, pointing to the widespread literary phenomenon of apocalypses (1981, pp. 61–62).

Though Schäfer's skepticism is certainly warranted, I find the distinctive features spread throughout this particular apocalypse remarkable, because they do not fully correspond to themes of interest found in other writings of the same genre that normally attack the emperor and the imperial cult. Equally remarkable of this apocalypse is its unique use of the construct "House of Israel," which also appears in some of the Bar Kokhba letters (see Goodblatt 2006, 135–36; Eshel, Eshel, and Yardeni 2009). Bourgel takes this "ecclesiological" language as evidence that the author(s) of *Apoc. Pet.* discusse(s) issues that are viewed as internally affecting the Jewish People (2009, 331).

Bauckham identifies two themes in chapters 1 and 2 of this apocalypse: 1) the distinction between the true and false messiah and 2) the theme of martyrdom. For Bauckham, the false messiah described in the *Apoc. Pet.* cannot be a Roman emperor, because Christian apocalyptic texts always make much of the imperial cult when depicting emperors. The false messiah of the *Apoc. Pet.*, by contrast, does not demand worship (this complies with the portrait of Bar Kokhba suggested by Oppenheimer), but merely claims to be the messiah. As for the theme of martyrdom, the author develops this idea with the parable of the fig tree, as found in Matthew 24. Bauckham reads the fig tree in the *Apoc. Pet.* as representing the "house of Israel." The sprouting twigs of this fig tree herald the end of the world and represent the martyrs who will die at the hands of the false messiah.

Bauckham asserts that this theme can be more clearly understood if we situate the author and his readers at a time when the false messiah had already appeared and had put some "Jewish Christians" to death. Goodblatt agrees that the *Apoc. Pet.* refers to the persecution of followers of Jesus by Bar Kokhba, but offers an alternative hypothesis, suggesting that such a pursuit was the outcome of priestly influence upon Bar Kokhba. Indeed, Goodblatt posits a strong priestly support for Bar Kokhba. It was, after all, in the interest of the priests to see the Temple rebuilt. And since only the priests were known to have previously persecuted followers of Jesus, Goodblatt maintains that they played an integral role in fermenting persecution against them during the Second Revolt (1983, 11).

Because nothing is said about the final outcome of this false messiah, Bauckham posits that the *Apoc. Pet.* was written during the Second Revolt, before it had ended, "when Bar Kochba's military success against the Romans persuaded many Jews that he must be the Messiah and some Jewish Christians were being carried away by this enthusiasm for an enterprise apparently blessed with divine aid" (1998, 231). If we accept Bauckham's thesis, it could be taken as partial evidence for the participation of at least some Jewish followers in the Bar Kokhba Revolt, because the author condemns certain individuals of his group as traitors and followers of a false messiah. Whether such followers of Jesus retained their faith in Jesus cannot be ascertained. Maybe some Jewish followers of Jesus did not actively support the war by bearing arms, but silently hoped that it could lead to the eschaton they were long awaiting. These remain speculations. In his study of the *Apoc. Pet.*, Buchholz suggests that some followers of Jesus may have viewed Bar Kokhba as Jesus the messiah returned or as a military precursor preparing the way for the second advent (1998, 286).

The controversy in the *Apoc. Pet.* also may have revolved around other issues besides messianism. In *Apoc. Pet.* 16, the author stresses that the true Temple is the one built by God, not by man, and then provides a description of the credentials of the true messiah. Bauckham reads the emphasis on the true Temple and true messiah as the author's condemnation of Bar Kokhba's attempt to rebuild the Temple in Jerusalem (1998, 233). The position advocated in *Apoc. Pet.* against the Temple would not have been completely different from that of the *Epistle of Barnabas*, if, as some scholars believe, the latter was written with a "Jewish Christian" audience in mind in an attempt to dissuade them from remaining attached to the literal observance of the Torah (Claude-Mimouni 1998, 191).

In *Barnabas* there appears an enigmatic sentence that possibly alludes to the reconstruction of the Temple in Jerusalem around the time of Hadrian, perhaps right before the revolt (*Barn.* 16:3–4). This obscure passage has been understood in various ways, however, and it is difficult to make positive assertions about its historical referents (Horbury 1992). Nevertheless, it is significant that the author of *Barnabas* exerts himself considerably in his letter to spiritualize a variety of Mosaic commandments. Could this be because some Jewish followers of Jesus from his time, around the beginning of the second century, remained attached to the Torah?

Some Jewish followers of Jesus, because of their attachment to the literal observance of the Torah, might have sympathized with the goal to rebuild the Temple presumably promoted by Bar Kokhba, and the authors of both *Barnabas* and *Apoc. Pet.*, unhappy with such devotion, would have sought, each in his own way, to turn the gaze of the audience elsewhere.

CONCLUSION

The question about the "Jewish Christian" response to the Bar Kokhba Revolt has often been dominated by doctrinal considerations. This is due in part to the influence of the patristic authors, who, beginning with Justin Martyr, "christologized" the image of Bar Kokhba and interpreted his revolt against Rome in ways that served their ideological purposes. In one passage, however, Eusebius simply states that the followers of Jesus refused to participate in the war and were consequently persecuted by Bar Kokhba.

This led the late Israeli scholar Alon (1984, 2:628) to posit that Jewish followers of Jesus who did not support the war were not persecuted by Bar Kokhba because of their belief in Jesus as the true messiah, but because of their refusal—along with others—to participate in the war. In other words, they were persecuted as draft evaders. Abramski (1961, 76) argues that followers of Jesus did not participate in the revolt because of pacifism. This belief, however, did not prevent Christians in the long run from fighting in the Roman army (which eventually became Christian). Indeed, it is surprising that patristic authors (e.g., Tertullian, *De corona militis*) do not present the ideal of Christian pacifism as the reason for not joining the Roman army. Helgeland (1974) shows that the church fathers of the first three centuries objected to enlistment in the Roman army because of the idolatrous and polytheistic practices observed by the Roman legions.

There would of course be no such problem for Jewish followers of Jesus who wished to fight in a Jewish army under a Torah-observant leader such as Bar Kokhba. Ultimately, the specific reasons for the refusal on the part of some Jewish followers of Jesus to support Bar Kokhba elude us. They could have stemmed from a cluster of christological, eschatological, ethical, and pragmatic considerations as well as social-political factors.

Hopefully this investigation has made a small contribution to the ongoing discussion on the "parting of the ways" between Judaism and Christianity. It is laudable that newer paradigms now exist for constructing a more nuanced relationship that avoid isolating a single event as the decisive moment for a complete schism between all Jews and Christians (see Reed and Becker 2007; Boyarin 2004; Lieu 2002). As far as we can determine from the extant primary sources, only Justin Martyr seems to have readily and quite rapidly appropriated the Bar Kokhba event to promote a particular Christian agenda. Other patristic authors viewed the Second Revolt as a determinative moment in "salvation history" only in hindsight, more than two centuries after the war occurred.

By contrast, during the immediate aftermath of the war relations between Jews and Christians probably did not radically and suddenly change everywhere. The only body in the Jesus movement to experience the immediate and dire effects of this terrible war was the Jewish *ekklesia* in Palestine, whose members—along with their fellow non-Christian Jews—were either dispersed or decimated by the Romans.

The reexamination of the Christian passages dealing with Bar Kokhba and the followers of Jesus has been fruitful in many respects. An inquiry that began with an interest in assessing the relationship of Jewish followers of Jesus to the Bar Kokhba Revolt proposed a more complicated scenario, more representative of the complex human experience (especially in times of war) and in harmony with the newer perspectives on the question of the "parting of the ways," which are now well under way. It has hopefully become apparent that when we approach the relevant Christian sources, we learn just as much as, if not more, about the patristic authors and their impact on the formation of Jewish–Christian engagement as we do about the Bar Kokhba Revolt and the Jewish followers of Jesus of that time.

NOTE

1. This chapter is based on a paper written for a seminar on the Bar Kokhba Revolt presented by Aharon Oppenheimer during his stay in 2008–2009 as a fellow at the Frankel Institute for Advanced Judaic Studies, University of Michigan. I would like to thank my friend Jonathan Bourgel, a former doctoral student of Oppenheimer, for sharing the chapter from his dissertation entitled, "The Jewish Christians in the Storm of the Bar Kokhba Revolt" (2009). We are both delighted to have independently reached similar conclusions, namely, that the Bar Kokhba Revolt (at least during and in its immediate aftermath) should not be interpreted as a watershed in the so-called process of the "parting of the ways," and that some Jewish followers of Jesus may have even participated in or at least supported the revolt. My research, more than Bourgel's, tries to highlight the patristic refraction and reification of the Bar Kokhba event in the formation of Jewish and Christian identities.

REFERENCES

Abramski, S. (1961). *Bar Kokhba, Nasi Israel.* Tel Aviv: Masadah.

Alon, G. (1984). *The Jews in Their Land and in the Talmudic Age (70–640 C.E.).* Translated by G. Levi. Vols. 1–2. Jerusalem: Magnes.

Bauckham, R. (1998). "Jews and Jewish Christians in the Land of Israel at the Time of the Bar Kochba War, with Special Reference to the Apocalypse of Peter." In *Tolerance and Intolerance in Early Judaism and Christianity*, edited by G. N. Stanton and G. G. Stroumsa, 228–38. Cambridge, MA: Cambridge University Press.

Bauckham, R. (1990). *Jude and the Relatives of Jesus in the Early Church.* Edinburgh: T&T Clark.

Bauckham, R. (1998). "The Apocalypse of Peter: An Account of Research." In *Aufstieg und Niedergang der römischen Welt*, edited by W. Haase, II: 25.6 (pp. 4712–50). Berlin/ New York: de Gruyter.

Benoit, P., J. T. Milik, and R. de Vaux. (1961). *Les grottes de Murabb'ât.* Oxford: Clarendon.

Bourgel, J. (2009). "The Jewish Christians in the Storm of the Bar Kokhba Revolt." In "Jewish Christians and Other Religious Groups in Judaea from the Great Revolt to the Bar-Kokhba Revolt," 243–331. PhD. diss., Tel-Aviv University.

Boyarin, D. (2004). *Borderlines: The Partition of Judaeo-Christianity.* Philadelphia: University of Pennsylvania Press.

Boyarin, D. (2009). "Rethinking Jewish Christianity: An Argument for Dismantling a Dubious Category (To Which Is Appended a Correction of My Borderlines)." *Jewish Quarterly Review* 99: 7–36.

Buchholz, D. D. (1998). *Your Eyes Will Be Opened: A Study of the Greek (Ethiopic) Apocalypse of Peter.* Atlanta, GA: Scholars.

Claude-Mimouni, S. (1998). *Le judéo-christianisme ancien: Essais historiques.* Paris: Cerf.

Duker-Fishman, R. (1984). "The Bar-Kochva Rebellion in Christian Sources." In *The Bar-Kochva Revolt: A New Approach*, edited by A. Oppenheimer and U. Rappaport, 233–42. Jerusalem: Yad Yitshak Ben-Tsevi.

Dunn, J. D. G. (2006). *The Partings of the Ways between Christianity and Judaism and Their Significance for the Character of Christianity.* London: SCM.

Eshel, E., H. Eshel, and A. Yardeni. (2009). "A Document from 'Year Four of the Destruction of the House of Israel' in Which a Widow Declared That She Received All Her Rights." *Cathedra* 132: 5–24.

Flusser, D. (1988). *Judaism and the Origins of Christianity.* Jerusalem: Magnes.

Goodblatt, D. (1983). "Did the Tannaim Support Bar-Kokhba?" *Cathedra* 29: 6–12.

Goodblatt, D. (1984). "The Title *Nasi* and the Ideological Background of the Second Revolt." In *The Bar-Kochva Revolt: A New Approach*, edited by A. Oppenheimer and U. Rappaport, 113–32. Jerusalem: Yad Yitshak Ben-Tsevi.

Goodblatt, D. (2006). *Elements of Jewish Nationalism.* Cambridge, MA: Cambridge University Press.

Heemstra, M. (2010). *The Fiscus Judaicus and the Parting of the Ways.* Tübingen, Germany: Mohr Siebeck.

Helgeland, J. (1974). "Christians and the Roman Army A.D. 173–337." *Church History* 43: 149–163, 200.

Horbury, W. (1992). "Jewish-Christian Relations in Barnabas and Justin Martyr." In *Jews and Christians: The Parting of the Ways A.D. 70–135*, edited by J. D. G. Dunn, 315–45. Tübingen, Germany: Mohr Siebeck.

Hritzu, J. N. (1965). *Dogmatic and Polemical Works*. Washington, DC: Catholic University of America Press.

Irshai, O. (1993). "Historical Aspects of the Christian-Jewish Polemic Concerning the Church of Jerusalem in the Fourth Century." PhD diss., Hebrew University of Jerusalem.

Jaffé, D. (2006). "La figure messianique de Bar-Kokhba: Nouvelles perspectives." *Henoch* 28: 103–23.

Lee, S. (1843). *On the Theophania or Divine Manifestation of Our Lord and Saviour Jesus Christ*. Cambridge, UK: Duncan and Malcolm.

Lieu, J. (2002). *Neither Jew Nor Greek? Constructing Early Christianity*. London: T&T Clark.

Mildenberg, L. (1984). *The Coinage of the Bar Kokhba War*. Aarau, Switzerland: Sauerländer.

Mor, M. (1991). *The Bar-Kochba Revolt: Its Extent and Effect*. Jerusalem: Yad Izhak Ben-Zvi.

Mor, M. (2002). "The Geographical Scope of the Bar Kokhba Revolt." In *The Bar Kokhba War Reconsidered*, edited by P. Schäfer, 107–32. Tübingen, Germany: Mohr Siebeck.

Oppenheimer, A. (1984). "Meshihiyuto shel Bar Kokhba." In *Messianism and Eschatology*, edited by Z. Baras, 153–68. Jerusalem: Merkaz Zalman Shazar.

Pervo, R. I. (2009). *Acts: A Commentary*. Minneapolis, MN: Fortress.

Reed, A. Y., and A. H. Becker, eds. (2007). *The Ways That Never Parted*. Minneapolis, MN: Fortress.

Roberts, A. (1991). *The Works of Sulpitius Severus*. Vol. 11 of the *Nicene and Post-Nicene Fathers of the Christian Church*, edited by P. Schaff and H. Wace. Edinburgh: T&T Clark.

Schäfer, P. (1981). *Der Bar Kokhba-Aufstand: Studien zum zweiten jüdischen Krieg gegen Rom*. Tübingen, Germany: Mohr Siebeck.

Schäfer, P. (2002). "Bar Kokhba and the Rabbis." In *The Bar Kokhba War Reconsidered*, edited by P. Schäfer, 1–22. Tübingen: Mohr Siebeck.

Schwartz, D. R., and Z. Weiss, eds. (2012). *Was 70 CD a Watershed in Jewish History? On Jews and Judaism before and after the Destruction of the Second Temple*. Leiden, Netherlands: Brill.

Skarsaune, O. (1987). *The Proof from Prophecy*. Leiden, Netherlands: Brill.

Skarsaune, O. (2007a). "Jewish Believers in Jesus in Antiquity—Problems of Definition, Method, and Sources." In *Jewish Believers in Jesus: The Early Centuries*, edited by O. Skarsaune and R. Hvalvik, 3–21. Peabody, MA: Hendrickson.

Skarsaune, O. (2007b). "Jewish Christian Sources Used by Justin Martyr and Some Other Greek and Latin Fathers." In *Jewish Believers in Jesus: The Early Centuries*, edited by O. Skarsaune and R. Hvalvik, 379–418. Peabody, MA: Hendrickson.

Stern, M. (1984). *Greek and Latin Authors on Jews and Judaism*. Vols. 1–3. Jerusalem: The Israel Academy of Sciences and Humanities.

Tomson, P. J. (2003). "The Wars against Rome, the Rise of Rabbinic Judaism and of Apostolic Gentile Christianity and the Judeo-Christians: Elements for a

Synthesis." In *The Image of the Judeo-Christians in Ancient Jewish and Christian Literature*, edited by P. J. Tomson and D. Lambers-Petry, 1–31. Tübingen, Germany: Mohr Siebeck.

Ulrich, J. (1999). *Euseb von Caesarea und die Juden: Studien zur Rolle der Juden in der Theologie des Eusebius von Caesarea.* Berlin: Walter de Gruyter.

Wilson, S. G. (1995). *Related Strangers: Jews and Christians 70–170 C.E.* Minneapolis, MN: Fortress.

Yadin, Y. (1971). *Bar-Kokhba: The Rediscovery of the Legendary Hero of the Second Jewish Revolt against Rome.* New York: Random House.

Yadin, Y. (2002). *The Documents from the Bar Kokhba Period in the Cave of Letters: Hebrew, Aramaic, and Nabatean-Aramaic Papyri.* Vols. 1–2. Jerusalem: Israel Exploration Society.

Yeivin, S. (1957). *Milhemet Bar Kokhba.* Jerusalem: Mosad Bialik.

CHAPTER 7

JEWISH APOCALYPTIC EXPECTATIONS DURING AND AFTER THE REVOLTS AGAINST ROME

Isaac W. Oliver

According to a rabbinic legend, four sages visited (probably in a vision) paradise. Ben Azzai looked and died. Ben Zoma went mad. The "other" (i.e., Elisha b. Abuya) "destroyed plants." Only R. Akiva entered in peace and departed in peace (*y. Hagigah* 2:1 77b; *b. Hagigah* 14b). My intent is not to explicate this passage, whose details are susceptible to various interpretations, but rather to signal a certain apprehension embedded within this story toward apocalyptic and mystical experiences and enthusiasm. According to this story, only one-quarter of the time do humans emerge unharmed from such experiences and remain sane. This rabbinic story is recorded in works written at least two centuries after the two Jewish revolts in Palestine (ca. 66–70 and 132–35 CE) and the uprisings in the Diaspora during the reign of Trajan (ca. 115–117 CE), a time when expectations of the end of time ran high among many Jews, as the composition of various apocalypses attests (2 Baruch, 4 Ezra, Revelation of John, etc.).

In hindsight, such rabbinic reservations should come as no surprise. The rabbis knew that these wars had only led to the death of thousands of Jews (as exemplified, for our purposes, by Ben Azzai), psychological and emotional trauma (embodied by Ben Zoma), even heresy, and one might add apostasy (incarnated by the legendary Elisha b. Abuya, dubbed the "Other"). Only Akiva's peaceful demeanor, which for purposes of illustration mirrors a certain type of "eschatological quietism," guarantees Jewish survival and well-being.

In this chapter I try to highlight the impact of the revolts on the apocalyptic expectations of Jews living during and right after this tumultuous period.

The term *apocalyptic* has been subjected to various definitions throughout its long use in the history of research, be it in reference to a literary genre, a worldview, a movement, or a conflation of all three (Collins 1989, 8–13; Boccaccini 1991, 126–60; Portier-Young 2012). A time may come when such terminology will have to be discarded altogether, given the confusion and disarray it has generated. Here I am interested in exploring the eschatological-messianic dimension often associated with this epithet and its intersection with Jewish "nationalism" (Goodblatt 2006, 14). I therefore do not discuss the mystical and esoteric aspects appearing prominently in Jewish and Christian apocalypses, some of which show little interest in eschatology (Adler 1996a, 30).

I can only discuss here in broad terms how the repeated failures of the Jewish uprisings against Rome affected the eschatological, messianic, and nationalist expectations of Jews as expressed in "historical apocalypses," viewed by some as literature of resistance par excellence (Portier-Young 2011), and other literary works. The following survey is by no means exhaustive, but is intentionally eclectic, though I hope it is sufficiently representative of some of the main trajectories that emerged during and immediately after the bloody confrontations between Jews and Romans.

DEVASTATION AND APOSTASY

First of all, we should remember that the two Jewish revolts in Palestine as well as the uprisings in the Diaspora cost the lives of hundreds of thousands of Jews and radically affected many others, who were either deported, were sold as slaves, or sought asylum in other parts of the Mediterranean basin and Mesopotamian regions. Those sixty years of bloody confrontation have no parallel in the Roman world (Eliav 2006, 571). After the First Revolt, all Jews, including those in the Diaspora, had to pay the *fiscus Judaicus*, a tax used for the maintenance of the pagan temple of Jupiter on the Capitol in Rome, a humiliating punishment indeed (Heemstra 2010). Some Jews tried to conceal their Jewish identity to avoid paying the tax (Suetonius, *Life of Domitian* 12:2).

In Judea proper, Josephus describes with vivid and terrifying detail the suffering scores of Jews underwent during and after the First Revolt: many were slaughtered, others sold into slavery or sent to work in mines and quarries, while still others were taken to theaters where they were devoured by wild beasts or the sword (*Jewish Wars* [JW] 6:414–20; cf. Apoc. of Abraham 27:1–6). The Second Revolt, also known as the Bar Kokhba Revolt, was no less brutal, leading to the eventual banishment of all Jews from Jerusalem, while the uprisings in the Diaspora contributed to the decline of the once prosperous and populous Jewish communities in North Africa.

It is quite possible, then, given the brutal consequences and discriminatory policies, that some Jews gave up on Judaism and their Jewish identity altogether

(Schwartz 2001). Indeed, the author of 2 Baruch, writing sometime between the two Jewish revolts in Palestine (Henze 2011), bemoaned what he saw as an apostasy from Judaism, regretting that many of his people had ceased observing Mosaic statutes by casting away the "yoke" of the Law and mingling with the seed of the nations (2 Baruch 41:3; 42:4). The question of theodicy must have weighed upon the hearts and minds of many Jews as they wondered about the repeated failures to secure liberation and mourned the destruction of the Temple in Jerusalem, the abode where God was supposed to dwell among the chosen people of Israel.

After decades of confrontation, centuries of foreign domination, and the failure of prophetic predictions promising restoration to crystallize, some Jews must have given up not only on their messianic hopes, but on Judaism altogether, gravitating toward the Gentile world in search of better answers and social-economic opportunity, particularly after 135 CE (Goodman 2007, 501). Some might have become "Epicureans," a term used by Jews such as Josephus (*Jewish Antiquities* 10:209, 277–80) and the rabbinic sages (*m. Sanhedrin* 10:1) in a derogatory manner to condemn those who denied divine providence. Others may have even felt betrayed by apocalyptic ideology and concluded that the creator, as described in the Mosaic Torah, had prevented them from recognizing spiritual truths about supreme reality, thought it is impossible to posit this thesis with any certainty, as the origins of "Gnosticism," with its many non-Jewish facets and modes of expression, elude us (King 2003).

Nevertheless, it is still possible that certain forms of Gnostic expression proved attractive to Jews frustrated with apocalyptic visions that never materialized (Ehrman 2006, 115–20; Pearson 1990). Frankfurter signals many literary continuities between Jewish apocalypses and Gnostic texts, and one could argue that after 117 CE, when much of Egyptian Jewry was destroyed, only those individuals who no longer identified themselves as Jews composed "neo-apocalyptic" or "proto-Gnostic" texts in that region. Frankfurter, however, maintains that "[o]ne can distinguish Gnostic from apocalyptic readings of biblical scripture in terms of a transvaluation or inversion of Torah and its narrative themes and figures; but one cannot extrapolate from these transvaluations to establish which authors were inside and which outside 'Judaism,' especially in Alexandria" (1996, 162).

KEEPING THE "APOCALYPTIC FAITH"

In the face of destruction, other Jews insisted on rehearsing God's control over history to account for Jewish suffering and provide hope for eschatological restoration. Thus, 2 Baruch rehearses the common trope concerning Israel's failure to heed God's commandments, calling for collective repentance with the promise that God will send the messiah and exalt Israel above all nations (chs. 32, 42–44, 72, etc.). Most Jewish and anti-Roman is the Revelation of John (Marshall 2007; Pagels 2012), which acquired its final form after 70 CE. The destruction of Jerusalem by the Romans, which clearly displeased the author, provided ample opportunity for him to identify Rome as Babylon (cf. 1 Pet. 5:13). This identification also occurs in 2 Baruch and 4 Ezra, which are both placed in the context of the Babylonian destruction of the First Temple. Unlike 2 Baruch, the book of Revelation does not focus so much on the issue of Torah praxis, though its author despises those who neglect certain aspects of the Law (Rev. 2:20; cf. 14:12). Instead, the author of Revelation emphasizes showing devotion to God and the messiah rather than to Rome and the Roman emperor (e.g., 13:1–10). Like 2 Baruch and 4 Ezra, the author of Revelation speculates about the end of times.

Although the author of Revelation knows that Jesus was crucified decades ago, he refuses to give up on apocalyptic hope, insisting that the risen messiah will come with the clouds, and that every eye will see him, even those who pierced him (1:7). These works show that the failure of prior apocalyptic dreams to materialize does not necessarily lead to immediate incredulity or apostasy. On the contrary, out of great disappointment can emerge newly contrived apocalyptic visions that will always view previous tragedies as proof of the dawning of the eschaton. For those who are able to hold onto to such belief, no tragedy, however great, can eliminate the confidence that God is indeed in control of history and will soon reward the righteous and punish the wicked.

The author of 4 Ezra, however, seems to have been on the brink of becoming an "agnostic." This work earnestly and honestly tackles profound theological and existential questions raised by the destruction of the Temple and human suffering, but in the end, so it seems, holds onto an apocalyptic worldview that promises salvation and restoration, albeit to a small elite within Israel that has been set aside by God to enjoy such blessings (but see Hogan 2008). Like the book of Revelation, which focuses on the history of the Roman Empire and its eventual demise (Rev. chs. 13 and 17), so too does 4 Ezra speculate about the exact time when Roman power will end, hinting in his vision of the multi-headed eagle that the Roman Empire would soon collapse, perhaps around the time of Trajan (Ableman 2012).

The ideology espoused in such apocalypses undoubtedly inspired anti-Roman resentment and probably even fueled violent uprisings against Rome, though some apocalyptic texts seem at times to envision God as directly inflicting punishment on the nations (e.g., 4 Ezra 6:22–28; cf. Apoc. of Abraham ch. 31), while others envisage humans participating (with heavenly assistance) in warfare (e.g., the *War Scroll*, a pre-70 CE text). Indeed, the Diaspora Revolt of 115–117 and the Bar Kokhba Revolt may be understood in part as attempts, energized by eschatological fervor, to restore the Temple

(Goodman 2007, 476–91; 2012, 516), though more down-to-earth and pragmatic motivations on the part of certain Jews to have their privileges and cultic system restored after they were removed in 70 CE should not be underestimated (see chapter 6 in this volume).

In the end, however, some Jews felt that repeated announcements of imminent apocalyptic showdowns, coupled with violent confrontations, only endangered the survival of the Jewish people, who experienced in very concrete terms the overwhelming military might of the Roman Empire. In such circumstances, more accommodating, subtle, yet subversive stands toward Rome were devised that sought to preserve Jewish expression and identity without foolishly bearing arms against Rome.

ALTERNATIVE STRATEGIES

Already before the Bar Kokhba Revolt had erupted, the Jewish author who wrote the Gospel of Luke and the Acts of the Apostles (Oliver 2012; Wolter 2008; Jervell 1998) was discouraging his audience from speculating about the exact time when the kingdom of Israel would be restored (Acts 1:6). This does not mean that the Jewish author of Luke-Acts had given up on the hope of Israel's eschatological restoration. Like the rabbinic sages, "Luke" only discourages calculating about the end of time, because this might lead to disappointment or futile uprisings against Rome. However, Luke never refutes the notion that Israel will one day experience collective liberation. Indeed, he laments that many Jews have been taken as captives by Rome and that Jerusalem is trampled by the Gentiles (Luke 21:24). Luke's Jesus *weeps* over the siege and destruction of Jerusalem (19:41). But a time will come when the cup of the Gentiles will reach its full (Luke 21:24), and Jerusalem will finally welcome the (returning) savior with the psalmic and prophetic words, "Blessed is he who comes in the name of the Lord" (Luke 13:35). At that time, when the heavenly Son of Man comes in the clouds (Luke 21:27), God will heal and restore the Jewish people (Acts 28:27; Bovon 1992; cf. Merkel 1994, 396). The return of the heavenly Son of Man can only mean bad news for the rulers of this world, including the Roman Empire (Acts 4:25–26; Luke 9:26, 21:24).

Luke's claim that Jesus reigns on high in heaven challenges Roman earthly claims about ultimate power and authority. This relocation of ultimate authority enables Luke and his readers to engage in nonviolent resistance against Rome. Instead of speculating about the end of time or foolishly daring to fight powerful Roman armies, Luke channels Jewish zeal toward the proselytization of the Roman Empire: Jesus's Jewish disciples serve as ambassadors preaching the gospel in Jerusalem, Judea, Samaria, and the extremities of the earth (Acts 1:8). According to this geographical scheme, Jerusalem lies at the center of the world, not Rome, which is to be found somewhere at the ends of the earth vis-à-vis the holy city of Jerusalem, the navel of the world according to Luke's conception of time and space. This perspective contests Roman claims of the centrality of their beloved capital, Rome, and competes with Roman aspirations of conquest, albeit in a nonviolent fashion: Rome, for Luke, is the ultimate target of evangelization. Jesus's disciples outmatch Roman expansion by reaching regions of the world (e.g., Ethiopia, through the conversion of the Ethiopian eunuch in Acts 8:26–39) that Rome can only imagine controlling. By the end of Acts, Paul appears to have largely fulfilled the task of preaching the gospel to all nations: arriving from Jerusalem, he witnesses about Jesus's kingdom in the very heart of the Roman Empire. It is the subversion of Rome through its conversion.

Josephus, a contemporary of Luke, also avoids overtly speaking of the final eschatological demise of Rome. This is understandable, because Josephus found himself in a most delicate spot, having participated in the First Jewish Revolt only to then find refuge under Roman wings. He also wrote about the siege and destruction of Jerusalem, which he personally witnessed, all while under Roman patronage. Caught in this awkward and delicate situation, Josephus was careful in his writings to please Roman sensibilities while simultaneously defending his moral integrity in the face of Jewish allegations about his opportunism. Curiously, Josephus interprets Numbers 24:17–19, full of messianic connotations for many Jews in antiquity (e.g., 1QSb 5:27; 1QM 11:6–7; *y. Ta'an.* 4:6 68d), as applying to the Roman Emperor Vespasian (JW 6:312–13).

For Josephus, as for many other Jews, the Romans succeeded in destroying Jerusalem only with God's permission (as a divine punishment against the Jewish people). Accordingly, Josephus fashions Vespasian into a new Cyrus in reverse, who, instead of bringing the Jews back from exile to worship their deity in Jerusalem, has their Temple destroyed. Josephus even has Titus credit the God of Israel for the Roman conquest of Jerusalem (JW 6:411). But this positive portrait of Roman imperial power does not fully conceal Josephus's secret belief in its eventual demise. Josephus greatly admires the prophet Daniel and writes extensively about the apocalyptic book ascribed to this figure (JW 10:203–10, 267–81). He recounts Daniel's famous vision about the statue, boasting about Daniel's prophetic accuracy, claiming that all the historical events "foretold" in that vision have materialized, including the Roman conquest of Israel.

What Josephus wisely avoids interpreting is the symbol of the stone that in the end of times is supposed to fall upon the statue and shatter it into pieces, conveniently arguing that his task as a "historian" is not to describe the future but only to write about things past and present ([JW] 10:210). It is possible that he cautiously avoids speculating about future prophecy in order to avoid fomenting unrest among anti-Roman Jewish political factions (Adler 1996b, 214). However, the Josephan praise for Daniel and his prophetic foresight also implies in disguise the eventual demise of Rome. Just as much as Josephus asserted the "accurate" fulfillment of past prophecies, he probably believed in the crystallization of future Danielic promises, and there is no reason to believe that he had completely given up hoping for the restoration of Jerusalem and the Temple. Interestingly, Josephus focuses on the Temple when he defends and describes the beliefs and practices of Judaism, speaking of this institution in the present and future, as if it were still operating (*Against Apion* 2:193–94).

Many of the sages mentioned in the earliest rabbinic works, namely the Mishnah, Tosefta, and Halakic Midrashim, lived during and after the tumultuous period of 70–135 CE. They could not have remained indifferent to this state of political affairs. Surprisingly, the first rabbinic document, the Mishnah, makes little reference to eschatology and messianism (but see *m. Sotah* 9:15). The same holds true for the Tosefta, traditionally viewed as a supplemental work to the Mishnah. Part of the reason for this silence may be the literary genre and the types of topics surveyed in such documents, which served, among other things, as curricula for the study of Jewish law. Often this silence has been explained in light of the repeated defeats of the Jews by Rome (Neusner 1984; Schiffman 2011).

The Tannaim (the rabbinic sages of the first two centuries CE) had vividly witnessed the tragedy of such events. They saw how repeated messianic uprisings had led to destruction, suffering, banishment, and death. Accordingly, they devised and adopted an alternative way of dealing with this harsh reality. They chose to turn inward, withdrawing into their academies, where they found an intellectual and emotional refuge that enabled them to construct an intricate and sanctified way of living that could preserve Israel as it continued to await salvation.

Like Luke, and to a certain extent Josephus, the rabbis discouraged speculating or calculating about the end of times. Thus, the *Mekilta de-Rabbi Ishmael* declares that no one knows the time "when the kingdom of David will return to its place and when this wicked kingdom (i.e., Rome) will be uprooted" (*Mekilta* Beshallah-DeWayisa Parashah 5). In the later Babylonian Talmud, R. Samuel b. Nahmani said in the name of a Tanna (R. Jonathan): "Blasted be the bones of those who calculate the end" (*b. Sanhedrin* 97b). Instead, the Tannaitic sages delved into the world of halakah. Remarkably, they focused on the administration and rituals associated with the Temple cult in great halakic detail. Some suggest that the Mishnaic report of the Temple ritual served either as a historical record or for the purpose of easy reference in the event of its restoration (Safrai 1998). We might add that the discussion of the Temple, its dimensions, rituals, and sacrifices, enabled the rabbinic sages to deal with the trauma and vacuum left in the aftermath of 70 CE.

Such discourse and retention could have functioned as "damage control," providing a certain sense of continuity in face of uncertainty. On the other hand, Schwartz (2007, 143–44) notes that the Mishnaic tractate *Avot* does not even refer to the Temple when it discusses the handing over of the Torah from Sinai. It seems to move from a Temple-centric worldview to a conception of the world without the Temple. This transition derives from a willingness to momentarily rescind territory as essential for forming Jewish identity. As Hirshman (1996, 55–58) argues, the Tannaitic sages emphasized instead the importance of observing "portable" commandments such as the Sabbath and circumcision. These commandments became essential for the preservation of Jewish identity, as they could be observed anywhere in the world even without the Temple standing.

APOCALYPTIC EPILOGUE

It has been said that "insanity is doing the same thing over and over again but expecting different results." For some Jews, apocalyptic messages announcing the imminent arrival of the messiah, the eschaton, and the final judgment could be convincing and enticing for only so long. Many Jews of the first century CE had seen their share of itinerant preachers and messiahs, and they could only bear so many military defeats and punishments before ceasing to heed apocalyptic cries of "wolf." Indeed, after the Bar Kokhba Revolt, we no longer hear of Jewish uprisings or wars for independence. Palestine from the third century onward became a remarkably quiet region, fully integrated into the Roman Empire. In this peaceful atmosphere, Jewish society was able to recover from its previous wounds and flourish once again. However, after a period of relative stability, some Jews were able to readopt, however timidly, apocalyptic forms of messianic hope (Schiffman 2011), reminding us that visionaries see apocalyptic dreams not only in nightmares, but also during nights of relative calm and rest.

REFERENCES

Ableman, O. (2012). "Multi-headed Beasts and the Roman Emperors: Eschatological Antagonists in 4 Ezra 11–12 and Revelation 13 and 17." Paper presented at the Enoch Graduate Seminar, University of Notre Dame, Indiana, June 20.

Adler, W. (1996a). Introduction to *The Jewish Apocalyptic Heritage in Early Christianity*, edited by J. C. Vander Kam and W. Adler, 1–31. Minneapolis, MN: Fortress.

Adler, W. (1996b). "The Apocalyptic Survey of History Adapted by Christians: Daniel's Prophecy of 70 Weeks." In *The Jewish Apocalyptic Heritage in Early Christianity*, edited by J. C. Vander Kam and W. Adler, 201–38. Minneapolis, MN: Fortress.

Boccaccini, G. (1991). *Middle Judaism: Jewish Thought, 300 B.C.E. to 200 C.E.* Minneapolis, MN: Fortress Press.

Bovon, F. (1992). "Studies in Luke-Acts: Retrospect and Prospect." *Harvard Theological Review* 85: 175–96.

Collins, J. (1989). *The Apocalyptic Imagination. An Introduction to the Jewish Matrix of Christianity.* New York: Crossroad.

Ehrman, B. D. (2006). *The Lost Gospel of Judas Iscariot: A New Look at Betrayer and Betrayed.* Oxford: Oxford University Press.

Eliav, Y. (2006). "Jews and Judaism 70–429 CE." In *A Companion to the Roman World*, edited by D. Potter, 565–86. Oxford: Blackwell.

Frankfurter, D. (1996). "The Legacy of Jewish Apocalypses in Early Christianity: Regional Trajectories." In *The Jewish Apocalyptic Heritage in Early Christianity*, edited by J. C. Vander Kam and W. Adler, 129–200. Minneapolis, MN: Fortress.

Goodblatt, D. M. (2006). *Elements of Ancient Jewish Nationalism.* New York: Cambridge University Press.

Goodman, M. (2007). *Rome and Jerusalem: The Clash of Ancient Civilizations.* London: Allen Lane.

Goodman, M. (2012). "Religious Reactions to 70: The Limitations of the Evidence." In *Was 70 CE a Watershed in Jewish History? On Jews and Judaism Before and After the Destruction of the Second Temple*, edited by D. R. Schwartz and Z. Weiss, 509–16. Leiden, Netherlands: Brill.

Heemstra, M. (2010). *The Fiscus Judaicus and the Parting of the Ways.* Tübingen, Germany: Mohr Siebeck.

Henze, M. (2011). *Jewish Apocalypticism in Late First Century Israel: Reading Second Baruch in Context.* Tübingen, Germany: Mohr Siebeck.

Hirshman, M. G. (1996). *A Rivalry of Genius: Jewish and Christian Biblical Interpretation in Late Antiquity.* Albany: State University of New York Press.

Hogan, K. M. (2008). *Theologies in Conflict in 4 Ezra: Wisdom, Debate, and Apocalyptic Solution.* Leiden, Netherlands: Brill.

Jervell, J. (1998). *Die Apostelgeschichte.* Göttingen, Germany: Vandenhoeck & Ruprecht.

King, K. L. (2003). *What Is Gnosticism?* Cambridge, MA: Harvard University Press.

Marshall, J.W. (2007). "John's Jewish (Christian?) Apocalypse?" In *Jewish Christianity Reconsidered: Rethinking Ancient Groups and Texts*, edited by M. Jackson-McCabe, 233–56. Minneapolis, MN: Fortress Press.

Merkel, H. (1994). "Israel im lukanischen Werk." *New Testament Studies* 40: 371–98.

Neusner, J. (1984). *Messiah in Context: Israel's History and Destiny in Formative Judaism.* Philadelphia, PA: Fortress Press.

Oliver, I. W. (2012). "Torah Praxis after 70 C.E.: Reading Matthew and Luke-Acts as Jewish Texts." PhD diss.; University of Michigan.

Pagels, E. H. (2012). *Revelations: Visions, Prophecy, and Politics in the Book of Revelation.* New York: Viking.

Pearson, B. A. (1990). *Gnosticism, Judaism, and Egyptian Christianity.* Minneapolis, MN: Fortress Press.

Portier-Young, A. (2011). *Apocalypse Against Empire: Theologies of Resistance in Early Judaism.* Grand Rapids, MI: Eerdmans.

Portier-Young, A. (2012). "Apocalyptic Worldviews." Paper presented at the Nageroni Meetings, Milan, Italy, June 25–29.

Safrai, S. (1998). "Jerusalem and the Temple in the Tannaitic Literature of the First Generation after the Destruction." In *Sanctity of Time and Space in Tradition and*

Modernity, edited by A. Houtman, M. J. H. M. Poorthuis, and J. J. Schwartz. Leiden, Netherlands: Brill.

Schiffman, L. H. (2011). "Catastrophe or Utopia: The End of Days in Rabbinic Literature." Paper presented at the public session, End of Times: Fear or Hope, Catholic University of Milan, Italy, July.

Schwartz, D. R. (2007). "Josephus on the Pharisees as Diaspora Jews." In *Josephus und das Neue Testament*, edited by C. Böttrich and J. Herzer, 137–46. Tübingen, Germany: Mohr Siebeck.

Schwartz, S. (2001). *Imperialism and Jewish Society: 200 B.C.E. to 640 C.E.* Princeton, NJ: Princeton University Press.

Wolter, M. (2008). *Das Lukasevangelium*. Tübingen, Germany: Mohr Siebeck.

CHAPTER 8

THE PAULINE REVOLUTION: RELIGION THAT CHANGED THE WORLD

J. Harold Ellens

The story of Saul, who later came to be known as St. Paul, is a surprising, dramatic, and thoroughly intriguing narrative. He was apparently born sometime during the lifetime of Jesus and was raised in Tarsus in Syria. He was educated as a Pharisee under the famed Rabbi Gamaliel (Acts 22:3) and was given an important and authoritative position in the first-century Jewish community (Acts 22:5). He first comes to our attention as one of those present at the death by stoning of Stephen (Acts 7:58–8:2), a teacher and deacon in the nascent Christian church.

We next encounter him on a violent crusade against Christians in Palestine and Syria (Acts 8:3). Commissioned by the high priest and the entire council of elders in Jerusalem (Acts 22:3–5), he traveled to centers of Christian community and laid them waste (Acts 8:3). He imprisoned and punished both men and women for diverging from the Jewish ethnic community and its religious life. In this sense he seems to have been more urgent and aggressive about his Jewish faith than his fellow Pharisees were. He was a man of principle and action. Committed abjectly to his Jewish faith, he compulsively worked to literally exterminate those Jews who had accepted Jesus as the promised Messiah. He saw them as departing from the religious orthodoxy for which he stood.

On the occasion of his foray into Damascus to destroy the Christian congregation there, Paul had a radically life-changing, paranormal experience. Scholars cannot agree on exactly what happened to him on the road to Damascus; no one is certain what he was describing in his report on that event. What is clear, however, is that Paul experienced a remarkable confrontation with the postresurrection Jesus (I Cor. 15:8). Later (I Cor. 15:3–7). When describing what the disciples had previously seen and reported to him as postresurrection appearances of Jesus, Paul referred to such encounters as experiencing the presence of the glorified Christ.

He was quite clear what he meant by that terminology. The glorified Christ is Jesus Christ appearing in an ethereal or heavenly form after his death and translation into eternity with God. There are numerous implications in Paul's claim. First, the veil between time and eternity is more porous than usually supposed. Second, the state of life after life is such that persons who pass to it are not constrained by time, space, or materiality. Third, they can apparently manifest themselves in the arena of time and space in forms that are sufficiently similar to physical human beings that they can be observed as though they are in this present realm. Fourth, persons making such appearances from their eternal home are not immediately recognizable by ordinary humans, unless they make some gesture that reveals their identity. In none of the postresurrection appearance reports did anyone immediately recognize the person encountered. In every case Jesus had to "manifest" himself by some word or gesture.

Paul was certain that his life-changing experience involved three specific features. First, it was a personal meeting and discussion with the actual person, Jesus Christ. Second, it was a profound spiritual experience; that is, it cut through the defensive structures of his personality formation and grounded an entirely new sense of values in him at the character level, thus thoroughly infusing his life with an entirely new and different sense of meaning. Third, it turned him into a bold and uncompromising revolutionary within his ethnic and religious community and culture. This eventually led to his perceiving himself as a divinely called apostle to the Gentiles (Rom. 11:13).

What really happened to him, and what was its outcome? Paul's conversion on the Damascus road was not so much a matter of change in his nature, personality, or ambition. Rather, it was a radical shift in his values, belief system, mission, and objective. Apparently he was always an assertive crusader. When he was a thoroughly convinced member of the first-century Jewish ethnic community, cult, and culture, he was totally invested in killing Christians and exterminating what he considered to be a dangerous, heretical sect of infidels. After his encounter with Jesus, the Christ, he was the same assertive crusader, but with radically altered values, purpose, and goals. He became a revolutionary within the Jewish ethnic and cultic community, promoting the notion that Jesus of Nazareth was indeed the promised Jewish Messiah, as Jesus's disciples had been proclaiming.

What turned Paul from persecutor to promoter of this innovative Jewish sect soon to be called Christianity was a fundamental shift in his belief system and hence in his entire worldview. Having seen Jesus alive and well, he was wholly persuaded of the resurrection as the disciples testified to it. He was clearly aware that the resurrected Jesus was not the body that had been retrieved from the cross and temporarily stored in a friend's tomb. Jesus's resurrected state was an entirely different phenomenon. It was a glorified, heavenly, ethereal, transcendent reality, capable of manifesting in a recognizable form in this world. Paul declared (1 Cor. 15:42–46), as did Peter (I Pet. 3:18–19), that Jesus died in the flesh and arose in the spirit. He would find thoroughly objectionable the arguments over the last twenty centuries insisting upon or denying the bodily resurrection. It is most likely that the recent archaeological discoveries of ancient ossuaries and papyri by James Tabor and his colleagues, referring to the human life and permanent tomb of Jesus, are literally authentic references to Jesus of Nazareth (Tabor 2012).

Paul was sure that he had seen Jesus personally and understood that he was now a transcendental reality of an eternal nature, rather than merely a mortal reality of a mundane nature. That shift in perspective, based on his life-transforming experience, seems to have been the key factor in the course and outcome of Paul's new life. It was the root and ground of his revolutionary role in the rise of Christianity as we know it. As far as we know, Paul was the first to write anything about Jesus. Seven of his documents are available, all written between the death of Jesus about 30 CE and the destruction of Jerusalem by Titus in 70 CE.[1]

His narratives on the nature and meaning of Jesus's life and ministry definitively shaped the revolutionary new religion. He caught the essential thrust of the posture of God toward humankind that Jesus endeavored to promote. Jesus had refused to back down from that claim, and that got him tacked up on a Roman cross on a windswept Judean hill. It all had happened in a backcountry of virtually no noteworthiness, among a people who were a chronic gnat in the armpit of the Roman Empire. Nonetheless, Paul's assertive mission, focused on the fact and nature of Jesus' resurrection, produced three million Christians by the end of the apostolic age and ten million by the end of the third century.

It is clear that what empowered Paul was his experience with the resurrected Christ and his discernment of Jesus's claim that God's grace, goodwill, and forgiveness was radical, unconditional, and universal (Eph. 2:4–9, Rom. 14:11, Philem. 2:10–11). Five religions were competing for the attention of the Roman people in the times of Paul and the other apostles. First, diasporic Judaism was quite effective in adding Greek and Roman proselytes to its fold throughout the empire. The Jews held a sinecure from Rome to practice their religion without disturbance as long as they paid a special tax for that privilege. Second, the Emperor Cult was enforced with varying degrees of severity all over the Roman world, depending on who was emperor at any given time. Third, Mithraism, a Persian religion with many liturgical and theological characteristics similar to those of Christianity, was popular in the Roman army as well as among the general citizenry. The fourth religion was the Jesus movement, which slowly became the formally established Christian religion by the end of the apostolic age. The fifth religion poised to dominate the era was middle Platonism, soon to be transformed by Plotinus and Porphyry into Neoplatonism.

Each of these religions positioned itself, with more or less intensity, to become the favored monotheism. Had it not been for the Pauline revolution in Judaism, it is likely that Mithraism or Neoplatonism would have prevailed as the world religion, with Hellenized Judaism as a notable second. It was surely Paul's aggressive missionary efforts that spread Christianity beyond Palestine and Syria to permeate and pervade Asia Minor, becoming established in all the major cities. Moreover, this approach carried the faith to Greece and Italy. In each place where Paul planted an inquiring Christian community, the religion caught fire, spreading with surprising speed. By the end of the third century the Roman army was made up largely of Christian soldiers.

What was so appealing about this new religion, and why did it produce such a dramatic revolution, despite being repeatedly persecuted and repressed by imperial edicts? A graduate student of mine at the University of Michigan some years ago was so intrigued by these questions that he wrote his master's thesis about it. He was a very skilled researcher and writer and produced a fine study. His conclusion was that only Christianity offered a message and worldview in which God visits us in human form, a God who walks in our shoes, endures the tragic adventure of our lives, and embraces us all in divine forgiveness when we falter or fail (John 3:13–18, Rom. 8, Mic. 7:18–20). This student was headed in the right direction in his research and conclusions.

The mystery religions of Greece and Rome had largely run their course by Paul's time, except for the mystical and mysterious Mithraism, which had gained popularity. The Emperor Cult was quite obviously merely political manipulation and coercion, which could not link anyone to the transcendent and eternal or satisfy the universal and irrepressible human hunger for proximate and ultimate meaning. Judaism was an intriguing monotheism, but was limited by being rather exclusive, despite its Hellenization and diasporic diversity. Moreover, its dietary laws and nomistic nature must have seemed rather garish and contrived to the sophisticated Roman communities. It was a religion aimed at the head rather than at the heart, which did not inspire ultimate devotion or gratify the heart's hunger for meaning and a personal relationship with the transcendent world and God.

None of these religions suggested that God is directly involved with us in our life's journey, but Christianity did. No other intimated that God has revealed himself and the heavenly mysteries to humans directly. They did not propose that God invests our spirits with himself as divine spirit, as Christianity claimed. Mithraism proposed that God became present to us each time we celebrated the Mithraic liturgy, but he was represented symbolically in that cultic practice in the form of a sacrificed bull. This was probably too much like the mystical leftovers of the mystery religions to afford much spiritual gratification, compared with Christianity's God, who visited us, suffered our kind of life, maintained his integrity, and upon being done in by those who feared him and failed to catch his message, visited us again as a resurrected and glorified heavenly person.

Paul's story initially must have been a remarkable shock to all who heard it. Moreover, when he combined it with a previously completely unheard of and unimagined possibility that God is in no way a threat to humans but is inherently a God of grace, acceptance, and forgiveness for every human being, no matter how he or she has lived (Rom. 8), that must have seemed like surprisingly good news. I believe that it was this unique notion of God that converted Paul and revolutionized his world. Both the Gospel of John and Paul's Epistle to the Romans proclaim this radical, unconditional, and universal grace of God.

For Paul, radical grace meant that God's forgiving acceptance of each and every human overcomes all our pain, ego assertiveness, self-justification, narcissism, neurosis, fear, guilt, and shame to resolve the central pain and perplexity that is at the center of our psyches. That is God's acceptance of us all as he removes all fear, guilt, and shame from the equation of our relationship with him, deflates our sense of the need to measure up, and neutralizes all issues that induce the need to make ourselves right *with* or *for* God.

Paul's notion of the unconditional nature of God's grace is equally spectacular and surprising. Only God could have thought of the idea of grace. Humans believe in our heart of hearts that this is a *quid pro quo* world. Doing good will pay off. Doing bad will be punished. Paul's announcement definitively asserts that that is not the way God operates (Rom. 8; Eph. 2).

Micah, the Old Testament prophet, declared doxologically that God "tramples our iniquity under his feet and casts all our sins into the depths of the sea," where they are totally irretrievable forevermore. Micah, John, and Paul assert that this grace of God is uncalculating. It is not gauged by the quality of human lives, but is measured by the quality of God's integrity in assuring us the certainty of salvation. It is Paul who declared that, "By grace we are saved, through faith, and that not of ourselves. It is a gift of God, not from our good behavior, lest anyone of us should boast that we had earned God's favor" (Eph. 2:8–10).

For Paul, his experience and vision of God's grace as universal meant that no one is ever lost from God's grace and goodness. We cannot sin ourselves out of God's grace! We cannot squirm out of God's long embrace! The perplexity and finally the delight of those early Christians lay in Paul's assurance to them that even the oppressive emperors and those who violently carried out their edicts would ultimately be embraced by God's forgiving grace and share the blessed eternal world with all of the faithful. Paul repeatedly declared, throughout his epistles, that in the end, as we make the transition into life after life, "every eye will see God, every knee will bow in worship of God, and every tongue will confess that Christ is Lord to the glory of God." No sheep will be lost from the fold. Hitler, Stalin, and Osama bin Laden will be in heaven, making our simple-minded imagining of that eternal world infinitely expanded and more joyful in realizing that God's grace is so forgiving that it can embrace every wretched human, whether he or she has previously heard of the Christian gospel or not.

That was the revolutionary claim that Paul made everywhere he went. He realized that it was this claim for which Jesus had stood; when Jesus would not compromise that claim, he found himself at cross purposes with the entire religious establishment of his day. The religions afoot in the world then and now prefer(red) a threatening God and conditional grace. According to Paul, it is fine to do good, but that is not important to God; measuring up is not necessary in his religious rubrics. Doing good is not part of the ultimate equation of divine grace.

It is not surprising that this was a revolutionary idea in the ancient world. Every other religion held that God is a threat. Only Paul's form of Christianity realized that "God is unconditionally for us, not against us" (Rom. 8:31). Not all forms of early Christianity agreed with Paul. The Synoptic Gospels, Matthew, Mark, and Luke all described Jesus's life and work as standing for a conditional grace in which history would end with a cataclysmic Second Coming of the Son of Man (Jesus) as the final judge. He will end history as we know it on a horrific Judgment Day. He will gather the righteous into God's eternal kingdom and exterminate the wicked. They described a *quid pro quo* world. They did not know about the essence of Jesus's message and ministry as Paul grasped it.

This is not surprising. Despite being tutored by Jesus for about three years, they never got over their notion that he was destined to establish a political, social, and military kingdom in Jerusalem. They expected and desired that he would resurrect the golden age of David's kingdom of 1,000 years before. The Synoptics expected Jesus to raise a popular revolution, defeat the Romans, throw them out of Palestine, and reestablish Israel as a politically independent and economically prosperous nation. The biblical narrative indicates that even after Jesus's death and resurrection the disciples asked him, the last time they saw him, whether he was now, after his spectacular weekend, going to establish David's kingdom in Israel. To the bloody end they just did not get it.

What should surprise us is that both Paul, the first to write about Jesus, and John, the last to write about his person and ministry, did understand. John's gospel, written fifty or sixty years after Paul's epistles, declares that before God created the world he determined that in this trial and error experiment of evolutionary history, he would embrace every human in his saving grace. In John's gospel there is no Second Coming, no final judge, no Judgment Day, no termination of history, no catastrophic divine intervention, and no extermination of the wicked. Jesus came to save the whole world with his proclamation of God's word of grace, fortunately grasped by Paul. All wicked persons and all of us who fall short of our ideal possibilities are assured by John's gospel that God disposes of all wicked persons and all wickedness by completely and unconditionally forgiving the wicked and wickedness.

The revolutionary nature of this Pauline proclamation was nailed down by his claim that Jesus had appeared to his disciples from his heavenly abode after his crucifixion, reassuring them of the certitude of God's grace. Paul claimed he knew this to be true because he himself had seen Jesus and had a definitive conversation with him on the Damascus road. No wonder this kind of spirituality caught fire throughout the ancient world. It addressed the full spectrum of hungers of the human spirit for a sure sense of the meaning of life and certified the realities of life after life.

It is a tragedy that the imperial church of Constantine and subsequent Catholic tradition lost its grip on the Pauline witness to radical, unconditional, and universal divine grace, pushing the Christian religion back into the rubrics of the Synoptics and inherent pagan lust for a *quid pro quo* world. It is a double tragedy that the primary motive for this regressive shift was the desire to employ a threatening God to increase the church's power, authority, and wealth as it developed from the witnessing community before 300 CE to the oppressive imperial enforcer after 300 CE. Paul's unique revolution was lost, rediscovered by some of the monastic orders, and momentarily rediscovered in the Protestant Reformation, only to be lost again to Reformed and Lutheran scholasticism.

The only form of Christianity capable of revolutionizing society and human life is Paul's kind of proclamation of God's universal grace. Paul's revolution was driven by one radically innovative idea that quickly became a comprehensive worldview, imbuing its adherents with a gratifying sense of meaning and certitude, temporal and eternal. It worked like a fire of the spirit in each human soul that embraced it.

NOTE

1. 1 Thess. (ca. 51 CE), Phil. (ca. 52–54 CE), Philem. (ca. 52–54 CE), 1 Cor. (ca. 53–54 CE), Gal. (ca. 55 CE), 2 Cor. (ca. 55–56 CE), Rom. (ca. 55–58 CE).

REFERENCE

Tabor, James. (2012). "The Jesus Dynasty." *TaborBlog.* http://jamestabor.com/category/jesus-dynasty/.

CHAPTER 9

THE PROTESTANT REFORMATION: A FAILED REVOLUTION

Raymond J. Lawrence

The sixteenth-century Protestant Reformation was both an attack on the foundations of medieval Roman Catholic religion, using the Bible as the instrument of critique, and a sexual revolution against centuries of Catholic repression of sexual pleasure. The former was a limited or modest success. The latter was a failure, unless one argues that a partial success finally occurred half a millennium later in the form of the sexual revolution of the mid-twentieth century.

In the scholarly world the sexual revolutionary content of the Reformation has generally been treated as a taboo subject. Scholarship, particularly theological scholarship, has been for the most part embarrassed by the sexual behavior and values of some of the Protestant reformers. Luther and the Anabaptists were astonishingly favorable toward sexual pleasure; Calvin and his tribe were quite stringent in permitting it. Each of the Protestant reformers was of course exiting a medieval Catholic value system that was massively repressive and yet quite ambiguous. Sexual pleasure for its own sake was categorically impermissible, yet homosexual social structures in the literate class were universal and thus ineluctably encouraged homosexual relations. The aristocracy on the upper end and the peasant class on the lower were mostly left to their own devices, practically speaking.

From the perspective of the broad sweep of Judeo-Christian history, including its Islamic spin-off—the so-called Abrahamic faiths—the nature of the curve in sexual valorization is clear. Jewish religious tradition has been relatively consistent in its guilt-free, affirmative stance toward sexual pleasure. Christianity utterly reversed that posture, evolving eventually into the world's most negative religion regarding sexual pleasure of any sort.

The emergence of Islam in the seventh century CE in turn reversed that Christian reversal, at least for Muslims. In certain respects Islam, with its aniconic posture and affirmation of sexual pleasure, was the revival of a kind of Jewish sexuality, in a new form. "Jewish heresy" is perhaps a good label for Islam. Islam owes more to the biblical and Talmudic traditions than it does to Christianity, even if all three religious groups are referred to as "the people of the book," namely the revered Abrahamic Bible. Whatever Islam is, it is a biblical religion that is indebted to the biblical texts, though certainly not to historical Christianity. Islam and Judaism have more in common than either has with Christianity.

The Bible, which could be called the Judeo-Christian-Muslim Bible, is astonishingly positive in its appreciation of sexual pleasure, in spite of negative misreadings of that same Bible by Christian tradition generally. One of the most telling stories of sexuality in the Bible is that of King David and Abishag, which is rarely if ever discussed or preached about in Christian contexts (1 Kings 1:1–4). When David was in geriatric decline, a delegation was sent throughout the kingdom seeking a beautiful young maiden to send to his bed in hopes of reviving the old man. Abishag was found and sent. She got into his bed, but her stimulating presence did not cure David of his decline. The text in 1 Kings reports that David did not have intercourse with Abishag. The Talmudic rabbis take another view. The tale of Abishag is a beautiful one. It surely warms the heart of any red-blooded aging male. What else in the world could equal her power to revive the spirits of a failing man?

This story also highlights the extraordinary gulf that exists between biblical ways of looking at sexual pleasure and how Christianity has generally viewed it. It is difficult to imagine a practicing Christian today tolerating a twenty-first-century repetition of the Abishag–David tryst, even for the sake of longevity.

The story of Abishag and David is not some obscure, off-the-beaten-track tale incongruent with the rest of biblical tradition. Rather, it rests right in the middle of that tradition. Sexual pleasure was consistently viewed as a God-given blessing to which everyone was entitled. As in everything else, of course, males trumped females. Gender equality was not on the proverbial radar. Patriarchy was generally accepted unquestioningly, Jesus being an arguable exception.

Although opposition to patriarchal privilege is mostly absent from the biblical narrative, some of the sayings and reported actions of Jesus do suggest a challenge to it. Jesus seems more at home with women than with men. He appears to have had more female disciples than male. He traveled with women and consorted with women of ill-repute, to the chagrin of some of his close male followers. It may well be that Jesus was considerably more liberal in his gender and sexual relationships than the texts reveal, especially as the texts themselves were put down in writing a generation or more after his death. It is not far-fetched to conjecture that Jesus was something of a women's liberationist. Such a public stance would have been grounds enough to execute him as a common criminal. Nothing enrages people in virtually any culture more than tampering with sexual and gender boundaries and prerogatives. Furthermore, the biblical texts as they stand do not go very far in explaining exactly why Jesus was executed. The Roman imperial authorities and the Jewish religious authorities are both depicted as being on some level vexed by Jesus, but it is certainly not clear exactly what about him bothered either of them. Sexual radicalism and/or empowerment of women would clearly be enough to earn the censure of both power groups. Such a sexually radical Jesus is not portrayed explicitly in the texts, although a number of incidents suggest this radicalism. (In the early 1980s Elizabeth Schussler-Fiorenza was the principal scholar to make this claim.) And since the texts themselves were all written decades—or in some cases generations—after Jesus's death, they were very likely cleaned up by subsequent generations. All traditions typically engage in posthumous softening of the edges of their heroes and leaders, and there is no reason not to assume that the Jesus of the existing texts was a somewhat sanitized portrait of the real man.

The historical formation of Christianity itself was a juggernaut of opposition to Judaism, propelled by powerful anti-Semitic impulses. As the earliest Jesus followers, who were all Jews, began accepting Gentiles, conflicts arose over whether these adherents should be required to become full-fledged Jews as well. The hard-liners argued for requiring circumcision for converts. This argument morphed into the eventual separation of Judaism and Christianity, a subsequent cold war between the two religions, and ultimately virulent anti-Semitism. The fuel for the latter has usually been sexual. The energy for this anti-Semitism was plausibly, even likely to have been rooted from the start in disdain for Jewish sexual attitudes and values. The Christian Bible is an entirely Jewish document, even if the New Testament is a somewhat heretical form of Judaism. It is astonishing that the central sacred literature of Christianity is entirely Jewish, while at the same time Christianity evolved rather early into a powerfully anti-Semitic religion. (The latter case has been persuasively argued by James Carroll in his landmark *Constantine's Sword: The Church and the Jews.*)

The focal point of that anti-Semitism was and remains sexual, the sly innuendo through the centuries that Jews were sexual deviants. The charge of Jewish sexual deviance was bandied about in Imperial Rome and lived on through the centuries in Christianity. The positive spin Judaism put on sexual pleasure, culminating in the Song of Songs, was repugnant to Roman imperial ideology. Polygamy was considered reprehensible. Jews, with their polygamy, were religious and sexual misfits in the monogamous Roman Empire. This early sexual slur against Jews permeates all of Christian history. In the mid-twentieth century the sexual anti-Semitic trash talk of Adolf Hitler and his Nazis only brought out into the open what Christian leaders had been saying about Jews for centuries.

In the entire Christian Bible, from Genesis to Revelation, there is not a single command to practice monogamy, nor a single condemnation of polygamy. Unmarried males were viewed with suspicion. Unmarried females were considered bereft of divine beneficence. How Christianity succeeded in radically reversing this posture while venerating the same texts is a stunning instance of legerdemain. The biblical texts were spun by Roman and medieval exegetes to support a massive assault on sexual pleasure of any sort in one of the most remarkable reversals in human history. This sleight of hand was accomplished by focusing mostly on what is not rather than on what is written in the texts. For example, the presumed celibacy of Jesus and Paul is entirely spurious, with no foundation in written accounts, and this in a culture where males who declined to marry were viewed with great suspicion. Paul appears to address his "spouse" in Philippians 4:3, but the interpretation and translation is somehow twisted, without any linguistic or etymological support, to mean something other than spouse. The biblical texts in their entirety fall barely short of stating boldly that one should have as much sexual pleasure in life as possible, as long as the object of one's sexual pleasure is treated with justice. But somehow Christians have been trained to hear quite the opposite, an astonishing reversal of the texts.

In support of the conjecture that Jesus was killed for tampering with the sexual codes—is the puzzling existence of the fish symbol, which was widespread in the earliest Christian churches and has been authenticated through archaeological finds. The fish predated the cross as the central Christian symbol, but it fell out of use by the time the imperial state began to tolerate and finally adopt Christianity as the imperial religion. The fish is a blatantly sexual symbol, associated with both the unconscious and coitus. Its association with sex and the unconscious can be seen in cultures the world over in archaeological remains.

Furthermore, we know that the fish was a powerful sexual symbol in imperial Rome at the time of Jesus. The Romans ate fish on Fridays to commemorate Venus, the goddess of love and sex. Of course the Christian church later essentially baptized the practice of Friday fish eating and simply spun it a different way. Instead of eating fish to celebrate sexual pleasure, Christians ate fish instead of meat to remember Jesus's crucifixion, replacing fantasies of coitus with fantasies of death.

When the earliest Christians adopted the fish symbol—the rationale for which does not appear in any of the texts—they surely knew what the fish represented to imperial Romans. They had to know its sexual connotations.

This leads to the obvious conclusion that at least some part of earliest Christianity was a sexual liberationist movement, now essentially lost to us. Thus I argue that the earliest Jesus movement was a sexual and gender liberationist movement that failed, prefiguring a similar failure in the sixteenth century.

In the march of history many individuals and groups have challenged Christianity's negative reading of sexual pleasure. The first three centuries of Christianity were marked by considerable variety, almost certainly far more than is evidenced in the surviving documents. For the first three centuries no central Christian authority existed. Various divergent practices and traditions began with conflict between Paul, the internationalist, and Peter, the leader of the Jerusalem and Torah-abiding followers of Jesus. As the decades and centuries passed, variations in the communities that professed to follow Jesus multiplied. Much, and probably most, of the record of such divergent groups is lost. Nevertheless, many fragments remain, attesting to the extremely wide variety of practices of disparate Christian communities and congregations.

Much of the fragmentary information from the first three centuries of Christianity is sexually inflammatory, some of it astonishingly vivid. Charges of sexual libertinism among "heretical" Christians abounded in the early years. The label came from the vanquishers, not the vanquished. The latter are not able to speak for themselves. As the saying goes, history is written by the winners.

The fate of Theodore of Mopsuestia is a case in point. An early fourth-century bishop, Theodore was something of a liberal, and he set himself against the sexual negativism of Augustine. History knows of Theodore only from the words of those who condemned him. In this case he is not accused of sexual libertinism, as were many others who were condemned, but rather of being too liberal and declining to fully enforce monastic discipline. Theodore's fate is a good example of what happened to those who failed to toe the party line. The irony in Theodore's case is that the hysterical charges against him made by Augustine and others, who became the only source of our information about him, actually make him look good. Clearly that was not Augustine's intention.

If the first three centuries were a time of Christian variety, the fourth was a time of right thinking enforced by the power of imperial Rome. For the first time the power of the state assisted Christians in killing other Christians for their divergent views or practices, the Donatists of North Africa being the first known victims of such Christian-on-Christian purges. From the fourth century on it was dangerous in Europe to be anything other than a government-approved Christian.

In tandem with government backing for proper Christian beliefs and practices, along with civil punishment handed out to those practicing divergent forms of Christianity, came a new guiding ethical principle. Sexual pleasure was enthroned as the principal root and source of all evil. *"Ecce unde,"* wrote Augustine. "That's the place!" Sex is the place where original sin enters the human experience. Thus from Augustine onward, until the sixteenth century, abstinence from sexual pleasure became the primary mark of those worthy to be considered the most religiously devout. After Augustine, for about a millennium the religious leadership, which was also the intelligentsia, those who could read and write, was confined to monastic life in single-gender communities. Naturally rebels appeared here and there. And there were periods when homosexuality flourished relatively unrestrained, although under the radar, as John Boswell documents. Single-gender monastic life was quite conducive to homosexual liaisons, whereas heterosexual liaisons in that environment were exceedingly difficult. In fact, one suspects that medieval Christian life was purposely designed to promote homosexuality.

Only four known figures stand out in that millennium as dramatic dissenters from the official religious denigration of sexual pleasure: Peter Abelard, Heloise, Theresa of Avila, and Juan de la Cruz. Theresa and Juan were not explicit, but the circumstantial evidence is persuasive. Both Abelard and Heloise wrote openly about their sexual relationship and were both affirming of it. The love affair began when Abelard was a teacher at the cathedral and Heloise was his teen-aged student. Abelard was violently attacked and castrated, which probably also involved a penectomy. Yet their love for each other continued throughout their lives. They were victims of a culture unable to view sexual pleasure as more than a work of the devil. Theresa's account is more opaque and does not directly discuss her sexual behavior, but the innuendo is unmistakable. Juan's poetry is highly erotic, but not confessional. Both Theresa and Juan were brought before the Inquisition and charged with sexual activity. Theresa talked her way out of it; Juan was imprisoned and finally died in disgrace and exile.

Others throughout the centuries undoubtedly challenged the perverse denigration of sexual pleasure in medieval Catholic life, but whoever they were, they are lost to history. Martin Luther single-handedly and openly challenged a millennium of religious denigration of sexual pleasure in the early sixteenth century. His was the revolution that failed. The reasons for that failure were complex.

Martin Luther began the Reformation by challenging what he considered abuses by the leadership of the Roman Catholic Church. He employed the Bible and biblically based theological principles to criticize the role of church leadership. Particularly objectionable to Luther was the use of indulgences, certificates that could be purchased against past or future sins. He considered this mechanistic approach to misbehavior contrary to biblical and theological principles. For Luther, a good conscience came from faith and a belief in forgiveness, not in the collecting of credits. The Vatican in Rome did not take such criticism well, and a struggle ensued.

The context of this argument was early Renaissance Europe, a time when culture itself was moving out of the constraints of the medieval period into openness and liberality. Change was in the air, which can be vividly seen in the plastic arts. The stylized human figure of the medieval icon gradually began to give way to naturalistic portrayals of human flesh in art and sculpture. The Renaissance was a time of new discovery and awakening to the beauty of the human body as well as of nature itself. It also involved the reassertion of human reason in tension with established dogma. Luther harnessed the energy of the Renaissance and used it to undermine established authority centered in the Vatican.

As Renaissance art vividly demonstrates, the emerging new era was one of sexual awakening. Leo Steinberg (1983) demonstrates in his landmark work the surprising new sensuousness in early Renaissance art. The Virgin Mary and other biblical women became expressions of and objects of sexual desire. Even portrayals of Jesus began to show him as a sexual person, often in the most vivid fashion. A powerful sexual revolution was taking place during the Renaissance, portrayed in art, and it affected the clergy. Not only was the necessity to be obedient to Rome called into question; those in the religious life decided that they would no longer deprive themselves of a sexual life, and they began voting with their feet. Large numbers of monks and nuns began leaving convents and monasteries.

Many of the escapees looked to Luther for guidance and help. As a result he turned his monastery in Wittenberg, a large multistory complex, into a halfway house and marriage bureau for escaped nuns. And *escape* is not too strong a word. Some stuffed themselves into empty fish barrels to be hauled away, as a safe means of leaving the convent. Those who had families to take them in were fortunate. Without a man to protect her, a mature, unattached woman in the early Renaissance social order was highly vulnerable. Luther therefore set out to find husbands for the nuns, some of whom had risked their lives to escape.

Luther himself did not intend to marry as he moved from monastic life to his position as leader of the German Reformation. With a death sentence on his head, he did not think he was an appropriate husband for any woman. His views on sex and marriage evolved as time passed. In the early years he regarded marriage as a lesser calling than celibacy. But by 1522 he was calling for monastics to abandon that life. In 1524 he abandoned his own monastic habit. Six months later, in June 1525, he was married. And he eventually came to see that, as he put it, there is nothing more fictitious than the fictitious chastity of monastic life.

In his role as matchmaker of Wittenberg, Luther was very busy. But unexpectedly, and to the surprise of his colleagues, he married Katharina von Bora, after she was jilted by her fiancé, Jerome Baumgaertner. For reasons unknown, Baumgaertner never returned from a journey after they became engaged. We can even assume that Katy had already consummated her relationship with her fiancé. Luther admitted later that he was not in love, and it seems that he married Katy out of a sense of social justice or even pity.

The marriage between Katy and Martin turned out to be a good one, of surprising equivalency. In their "table talks," she even bantered with Luther about polygamy. When Luther speculated that polygamy was approved in the Bible and should perhaps be brought back into practice, she threatened to leave him and all their children. The written record leaves the impression that it was a lighthearted conversation, not a threatening one. Katy was a strong companion to Luther all the rest of his life. Her statue deservedly stands in the courtyard of the Wittenberg monastery, signifying her importance to Luther and the Reformation.

Luther's marriage marked the point of no return for him and was decisive for the Reformation. Philipp Melanchthon and other colleagues of Luther had urged him not to marry because they realized that his marriage would represent an irrevocable break with Rome, ending any hope for reconciliation between the Vatican and Protestants. By church law, having sexual relations with a nun was a capital offense. Luther was of course pilloried by conventional Catholics for his marriage, caricatured as driven by lust, but he took this contempt as a badge of honor. He came to see the affirmation of sexual pleasure as a major component of the Reformation. The idea that religious leaders should enjoy the benefits of sexual pleasure became the central claim and offense of the Reformation. Theories of faith versus works in the salvation of the soul, the arguments that had originally sparked the Reformation, could have been settled by a theological concordat. The theological rift might have been patched up. But the marriages of priests, monks, and nuns and the emptying of monasteries and convents could not be undone. In the eyes of the Roman Catholic leadership, the Protestant Reformation became a revolution that could not be negotiated away.

In many respects Luther became quite modern in his thinking about sex. His discussions with his wife about polygamy were not entirely theoretical. He had used his religious authority to approve the bigamy of Philip of Hesse and was criticized for it. Luther was not a literalist about sexual fidelity in marriage. When a woman approached him whose husband was impotent, he advised her not to divorce the man, but to take a lover, preferably a brother-in-law, first getting her husband's permission. If the husband refused, Luther recommended she find another man and flee to another province.

Luther also proposed that religious leaders get out of the business of approving marriage and divorce. "As soon as we begin to act as judges in marriage matters, the teeth of the mill wheel will have snatched us by the sleeve and it will carry us away to the point where we must decide the penalty. Once we have to decide the penalty, then we must also render judgment about the body and goods, and by this time we are down under the wheel and drowned in the water of worldly affairs."

He was earthy, direct, uninhibited, and playful in matters of sexuality. He even cited approvingly the popular proverb, "If the wife refuses, let the maid come." He expressed distaste for big-breasted women, who he said promised much and produced little. When Luther was invited to the wedding of his dear friend Georg Spalatin, who was to marry a woman also named Katy, he was unable to attend. The journey would have taken him through Catholic-controlled territory, risking arrest and probably execution. He was a wanted man on several counts, in addition to having defiled a nun. As a substitute for attending the wedding, Luther proposed that he and Spalatin simultaneously have intercourse with their respective Katies. "I will calculate how long it will take my courier to reach you. The very night you receive this letter you penetrate your lovely Katy and I will penetrate mine. Thus we will be united in love." From the text it is not clear whether the Spalatin marriage ceremony had yet taken place. In any case, that would not have made much difference to Luther.

Luther did not make it home alive from his last journey, to Eisleben, where he planned to help settle a political dispute. On that journey he wrote to Katy that he suffered only from the resistance of the beautiful ladies, which he said prevented him from any fear about his virtue. Whether playful or serious, this reveals a Luther who took sexual pleasure as it ought to be taken, as a natural act that should be enjoyed to the utmost, and abstinence from which should be considered no religious virtue.

He was astonishingly candid about his own libidinal urges. His sexual freedom was a major driving force in his life and a large part of the energy behind his attack on medieval Catholicism. As Friedrich Nietzsche said, "Perhaps Luther's greatest merit was to have had the courage of his sensuality (in those days one spoke, delicately enough, of 'evangelical freedom')." The popular sixteenth-century ditty, "Who does not love wine women and song, remains a fool his whole life long," often attributed to Luther, may not have been Luther's creation, but it certainly captures his spirit. He was utterly enthusiastic about sexual pleasure, and he was not wholly convinced that it had to be constrained within the boundaries of monogamy. In that regard, Luther and Calvin were worlds apart.

It is noteworthy that modern attacks on Luther by partisan Catholics have generally focused not on specific religious doctrines as such, but on his sexuality, charging Luther with "a diseased, oversexed soul," for example. Such attacks are quite to the point. Everything Luther stood for could easily be absorbed by the Vatican except his affirmation of sexual pleasure and with it, his contempt for celibacy and the "fictitious chastity of monastic life."

By taking that stance Luther had severed the tap root of historic Catholicism, which had been set in place by Augustine's *"ecce unde."* But subsequent generations of Lutherans followed an expurgated Luther, whose sexual freedom was quickly forgotten.

Martin Luther, and John Calvin after him, became the two central figures of the Protestant Reformation. Each appealed to the authority of the Bible in critiquing the medieval Catholic Church. They shared a common view of the necessity for reforming Christianity, but Calvin was generally more radical than Luther in his deconstruction of medieval Christian tradition. He advocated more power for the congregation and less for the clergy. Calvin may never even have been ordained as a cleric; if he was it was an event that everyone seemed to forget. However, he unquestionably functioned as a cleric. In fact, for the last two decades of his life he was the preeminent cleric of Geneva. Calvin, more radically than Luther, deconstructed the Catholic mass, demystifying it further than Luther did. The mystical Eucharist of medieval Catholicism became a memorial meal in the Reformed tradition of Calvin. Thus even today the Lutheran liturgy, the authority of the clergy, and the ecclesiastical structure of Lutheranism more closely resemble the medieval Catholic Church than Reformed churches, which look to Calvin as their authority.

Calvin, born in 1509, was twenty-six years younger than Luther and became active slightly later in life. He had barely come into his own by 1546, the year Luther died. He held Luther in high esteem, but the two never met. Calvin read Luther in translation, not being fluent in German. He probably never had access to Luther's casual conversations or to his posthumously preserved "table talks." Had the casual, free-speaking Luther been accessible to Calvin, he would likely have been scandalized by Luther's personal freedom, especially on matters of sexuality.

Though in agreement on the need to reform Christianity, Luther and Calvin were worlds apart in personality. Their respective personalities were not an irrelevant factor in the development of the Reformation. As Reformation historian Pierre Chaunu is reported to have said, Calvin was not someone you can imagine having a glass of beer with. That would not likely be a comfortable tête-à-tête. He was brilliant and intense, but available information suggests that he had little time for or interest in casual conversation. Luther, on the other hand, was someone with whom sharing a beer, or even several beers, would probably have been a delight. He was candid and outrageously playful. It is difficult to imagine that the two men would have been able to enjoy each other's company.

On matters of sexuality, Luther and Calvin were worlds apart. Calvin, like Luther, rejected the medieval Christian tenet that sexual abstinence was a mandatory virtue for those in religious leadership. Both viewed celibacy as a misguided requirement. But Calvin, unlike Luther, valued celibacy for those who could commit to it. He even considered celibacy a higher calling for those who could adhere to it. He was happily celibate for most of his own life and was likely sexually abstemious at times even during the brief decade when he was married. In his teachings, unlike Luther, Calvin promoted extremely rigorous religious controls on the acceptable contexts for sexual pleasure. He limited sexual pleasure to the strict boundaries of monogamy and had little tolerance for premarital or extramarital sex. He was quite troubled by Luther's willingness to tolerate polygamy in certain cases. Calvin was even troubled by Jesus's leniency toward the woman taken in adultery, fearing the story would become an excuse for sin. He was scandalized by a seventy-year-old Geneva woman who confessed to being still interested in sexual relations.

Calvin was quite willing to shape the social life of Geneva to conform to his view of proper Christian behavior. Thus he made war on public baths in 1549, labeling them haunts of perdition because they admitted men and women together. Calvin referred to the baths as places where cleanliness served as a pretext for lewdness. He used his influence to convert the baths of Geneva into single-gender operations, with men and women bathing on alternate days. Calvin led the church to pressure the state to enforce sexual discipline in the community at large, and he supported implementation by civil authorities of public punishment for those who flouted what he considered Christian rules of sexual behavior. Calvin's program for social control on matters of sexual conduct was not far removed from the Vatican's.

The Geneva of Calvin's day was not a theocracy, though it may have felt like one in many respects. Church and state were separate. The Consistory was the authoritative body of the church, and the Council that of the state. The Consistory had influence over the Council, but did not dictate to it. The Consistory had more independence in Geneva than in any other Protestant city of the early Reformation. And it had influence; its moral judgments were typically implemented by the Council.

Through the Consistory Calvin imposed his libidinal negativity on Geneva as a whole, and subsequently of course on Reformed Protestantism generally, even into present times. Calvin also extended ecclesiastical control over marriage and who was eligible to marry. For example, an old man was not permitted by Calvin to marry a young woman.

In Geneva Calvin was as obsessive about controlling the terms of matrimony as the Roman Catholic Church that he had abandoned. He prohibited weddings on any day when communion was celebrated, echoing the medieval rule of weddings being prohibited on any of the sixty-odd holy days. Brides were prohibited from wearing a veil if they had "fornicated" prior to marriage. And in Calvin's view, it was the community's business to know who had fornicated prior to the marriage ceremony. On the other hand, his humanism revealed itself in his teaching that both husband and wife "surrendered their bodies to each other." Calvin was a controlling and sexually repressed humanist. Luther was a sexually liberated Ur-Christian.

Under Calvin's sway, Bibles had to be placed in every tavern. While sexual misbehavior was condemned by the Consistory, it was left to the Council to implement the more draconian forms of punishment. People were banned from the city by the Council for sexual misconduct as well as other offenses. During Calvin's last decade several women were drowned as punishment for committing adultery. For his disbelief in the Trinity, Servetus was burned at the stake by the judgment of the Council. Calvin did not sentence him to death, but certainly if he had called for restraint, the execution would have been halted. A saying made the rounds: "Better the Spanish Inquisition than the Geneva Consistory."

A great irony is that Calvin was broadly speaking a more radically biblical humanist than Luther. However, Calvin's flawed and essentially medieval posture toward sexual pleasure gutted his humanism and ultimately morphed his biblical humanism into Protestant Puritanism. As Heiko Oberman (2003) so vividly wrote about subsequent generations of Reformed Christians throughout the world, "these international Calvinists were hardly aware that in their baggage were treasures of that monastic past which Luther, with such fear and trembling and inner pain, had foresworn. . . . This medieval heritage is misnamed 'Protestant Puritanism.'" On matters of sexual behavior, Calvin's humanism rarely manifested itself, and in this respect he was poles apart from Luther.

Calvin, a Frenchman, was invited by William Farel to come and work in Geneva in 1536 to promote the Reformation. Geneva was a small town of 13,000, much smaller than London, Paris, and Rome, with their populations of about one million. Calvin lasted only two years in Geneva and was exiled because of his insistence on moral (mostly sexual) discipline in the church. But in 1541 he was invited back, again at the strong urging of Farel, became a citizen, and remained in Geneva as principal religious leader until his death in 1564.

Protestantism in its various forms was in constant turmoil about which religious traditions were acceptable and which were not. Calvin took a strict position, looking to the biblical record for guidance. Among Protestants in Bern, for example, unleavened bread was used in communion (following Roman Catholic practice), bridal garments were permitted, and medieval religious holidays were observed. Calvin tolerated none of that in Geneva. Nor would Calvin countenance notions of a "real presence of Christ" in the Lord's Supper, as Lutherans were wont to accept. He argued that Christ remains in heaven and does not come down to dwell in the bread, leavened or unleavened. He also rejected the Nicene Creed as a human concoction. Calvin sought to "exterminate as much as possible any residue of Popish superstition." He had good credentials as a radical liberal opponent of Rome in most respects, but on issues of sex, Calvin and the Vatican were not far apart.

He apparently did not court anyone before he was thirty. By his own account he was not afflicted with lust: "Lack of continence would not be the reason . . . for marrying. No one can charge me with that." Later in life, after the death of his wife, he wrote: "It is now eighteen months since the death of my wife, a woman of matchless type, and ever since I have again been practicing celibacy, and not unwillingly. . . . I am not one of those insane lovers who, once smitten by the first sight of a fine figure, cherishes even the faults of his lover. The only beauty that seduces me is of one who is chaste, not too fastidious, modest, thrifty, patient, and hopefully she will be attentive to my health." William Farel, Martin Bucer, and other fellow reformers at Calvin's request worked hard to find a wife for him. Several women were brought to him for review, but none passed muster. Only when he decided to give up looking did he meet on his own one Idelette de Burre, an Anabaptist widow with two children. She was savvy, sociable, respectable, and "actually pretty," Farel noted with surprise.

Calvin's last letter was written to his longtime colleague and friend, Farel, on May 2, 1564. Though Farel had been one of several close friends and allies in his work of reforming the church, Calvin had been lately estranged from him. The problem was that Farel, to Calvin's dismay, had in his old age married a young woman. Calvin had little tolerance for any but the most restrained and conventional forms of sexual pleasure, and he was offended by Farel's action. Nevertheless, Farel hastened to Calvin's deathbed for a touching farewell.

Philip Benedict (2001) points out that Calvinism as it spread after his death carried with it an inordinate amount of attention to sexual desire. In the century following Calvin's death a great deal of attention was paid to sexual behavior by Reformed churches beyond Geneva, as they inherited Calvin's spirit. By 1700 the disciplinary cases presented to the Amsterdam Kerkeraad virtually equaled the total of all other forms of discipline. The Calvinist attitude toward sexual behavior became embedded not only in Dutch Reformed tradition but in all of Protestantism. What remains of Protestantism's sexual ethics in the twenty-first century is indebted to Calvin. The shaming of homosexuals, and of heterosexuals for any form of nonmarital sexual pleasure, is a direct inheritance from the abstemious Calvin.

The more radical Calvin demystified the church. Its public worship morphed into more of a community meeting focused on a study of the Bible. The mass was turned into a communal breaking of bread, more closely resembling the account of Jesus eating with his disciples at the last supper.

This demystification has continued in the Reformed tradition today. Churches in the Calvinist tradition have religious services that are more like a community meeting than a mysterious rite, "the holy mysteries" of Catholics. The cleric is a "teaching elder," as distinguished from the "ruling elder," with none of the accouterments of priestly authority. And of course the ruling elder, on paper at least, holds the balance of power in the congregation. Thus we can see that Calvin was the more radical reformer, particularly compared with other mainline Protestant groups that more closely mimic Roman Catholic rites and polity.

As bad money drives out good, so does negativity toward sexual pleasure drive out the positive. With rare exceptions, cultures and religions the world over, like people, are typically conflicted and often guilt-ridden over sexual pleasure, some more than others, and those in the Jewish tradition less than most. Thus as the Reformation churches spread after the sixteenth century, the negative sexual posture of Calvin overcame the positive sexual posture of Luther and the Anabaptists. Luther's own sexuality became an embarrassment even to the eponymous Lutherans.

The sexual liberationist aspect of the early Reformation was its heart and soul. Exuberant and playful Martin Luther, the priest who married the nun, who deliberately put his finger in the eye of the pope and brought down an additional death sentence on his head, was the preeminent reformer. Luther turned on its head Augustine's doctrine of sex as the root of sin—*ecce unde*, "that's the place" where sin begins. His polymorphous sexuality was an even more potent challenge to Roman Catholic magisterium than any arguments the various reformers were able to muster. That voice of Luther is now mostly forgotten by Catholics and Protestants, essentially lost to history. Catholic and Protestant alike today speak mostly with one sex-phobic voice. A constrained, abstemious, and tightly controlled sexuality remains the de rigueur principle of essentially all current manifestations of Christianity. Calvin's pinched and stingy posture toward sexual pleasure triumphed in all of Protestantism, Lutheran as well as Reformed. Thus Luther's revolution failed. We need him to return and do it all again, one more time.

REFERENCES

Benedict, Philip. (2001). *Christ's Churches Purely Reformed: A Social History of Calvinism.* New Haven, CT: Yale University Press.

Boswell, John. (1987). *Christianity, Social Tolerance, and Homosexuality.* Chicago: University of Chicago Press.

Bouwsma, William J. (1988). *John Calvin.* New York: Oxford University Press.

Cottret, Bernard. (2000). *Calvin: A Biography.* Translated by M. Wallace McDonald. Grand Rapids, MI: Eerdmans.

Schussler-Fiorenza, Elizabeth. (1984). *In Memory of Her: A Feminist Theological Reconstruction of Christian Origins.* New York: Crossroads.

Godfrey, W. Robert (2009). *John Calvin: Pilgrim and Pastor.* Wheaton, IL: Crossway Books.

Gordon, Bruce. (2009). *Calvin.* New Haven, CT: Yale University Press.

Lawrence, Raymond J. (1989). *The Poisoning of Eros: Sexual Values in Conflict.* New York: Augustine Moore Press.

Lawrence, Raymond J. (2007). *Sexual Liberation: The Scandal of Christendom.* Westport, CT: Praeger.

Mackinnon, James. (1962). *Calvin and the Reformation.* Edinburgh: University of Edinburgh–Russell and Russell.

Oberman, Heiko A. (1989). *Luther: Between God and the Devil.* New Haven, CT: Yale University Press.

Oberman, Heiko A. (2003). *The Two Reformations: The Journey from the Last Days to the New World.* Edited by Donald Weinstein. New Haven, CT: Yale University Press.

Steinberg, Leo. (1983). *The Sexuality of Christ in Renaissance Art and Modern Oblivion.* New York: Pantheon.

Witte, John, Jr., and Robert M. Kingdon. (2005). *Collected Works, Sex, Marriage and Family in John Calvin's Geneva.* Vol. 1, *Courtship, Engagement and Marriage.* Grand Rapids, MI: Eerdmans.

CHAPTER 10

A FORGIVENESS MINIREVOLUTION: REVIEWING A HISTORICAL AND SCIENTIFIC MOVEMENT

Everett L. Worthington Jr., Caroline Lavelock, Daryl R. Van Tongeren, Jeni L. Burnette, and Kayla Jordan

INTRODUCTION

Between 1984 and 2012 a scientific subfield that investigated forgiveness grew rapidly. This empirical inquiry, with its humble beginnings in religion, suddenly began to be pursued by psychologists. This unusual transformation, which virtually never happens in science, resembles a revolution. Building on this idea, we start by drawing on historical lessons of relevance for both researchers and activists who wish to advance the scientific study of forgiveness. We then apply these empirical findings to crucial political and societal processes. We parallel the revolutionary years and postrevolution establishment of America with the birth, development, and solidification of the scientific study of forgiveness. We then suggest that science can take the next step in the continued development and application of forgiveness.

EXPOSITION

Amid the stories of massive societal upheavals told in these volumes, our recounting of the relatively recent "forgiveness revolution" may seem less meaningful, especially considering that forgiveness has not always been considered a practical solution to conflict and upheaval. For example, the world was uninterested in forgiveness after World War II, giving us Nuremberg and war crimes trials. However, in more recent years Desmond Tutu's conclusion at the end of the South African Truth and Reconciliation Commission (TRC) hearings, and throughout the hearings, was simple: without forgiveness, there is no future. How did we travel from Nuremberg to Johannesburg, from wanting to rip offenders into pieces to wanting to pursue peace?

In this chapter, in addition to examining historical and societal shifts, we suggest that a parallel movement in science contributed to the more widespread acceptance of forgiveness. Specifically, we focus on what we call a minirevolution in a subfield of psychological science in which scholars began to study forgiveness (which had long been considered within theology and politics and had little traction with psychologists). As the study of the topic gained momentum, the political and societal ramifications intensified. In this chapter, drawing on the historical shifts and revolution of empirical inquiry, we seek to address three main topics. First, we analyze the last thirty years of forgiveness research, focusing on the evolutionary foundation of the movement. Second, we examine the (r)evolution and conclude that it has thus far been only a minirevolution, as yet not fully realized. Third, we compare the forgiveness (r)evolution to the American Revolution in hopes of providing lessons from history that can inform researchers and activists about next steps in advancing an agenda of peace that includes the findings from the scientific study of forgiveness.

THE EVOLUTION OF REVENGE AND THE POSSIBILITY OF FORGIVENESS: MCCULLOUGH'S REVENGE VERSUS FORGIVENESS ARGUMENT

McCullough (2008) has argued that evolution of group-dwelling animals made the development of forgiveness possible. Humans have long lived in groups to help combat the advantage of predators, who could easily pick off individuals (Cacioppo, Fowler, and Christakis 2009). At times revenge is also a necessary component of preventing future acts of exploitation. For example, McCullough argues that vengeance is needed for a group to punish norm violation, individual advantage taking, and free riding on the backs of others' labor in order to handle transgressions that violate external boundaries and internal normative boundaries. Because of the pull to ensure individual survival, there is inevitable conflict surrounding resources one individual or group needs (or wants) but does not have or deserve. In dealing with these conflicts, although injustice must be punished, some sort of reconciliation is also needed to keep the group cohesive. We examine both the revenge and benevolent components of this evolutionary balance.

Vengeance and the Rise of Justice

The societal costs of vengeance. Although revenge has its evolutionary adaptations at the individual level, helping to deter future exploitation, a society that is founded on violent vengeance is likely to be short lived. Wars with neighbors erupt when boundaries of groups become closer together. Killing (weakening the group) and injury (weakening individuals and making them subject to predation) become not only inevitable but frequent. Injury and killing might not occur just in border disputes, but also within in-groups as individuals struggle for resources and access to desirable mates. Free riders must also be punished, and advantage taking must be discouraged. Conflicts between group members for priority of access to resources—whether for eating or mating—must be resolved. If there are no structural ways to avoid in-group conflict or reconcile it when it does occur, then the group will be decimated from the inside until there is no group.

Individual and societal strategies that limit violence. This "escalating cost" of vengeance has led to individual evolutionary adaptive strategies as well as societal level mechanisms. For example, numerous reconciliation strategies have been developed and are practiced across species (Sapolsky and Share 2004). Frans de Waal and his colleagues have detailed many such strategies within several types of primate groups, including gorillas, chimpanzees, various monkeys, and bonobos living in captivity (de Waal 1989; de Waal and Pokorny 2005). These reconciliatory acts are also adaptive for humans, as they repair valuable relationships that have downstream benefits (McCullough 2008). In addition, through their own social evolution, societies have developed justice and reconciliation systems, justice motives, and forgiveness experiences to regulate both society and individuals. We elaborate on two such control structures that establish justice at the societal level.

Rex lex. Within in-groups, justice and sharing are necessary, requiring the patrolling of boundaries against interlopers who would take resources or power. One way to achieve this is through power hierarchies. *Rex lex* literally means the "king is law," which suggests that one person controls access to resources. Power, whether monetary, physical, military, or police, is the currency of social control. Sometimes control has been determined by intellectual power (e.g., the control of medieval Europe by the church) or virtuous power (e.g., leadership of ancient Greek civilizations by admired leaders). Power-based control resides in groups that progressively widen. Kin groups often surround the alpha leader as the inner circle of the whole group, and less-related but trusted groups protect the resources of the individual and his or her inner circle of kin, becoming the second layer of the circle. The in-group must also patrol its inner daily workings against those from within who would monopolize resources and seek to usurp power, act with unhelpful self-interest, or take advantage of other in-group members. Justice in *rex lex* societies is based on power and force.

Lex rex. A social contribution of liberal democracy is a shift from *rex lex* to *lex rex*—"law is king." Constitutional rule, articulated laws, and precedents become superior to the ruler or the ruler's police or armed forces. Justice is important for the way society thinks about transgressions and control, and it must be developed to serve as a moderating force for individual self-interest and the interest of groups that try to establish power-based control. Enforcement of transgressions is based on positions (e.g., king or president), not kin groups, and those who occupy the positions change, but are always subject to the rule of law.

In summary, an evolutionary perspective suggests that humans have developed the capacity for relationship repair to maintain valued relations. In addition, social groups must have some mechanisms to punish boundary and rule violations from within or without, and they must have some way of reconciling with in- and out-group transgressors, lest they become depleted by continual struggle and war (McCullough 2008).

Thus, although evolution prepared humans for both justice and reconciliation (and thus for forgiveness as one internal experience that makes reconciliation more likely) in ongoing, valuable relationships in which future exploitation was unlikely, we suggest that *societal pressures* have contributed to both justice structures (like *lex rex*) and forgiveness as a preferred choice of relational repair. Evolution in combination with specific social and societal adaptations interacted in the formation of justice and forgiveness. We also recognize that there are multiple ways that social order can be maintained through those mechanisms of boundary patrol and reconciliation. For example, a tyrant could patrol boundaries through harsh and vicious punishment of rule violators, which deters other rule violators. Alternatively, laws could restrain wrongdoers (rather than harshly punish them) or could set up incentives for rule obedience. In addition to individual evolutionary perspectives and the multitude of societal level enforcements of forgiveness, there are also cognitive mechanisms relevant to the practice of forgiveness.

Cognitive Mechanisms of Relational Repair That Facilitate Forgiveness

Theory of mind. The development of many psychological mechanisms depends, in part, on the theory of mind and the concomitant rise of cognitive perspective taking and emotional empathy. Cognitively, individuals who can imagine the mind of the perpetrator and see their own propensity to do likewise can begin (at least somewhat) to excuse or even justify the perpetrator's wrongdoing. Emotionally, they may sympathize with the offender as they come to understand the perpetrator's perspective.

Sometimes, however, perpetrators do unimaginable evil (Milgram 1974; Oliner and Gunn 2006). Even if the evil is imaginable, some acts are so egregious that one cannot supplant the desire for justice. In such cases, historically, vengeance—or in more civilized settings, the thirst for punitive, retributive justice—ruled. Cognitive mechanisms can be recruited to justify demands for justice or vengeance, and appeals to divine justice or divine vengeance are common among religious and spiritual individuals with highly developed justice motives. Theory of mind suggests that severe retribution or justice would prevent recurrence of transgressions. If potential perpetrators—or observers—saw that transgressions would be met with harsh justice or retribution, without mercy, then (says theory of mind) perpetrators would not repeat crimes, nor would potential perpetrators commit crimes in the first place.

Deterrence theory still governs the criminal justice system, even though it is not always effective, especially for hardened criminals. It might also result in many negative unintended consequences (e.g., fear of parents, authoritarianism, the tendency to abuse one's own children).

Collectivistic self-construal. People might simply elevate the needs of the collective over one's individual sense of peace and well-being. Cultures in which people construe themselves to be collectivistic frequently adopt this strategy. Cultures that are more individualistic tend to pursue individual goals at the expense of communal goals more frequently when the two might conflict. This, of course, oversimplifies people's self-construal. All people see themselves both as individuals who have individual needs and simultaneously as members of a variety of interlocking social collectives—from family, to extended family, to circle of friends, to political and community organizations, to religious organizations, to states, to ethnic groups, to nation-states—as well as maintaining a sense of optimal distinctiveness in their group (Brewer 1991). Their sense of group identity, however, differs depending on the group; the norms in the group; and their own individual beliefs, training, and valuing of the virtues.

Forbearance. In some groups the norm is to hotly pursue justice. In others it is to forbear, or to suppress negative emotional expression for the sake of group harmony. In individualistic cultures, emotional suppression for the sake of group harmony is probably emotionally taxing. Suppressed emotions may take a toll on the health and emotional equanimity of the suppressors. However, in collectivistic societies, suppressing emotional expression for the sake of group harmony is the norm. Such individuals practice suppression from birth, and forbearance becomes second nature to them. Negative health consequences and effects on emotional equanimity are likely to be greater for emotional expression than for suppression.

Acceptance. Acceptance relinquishes one's control over bringing about justice or restoring relationships. For some, acceptance is motivated merely to end the pain or struggle and put the past behind them. For others, acceptance is a positive coping strategy to let go of stress so that more important goals can be pursued. Acceptance can arise from Christian efforts to surrender control to God, and from Hindu and Buddhist (and secular philosophies deriving from those religious positions) notions of embracing a sense of karma (i.e., unremitting justice) or dharma (i.e., sacred duty). Acceptance can involve the (sometimes futile, sometimes effective) hope that disengagement will lead to peace; however, acceptance can also be an active striving to forbear, tolerate the opposition, and disengage one's emotions from the possible outcomes.

The Variety of Responses to Relational Offenses

Relationships are often restored using any of a variety of the methods reviewed here: violence and threats of violence within dominance hierarchies, *rex lex* social order, *lex rex* law-driven society, communal norms that direct either relational repair or dissolution, cognitive readiness for relational repair through theory of mind leading to deterrence or empathy, collectivistic self-construal, forbearance for the sake of the collective, and acceptance. These methods stem from evolutionary, societal, and cognitive perspectives. Importantly, they do not necessarily mean that forgiveness will be a socially approved mechanism for relational repair. Forgiveness is one of many relationship repair strategies that is evolutionarily prepared but socially dictated.

In addition, we suggest a religious component to the forgiveness movement. Although Christianity did not invent forgiveness, as numerous religions, cultures, and philosophies have espoused forgiveness throughout human history, we suggest that Christianity contributed to a theological foundation and perhaps the first widespread societal acceptance of forgiveness as a mechanism leading to relationship repair. Constantine's conversion in the fourth century CE, adopting and turning Christianity into the law of the land in Europe and North Africa, was the "tipping point" that spread the forgiveness contagion into Western culture.

In conclusion, we suggest that forgiveness and justice are rooted in evolution, but the degree of its social use depends on cognitive adaptations, religious history, and societal circumstances. This merging of an evolutionary perspective with a societal revolution raises new questions. First, is forgiveness good for a country? Does a forgiveness-accepting and forgiveness-promoting society benefit more than a strict, mercy-free, justice-oriented society? Second, under what conditions might a country be dominated by vengeance versus forgiveness? Third, what social and political conditions are needed to bring about a forgiveness revolution within and between countries? Fourth, could forgiveness ever be practiced in widespread fashion? What is the ideal balance of forgiveness and justice? We address each of these issues in the next section.

FORGIVENESS AS A SOCIAL AND SOCIETAL GOOD

Not everyone is an advocate for forgiveness. Some think that it is useful only in a few circumstances (Lamb and Murphy 2002; Murphy 2003). This section examines forgiveness as a social and societal good.

Is Forgiveness Good for a Country (and for the World)?

Assumptions. Several assumptions are implicit in our arguments from this point forward. First, we assume that societies are capable of both relationship-rending and relationship-restorative acts. *Relationship-rending acts* by a state or group (e.g., political organization, religion, special interest group, or group of collective of organizations) include fear-based repression of out-group members due to perceived threats against autonomy of the state, vengeful or punitive retaliation for perceived wrongdoing, economic Darwinian selection that eliminates weak states through inability to survive in the global marketplace, aggressive dominance-imposing power grabs within and between states and groups, and maintenance of status quo via repression of dissident voices. *Relationship-restorative acts* include reconciliation between opposing parties, restorative justice procedures, impartial world judicial procedures that settle differences with minimal force, and peace-keeping force when violence within or between states threatens to become excessive.

Second, we assume that there is no global acceptance of relationship-restorative conditions and no global renunciation of relationship-rending conditions. Third, we assume that increasing acceptance of relationship-restorative and renunciation of relationship-rending conditions is a good and reasonable goal. Though we *can* never, and perhaps *should* never, completely reject relationship-rending conditions, the suffering in the twentieth century from war and violence suggests that we are not yet at optimal balance.

Fourth, we assume such conditions require some relinquishing of the autonomy of nation-states. Furthermore, some adoption of a *telos* that sets world peace as its goal is necessary.

Fifth, we assume that parties in political power want to retain that power, and people who feel economically, socially, and politically disadvantaged tend to want to change political structures. This implies that governments might desire global peace conditions, but people who feel disadvantaged might desire change. Some balance is necessary.

Sixth, this tension, created by shifts of power and resources, liberty and oppression, and stability and change, means there will likely never be a completely peace-filled time. However, peace, stability, and social justice may allow inequities and oppression to be minimized and subject to change.

Why Is Forgiveness a Potential Step Forward for Social Evolution?

Many ways of restoring peace—imposing force to quell dissent, truces, urging forbearance, accepting inequities and "necessary" evils, waiting in discontent for power, and subverting authority or engaging in violence—are aimed at a return to preconflict equilibrium (which might involve angst, terror, and inequity). Forgiveness, on the other hand, may offer a road to reconciliation and individual and societal healing.

Forgiveness involves two internal processes (Exline et al. 2003). *Decisional forgiveness* involves a decision to behave prosocially and treat the offenders with human dignity. *Emotional forgiveness* is the process of replacing negative unforgiving emotions and motivations with positive, other-oriented emotions and motivations. Socially, these forgiveness experiences might (but do not have to) accompany restorative social processes (Schönbach 1990; Waldron and Kelly 2008). For example, offenders might express empathy for pain caused, apologize, give a relationship-restorative account of wrongdoing, take responsibility for the conflict, offer restitution, seek reconciliation, pledge not to repeat the offense, seek forgiveness, and if offered, receive the offered forgiveness with grace and gratitude. Victims might make sensitive reproaches (i.e., requests for the offender to explain his or her behavior), listen nonjudgmentally, empathize with the offender's circumstances, communicate their decisions or emotional experiences of forgiving, and act mercifully instead of requiring strict justice. Yet despite these options, neither decisional nor emotional forgiveness might be internally experienced.

When an individual forgives an offender, this does not imply that the forgiver cannot be a staunch and impassioned defender of retributive, restorative, or social justice (Worthington 2009). Justice is always a social phenomenon, and one can pursue and support justice socially without harboring negativity for the transgressor. Justice is usually best administered impartially rather than empowered by negative and vengeful emotion—*lex rex* rather than *rex lex*.

Mercy is an act by one with the authority to administer or recommend less restitution or punishment than might be strictly required (Gartner 2011). Empathy helps the merciful actor see that suffering by the offender might not equate to justice. Sympathy helps the merciful actor feel sorry for the offender and want to apply less punishment or restitution, in order to rehabilitate the offender. Compassion helps the merciful actor turn sympathetic feelings into merciful actions. Altruistic love helps the merciful actor focus on the needs of the offender and put aside the merciful actor's own agenda, out of humility, to help bring beneficial consequences to the person deserving of judgment or condemnation. In short, then, emotional forgiveness—the replacement of unforgiving negative emotions and motives with positive, other-oriented emotions and motives—can move the world closer to *lex rex* and away from *rex lex*.

Thus, promoting forgiveness is indeed a step forward for social evolution. Forgiveness is pressured by evolutionary history (but so are vengeance, justice, and self-interest). Although those pressures seem too distal to exert major influence today, there is some evidence of selective advantage (McCullough et al. 2010). Forgiveness is advantageous both to the individual and society. Evolutionary and historical movements have made forgiveness possible. For example, forgiveness—as a cardinal virtue of Christianity—has spread to other religions and societies.

What Forces Could Spread Forgiveness?

Before suggesting various ways to spread forgiveness, we hasten to clarify that any revolution requires a confluence of social, intellectual, and political conditions. Political events that require and elicit peacemaking make forgiveness urgent. People with a vision for forgiveness and what it can accomplish, and with energy and resources to realize that vision, are essential. A population attuned to receiving a message of forgiveness, as McCullough (2008) has argued, is evolutionarily prepared, but forgiveness must be socially cultivated and nurtured. If not, then any of many other mechanisms will be enacted to yield relationship restoration.

Cultivate relationship value and reduce risk of future exploitation. To nurture forgiveness, building on an evolutionary perspective, *relationship value* must be cultivated and *risk of future exploitation* eliminated or significantly reduced to make forgiveness a viable option. Political, social, and scientific structures (i.e., electronic technology, organizations, and networks) must be established so that resources can be brought to social and political issues that could benefit from forgiveness. Conditions within psychological science that promote the study of forgiveness (i.e., the recent rise in positive psychology) are also needed, such as funding, resources, and publication outlets. Through those various social and societal mechanisms, forgiveness might be nurtured.

Leadership. We believe that the world naturally gravitates to the primitive use of power. Modulation of that primitive urge for power is the essence of civilization, of which the move from *rex lex* to *lex rex* is an illustration. Because it is more natural to revert to power than to more civilized relations, leadership is needed to move people toward more forgiveness. According to Fears (2007), excellent leaders are characterized by four qualities: (1) foundational moral principles and virtues that they consistently use, (2) a moral compass that rights itself in emotional conflict, (3) a compelling vision of the future, and (4) an ability to promote consensus among people to pursue that vision.

People like Nelson Mandela and Desmond Tutu have exhibited these characteristics. Many people complained about the South African Truth and Reconciliation Commission (TRC) because of Tutu's public imposition of his Christian principles and the TRC's inability to provide adequate reparations to victims of apartheid (Chapman and Spong 2003). Yet it is our view that the TRC was a great social innovation of the twentieth century, with far better prospects for restoring social order than truth commissions such as the Nuremberg trials, which pursued wrongdoing with a will to punish and humiliate. The Treaty of Versailles after World War I is another poor example of restoring stable social order; its punishment and humiliation through raw power merely laid the foundation for World War II.

Employment of restorative justice. The principles of restorative justice, at the societal level, seem to advance the peace process. Of course principles within the TRC cannot be simply transplanted into all societal conflicts. In Rwanda, the 800,000 murders involved a number of transgressions that were too large to allow the type of public hearings used by the TRC, so Rwanda localized truth and reconciliation in local hearings. These hearings were criticized as resulting in intimidation and social suppression of the voices of victims and their families, but they also accomplished much good (Brounéus 2008).

Communities that practice forgiveness. Forgiveness can be organized from the top down or from the bottom up. As hostilities between warring parties wind down, leaders can engage in Track I diplomacy (Montville 2001). This occurs between leaders and results in cease-fires, truces, or agreements to end future hostilities. Such Track I diplomacy might stop or delay killing and violence, but other, bottom-up experiences are needed to make changes run deeper and wider throughout society. Montville (2001) and Botcharova (2001) suggest that Track II diplomacy is a helpful bottom-up peacemaking strategy. This brings together groups of opinion leaders from each side of the dispute to tell their stories. Through being heard and developing a sense of empathy for those on the other side, the leaders' attitudes can be transformed. They can then carry their understanding of the other side back into their groups and spread attitudes of acceptance, or at least forbearance.

Worthington and Aten (2010) argued that the spread of peaceful attitudes could be accelerated and expanded beyond Track II diplomacy. They advocated psycho-educational groups about forgiveness led by group leaders who had participated in Track II diplomacy, and they termed this Track III diplomacy. This could promote forgiveness within in-group meetings with like-minded members (such as members of a local community) rather than when out-group members were in a group providing a strong stimulus to vengeance or hate.

Vehicles of transmission that move beyond religion. Revolutionary ideas and acts must be transmitted across groups. Historically, forgiveness has been transmitted by religion. However, forgiveness has recently been unmoored from religion, becoming more a part of secular culture (Koenig, McCullough, and Larson, 2001). If forgiveness is to become an established revolution, secular means of transmission are necessary. First, scientific studies and dissemination of results through media are needed. This requires (a) investigators; (b) government, foundation, and philanthropic funding; (c) scientists with media savvy to disseminate results; (d) global scientific infrastructure that provides support for indigenous investigators to conduct research on forgiveness and disseminate results; and (e) global collaborations between established forgiveness researchers and nations with less-developed scientific infrastructures. Second, nongovernmental organizations (NGOs) are needed to promote activism and spread knowledge among scientists, activists, and public audiences. Third, technology must be used strategically. Web, social media, e-mail, and mobile devices can deliver and facilitate communication. Interventions must be adapted for electronic media using interactive technology, virtual reality, workbooks, and psycho-education via e-books. The topics of forgiveness and reconciliation must resonate with researchers, journals, and funding sources to sustain progress. Scientific progress occurs as scientists (a) innovate and (b) thoroughly investigate new areas by systematic studies. Each innovation must be noble enough to attract and sustain new researchers and provide enough depth to allow scientists to exploit it.

In this section we argued that forgiveness is often an overall social and societal good (though not always). We suggested some reasons that it might advance world peace. Finally, we identified several mechanisms that would be needed for forgiveness to spread societally, including cultivating valuable relationships and reducing the risk of exploitation in countries and within individual relationships, good leadership to galvanize a movement, employment of restorative justice, the presence of viable communities that practice forgiveness and serve as a model for other communities, and vehicles of transmission other than religion (e.g., scientific transmission, political advocacy). In the following section we explore how these have played out in recent history by analyzing the forgiveness minirevolution from 1984 to date.

ANALYSIS OF THE FORGIVENESS MINIREVOLUTION, 1984 TO DATE

We suggest that the increase in the presence of forgiveness on the world stage is more of a minirevolution than a sustainable revolution. Forgiveness researchers have begun to systematically exploit and develop it. The infusion of forgiveness into the societal and political realm is substantially greater than in the 1980s, yet the transformation is far from complete. We parallel the revolutionary founding of the United States with the twenty-eight-year forgiveness minirevolution. Our goal is to inform researchers and activists of new ways to find progress.

Founding

Christopher Columbus discovered a land that would become a refuge from dissatisfaction in Europe. Novel possibilities inspired the colonization of Virginia (1607) and Massachusetts (1620), and these settlers crucially proved that in a different setting, they could succeed.

In the mid-1980s there was growing dissatisfaction with the progress of mental health treatment. De-institutionalization and managed mental health were on the horizon, psychopharmacology was making great strides, and psychotherapy had been progressing since the 1950s, including the conceptualization of evidence-based practice. Enter theologian Lewis Smedes (1984), an unlikely leader of a mental health treatment modality. He was a theologian and author who wrote beautiful trade books, such as *Forgive and Forget: Healing the Hurts We Don't Deserve*, making a new therapeutic argument: that forgiveness could be self-therapy.

After Smedes's Columbus-like invitation, two research groups established settlements, showing that forgiveness research could succeed. Enright paralleled Kohlberg's (1981) stages of reasoning about justice, creating stages of reasoning about forgiveness. He also developed an intervention (Hebl and Enright 1993) that became Enright's Process Model (Enright and Fitzgibbons 2000). McCullough and Worthington wrote reviews (McCullough and Worthington 1994) and an intervention that became Worthington's (2006) REACH Forgiveness Model (McCullough, Worthington, and Rachal 1997).

Early History

After establishing settlements in Virginia and New England, the pioneers began to cross the Appalachians. Similarly, after Smedes's and Enright's pioneering efforts. in forgiveness research studies, began to proliferate. McCullough, Exline, and Baumeister (1998) located fifty-eight studies on forgiveness, widely scattered across developmental, social, personality, and clinical psychology.

Revolution

By 1776 the colonies were well established, and their relationship with England had been fortified through the French and Indian War. This relationship had become strained, and Samuel Adams, a disciple of John Locke, argued strongly in written prose for government based on Lockean principles, responsive to the people. Adams realized that to disconnect the colonists from their attachment to England, he had to sever the ties that bound the colonists to the past. That tie was the idea that England had the best interests of the colonists in mind.

Adams abandoned ineffective pamphleteering as a mind-changing strategy and instead organized the Sons of Freedom, opposed the Stamp Act, and engineered the Boston Tea Party, using his writings not just to change minds, but also to chronicle the repressive acts of England and stir up opposition. Each act instigated by Adams provoked England into more repressive and self-interested responses, until at last soldiers shot into a crowd of people (which Adams immediately labeled the Boston Massacre). Repression was further provoked when the colonist group of minutemen opposed the

British troops at Lexington, and "the shot heard round the world" led to open fighting. Adams had severed the tie that ideologically connected many colonists to England by revealing the latter's stark self-interest.

The American Revolution erupted, and for much of the war, things appeared glum for the colonies. The British had one of the strongest armies in the world; the colonies largely used guerrilla warfare complemented by armies that rarely engaged the British troops in combat. A bad winter at Valley Forge and poor financial support of the colonies' troops almost led to defeat. Eventually, dogged guerrilla fighting by the colonists and resources from France led to British surrender.

Smedes's (1984) book was a similar revolutionary instigation, though he did not intend it that way. The popular belief in 1984 was that forgiveness was merely religious, but Smedes's book convinced psychotherapists to embrace forgiveness as something anyone—not just the religious—could do for self-benefit. Religion tends to be more collectivistic and other-oriented, typically considering the transgressor without recognizing benefits for the forgiver. Forgiveness was a gift, embodied in a community—the "body of Christ" (as Jones [1995] later argued), and done in grateful response to having been forgiven by God.

Therapeutic forgiveness severed the tie between forgiveness and each of these elements of religious forgiveness. It allowed science to be applied as a new method of understanding forgiveness. All major religions endorsed and promoted forgiveness, and despite their differences, this produced much good over the centuries. However, religious understandings of forgiveness had become stagnant, and something new was needed to provide a fresh perspective on forgiveness. The scientific approach provided such new insights. Religious people maintain the traditional views of forgiveness, although new scientific insights have been compatibly incorporated into religious understandings. The forgiveness minirevolution only slightly changed the traditional religious understanding of forgiveness. Many researchers investigated traditional religious understandings of forgiveness using scientific methods, revealing that they were often accurate and helpful. Thus, there was an *evolution* of Christian (and other religions') understanding of forgiveness. The *revolution* in forgiveness came about in the secular realm. That population went from rejecting forgiveness (or practicing it because of a vestige of traditional Christian influence) to embracing it as therapeutic and productive of physical, mental, relational, and spiritual health.

One major factor in bringing about the secular revolution of forgiveness research was—analogous to the political fallout between England and the colonies—social upheaval. Two were noteworthy: first, the USSR's war in Afghanistan created economic pressure and led to the collapse of Soviet communism, the dismantling of the Berlin Wall, and the breakup of the Soviet Union. Former enemies (i.e., communism and democracy) had to learn how to coexist peaceably. Second, former enemies were beginning to negotiate peace in Northern Ireland and South Africa. The world seemed poised on the brink of global reconciliation between 1989 and 1994 and receptive to learning about forgiveness. However, progress stalled with the 1994 massacre in Rwanda, in which 800,000 people were in killed in a hundred days.

Revolutions must gain support not only from the grass roots of the population, but also from secure resources. In 1997 the John Templeton Foundation (JTF), under the visionary leadership of John M. Templeton Jr., issued a $2 million request for research proposals. The flood of proposals prompted an additional $1 million grant by the JTF. Templeton also formed Campaign for Forgiveness Research, raising additional funds from fourteen funding partners, including the Fetzer Institute. In all, over $9 million was applied by the JTF, the campaign, and several partners to fund the research on forgiveness, creating an army of forgiveness researchers.

Postrevolution Unification

Once the Revolutionary War had ended (1780), leaders had either to step aside or change into peacetime founders. Some, like Washington, Adams, and Jefferson, made the transition. Others, like Samuel Adams and Thomas Paine, did not. Still others, like James Madison and Alexander Hamilton, had little impact during the revolution, but emerged as great founders of the new nation.

Similarly, in the forgiveness revolution, some revolutionaries continued to be extremely productive, such as McCullough, Enright, and Worthington. Some faded from visibility, like Smedes and many who had written about psychotherapy in the early years (e.g., Davenport 1991; Hope 1987). Other new faces became highly visible, and most who established very active research programs were funded initially by the JTF and Fetzer initiatives, Campaign for Forgiveness Research, or one of the funding partners. For example, Fincham has established a remarkable research career in studying forgiveness in marriages and has also initiated research programs in forgiveness for numerous other post-docs and colleagues. Several interventions were developed and have been tested, including Luskin's (2001) *Forgive for Good* and DiBlasio's (2000) decision-based forgiveness.

Studies of forgiveness in real-world political systems have flourished (for a review, see Burnette et al. 2012; Cairns, Hewstone, and Niens 2005; Lavelock et al. 2012; Staub 2005; and Worthington and Aten 2010), yielding numerous lessons in the peace process. First, reconciliation should be the aim, not just forgiveness (Worthington and Aten 2010). Second, Track I diplomacy—official, agreed-upon procedures—is a necessary first step (Montville 2001). Third, Track II diplomacy—informal and formal ways to bring together opinion leaders from each side—is helpful for spreading peace (Botcharova 2001; Kuriansky and Elisha 2007). Fourth, in-group and out-group contact on superordinate goals is important in changing attitudes. This can occur through activities like cooking and camping (Kuriansky and Elisha 2007), sports (Darnell 2010), shared activities (Anderlini 2007), and meeting members from the out-group who have lost loved ones, allowing for reshaping of out-group prejudicial narratives. Fifth, attitudes toward societal or personal justice can influence peace and unity (Durrheim et al. 2011; Lillie and Janoff-Bulman 2007). Sixth, Track III diplomacy—in-group psycho-educational forgiveness groups aimed at forgiving members of the out-group—can help people with similar group identity to forgive (Worthington and Aten 2010). Seventh, sustaining peace, or social change, is often more difficult than instigating it. Programs in Track I, Track II, and Track III diplomacy must be systematically examined to ensure that they last (Salomon 2011). Forgiveness programs will undoubtedly appeal to different constituencies within each group, and reaching all involved groups is vital to achieving stable peace. Eighth, silence and ignoring prejudices, differences, and past hostilities are likely to fail (for a review, see Liem 2007). Dialogue and co-constructing a new shared narrative of past, present, and future are necessary for stable peace. Finally, a variety of virtues is needed to sustain peace, including forgiveness, restorative justice, and humility (Davis et al. in press; Worthington 2009).

Forgiveness is not always good for individuals, and communication of forgiveness is not always good for society (Lamb and Murphy 2002). An example of when forgiveness is not helpful for individuals is when they mistake forgiveness (an internal experience) for the communication of forgiveness (a behavior). As Lamb and Murphy (2002) observe in many cautionary settings, the communication of forgiveness (i.e., saying, "I forgive you") in the event of a serious injustice to an abuser not only provides license to the abuser to abuse again, but can make the communicator feel guilty and ashamed. On the other hand, an understanding of forgiveness properly could allow a victim of abuse to forgive and not have to deal with the negativity and stress of unforgiveness (Worthington 2006), but could still permit the victim to demand that the offender face justice and behave responsibly in the future. Even if the victim understands forgiveness properly as an internal experience, he or she might experience other negative psychological and social effects from forgiving due to unconscious forces and the reactions of others in that person's world. Thus, from a practical point of view, it is not advisable to argue that forgiveness (and especially the communication of forgiveness) is beneficial in all circumstances.

LESSONS LEARNED FROM THE FORGIVENESS MINIREVOLUTION

Virtually all those involved in starting and prosecuting revolutions believe they are good for society. The difficulties of successful revolution are

(1) overcoming state inertia through instigators who act appropriately so as to lead and inspire followers; (2) waging the revolution against an often better equipped, trained, and supported establishment and winning the support of the populace; and (3) stabilizing the new order so that it can be sustained against the challenges it must face.

The study of forgiveness is a minirevolution that has met these three difficulties. It has already produced a literature that tells us more about forgiveness than we knew before, and it has developed interventions to help individuals and groups forgive. It has also discovered some conditions under which forgiveness is not always optimal. And it has elaborated on the potential individual and societal benefits of forgiveness when enacted under the right circumstances. In addition, although forgiveness does not necessarily imply reconciliation or peace, it makes both more likely (Tutu 1999). The study of forgiveness is now informing real-world interactions that can contribute to an important revolution: quick, frequent, thorough, and lasting peace. Life will always have war and heartache. Yet forgiveness, with its evolutionary adaptations, religious roots, and historical foundations, now takes the next step—revolution—in which a new power (i.e., science) can advance peace and reconciliation.

How did this occur? The ideas of Smedes (1984), early psychotherapists, and researchers laid the foundation, even though there was no intention to create a revolution that freed forgiveness from its almost exclusive association with religion. Events in the political sphere (i.e., the fall of communism) gave wider scope to the idea that (1) to forgive is human and (2) scientific study could deepen both understanding and application of secular forgiveness. Third, the involvement of visionary leader John M. Templeton Jr. and the application of the financial and managerial resources of the JTF brought other "revolutionaries" into the forgiveness movement. Fourth, the practical fruits of the research of multiple scientists solidified and sustained the minirevolution. Fifth, the secular, science-driven minirevolution of forgiveness did not oppose itself to the traditional religious view of forgiveness, but rather supplemented and complemented it, akin to the establishment of effective power sharing between former disputants. Furthermore, the media and the method of public sharing of forgiveness findings have served as impartial mediators.

In closing, we suggest that the minirevolution of secular, science-driven forgiveness is one informative case study of revolution. By analyzing it, we hope to have shed some light on successful and unsuccessful revolutions covered in these volumes.

REFERENCES

Anderlini, S. N. (2007). *Women Building Peace: What They Do, Why It Matters*. Boulder, CO: Lynne Rienner Publishers.

Berger, P. L. (1999). "The Desecularization of the World: A Global Overview." In Peter L. Berger (Ed.), *The Desecularization of the World: Resurgent Religion and World Politics* (pp. 1–18). Washington, DC: Grand Rapids: Eerdmans—Ethics and Public Policy Center.

Botcharova, O. (2001). "Implementation of Track Two Diplomacy: Developing a Model of Forgiveness." In *Forgiveness and Reconciliation: Religion, Public Policy, and Conflict Transformation*, edited by R. G. Helmick and R. L. Petersen, 269–94. Philadelphia: Templeton Foundation Press.

Brewer, M. B. (1991). "The Social Self: On Being the Same and Different at the Same Time." *Personality and Social Psychology Bulletin* 17: 475–82.

Brounéus, K. (2008). "Reconciliation in the Great Lakes Region: Some Thoughts on Key Topics, Agendas, and Challenges." Paper presented at the meeting of the John Templeton Foundation ad hoc Task Force on the Possibility of Research in Rwanda, Nassau, Bahamas, June 3.

Burnette, J. L., D. R. Van Tongeren, E. O'Boyle, E. L. Worthington Jr., and D. Forsyth. (2012). "Correlates of Inter-group Forgiveness: A Meta Analysis." Unpublished manuscript, University of Richmond, Virginia.

Cacciopo, J. T., J. H. Fowler, and N. A. Christakis. (2009). "Alone in the Crowd: The Structure and Spread of Loneliness in a Large Social Network." *Journal of Personality and Social Psychology* 97 (6): 977–91.

Cairns, E., T. Tam, M. Hewstone, and U. Niens. (2005). "Intergroup Forgiveness and Intergroup Conflict: Northern Ireland, a Case Study." In *Handbook of Forgiveness*, edited by Everett L. Worthington Jr., 461–75. New York: Brunner-Routledge.

Chapman, A. R., and B. Spong, eds. (2003). *Religion and Reconciliation in South Africa*. Philadelphia: Templeton Foundation Press.

Darnell, S. (2010). "Power, Politics, and 'Sport for Development and Peace': Investigating the Utility of Sport for International Development." *Sociology of Sport Journal* 27: 54–75.

Davenport, D. S. (1991). "The Functions of Anger and Forgiveness: Guidelines for Psychotherapy with Victims." *Psychotherapy* 28: 140–44.

Davis, D. E., E. L. Worthington Jr., J. N. Hook, R. A. Emmons, P. A. Hill, R. A. Bollinger, and D. R. Van Tongeren. (in press). "Humility and the Development and Repair of Social Bonds: Two Longitudinal Studies." *Self and Identity* 12(1–2): 58–77.

de Tocqueville, A. (1969). *Democracy in America*. Translated by G. Lawrence. Garden City, NY: Doubleday.

de Waal, F. B. M. (1989). *Peacemaking among Primates*. London: Penguin Books.

de Waal, F. B. M., and J. J. Pokorny. (2005). "Primate Questions about the Art and Science of Forgiving." In *Handbook of Forgiveness*, edited by E. L. Worthington Jr., 17–32. New York: Brunner-Routledge.

DiBlasio, F. A. (2000). "Decision-based Forgiveness Treatment in Cases of Marital Infidelity." *Psychotherapy* 37: 149–58.

Durrheim, K., J. Dixon, C. Tredoux, L. Eaton, M. Quayle, and B. Clack. (2011). "Predicting Support for Racial Transformation Policies: Intergroup Threat, Racial Prejudice, Sense of Group Entitlement and Strength of Identification." *European Journal of Social Psychology* 41 (1): 23–41.

Enright, R. D., and R. P. Fitzgibbons. (2000). *Helping Clients Forgive: An Empirical Guide for Resolving Anger and Restoring Hope*. Washington, DC: American Psychological Association.

Exline, J. J., E. L. Worthington Jr., P. C. Hill, and M. E. McCullough. (2003). "Forgiveness and Justice: A Research Agenda for Social and Personality Psychology." *Psychology and Social Psychology Review* 7: 337–48.

Fears, J. R. (2007). "Why We Study History." *The Wisdom of History*. Chantilly, VA: The Teaching Company. [audiotapes]

Gartner, A. L. (2011). "Sweet Mercy: A Scientific Investigation." PhD diss., Virginia Commonwealth University, Richmond.

Hebl, J., and R. D. Enright. (1993). "Forgiveness as a Psychotherapeutic Goal with Elderly Females." *Psychotherapy* 30: 658–67.

Hope, D. (1987). "The Healing Paradox of Forgiveness." *Psychotherapy: Theory, Research, Practice, Training* 24: 240–44.

Jones, L. G. (1995). *Embodying Forgiveness: A Theological Analysis*. Grand Rapids, MI: Eerdmans.

Koenig, H. G., M. E. McCullough, and D. Larson. (2001). *Handbook of Religion and Health*. London: Oxford University Press.

Kohlberg, L. (1981). *Essays on Moral Development*. Vol. 1, *The Philosophy of Moral Development*. New York: Harper.

Kuriansky, J., and T. Elisha. (2007). "Cooking, Climbing, Camping, and Other Creative Cooperations between Palestinians and Jews: Successes and Challenges." In *Beyond Bullets and Bombs: Grassroots Peacebuilding between Israelis and Palestinians, Contemporary Psychology*, edited by J. Kuriansky, 227–42. Westport, CT: Praeger.

Lamb, S., and J. Murphy, eds. (2002). *Before Forgiving: Cautionary Views of Forgiveness in Psychotherapy*. New York: Oxford University Press.

Lavelock, C. R., E. L. Worthington Jr., J. L. Burnette, D. R. Van Tongeren, D. J. Jennings II, C. L. Greer, Y. Lin, and M. Y. Ho. (2012). "Forgiveness and the Psychology of Peace." In *Psychology of Peace*, edited by Emir L. Kovacevic and Jusuf J. Medvjed, 1–71. Hauppage, NY: Nova Publishers.

Liem, R. (2007). "Silencing Historical Trauma: The Politics and Psychology of Memory and Voice." *Peace and Conflict* 13 (2): 153–74.

Lillie, C., and R. Janoff-Bulman. (2007). "Macro Versus Micro Justice and Perceived Fairness of Truth and Reconciliation Commissions." *Peace and Conflict* 13 (2): 221–36.

Luskin, F. M. (2001). *Forgive for Good: A Proven Prescription for Health and Happiness*. San Francisco: Harper.

McCullough, M. E. (2008). *Beyond Revenge: The Evolution of the Forgiveness Instinct*. San Francisco: Jossey-Bass.

McCullough, M. E., J. J. Exline, and R. F. Baumeister. (1998). "An Annotated Bibliography of Research on Forgiveness and Related Topics." In *Dimensions of Forgiveness: Psychological Research and Theological Speculations*, edited by E. L. Worthington Jr., 193–317. Philadelphia: Templeton Foundation Press.

McCullough, M. E., and E. L. Worthington Jr. (1994). Encouraging clients to forgive people who have hurt them: Review, critique, and research prospectus. *Journal of Psychology and Theology*, 22, 3–20.

McCullough, M. E., E. L. Worthington Jr., and K. C. Rachal. (1997). "Interpersonal Forgiving in Close Relationships." *Journal of Personality and Social Psychology* 73: 321–36.

McCullough, M. E., L. R. Luna, J. W. Berry, B. A. Tabak, and G. Bono. (2010). "On the Form and Function of Forgiving: Modeling the Time-forgiveness Relationship and Testing the Valuable Relationships Hypothesis." *Emotion* 10: 358–76.

Milgram, S. (1974). *Obedience to Authority*. New York: Harper & Row.

Montville, J. (2001). "Religion and Peacemaking." In *Forgiveness and Reconciliation: Religion, Public Policy, & Conflict Transformation*, edited by R. G. Helmick and R. L. Petersen, 161–82. Philadelphia: Templeton Foundation Press.

Murphy, J. G. (2003). *Getting Even: Forgiveness and Its Limits*. New York: Oxford University Press.

Oliner, S. P., and J. R. Gunn. (2006). "Manifestations of Radical Evil: Structure and Social Psychology." *Humboldt Journal of Social Relations* 30 (1): 108–43.

Salomon, G. (2011). "Four Major Challenges Facing Peace Education in Regions of Intractable Conflict." *Peace and Conflict* 17 (1): 46–59.

Sapolsky, R. M. (2005). "The Physiology and Pathophysiology of Unhappiness." In *Handbook of Forgiveness*, edited by Everett L. Worthington Jr., 273–303. New York: Brunner-Routledge.

Sapolsky, R. M., and L. J. Share. (2004). "A Pacific Culture among Wild Baboons: Its Emergence and Transmission." *PLoS Biology* 2: 534–41.

Shönbach, P. (1990). *Account Episodes: The Management or Escalation of Conflict*. New York: Cambridge University Press.

Smedes, L. B. (1984). *Forgive and Forget: Healing the Hurts We Don't Deserve*. San Francisco: Harper & Row.

Staub, E. (2005). "The Origins and Evolution of Hate, with Notes on Prevention." In *The Psychology of Hate*, edited by R. J. Sternberg, 51–66. Washington, DC: American Psychological Association.

Tutu, D. M. (1999). *No Future Without Forgiveness*. New York: Doubleday.

Waldron, V. R., and D. L. Kelly. (2008). *Communicating Forgiveness*. Thousand Oaks, CA: Sage.

Worthington, E. L., Jr. (2001). "Unforgiveness, Forgiveness, and Reconciliation and Their Implications for Societal Interventions." In *Forgiveness and Reconciliation: Religion, Public Policy, & Conflict Transformation*, edited by R. G. Helmick and R. L. Petersen, 161–82. Philadelphia: Templeton Foundation Press.

Worthington, E. L., Jr. (2006). *Forgiveness and Reconciliation: Theory and Application*. New York: Brunner-Routledge.

Worthington, E. L., Jr. (2009). *A Just Forgiveness: Responsible Healing Without Excusing Injustice*. Downers Grove: InterVarsity Press.

Worthington, E. L., Jr., and J. Aten. (2010). "Forgiveness and Reconciliation." In *Postconflict Rehabilitation: Creating a Trauma Membrane for Individuals and Communities and Restructuring Lives after Trauma*, edited by Erin Martz, 55–72. New York: Springer.

CHAPTER 11

REVOLUTION, THE SACRED, AND THE SECULAR

Richard Fenn

The sacred emerges in moments and situations in which an individual or a group, even a people or an entire nation, experiences the presence or absence of a person or object as signifying life or death. The most obvious example is the Neolithic response to the setting of the sun on the longest night of the year and its subsequent rising; its presence and absence are indeed a cause and not only an emblem of life and death. These Stone Age communities, gathered in the circles of standing stones, held torches embodying as well as signifying the light of the absent sun itself. In archaic Greece standing stones embodied and signified the presence of one who was absent on a journey and might or might never return. They were a form of the double, like the wax effigy of the dead king, which in the absence of the king's corpse, for a time received the sacrifices and offerings of the community. Similarly, a relic was animated by the spirit of a dead saint, a real presence that also connoted a real absence.

Thus the sacred, like a standing stone on an ancient Greek roadside that embodied the vital presence of someone known to be dead or absent, may lose its sanctity if the one personified fails to come when called or to otherwise be accessible. Similarly, the very grounding of that real presence, like the statue of Athena in the Parthenon, may become more like a copy or an image than a real presence. The sacred may become less accessible and authentic over time, just as it can lose authority even though its grounding becomes more permanent and secure.

The sacred enjoys a half-life, even when it is the presence and absence of the sun that is being celebrated or mourned, invoked or lamented. The winter solstice, ending in the rebirth of the sun, is followed by the summer solstice, in which the light of the world once again begins to run out of time. The standing stone embodying and conveying the presence of one who is absent, or the spirit of one departed, is eventually transformed into a statue on the Acropolis that is no more than a certified copy of the heavenly divinity. A relic may no longer embody or transmit the spirit of an ancestor or a saint; ancestors have a life of their own and may choose not to be evoked; invocations to the saints do not always produce the desired effect, or any effect at all. If a saint's tunic is no longer able to ground the being of a holy order or monarchy, perhaps the saint's jawbone will.

The capacity of the sacred to signify and effect both presence and absence, life and death, may be primarily of intense, personal, and local significance, or it may instead be collective. When a psalmist intones, "Lift up the light of the countenance upon me, and I shall be whole," there is no doubt that the presence or absence of the divine is also essential for life. Without the light of the divine countenance the soul, no longer whole, begins to disintegrate, like the psyche of a prisoner in solitary confinement.

If a monastic order or entire community intones these words, it is their collective existence that is at stake. Like the presence or absence of a flag over Fort Sumter, whether it "yet waves" may both signify and embody the fate of a people and a nation. When women in Syria and Egypt sewed crosses next to the crescents on their nations' flags, they were personally, and perhaps at some risk to themselves, identifying the Christian icon of life in the midst of death with the Islamic sign of collective identity. When women and men in Syria marched in the streets proclaiming that they themselves embodied the identity of a twelve-year-old boy whose mutilated corpse had been returned to his father by Syrian intelligence, they were once again, at great personal risk, embodying life in the midst of and yet transcendent over death, in an act that was at once corporate and deeply individual.

As these two examples from Syria indicate, in a revolutionary situation the sacred may be embodied in symbols and icons, images, and monuments that are of both collective and profound personal significance. On the other hand, the sacred may be embodied in a crowd of people who, identifying with the victim of the regime, are opposing their experience of the sacred to that of the political and cultural center.

Under these latter conditions it is fair to say that the soul of a people is at stake. That is an expression of peculiar relevance to recent events in Northern Mali, where a new Islamic regime is systematically destroying the sacred monuments and artifacts of the people. In a story for Independent Television News carried in the United States by the PBS show *NewsHour*, Lindsey Hilsum reported, "Mali, one of the most culturally diverse countries on Earth, a land of music, mud mosques, ancient Islamic manuscripts, animists, all now under threat." Referring to a group called the Hunters, whose use of rifles is largely ceremonial and whose traditions extend a millennium into the past, Hilsum noted: "These men see themselves as Muslims, but they mix their Islam with animism, traditional culture, and they know that, if the Islamists came down from the north to here, then they'd be the first target. But they're an essential part of Malian culture." According to Samuel Sidibe, the director of the National Museum of Mali in Bamako: "The Taliban destroyed the Buddha in Afghanistan. What happened to Timbuktu is quite the same, of course. Heritage is important for people because we all need to have the sense that we have an existence in the past. And if someone wants to destroy this idea of the past, I think it's clear that this one, this person wants to destroy the soul of Malian people" ("Islamic Militants" 2012).

This account documents the authenticity of these Malian formations of the sacred: the music and the instrument, the hunters, their rites and rifles, the sculpture, the tombs, and the animist practices. Their source is immediately accessible in the individuals who put their own lives at risk to affirm the capacity of life to transcend death. That in these acts death is inseparable from and confused with life is as inevitable as that the absence of the crucified Jesus, or of the Syrian boy tortured to death by the Syrian regime, is felt intensely as a real presence. The authenticity of invocations of the sacred may be diminished as the performance becomes more theatrical than potentially fatal, and when the absence conjured into presence may or may not be considered real by those whose devotion or sacrifice is being solicited by the enactment of the sacred.

When religion loses its ownership and control over the sacred, even forms of the sacred once enshrined within a religious tradition may become both subversive and potentially revolutionary. In modern societies religion has been most visibly losing its ownership and control of the sacred ever since the Reformation, although in the Middle Ages there was ample and often intense opposition by those who evoked the sacred on the periphery against its more highly institutionalized and centralized formations. In Mali the people are defending their own forms of the sacred, because their society, as they once knew it before the Islamic takeover in the North, was secular. According to one of the students interviewed in the Hilsum report, "We're a democratic, sovereign, secular republic. We never expected anyone to impose Sharia on us. We're in our own country, so we should be free to behave as we wish" ("Islamic Militants" 2012). Thus a secular and democratic society was providing a sanctuary for the sacred enshrined in the animist, Suf'i, and warrior culture of the people, and the notion of the people itself had acquired a collective sanctity of its own. All of these were opposed to the religious culture of the Islamist jihadis.

In thinking about the relationship of the sacred to the secular or of the traditional to the modern, we therefore have to suspend our usual categories and the judgments that issue from them. Only a poststructural as well as a post-postmodern viewpoint will begin to unscramble the assumed connections and differences between modernity and the past, or between the secular and the sacred. It is precisely such a renewed sorting of perspectives that Susan Rasmussen, in one of the most perceptive articles yet written about religion in Africa, suggests:

> There remains much unfinished business in theorizing sacred, secular, and related concepts. How do post-structural anthropologists, wary of binaries and reifications, know whether to ascribe the terms "sacred" and "secular" to particular concepts, ideologies, and settings? . . . the secular is not merely a space remaining from, or neatly opposed to, the sacred and/or religion. Yet the reverse also holds true, for what is sacred, or something approximating it, is not merely a space left over from or neatly opposed to the secular. Nor are these concepts static or sequential. The secular does not always emerge in linear fashion during social change, as more "modern" than the sacred. The sacred is not necessarily more or less "traditional" than and does not always precede other domains. (2007, 185)

I have noted elsewhere that in France revolutionary rhetoric used terms like *patrie*, the Constitution, the people, or the Nation to identify the sacred, terms that have been considered to be secular not only by traditionalists and religious intellectuals, but also by sociologists and anthropologists, as if secularity were a term opposed not only to the religious but also to all forms of the sacred.

But the conventional oppositions do not help us identify the sacred when it is neither profane or secular on the one hand nor religious on the other. Least of all does conventional terminology help to identify the sacred when its enemies are clearly religion or the religious. As Susan Rasmussen reports:

> These different religious orientations within Tuareg society appear in debates and dilemmas over conduct within *al hima* lands, Islamist reform, and in perceived opposition between *al hima* and what Tuareg alternately call Christian.
>
> The laws of Niger and Mali favor separation of religion and the state. Many officials and many Tuareg, particularly French-speaking intellectuals, described these governments as "laique" using, significantly, the French term for secular. Government pamphlets describing the secular court system; for example, family and gender-related statutes use this term. . . . Most people, however, do not make a rigid distinction between sacred and secular, or religious and non religious. In fact, the closest approximation to

laique and secular in Tuareg discourse is the Tamajaq term for Christian. (2007, 190–91)

It is precisely the need to identify the sacred within revolutionary situations that moves Rasmussen to call for a radical rethinking of the sacred and its relationships to the profane, the secular, and religion itself. To contribute to that rethinking is the purpose of this chapter.

When the sacred is evoked personally and collectively against a regime, a social order may be subject to dissidence, rebellion, and perhaps revolution. Under some conditions protest occurs within the same religious framework as that used to provide legitimacy to the regime; cases in point are the populist Islamic tradition in Mali, combined with elements from Malian animist and warrior cultures, as well as the protest in a Moscow cathedral by the Pussy Riot band invoking the Holy Mother against Vladimir Putin. The sacred thus marshaled against its own religious institutions resembles the protest in Rumania that unseated the Ceaucescu regime. In that revolution a Protestant group on the Romanian periphery, with ethnic and linguistic differences from the Orthodox and Communist political and cultural center, launched the revolution.

Much depends on whether the sacred seeking control of the political and cultural center is in opposition to the center or operating within a common religious framework. In Syria the revolution is dominated by Sunnis opposed to the Alawite regime, itself related to the Shiite branch of Islam. It is thus opposing its own, Islamic form of the sacred against the centralized Islamic institutions, but it is doing so in the name of predominantly secular and prodemocratic social and political objectives. Even among Sunnis there are extremists, like those of Hamas and an Al Qaeda fringe that might conceivably achieve a more influential position later in the revolution. In Russia as well, the invocation of the Holy Mother by a group seeking a more open, secular, and democratic society opposes a political and cultural center consisting of a church in the same religious tradition that is uniting with the state to impose a highly traditional and authoritarian social order on the nation. A comparable situation exists in Northern Mali, where Muslims accustomed to a largely secular central authority and allied with indigenous forms of the sacred, such as monuments and tombs, animism and a warrior sect, are fighting Islamicists who are imposing their own version of Sharia law.

The question in each of these contexts is whether a form of the sacred will dominate that is owned and controlled by traditionally religious authorities identified with the political and cultural center, who seek to monopolize all forms of the sacred, or whether a form of the sacred will prevail that is authentic, accessible, popular, democratic, and resistant to institutionalization as well as to being monopolized or controlled from the center.

The pattern of comparable forms of the sacred inhabiting and energizing, even legitimating, opposing centers and peripheries can also be found in ancient Greece. What has sometimes been called the "sacred revolution" was a revolution in the social location and function of the sacred. As the heavens became differentiated from the earth, or society from nature, the living may also have been increasingly separated from the dead; monuments like standing stones or effigies, forms of the double, may have signified the vital presence of the departed and absent. Eventually the double, in the form of an effigy, embodied the vital presence of the dead king, and to that double devotions were made for some time after the royal person had been buried. However, the double, in the form of a standing stone, also stood for the vital presence of the departed, whether dead or merely absent on a journey, and these stones could be found along the roadside and in remote parts of the country.

To put it another way, to the sacred revolution, permitting the differentiation of the heavens from the earth may also have allowed other forms of differentiation to be imagined, whether the separation of the natural from the supernatural or the center from the periphery. For example, once centered in the hearth in the household of the chief, the sacred may have been allowed to be imitated in the hearths of private households and leading citizens. That is, in ancient societies the sacred may have been contested, with one form becoming increasingly local or even domestic, accessible, and yet vulnerable to absence and death, while the other continued to be centralized, grounded in authoritative social centers, and accessible at the center of the polis only to those qualified to have such access. Only when the sacred was identified with the hearth at the center of the polis might it have been able to unite the center with the periphery.

What matters for our understanding of both revolution and the sacred is that the latter may be a source of apparent sacrilege, whether committed by the center against the periphery or by groups and individuals in opposition to the center. Certainly jihadist regimes that have overtaken the center of particular regions or societies have committed sacrilege against all other forms of the sacred, just as Sunnis in Iraq have destroyed Shiite shrines. Conversely, the revolutionary potential of sacrilege by the periphery against the center has characterized the recent protest by the Russian feminist band Pussy Riot, against the regime of Vladimir Putin at the Moscow cathedral that he had chosen as his sanctuary.

When in late February 2012 members of the feminist punk rock band Pussy Riot danced on the altar of the Cathedral of Christ the Savior in Moscow, they chanted three times, "Holy Mother! Send Putin packing" (Mackey and Kates 2012). Their brief theatrical performance attacked not only the Putin regime's claim to legitimate traditional authority, but also the patriarchal authority of the Russian Orthodox church, headed by a former official of the KGB, and of the Putin regime itself.

From the viewpoint of the center, Pussy Riot's crime was blasphemy and sacrilege. The ancient past was evoked to transform the present by relegating the regime of Vladimir Putin to the immediate past. The protesters' plea for aid from the Holy Mother had been addressed to a spiritual personage evoked as if she were indeed present, in the full awareness that the Virgin Mary died about two thousand years ago. No wonder that, according to the *New York Times*, the judge who sentenced the protesters to a number of years in jail, Marina Syrova, "described the women as posing a danger to society and said they had committed 'grave crimes' including 'the insult and humiliation of the Christian faith and inciting religious hatred.'" Indeed, in the eyes of the Russian Orthodox church, "'What happened is blasphemy and sacrilege, the conscious and deliberate insult to the sanctuary and a manifestation of hostility to millions of people'" (Herzenhorn 2012). Indeed, their primary offense had been blasphemy.

Conversely, in the opinion of an editorial writer for the left-wing *Gazeta.ryu*, an online newspaper identified with the worldwide Occupy movement, the trial was reminiscent of the early Middle Ages: "The case . . . proceeded according to Byzantium church convocations of the millennium before last" (Zagvozdina 2012). Certainly the statements read by the members of Pussy Riot at the conclusion of their trial evoked the sacred over and against Russian Orthodox religion and its collusion with the state.

Charged with sacrilege and blasphemy by both the church and the state, the band at first failed to receive more than ambivalent support from Russian public opinion, until the actors' authenticity was confirmed by their willingness to be jailed for their alleged blasphemy. The potent revolutionary implications of the band's performance later emerged in their statements at their trial, when they aligned their action with the sacrifice of Jesus, who before them has been crucified for blasphemy against the church of his time and the state. Indeed, some of the band members took their authority from the biblical wisdom tradition and its capacity to deepen the individual's sense of his or her own being in fundamental solidarity with all other humans and the creation itself.

In aligning themselves with this tradition, they cited passages from the New Testament that make divine wisdom immediately accessible to those who seek it. As one of the band members put it in her closing statement at the trial: "This motivation is best expressed in the Gospels: 'For everyone who asks receives; the one who seeks finds; and to the one who knocks, the door will be opened.' [Matt. 7:8] I—all of us—sincerely believe that for us the door will be opened. But alas, for now the only thing that has happened is that we've been locked up in prison" ("Pussy Riot Closing" 2012).

Open-mindedness, humility, the art of questioning, the capacity to develop inward sources of inspiration and authority, humility, and a passion for the truth are the fruits of the spirit of wisdom. In their closing statements, the dissidents evoked all who had suffered or been martyred for the truth, from Socrates to Jesus to Dostoyevsky. Just as Jesus and the first Christian martyr, Stephen, had been killed for blasphemy and for offenses against religion and the law, so were they being punished:

> Have you forgotten under what circumstances Stephen, the disciple of the Apostles, concluded his earthly life? "Then they secretly induced men to say, 'We have heard him speak blasphemous words against Moses and against God.' And they stirred up the people, the elders and the scribes, and they came up to him and dragged him away and brought him before the Council. They put forward false witnesses who said, 'This man incessantly speaks against this holy place and the Law'." [Acts 6:11–13] He was found guilty and stoned to death. I also hope that you all remember well how the Jews answered Christ: "It is not for good works that we are going to stone you but for blasphemy." [John 10:33] And finally we would do well to keep in mind the following characterization of Christ: "He is demon-possessed and raving mad." [John 10:20] ("Pussy Riot Closing" 2012)

Thus, when a periphery opposes its own symbols of the sacred to the symbols and institutions of the political and cultural center, even when the center and periphery legitimate themselves through the sources of the same religious tradition, the periphery commits what the center calls blasphemy or sacrilege.

Alone among those at the trial, the members of the dissident band were free to speak their minds; the other participants were slaves of the state, alienated not only from the truth but from themselves:

> I think that religious truth should not be static, that it is essential to understand the instances and paths of spiritual development, the trials of a human being, his duplicity, his splintering. That for one's self to form it is essential to experience these things. That you have to experience all these things in order to develop as a person. That religious truth is a process and not a finished product that can be shoved wherever and whenever. And all of these things I've been talking about, all of these processes—they acquire meaning in art and in philosophy. Including contemporary art. An artistic situation can and, in my opinion, must contain its own internal conflict. And what really irritates me is how the prosecution uses the words 'so-called' in reference to contemporary art. ("Pussy Riot Closing" 2012)

After being convicted of obscene behavior and sentenced to jail for three years, one of the activists, Nadezhda Tolokonnikova, proclaimed, "'We are happy because we brought the revolution closer!' A police officer snapped back, 'Well done'" (Herzenhorn 2012).

BEYOND SACRILEGE

The revolutionary potential embedded in the sacred itself derives from its capacity to invoke the absent and the dead as if they were vitally present, and in so doing not only to re-create the past within the present, but to initiate an unauthorized future. For the sacred to embody an absence in the form of a presence in such a way as to blur the distinction between life and death, it is necessary for any performance of the sacred to suspend all ordinary conventions for experiencing and interpreting the passage of time. An absence can only be a presence, and death can only be identified with life, if the ordinary sequence of events is suspended; that, of course, is precisely what a rite, properly performed, accomplishes. The sacred moment is not about to be outmoded by a later moment, but stands on its own ground outside the passage of time, immune to replacement or to being effaced by the inevitable sequences of *befores* into *afters*. That moment consisted of a two-minute video of Pussy Riot dancing obscenely in the cathedral, on the basis of which the court sought to justify its verdict of blasphemy.

Furthermore, the erosion of the difference between life and death, presence and absence, requires that the past and the future be fully integrated into the present. That is why one of the protesters could announce that the revolution was already closer at hand than it had been before their dance in the cathedral. Not only had an unauthorized future been inaugurated, but the regime had been allocated to the past. Thus online commentary by an editorialist for *Gazeta.ru* compared the judgment of the court to the procedures of the Byzantine ecclesiastical court. No wonder it had been dismissed by the verdict of global public opinion.

THE SECULARITY OF THE SACRED

If we are to understand the revolutionary and counterrevolutionary potential of the sacred, we need to recognize how the sacred may be indissolubly connected with the secular. In their demonstration at the cathedral, the protesters proclaimed that the Putin regime, through the KGB, had deployed the cathedral as a stage setting to give their illegitimate government the trappings of legitimacy; indeed, in an interview granted months before the protest, one of the members of Pussy Riot had deplored the close connections between the patriarch of the Russian Orthodox church and the Putin regime, not to mention his sporting a $40,000 watch in flagrant disregard for the Russian poor. In the same interview the activist stated a wide range of clearly prodemocratic views:

> Our political ideal is a developed civil society where people are aware of their rights and interests.

Politicians must depend on their electorate. Today, a small number of people have taken power by force in Russia, they now change laws to keep control of the country. They have not asked Russia's citizens, whether they want prolongation of presidential term to 6 years or not. Why didn't they conduct a referendum? Russia does not have democracy now. . . . We must change the judicial system first. Democracy is impossible without an independent judicial system. An education reform, and cultural reform are also needed. Putin pays attention to anything but culture—museums, libraries, culture centers are all in awful conditions. (Zagvozdina 2012)

There is no mistaking the inner, deeply individualized authority of the protesters. As one of them stated in her closing statement:

When I was involved with organizing the ecological movement, I became fundamentally convinced of the priority of inner freedom as the foundation for taking action. As well as the importance, the direct importance, of taking action as such. To this day I find it astonishing that, in our country, we need the support of several thousands of individuals in order to put an end to the despotism of one or a handful of bureaucrats. I would like to note that our trial stands as a very eloquent confirmation of the fact that we need the support of thousands of individuals from all over the world in order to prove the obvious: that the three of us are not guilty. ("Pussy Riot Closing" 2012)

In a revolutionary situation, only when the sacred formally aligned with the center begins to distance itself from political and cultural sources of power is it possible for the sacred to embrace a radical secularity. For example, some, if not all, of the largely Sunni rebels in Syria live without ideology and act with no other authority than their desire and respect for both life and death. In an article in the online *Guardian*, a Sunni sheikh named Omar asks his Alawite captive, one Barakat, whether there is hatred between them: "'Do you hate us because we're Sunnis?' asked Omar. 'No, my sheikh, I swear,' replied Barakat, leaning forward to touch Omar on the knee to press his point. 'I don't hate you at all. The regime created all these hostilities. We had always gotten on as communities. Who buried our dead after the fighting, the regime? They were nowhere to be seen. It was your men who dug the graves and gave my men a burial'" (Martin Chulov).

In the midst of battle, fighters have no need to distinguish themselves from others who also belong to a secular world that is always passing away. There is no salvation from the passage of time. Revolutionaries and their combatants do not need the times mediated to them by an authorized calendar of precedents and priorities; neither do they have to stand on ceremony, satisfy old loves or grievances, or wait for a final verdict on their thoughts or actions. They live in the immediate moment with the knowledge that it has lasting import and consequence.

Thus, in a dissolving social order, the sacred takes on the immediacy and authenticity of the profoundly personal, local, and fateful. Reporting for the *New York Times* from Syria, Samar Yazbek described a particular group of rebel fighters:

> They weren't Islamic fundamentalists. I've encountered very few Islamist groups and have not observed any connection to Al Qaeda or Salafism, a movement based on a rigid, austere interpretation of Islam. The young men there told me that a few Salafi jihadis had started to appear recently, but that they did not constitute a significant number. As we were sitting out on the balcony overlooking an olive orchard, the bombs started falling all around us. Nearby, the town of Taftanaz was being shelled; we could see it from the balcony. I asked the head of the division, who'd prepared dinner for us, "Aren't you afraid that a bomb might fall on your heads right now?" He replied: "We aren't afraid. Death has become a part of our lives." As we dined, the main topic of discussion was Aleppo, Syria's most populous city. A number of the young men present were from the besieged neighborhood of Salaheddin and were getting ready to return. They refused to let me go with them for fear of the looming battle. (Yazbek 2012)

In this situation presence and absence are indeed experienced as a matter of life and death: both are personal and depend on locale; either may be fatal.

Under these conditions immediacy achieves a certain universal pity or compassion along with its freedom from deference or obligation to the past and the future. Speaking of the rebels with whom she dined in Syria, Samar Yazbek (2012) continued:

> I was the only woman among them, and the young F.S.A. men treated me like part of the group. During that meeting it became clear that it's a mistake to consider the F.S.A. as a single bloc. It is a hodgepodge of battalions, including secularists, moderate Islamists and all-too-ordinary people who joined up to defend their lives and their families.
>
> At the end of our journey back to Saraqib, the commander told me, "We are one people, we and the Alawites are brothers. We had never thought about the sort of things that the regime is trying to stir up." (Yazbek 2012)

There is a real presence among those who recognize each other without social institutions that protect them from the full force of the passage of time. Institutionalized sanctity not only mediates the passage of time, but also puts up barriers between those who have unequal priorities or chances of surviving the passage of time. The highly personal, local, accessible form of the sacred, grounded finally in the individual, makes each person unique, perishable, and with claims to priority equal to those of others in the same context. When protesters in Moscow marched, chanting, "We exist," they held iPods above their heads rather than the traditional display of icons that once emboldened demonstrators against the forces of the czar. I regard the iconic iPods as a sign of the emergence of a people who in the face of death hold their lives and personhood sacred.

Without the protections, priorities, and barriers of the shrine and the sanctuary, all, whether Muslim or Jew or Christian or Hindu, find the sacred in the psyche, which is both accessible and vulnerable, immediate and yet elusive, highly individual, present and yet partially absent, the ephemeral ground of every human being.

The emergence of the sacred in revolutionary situations is rendered all the harder to identify, then, because the rhetoric of the revolutionaries may appear to be secular in the sense of being opposed to traditional religious authority, yet it may evoke a notion of the people that, from a sociological perspective, resonates with the sacred. For example, the forces opposing the church have long been labeled secular, precisely because they were opposed to the religious. It is only recently that these so-called secular forces have been labeled, properly labeled, I would argue, as forms of the sacred. Lynn Hunt, in "The Rhetoric of Revolution in France," has noted that the idea of the "Nation was perhaps the most universally sacred, but there were also *patrie* [fatherland], Constitution, Law, and more specific to the radicals, regeneration, virtue, and vigilance. Uttered in a certain tone, or included in a soon familiar context, such words bespoke nothing less than adherence to the revolutionary community" (Hunt 1983). In the midst of rebellions or revolutions, these emerging forms of the sacred may have been identified as secular because of their opposition to traditionally religious forms of authority, such as the monarchy and the church: the sanctity of the nation or the people, of the *patrie* or the constitution, having long been obscured by the conflict between religion and secular authorities in the West.

THE SACRED AS THE DIFFERENCE ENDING ALL OTHER DIFFERENCE

The task of identifying the sacred in revolutionary situations is difficult in part because the usual differences and oppositions are moot or irrelevant. The alliance of Copts and Muslims in Egypt, evident in the sewing of crosses next to crescents on the Egyptian flag, is a case in point. Indeed, the nation of Egypt, or the Egyptian people, may be an emergent form of the sacred that will eventually transcend or even trump sectarian differences within and between religious traditions in Egypt.

When the sacred takes on forms that are antitraditional, it may violate precedent and suspend or finish the past while inaugurating the future. These forms or expressions are not formally ritualized and may the more easily be confused with commonplace notions of secularity. That is because antitraditional forms of the sacred ignore or transcend the flow of time, disregard the sequence of befores and afters, and seem to be novel and ephemeral. Revolutionary forms of the sacred emerge in moments and events that constitute in themselves both an end and a beginning. The sacred thus marginalizes and transcends other perspectives regarding historical continuity, development, purpose, and completion.

Revolutionary forms or expressions of the sacred do not seek to justify themselves by appealing to precedents. They take their uniqueness straight without claiming to be heirs of past generations or societies and thus entitled to claim a certain priority for themselves; neither do they stand on ceremony and keep others waiting on the basis of the society's notions of priority. They increase the capacity and demand for immediacy on the part of individuals and groups disadvantaged and frustrated by social institutions like the state or the church. In so doing they suspend and overcome the social order's prescriptions for the relative priority and advantage of some over others. The realm of possibility itself opens up into the present, and what is no longer or not yet acquires a certain immediacy.

Because acts done in the name of revolutionary forms of the sacred suspend prior notions of the difference between cause and effect, or between means and ends, they are ends in themselves. The Moscow protest of Pussy Riot was both cause and effect, both a means and an end in itself, beyond any commonsense or authorized notion of what came before and what is to come after. If a moment is revolutionary, it is because it completes and yet supersedes the past, while initiating the future into the present. A moment that is both sacred and revolutionary constitutes both a new temporal and a new social order.

When societies begin to lose their ability to pretend that they can both embody the passage of time and transcend it, individuals and groups are more likely to begin to swim by themselves in the river of time, or to change the metaphor, individuals and groups come to their own terms with time. Free from a society's sense of priorities, they begin to assign their own. Once freed from the notion that sequences produce succession, they can challenge the authority of what came before to shape what comes after: the first becomes the last, and the last first. Individuals and groups that suspend the conventional or normative succession of befores and afters approved for reaching certain ends may find the sacred in feeding the hungry or healing the sick rather than in obligatory religious observance. Thus the basis for a universal compassion is laid as individuals find themselves immersed in the flow of time that bears all of them away. Their very secularity is the ground for the sanctity of their own and all others' being. No one will experience the world or know oneself as one does oneself, as each person bears the burden of time.

Such knowledge can be the basis for an extraordinary, even universal compassion. In India during the early 1960s, when Hindus and Muslims were killing one another in communal conflicts, encounters on the streets of an Indian city could prove fatal. In one city, Jabalpur, I was told, some Hindus and Muslims had resolved these encounters peacefully by saying to each other, "I, too, have children." I, too, am a *before* who will be replaced by an *after*. I, too, long to be succeeded by children who will in the end replace me. I, too, am headed for death and want to live. In one's own secularity and that of others, one finds common ground for the sacred.

THE SACRED MOMENT AND THE RADICAL BREAK WITH TIME

Consider again the account of the meeting between a *New York Times* journalist of Alawite extraction with Syrian rebels, a moment in which both presence and absence signified and might cause either life or death for each person. Such a moment, beyond even these crucial and existential differences, sanctifies that which is unique and unprecedented in oneself and in others without making any person into a case of some more general type or a means to some end. As Henri Bergson noted of artists and musicians, such an indirect experience of what we cannot understand is "so rich, so personal, so novel" (1910, 18).

Directly, and without mediation of any kind, moments may occur that break through all preconceived notions and precedents, all the vestiges of the past in the present. Moments of compassionate recognition of the self in the other are unique within themselves and unprecedented, and they defy the legacy of restraints on love and compassion derived from the social orders of the past. They also initiate the possibilities for loving recognition that have hitherto been relegated to the future, in which alone it would be possible for souls to enter into a harmony of mutual recognition transcending all authorized social differences and connections.

For example, in the midst of the Holocaust of Jews under Nazi Germany, a stranger might have knocked on another stranger's door and said, "Here are my children. I beg you to take them, and with them this jewelry: all I have." In many cases, the response may have been an immediate, unreflective, uncalculating, wholehearted, and unreserved affirmation: "Yes, of course." Call it pity or compassion; it involved the whole of one person in response to the presence of another person's entire being. "True pity," writes Bergson, "consists not so much in fearing suffering as desiring it . . . in a transition from repugnance to fear, from fear to sympathy, and from sympathy itself to humility"

(1910, 19). They experience and treat their presence with and absence from one another as a matter of quite literally life and death, and they do so authentically and immediately, without the protection of invisibility and social distance and with neither a guarantee of permanence nor authorization.

Moments like this are both sacred and revolutionary. They constitute a *novum ordo seculorum*: a transition to a full awareness of the uniqueness of each person and of the moment, and of our common humanity, which consists of these irreducible differences. Rather than obey some social logic about the proper sequences to be expected or precedents to be followed, the people thus engaged with one another create an unprecedented sequence of before and after by their own initiative and their own response to one another. Instead of obeying some externally imposed logic about the precedents to be considered or the effects of their actions, they in fact determine the sequences from that moment on. Granted that they may not know what is to follow: the consequences may be murky, to say the least, as well as fateful. Nonetheless, in acting to set in train a series of consequences over which they have no foreknowledge or control, they introduce an entirely different temporal and hence social order.

Such moments are sacred, in Max Weber's sense of charisma. The hallmark of charisma, according to Weber, is its compelling disdain for precedents and normal procedures: a complete indifference to the careful calculation of the relations of means to ends and of causes to effects. The charismatic figure simply acts, and in so doing creates the past and the future. Jesus was also remembered as having urged his followers not to worry about their future, but to emulate the lilies of the field. In suggesting "Sufficient unto the day is the evil thereof," Jesus was saying that the stakes in any moment may be as high as the human can bear, that at any moment, but at no certain moment, individuals are confronted with choices between life and death that are as fateful for others as they are for themselves.

For the charismatic to live within the moment is to understand that there is no precedent, no proper sequence, no authorized priority, and no relevant calculation of causes and effects, of ends and means that prescribe or authorize action. The individual willfully thinks or acts or feels in a way that is indeed not only unauthorized but also unprecedented. Jesus was remembered as having said, "Moses said unto you . . . but now I say unto to you." So much for tradition. In so doing that person introduces a split into the stream of time: a divide between the past and the future.

Institutions that try to preserve precedent and to determine the sequence of means and ends, causes and effects, seek to sacralize moments without permitting them to become revolutionary. It is a dangerous thing when two or more people come together in this way. Their future begins from that moment on. To borrow language from the order of service for the solemnization of holy matrimony, when two individuals bind themselves together in marriage, they create a social unit that, they vow, supersedes and takes priority over all others. They, too, create a new thing under the sun; their existence as a couple united in sacred bonds was not there until they made themselves into such a unit. However, the institution of the church, by creating a liturgy, seeks to find precedent for the unprecedented. Although this couple has never before existed as a unit that takes priority over all others, its story can only be told by invoking far more ancient precedent. Those who are getting married under the auspices of the church may be officiating at their own service, but they are doing so in a way that invokes a divine order that establishes such precedents as the presence of Jesus at a wedding in Cana, or even the precedent of the creation itself, in which God created humans of both genders for one another.

Thus the church reminds them that they are following a past that has been long established before them, and that they are walking in an ancestral direction. They are walking forward into the past. Given the risks and uncertainties of marriage and the possibilities for sickness and death as well as for life, the new couple has far more in common with the Jewish mother who, acting without the comforts of precedent and foreknowledge, placed her children in the hands of a stranger for life.

Institutions thus tap the magical thinking that enables an individual to imagine that what came before in fact causes and authorizes what comes after. Thus a word or gesture is imagined to have caused what came after: a rainstorm, perhaps, or a death. The institutionalization of magical thinking thus induces individuals to feel as if their actions were foreordained by and modeled after actions taken hundreds or thousands of years earlier by those with the authority to undertake them. Institutionalized magical thinking thus deprives the individual of a sense of being underived and capable of engaging in unfettered action. People may even feel responsible for sins they have not committed, as if an angry thought were tantamount to a deed, the after to the preceding thought or wish being transformed into an outcome. Thus a subsequent death may be considered in retrospect to have been the meaning or outcome of a preceding presence of absence.

It takes a great deal of thought for individuals to assess for themselves whether there is any connection between the present and the past other than the merely sequential and therefore temporal. It also takes an act of the will to decide whether old passions and longings, old hurts and dreams, are worth keeping alive, to decide whether to allow them to impinge directly on the present or to relegate them to a "before" that has at last been finally superseded by the "after."

Certainly the mind's ability to magically connect what came before with what comes after gives a society the opportunity to play charades with time. If individuals were less prone to believing that there are causal connections to be found in sequences, a society's explanations of causality would have less resonance with those of the individual. If the mind were not already likely to find meaningful connections between befores and afters, there would be nothing for social orders to mimic: no mental images of sequence to turn into successions, recipes for linking means to ends, or ideas about causal relationships. Many are still living under the spell of sequences that through the eyes of religious conviction have become preludes to sequels, precedents of outcomes: the biting of a fateful mythic apple, for example. Millions consider Israel's conquest of the West Bank the fulfillment of an ancient, apocalyptic prophecy. Certainly the pretensions of some Americans to regard the United States as a new Israel are as old as the nation itself and have acquired new force from the convictions of the Christian Right. There are some conservative Christians who believe that America as the new Israel will rightfully succeed the old one when Armageddon comes to the Near East.

As I noted in the beginning of this chapter, in a revolutionary situation the sacred, as it emerges on the periphery of a social order, among the marginal and the distressed, may come into direct conflict with the sacred as institutionalized in the cultural and political center of a society. As we have seen, during the French Revolution there were indeed words, standing for the nation and the people, or for law and the constitution, that evoked the sacred in opposition to the church and the monarchy. It was so also in the American Revolution, as leaders like George Washington tried to convert an unprofessional and autonomous militia into the more disciplined ranks of a professional army: the sacred located in home and the farm thus was pitted against the more military, collective forms of sacred.

During the American Revolution, for example, some men were free to come and go at their own will and discretion, returning at times to their homes and farms regardless of what was happening in the war. Their commitments to revolutionary principles made them unreliable on the battlefield; they were devoted to their homes and their families, their farms and their fields. They may have been more like the more undisciplined militias in the Free Syrian army than the ranks of the Syrian regime's military. Other Americans were under the discipline of an army that was becoming almost as professional as the British. It took the potent rhetoric of a leader like George Washington to transform the blessings of liberty into the obligations of military service. We learn from the historian Robert Middlekauff that

> George Washington, their commander-in-chief, never tired of reminding them that their cause arrayed free men against mercenaries. They were fighting for the "blessings of liberty," he told them in 1776, and should they not acquit themselves like men, slavery would replace their freedom. . . . The challenge to behave like men was not an empty one.

> Courage, honor, gallantry in the service of liberty, all those words calculated to bring a blush of embarrassment to jaded twentieth-century men, defined manhood for the eighteenth century. In battle those words gained an extraordinary resonance as they were embodied in the actions of brave men. . . . By standing firm they served their fellows and honor; by running, they served only themselves. Thus battle tested the inner qualities of men, tried their souls, as Thomas Paine said. Many men died in the test that battle made of their spirits. (1980)

If such words of moral and patriotic exhortation now induce a "blush of embarrassment," it is because the grounding of the sacred was being changed, as in ancient Greece, from the domestic hearth to the hearth in the chief's household and at the center of the polis. The existential was becoming bound to the corporate: personal choice to widely shared and deeply held collective sentiments. As Middlekauff put it: "For those American soldiers who were servants, apprentices, poor men substituting for men with money to hire them, the choice might not have seemed to involve moral decision. After all they had never enjoyed much personal liberty. But not even in that contrivance of eighteenth-century authoritarianism in which they now found themselves, the professional army, could they avoid a moral decision. Compressed into dense formations, they were reminded by their nearness to their comrades that they too had an opportunity to uphold virtue" (1980, 147–48).

In contemporary American society, the sacred is not securely grounded in the institutions that define and reinforce public virtues or in days of collective remembrance that attribute the present to old sacrifices. Memorial Day itself has drifted slowly into more widespread nonobservance. Secularity pulls the collective ground from under the feet of personal sacrifice. Secularization has allowed collective amnesia, rather than memory, to efface or erase the presence of the departed and to erode the meaningful sequences of befores into afters.

If the sacred has a hallmark, it is, I have been arguing, the ability to create and legitimate sacrifice by eroding the difference between life and death. It takes a death to cause new life; ancestors must indwell the newborn, and the death of a lamb may preserve the nation from destruction. Conversely, new life requires a death to the past and original sin or a spiritual death, especially for young men, to the securities of the home. A nation begins to take on the aura of the sacred if, and only if, individuals who are born transform their birthright into the obligation to die for their country. The individual's entire life's trajectory, from life to death, is framed and shaped by the place in which he or she lives. As Andrew Del Banco has argued, under the influence of ideologues like Thomas Jefferson, the new United States became a "New Jerusalem," a new homeland and a new destiny, a universal mother for whom one would both live and gladly die (1999, 62). Jefferson himself spoke of the "native American" as a superior individual endowed with the virtues necessary for a republic, and others imagined their nation as having a common ancestry purified of the corruptions of a European class system (Del Banco 1999, 62–63). No wonder, then, that many began to imagine their nation in racial terms. As a sacred nation defined as a superior race, America became like Melville's vessel in *Moby Dick*, the *Pequod*: "a world conquering ship" that was becoming "a killing machine" (Del Banco 1999, 68).

I am making a very simple argument: The sacred emerges when individuals confuse the sources of life with death itself. That confusion is apparent in every form of sacrifice in which the one who makes the sacrifice is willing to surrender his or her life to gain eternal life. That is why the sacred emerges in the revolutionary moment, when the individual is willing to die for the people or for the nation that alone gives life meaning. Only when a nation becomes a motherland, a source of life itself, can it legitimately call for human sacrifice.

Under these conditions the sacrifices of the periphery become sacralized at the center. The nation that precedes the individual gives life to the individuals who are later born on national soil; their lives are spoken, even called, for from the outset. The existential becomes defined by the collective, and the collective acquires the existential meaning and sanctity as a source and double for the psyche. Violence becomes directed outward and away from the self and the nation toward others who are defined as unworthy: as pagans, for example, or as belonging to an unworthy race. The domestic hearth is subsumed under the collective hearth, the local graveyard is linked symbolically with the national cemetery, and the standing stone becomes a national memorial to those who have died defending the nation. The standing stone is assimilated to the effigy of the king as a double for the psyche. To be born an American is to share in the common hope that all other accidents of birth have no inevitable, material consequences. The American birthright endows the individual not only with political freedoms, but with freedom from the oppressive consequences of being governed.

When a people becomes sacred, its members encompass collectively both life and death. Their nation can call upon them to offer their lives for its sake, and death for such a nation is an entrance into a life eternal. The nation, as a double for the psyche, embodies the idea "that life is worth living only when it furnishes the mind with something worth dying for" (Del Banco 1999, 75). A new nation that sees itself as transcending the passage of time is in a position to call for sacrifice, but it needs heroes who are emblematic of this devotion to the sacred. As the periphery yields to the center, and the psyche identifies with a collectivity that engages in inhumane sacrifice, the revolutionary forms of the sacred begin to recede into the past; they become a before without a meaningful or causal afterward.

Only new forms of revolution, new revolutionary moments centered in the periphery, can retrieve the revolutionary ideal. Del Banco points out that some northerners found in John Brown and his men precisely such heroes. For Thoreau, he notes, "'These men, in teaching us how to die, have at the same time taught us how to live'" (Del Banco 1999, 74–75). As Del Banco points out, the nation had embraced a racial dream of itself as a people tied by ancestral links to the origins of virtue. In its midst, then, any distinctions based on a lesser notion of race could only violate Lincoln's exalted notion of the Union as a sacred communion. The Civil War was precisely such an attempt to externalize violence once and for all against evil as the enemy of the sacred nation.

Thus Del Banco tells us that "for Lincoln the Union was both symbol and incarnation of transcendence" (1999, 78). Lincoln himself went to great lengths to argue that the enemy was neither the South nor the North; rather, it was an evil that lay within the hearts of people that had to be expunged for the sake of the sacred nation itself.

The slave stood for the very opposite of the new American citizen, who imagined himself as having found on these shores a new motherland. The slave had no future other than death and would be forced always to live in a present that perpetuated the past. If America were to recover the revolutionary moment, it would have to become "the political incarnation of the idea of universal rights—of a new age when people 'who cannot trace their connection . . . by blood' to the birth of the nation nevertheless are as fully American as if 'they were blood of the blood, flesh of the flesh of the founders'"; thus Del Banco (1999, 79) sums up the idea of the new sacred nation in the words of Lincoln himself. If the nation could not offer the symbols of the sacred, it would not be worth either living or dying for, until there could be a more perfect union.

If there is a potential for the sacred to be the rallying point for a new revolutionary movement in the United States, it may be among those who, like their counterparts in Moscow and Damascus, Cairo and Tripoli, have risked their lives in order, as the members of Pussy Riot put it, to stop the lies. However, I expect the first wave of revolt to come from among the people in the United States with the lowest levels of what pollsters call social trust: "a belief in the honesty, integrity and reliability of others—a 'faith in people'" (Pew Research Center 2010).

According to polls taken by the Pew Research Center (2010), those with the lowest levels of social trust are to be found in the large cities, and they are young, poor, and poorly educated ("18% among those who describe themselves as the struggling class. . . . Some 50% of college graduates have high levels of social trust, compared with 28% of those with a high school education or less.") and disproportionately black and Hispanic, although the youngest and poorest whites also score very low on these measures of trust. The Pew Center notes that the lack of trust among younger Americans is alternatively ascribed to their youth or to when they came of age: "a life cycle effect—as people pile up more experiences and have more interactions with others, they become more trusting. Or it could be a generational effect—today's older adults may have come of age at a time when social mores and historical events provided a more fertile seed bed for social trust."

It was the nonvoters who, in Germany in 1933, voted in the Nazi Party, so it may well be that roughly 50 percent of the American electorate who, although eligible to vote, have hitherto stayed away from the polls. If they become newly enfranchised and mobilized, it will have been by the discovery that for the larger society they have become surplus people: truly expendable because they do not vote. The first wave of the rebellion may well come, then, after another young black person has been executed by a vigilante or killed by the police; or when a nonviolent, protesting veteran is savaged by the riot police; or when a despairing young man, like the street vendor in Tripoli, immolates himself because he finally understands how little his existence matters to those who control the larger society and have exclusive rights to its comforts and privileges. Their absence will be felt like a presence, and in their death they will acquire a vitality and a presence far more potent than they enjoyed while they were alive. Their deaths will become moments in which the normal succession of befores and afters is indefinitely arrested, and the long outstanding bills of the past and the long-awaited promise of the future will define the present. They will be the emergent form of the sacred. In saying this I can only hope that I am wrong. If what is left of the middle class joins them, it will be because of the lies that politicians have been telling them about their bills and policies; or that investment banks use to misrepresent the value of their securities; or that they have believed about their prospects for getting an education and a job, health coverage, and, eventually, a pension.

REFERENCES

Bergson, Henri. (1910). *Time and Free Will. An Essay on the Immediate Data of Consciousness.* London: Riverside Press.

Chulov, Martin. "Anger, Tears, and Forgiveness as Syrian Rebel and his Prisoner Share their Fears." *The Observer.* http://www.theguardian.com/world/2012/aug/11/syria-rebel-regine-sunni-alawite

Del Banco, Andrew. (1999). *The Real American Dream. A Meditation on Hope.* Cambridge, MA; London: Harvard University Press.

Herzenhorn, David M. (2012). "Anti-Putin Stunt Earns Punk Band Two Years in Jail." *New York Times*, August 17. http://www.nytimes.com/2012/08/18/world/europe/suspense-ahead-of-verdict-for-jailed-russian-punk-band.html?src=ISMR_AP_LO_MST_FB#h[TcbTcb].

Hunt, Lynn. (1983). "The Rhetoric of Revolution in France." *History Workshop* 15 (Spring): 78–94.

"Islamic Militants Destroy Malian Cultural Heritage, Purporting a 'Pure Islam.'" (2012). *PBS NewsHour*, August 23. http://www.pbs.org/newshour/bb/world/july-dec12/mali_08-23.html (accessed April 2, 2013).

Mackey, Robert, and Glenn Kates. (2012). "Russian Riot Grrrls Jailed for 'Punk Prayer.'" *New York Times*, March 7. http://thelede.blogs.nytimes.com/2012/03/07/russian-riot-grrrls-jailed-for-punk-prayer/.

Middlekauff, Robert. (1980). "Why Men Fought in the American Revolution." *Huntington Library Quarterly* 43 (2) (Spring): 135–148.

Pew Research Center. (2010). "Americans and Social Trust: Who, Where and Why," 2010 http://www.pewsocialtrends.org/files/2010/10/SocialTrust.pdf

"Pussy Riot Closing Statements." (2012). *N+1 Magazine*, August 13. http://nplusonemag.com/pussy-riot-closing-statements.

Rasmussen, Susan. (2007). "Re-Formations of the Sacred, the Secular, and Modernity: Nuances of Religious Experience among the Tuareg (Kel Tamajaq)." *Ethnology* 46 (3) (Summer): 185–203.

Yazbek, Samar. (2012). "In the Shadow of Assad's Bombs." *New York Times*, August 9, Op-Ed, A19.

Zagvozdina, Darya. (2012). "'Art and Politics Are Inseparable for Us': Interview with Pussy Riot, 27.02.12 19:57." *Gazeta.ru*, August 18. Edited by Karina Ayvazova .http://en.gazeta.ru/news/2012/02/27/a_4014157.shtml.

Chapter 12

Freud on Religion: Force of Oppression and Source of Resilience

Cassandra M. Klyman

Sigmund Freud was a revolutionary in the realm of investigating and understanding the individual's mental life, but he also was interested in how the intrapsychic life creates and interfaces with the group and indeed civilization as a whole. He was particularly interested in the establishment of religion and government as manifestations of the universality of much of early human experience. Both for the human race and the family, early certain structure remains necessary to foster the life of the human baby. The baby is born dependent on the nurturance and protection of its parents to survive, as the parents are also dependent upon the group.

To the infant and child the adult seems omnipotent and omniscient, quite godlike or monarch-like in his or her attributes, requiring compliance to avoid risking confrontation, with possible grave consequences. As the Dali Lama once said, "Without our mother's milk of human kindness we would have been dashed to the ground the first time we bit her breast." According to Freud, we survive because our fear of the more powerful one is greater than our conscious or unconscious desire to gobble up or devour both the giving and depriving parent and later to sexually connect with them. For the female those incestuous wishes toward the father are accompanied by the recognition of disparity of body size and the dread of what his large phallus could do to her small body. She is also afraid to lose the regard or incur the rage of an avenging mother. For the boy, shame about his inadequate little genitalia makes him worry about them getting lost or being bitten off or of being ridiculed by his mother, let alone the fear of his father's retaliation by castration. Freud called this the Oedipus complex, deriving the name from Sophocles's tragedy "Oedipus Rex." This first part of the Greek trilogy gives additional weight to the universality of this truth in Western civilization. With so much conflict that carries over to child and adult patients, these dilemmas are both internalized and externalized and are projected into fantasized realms, to the world of dreams, drama, religion, and politics.

Freud's documented interest in social anthropology goes back to an 1897 letter to Fliess (Draft N, May 31, 1897) discussing the "horror of incest," in which he generalizes that there is a strong and inevitable relationship between the growth of civilization and the suppression of instincts. And later that same year (December 12, 1897, letter 17) he wrote that immortality, retribution, and life after death are all reflections of our inner psyche projected outward and characteristically into the future and the world beyond.

In *The Interpretation of Dreams* there is a footnote (1905, sec. B, ch. V, S.E. 4, 217n) in which he discusses the derivation of the notion of monarchy from the social position of the father of the family. In *Totem and Taboo* (subtitled "Some Points of Agreement between the Mental Life of Savages and Neurotics"), Freud elaborates on his Oedipal hypothesis of the primal horde and the killing of the primal father as being the starting point for later social and cultural institutions. Though it was written in 1912, he regarded the last chapter as his favorite. He discussed it carefully in his *Autobiographical Study* in 1925 and quoted it in his final publication, *Moses and Monotheism* (1939). Taboos, he states in his preface, still exist among us as "moral imperatives," hardly conscious to us. Totems, on the other hand, have undergone many transformations, and only symbolic derivatives and hints remain. The two basic laws of totemism are not to kill the totem animal and to avoid sexual intercourse with opposite-sex members of the totem clan.

Over the centuries the totem animal has become the ruler of human societies. He is envied because of his privileges and yet protected against attempts to usurp his power by the fear that this could lead to dissolution of that society, and then the temptation would exist for an alien group to maraud and exploit the society's weakness for the promise of rapacious enjoyment of the spoils. This envy and protection are not inviolable, however, as the world history's proves.

What has allowed men and women to break the taboo against hurting the totem? Perhaps it is that "moral imperative" for freedom and justice that has instigated revolution in our time in Africa and the Middle East. Certainly it takes one person, impulsively or with premeditation, to violate the taboo, to risk becoming taboo himself, because he then possesses the dangerous attribute of tempting others to follow his example and himself becoming a leader. In turn, he arouses ambivalence among those who witness his daring. Disobeying a prohibition can be isolating, or on the other hand contagious, if the desires are intensely similar and shared. Disobedience thus can borrow enormous strength, because prohibited desire in the unconscious can shift from one thing to another, so the more renunciation one has had to experience, the more one is ready to explode and commingle.

Taboos are the ordinary measures of legislation, serving social purposes of protecting the chiefs' and priests' privileges and property. Freud examined the second part of James G. Frazer's *The Golden Bough* to study the taboos attached to enemies, chiefs, and the dead. They do have rules, demanding the appeasement of the enemy's souls or ghosts, placing restrictions on the slayer and requiring acts of expiation and purification by him via ceremonial observances.

Freud opined that this suggests that even before the Ten Commandments, savages had a living commandment of "thou shalt not kill." In the New Guinea Islands and among the Native North Americans, the victorious slayer had to be isolated, kept from the flesh of his wife and the meat of animals to guard against the smell of the blood of the slain so the hunter would not fall ill and die. More contemporary hooded executioners, like the public hangman in medieval society, are treated with similar anonymity. The unity of this derives from the emotional ambivalence toward the enemy—he is feared and envied, and we are in awe of his previous power.

Thus there is a taboo about rulers or their symbolic representations, who not only are guarded but must be guarded against, lest their magical powers, if touched, bring on terrible consequences. Such was the horror of a shoe being thrown at President George W. Bush when he visited Iraq or even the outcry about the artistic display of urine being poured on our flag. Contrariwise when the king's or queen's hand reaches out to actively touch someone, it can be experienced as a healing or blessing. It is not only written that Christ cured lepers, but during the reign of Charles II, the monarch was reputed to have touched close to 100,000 persons in search of a cure for their scrofula (tuberculosis or the king's evil).

The court/church/temple/mosque ceremonials primarily protect the ruler/pope/ayatollah from threat of danger despite his magical attributes. Why? Because when his magic does not always work for the well-being of his people, they become disenchanted—if he is their god, he should be their preserver. So the captor becomes captive, like the Japanese Mikado, who had to sit on the throne for hours, with his imperial crown on his head, like a statue, to ensure peace and tranquility in the empire; if he did otherwise, he was inviting great misfortune not only on himself, but on his people. Often the more powerful the leader, the more taboos he is bound to observe, particularly in movement and diet. This then evolved into the division of the original priestly kingship into a spiritual and temporal power to dilute the onerous restrictions on one individual or class. This arrangement gives rise to many contradictions "by which, incidentally, a savage intellect is as little disturbed as is a highly civilized one when it comes to such matters as religion and or loyalty" (Freud 1913–1914/1968, S.E. Vol. XIII, 48).

Freud submitted these observations to analysis, as if religiosity was similar to a patient with an obsessive-compulsive neurosis. He notes the excessive anxiety and solicitude that surrounds the taboo ceremonials are the symptomatic result of a compromise formation between affection and hostility. This solicitous overaffection is found in everyday life experiences, in a new mother–child relationship, or in a doting married couple, where there is domination in the guise of service. He quotes Frazer, who cited the savage Timmes of Sierra Leone. They elected their king and reserved to themselves the right of beating him on the eve of his coronation. They availed themselves of this privilege so heartily that sometimes the unhappy new monarch did not survive. Hence when the leading chiefs had a spite against a man, they elected him king, masking all this as a ceremonial (1913–1914/1968, S.E. Vol. XIII, 49). Certainly the suffering on the cross, the crucifixion passion, shows parallels.

Along with the notable ambivalence toward the ruler is the cognitive distortion or delusion of persecution. So if the ruler's absolute power is magnified to make him responsible for everything disagreeable—plagues, natural disasters, genocide—the individual may lose faith or work even harder to propitiate the one idolized. We see this happen with abused children, who cling to the abusive parent when Protective Services comes to the rescue: "It was my fault, I didn't listen.... I'll be better ... give me a chance." Or feeling worthy, we may cry out like Job and learn that it was just the roll of the dice, cursing, "Why me, O Lord?" And we look to see what taboo we have broken inadvertently so that we will not make the same mistake again if given that second chance.

The third powerful taboo (the first being the touching of enemies, the second the touching of rulers) is the touching of the dead. Those who have contact with the dead—victorious slayers, mourners, as well as those who do the burying—are considered taboo or unclean themselves and are subject to a boycott. In very primitive tribes they must grovel like animals or be fed by someone else almost as badly stigmatized. They may not have sexual intercourse for a period of time. By projection of the survivor's ambivalence, the dead then become evil spirits.

Certain taboos, if not all, arise out of the fear of temptation. The fact that the dead are helpless evokes expression of hostile feelings: "How dare you leave me, what have you promised that you can no longer perform," and so forth. It is unseemly to "kick the gravestone," so those temptations to dismember the dead must be kept in check by prohibition and proscription; hence the elaborate burial ceremonies found in every culture—even after cremation.

Other helpless members, like infants, or those we envy, like the beautiful or handsome adolescent, must undergo certain prescribed rituals—circumcision, baptism, confirmation or tortured rites of passage, scarifications, genital mutilation—to both express and inhibit greater community harm from the envious and tempted. Freud suggested: "It might be maintained that a case of hysteria is a caricature of a work of art, that an obsessional neurosis is a caricature of religion and that a paranoid delusion is a caricature of the philosophical system.... [T]hey endeavor to achieve by private means what is effected by society by collective effort" (Freud 1913–1914/1968, S.E. Vol. XIII, 73).

So religion is an oppressive but civilizing force, suppressing our hostile, aggressive impulses and licentiousness. It allows us to devour only a token, a symbolic piece of the totem, of the revered and idealized authority figure, in order to feel less blameworthy and allow us to hope for continued beneficence after Holy Communion or potlatch, rituals that, except under extreme circumstances, are practiced communally. In numbers there is strength and perhaps invincibility.

When the inevitable disillusion occurs with our earthly parents and they are seen as not able to give us all the nurturance and support they or we wish for, where do we turn? God, our "Heavenly Father," we ask, "give us our daily bread ... forgive us from evil, ... deliver us from temptation." The stronger our faith, the more we can endure. It is no surprise that those who regularly pray are physically healthier. They make use of a meditative mechanism that reduces their stress level, increases the alpha waves measured by an EEG, reduces their levels of cortisol to maintain insulin sensitivity, increases immunological defensiveness, slows heart rate, reduces blood pressure, and gives them hope. Hope to dream that the hereafter, if not the present, will be joyful. Besides the individual comfort with one's creator, there is the sense of community with fellow worshippers who share a bond of fellowship. Outreach to the needy, even across continents, brings satisfaction and solidarity.

Researchers (Theilman 1998; Curlin 2007; McFarland 2010) concur that although faith in a higher power has been sustaining society since time immemorial, it may have a special benefit for those with mental illness, especially depression and despair or the travails of the terminal phase of life. However, psychiatrists, as humanists, are not as open to these positive effects. This is probably because fewer psychiatrists than other specialists belong to organized religion, and they have too often seen the down side of hyperreligiosity in their paranoid and manic patients as well as "false" religious-numinous experiences in those with fronto-temporal dementias and epilepsies (Saver and Rabin 1997).

Contemporary religions, unlike totemism, do not emphasize exogamy, in which one is to marry only outside the clan. In fact, they encourage marriage within the group of believers. This may be because Western civilization has evolved other legal prohibitions against consanguinity (though historically these limits were abrogated for the privileged classes). This underscores Freud's point that there is no actual aversion to incest, but that the many regulations regarding it prove its innateness to man and his biological ancestors. He refers us to Charles Darwin's observations about gorilla bands, among whom there is competition to become the alpha male; the loser is expelled and must go off to mate elsewhere. Among primitive humans, Freud hypothesized that "brothers who had been driven out came together, killed and devoured their father and so made an end to the patriarchal horde," taking his life and his mate. United, they did something that would have been impossible to do individually. In the act of devouring him, they accomplished their identification with him and his strength. Freud went on to say, "The totem meal, which is perhaps mankind's earliest festival . . . was the beginning of so many things: social organization, moral restrictions, and religion" (Freud 1913,142–145). But because there had been affection for and admiration of this father, subsequently there was remorse and guilt; so the dead father became stronger than the living one. Hence our current concerns about minimizing martyrdom of our enemies, lest they become more venerated: there was no execution of Saddam Hussein and no pomp and circumstance surrounding bin Laden's burial.

Primitive peoples would choose an animal with which to memorialize the dead father and renounce their incestuous wishes in order to establish renunciation and reconciliation with him. This established a covenant wherein they were promised protection, care, and indulgence for not repeating the patricide. All later religions, Freud states, offer the same consolations. The commandment against patricide is elaborated into a general "thou shalt not kill," which also gives the prayerful a sense of relief and safety.

At the end of "Totem and Taboo" there is the often-quoted paragraph "in the meantime the concept of God had emerged, from some unknown source, and had taken control of the whole of religious life . . . the psychoanalysis of individual human beings, however, teaches us that . . . the god of each of them is formed in the likeness of his human father, that his personal relationship to God depends on his relation to his father in the flesh and oscillates and changes along with that relation, and that at bottom God is nothing other than an exalted father" (Freud 1913, 147).

From the feminist point of view we may ask, what about the great mother-goddesses? They may have preceded the father gods, but Freud, as so often with regard to ideas about women, does not even speculate about it, suggesting that it is more important to look at the father's role because it affected not only religion but all societal organizations that we know (149). To examine how the incestuous desire/prohibition was worked out, Freud suggests that as humans became involved with agriculture, they elevated Mother Earth to a new deity off whom they could live. Yet even then, her bounty would be cut off by symbolic derivatives of a wrathful father who caused drought and storms.

When Christianity first penetrated into the Persian Empire, it offered the idea of an alternate way to alleviate the guilt of the primal sin. Christ would sacrifice his own life for the redemption of others for their murderous impulses, the talionic law. Self-sacrifice speaks to blood guilt. And communion preceded by confession and forgiveness makes us feel whole again. It is that recurrent reminder that we can sin and be forgiven over and over again that makes the human psyche resilient.

In 1926 Freud received a letter from an American doctor, who had read his interview with G. S. Viereck, and subsequently reproached him for not having any religious belief and describing his own amazing conversion from nonchalant religiousness to ardent Christian faith. Responding in "A Religious Experience" (1928,167), Freud interprets the man's initial onset of cynicism about the goodness of God and the merits of continuing to go to church, came about as a result of his own Oedipal conflicts when he saw an "elderly, sweet-faced woman" headed to the morgue. According to Freud, his correspondent unconsciously experienced the woman as if she were his mother. He unconsciously blamed his father for her death, making him furious at his unconscious, fused father/God mental representation.

Ultimately he heard an inner voice warning him against such apostasy and giving him a revelation that made him return to his religion with complete submission. It seems clear that this would have had to be the outcome, for if the ill-treatment was related to childhood fantasies of primal scene material, in which he believed mother was being abused through marital sexual intercourse, it might foreclose his own ability to carry on his heterosexual pursuits in identification with his earthly father (Freud 1928, Vol. XXI, 168–72). Therefore he would have to make a rapid turnaround from being furious to becoming reconciled with God, his symbolic father, for the purpose of his own sexual gratification. Freud is said to have wished he could experience the oceanic bliss that some religious people feel, just as he wished he could appreciate music (but to both he was tone deaf).

What other consolations exist to help us through this earthly travail, besides sexual release? Art, science, and other intoxicating substances that alter our chemistry serve such purposes. For example, being in love is mediated through oxytocin, vasopressin, dopamine, and serotonin. Freud believed it was presumptuous to talk about the purpose of life other than about its biological dictates designed to keep the species going. Most secular people would say the purpose of life is the pursuit of happiness, however that is defined, and more modestly, the avoidance of displeasure. The extreme form of this goal may be the control of influences from the outside, renouncing the world in an asceticism such as is found among the Eastern practitioners of yoga, or simply in a life of quietness.

However, with the diminution of sensation and the repression of the wild perversity of forbidden things, life's intensity fades, and our physical beings do not achieve orgasm. A better way, Freud suggested, is to employ sublimation, the displacement of libido to heighten the yield of pleasure from sources of psychical and intellectual work and legitimate love. The religious Christian is taught to believe and say that the purpose of life is to love, honor, and serve God. The observant Jew knows he or she is to praise the lord by keeping not only his commandments but also his 652 mitzvoth. The Moslem knows he or she is to follow the five Pillars: Shahada (there is one god), Salat (prayers five times/day), Saum (fasting during Ramadan), Zakat (purifying tax), and Hajj (the pilgrimage to Mecca). The most radical of the Shi'ites believe and hope for an apocalypse so that the lost imam will return and bring paradise to earth. The Mormons have a ferocious work ethic, being "anxiously engaged in a good cause," so as to achieve self-improvement and divine approval, marked by the outward characteristics of prosperity without ostentation.

In *Civilization and Its Discontents* (1930, 21), Freud admits that religious ideas have arisen from the same needs as have all other achievements of civilization: to defend oneself against the crushingly superior forces of nature and to rectify the shortcomings of civilization. A person enters into this heritage of many generations and assumes it like the multiplication tables and geometry. It may be called divine revelation, but the father of psychoanalysis would argue that religion is an evolving legacy over the eons of human history in which man personified the forces of nature and therefore applied the same successful tactics used to manipulate, appease, and endear him to his parents. This is a lesson learned from earliest childhood, when we smile and cry to influence our environment.

Religious ideas are teachings and assertions about the reality that is most important and interesting to humans. Unfortunately the evidence or proof is based on trust alone, namely, that these ideas are real because our ancestors believed in them and wrote about them. We are forbidden to question these important assumptions, so we develop practical fictions that protect us from being confronted by our insignificance in the world (Freud 1927, Vol. XXI, 3–56). Illusions are created from human wishes. They are not identical to errors, which are subject to scientific inquiry. The truths contained in religious doctrine may be good but not God given. Unfortunately, when doubt enters we may be sadder and more distrustful, like the child who is told the stork brings babies. When she recognizes the deceit, she may become difficult because her parents have let her down. "Better to avoid such symbolic disguising of the truth in what we tell children . . . and not to withhold from them a knowledge of the true state of affairs commensurate with their intellectual level," Freud asserted (1927, Vol. XXI, 45). He strongly believed that the gods of logic and reason will then prevail.

The case of one of my patients exemplifies how religion can be an unusually significant therapeutic ally in recovery:

In the early 1980s an exasperated colleague referred his long-standing patient to me along with a case file about a foot-high. Mr. K had been hospitalized many times, treated with many different and repeated courses of medication and was now deemed treatment-refractory. Perhaps, thought my older mentor, my youth and enthusiasm would make me willing to take on the challenge. The patient presented as a man in his late thirties who looked aged and harried. He was short, muscular and slightly balding. Dressed as a hippie he looked unkempt and disheveled. Most notable was the wild stare in his eyes that indicated terror and perplexity. He could not meet my gaze nor did I really welcome it. His anxiety was manifest in his trembling soft handshake. He was candid about his history and resigned as he passed over the sealed box of records. His chief complaint now and for some time was that "God is pinching me, hard." He believed the pinching punishment was not so much for what he did but for his thoughts about people he knew, their close loved ones, and even people he met casually. It took him a long time to tell me what those thought were: "You'd be too horrified . . . I see them being skinned and their skin turned into lampshades!" "But as you gradually tell me, little by little, you will begin to trust me and then we can work together," I'd say, like coaxing a bad dream out of a crying boy.

He reported that Dr. S had once kicked his leg and I promised I would never hurt or even touch him, that we would talk, listen, and talk some more. Meanwhile I was wading through the reading of his records. They offered no enlightenment, just a swamp of failed procedures at the most renowned psychiatric centers, from the Institute for Living to the Clinton Valley Hospital in Pontiac, Michigan, a state institution where he was ware-housed for months and then released because he was no longer actively hallucinating.

Mr. K was seeing me twice a week and was no longer trembling. He would lie on the couch but knew he could freely turn around to look at me at any time. He kept checking and I was always there—with a quizzical frown, maybe a smile, sometimes a contemplative look but always engaged. I was establishing a positive therapeutic alliance that kept deepening and was sustaining for the hard work ahead. That hard work was sharing the historical narrative he related to me. Much of this was of his painful personal life history and the rest was of personalized Holocaust imagery where he was identified as the Nazi and others, his friends, their loved ones, and even total strangers were his victims. Because he did have vigorous athletic outlets for his aggression I was not often scared but mostly on the verge of tears for how he suffered as a child and suffered still. My murmurs and soft, "oh, ohs" or "I can stand it, continue," allowed the unfolding to go on.

His personal family history was that he had been born into a middle-class family whose trucks bore the family name around the Detroit area. His father had not chosen to be in the business and started his own manufacturing shop. My patient was the youngest of 5 siblings. Three brothers and a sister preceded him. After each pregnancy his mother became more mentally ill with severe anxiety, panic, and agoraphobia that was managed only by going to her daily psychoanalytic sessions. The rest of the time she remained in her room. At dinner each night the same scene repeated. My patient would shout "Momma, Momma" and run to bury his head in her. He felt her body tense and the other kids would yell mockingly, "Crybaby, crybaby." Dad would order him back to his seat. His mother would eat silently and glide back upstairs and the older brothers would give him a sharp poke or pinch as they left the table. Often my patient would not have been able to eat so the African-American maid would bring the left-overs to him and he recalls sitting on the heat register, picking at them, and rocking back and forth.

Before high school the father bought a home in the suburbs with a large side lot that he flooded so he and the boys could play ice-hockey. K developed speed, skill and cunning and established a respectful niche for himself. It would have been the time when other Jewish boys would have been having their Bar Mitzvahs but in this suburb there was not even a synagogue. Hockey teams drew few minorities and so K, after frequent nosebleeds, got a rhinoplasty that made him look as Waspish as his team-mates. Then there were Boy Scout Camps and he developed a love for the out-of-doors. There was an adolescent attempt to have a girl-friend and be sexual; but as his bad-luck would have it, when he was "making out" by a camp-fire his sneaker got on fire and the fiery experience became too literally hellish and haunting. After years of solitary sexual pleasuring with or without pornography, he tried to master that original experience by repeating it with girls much younger than himself under secretive conditions. This made him feel "like a dirty old man" and he despaired that he would always be alone.

He barely recognized his interest in Art but in the music of the Viet-Nam era he could resonate with the lyrics of protest and the poignancy of Joanie Mitchell. As soon as he graduated high school he joined the National Guard. In going through basic training he became addicted to "pot" and experimented with other drugs that made him blatantly psychotic. He was given an honorable medical discharge after a home furlough when he stood naked, masturbating, in front of his mother. By then Mom was herself mentally better and knew he needed good and intensive help. He pleaded for time up at their cabin in Northern Michigan instead, but was found there a couple of weeks later in a catatonic state. That's when the medical reports began piling up. Now I was seeing him a dozen years later.

He had created a friendship circle of jocks, who used him as the butt of their practical jokes. He had no awareness that he was creating new "brothers" to mock him and call him crazy. The original brothers were now quite distant and disowning, practicing law or running franchises, while he lived at home and worked part-time doing menial work for his father. This was mainly so he could maintain his health insurance.

Encouraged by me to have an annual physical exam, it was discovered he had a malignancy. I hoped his thyroid tumor might have contributed to his mental illness and its removal would be helpful but it was more the post-operative circumstances that were ameliorative.

First, the cancer itself was "framed" by the surgeon, as one of the best for a person to have with a likelihood of cure, and that seemed to be a blessing rather than a curse. Secondly, his parents were mildly attentive, at least his father visited and was dozing by his bedside when I came by to see him. Thirdly, his dinner had been brought early and I offered to feed him his soup and jello. I talked to him about how this different time in the hospital might be the beginning of a new start in his self-love, self-care, of kindness turning both inwards and outwards. Each spoonful was a corroborative modeling.

A past buddy of his who had "not been able to get his life together" had emigrated to Jerusalem the year before and was working in a kibbutz and invited him to come. K went and came back with a sense of Jewish identity he did not have before. He sought out an Orthodox Rabbi who had a warm and welcoming reputation. Rabbi S. invited K into his home for Shabbat dinner, accepted the fact that he stumbled even over the simplest prayers over the bread and wine; accepted that he barely talked to the adults but did play with the kids, and took them to sports events in gratitude. K began "lunch and learn" Torah study. No one laughed when he gave his own needlepoint creation to the Rabbi's wife. In sessions I had told him celebrity jocks like Rosie Grier did that for relaxation and some basketball players took ballet lessons. His "feminine" side stopped being a torment: no big brothers called him "sissy" to make him cry.

So we worked back and forth, present and past and present again.

Naturally the Orthodox community wanted him to marry. By this time he was working side-by-side with his father, had moved into his own home within walking distance of the "shul," was keeping the Sabbath except for smoking (after services), and had substituted racquetball for hockey as he needed more time for work, prayer, and "shul" attendance. He was "matched" with a young podiatrist and spent the next summer hiking, golfing and canoeing together. He surprised all three of us by offering her a large engagement ring she accepted. He brought her into the next session and wanted me to explain his problems to her, lest she should want to change her mind. I explained the symptoms of his past chronic severe and current sub-acute psychosis; re- assured her that small amounts of antipsychotic medication and ten years of therapy had brought it under control. She said she recognized his moodiness and episodic withdrawal but that she was resourceful and did not mind because they could have so much fun together at other times. I asked her what came to mind, in a scene, of their life together in 5 years. Her answer dismayed me: "I see us in a canoe. I'm standing up, laughing and splashing him with water." K had a rather conventional scene he described and neither were ready to consider the inherent control issues and ultimate capsizing of their marital vessel!

Within two years, S filed for divorce and a "get." She complained to her friends that their sex life was terrible and that K was a pervert who preferred masturbation to her. The following year she was married to an ex-boyfriend. K was broken-hearted, remorseful that he had been unable to talk to me about his sexual arousal conflicts. S was too big (similar to my average size), and he was attracted to women with small ballerina shapes (similar to his petite mother or the girl he had loved in high school, when he burned his foot). Maybe, he opined, he was just stuck with pornography that was now so freely available on the Internet.

A single man is an oddity within a religious community of large families. What could he do? Rabbi S, however, recognizing his mistake of pressuring K to fit in, backed off and only after a while encouraged K to try some "frum" dating sites. However, when he was age-matched there were few sylph-like Jewish ladies who fit his ideal of a slim fresh-faced natural beauty.

Nevertheless, he busied himself with studying for his adult Bar Mitzvah at age 50. He threw himself an all-inclusive party, with the ironic theme of St. Exuprey's *Petit Prince*. That novella is about a boy who went out into the world looking for knowledge and truth. "I made a journey from the military to Woodstock to Israel and I found truth and knowledge in the Torah." No one from his family was interested in attending. My husband and I went to the ceremony and finally Rabbi and I met and congratulated each other about Mr. K's significant personal accomplishments. Tangible accomplishments hung in the social hall: large tapestries of biblical scenes, and the even more noticeable warm regard the congregants had for him and his generosity from his prospering business.

The Chief Rabbi of Crown Heights, Brooklyn was another matter. He was a mystic and made no distinction between thought and reality. Wishes and feelings carried a moral weight. K and I had spent years altering whatever truth there is in the idea of "honi soit qui mal y pense" (evil is he who thinks evil). God no longer inevitably pinched him when K was annoyed or irritated or even when he thought "drop dead" regarding an unfair competitor. He seemed far away from the danger of a religious psychosis. However, Mr. K made the pilgrimage every year to stand in long lines hoping to have his soul read and hear the Rebbe speak. Might he even expect a blessing, a prediction that would come true? Fortunately for all of us, the most the Rebbe mumbled through his long beard the year before he died was to reassure K that he was a good man. I was so relieved.

Then at a high school reunion he met his high school sweetheart. They fell in love again but ultimately she was unable to accept his life style and he was unable to accept her continued pot-smoking. So he remained single. He chose his new mental stability formed by and founded in an old religion.

Mr. K, Orthodox Judaism, Psychoanalysis, and I have partnered now for several decades. The Chabad authorities agree that psychoanalysis has helped people because, like Judaism, it deals with the multiple facets and layers of inner personality. They differ, of course, with Freud's emphasis on sexuality and with his describing religion as similar to a neurosis. The authorities prefer Viktor Frankl's theory that the individual's primary motivation is to find meaning in his life. "Chabad" (Rebbe Schneur Zalman's teaching) puts instinctual (sexual and aggressive) desires and conflicts at a distance. "Chabad" does believe our emotions and behaviors are symptoms of what is happening in our minds and can be sympathetic to the parallel of ego/superego/id with person (guf)/Godly soul/and animal soul. However, the Tanya sees the underlying force to be the G-dly soul and that the guidance of the tzaddik (wise rabbi) makes the psychologist unnecessary.

How does this case history tie in with the overall theme of this chapter? On a personal/patient level it shows how religion, "God is pinching me, hard," was used in the service of undue oppression and then became a force of inner structure and resilience for this particular patient. On a grander scale, often there is a split between the secular and religious ruling bodies in nations and societies. This split dilutes the ambivalence/intensity toward authority. In England and France the divine right of kings gave way to a separation between church and state. It began and stayed that way in the United States. In Great Britain in 2012 we witnessed the diamond jubilee of Queen Elizabeth II, who has seen not only many prime ministers, but also Anglican clergy, come and go.

In the Middle East, particularly in Iran (formerly Persia), an unusual revolution occurred in which a secular government was overturned by a theological one. How did that come about? How likely is that to become the case in Egypt? Will the Moslem Brotherhood be moderate and responsible to all, as President Morisy's inaugural speech promised? How much of Israel's internal struggle is to keep the religious Right from having a dominant voice in the peace process? Recently the moderates joined with Prime Minister Netanyahu to require the Orthodox to perform their military service, but when that coalition fell apart, the Orthodox became even more adamantly opposed to giving up any land for peace, though they are not willing to lay down their lives for that principle.

In Jordan the moderate Moslem King Abdullah is constantly challenged by the more radically religious Moslems who are native and/or Palestinian and the recent tidal wave of poor immigrants from Iraq and Syria. The professional class from all Arab states is generally more secular in attitude. In Turkey a political/theological compromise is in the works. Currently Islamic fundamentalism is evident in the behavior and changing customs of women who are choosing to wear Islamic dress, travel only in groups, attend Friday prayers more often, wait in segregated bus lines, and abrogate the many freedoms gained when Mustafa Kemal Ataturk instituted legal equality in 1934 (Daftari 2012). Whether this is just a fad in imitation of the First Lady, who insisted on wearing a headscarf during her husband's political campaign; an expression of female solidarity; or true nationalism or religious assertiveness is yet to be determined.

A case in point in our own hemisphere is the history of Haiti. In 1791 enslaved African Americans rose up against the sugar colony of Saint-Domingue and burned lucrative sugar plantations that had brought the French more riches than the northern thirteen colonies had brought the British. Over half a million slaves, united by their voodoo faith and Creole language developed in bondage, overcame superior forces with guerrilla tactics, not just once, but later against Napoleon's army as well. They put a black nation on the map with a constitution that stated: "No white man, regardless of nationality, may set foot here. {in Haiti} . . as a master" (Jelly-Shapiro 2012).

The challenge to ruling incumbents is basically always the same. To what degree are they meeting the basic needs of the people for food, water, safety, and opportunity to better their standard of living? It may not really matter whether the ruler is secular or "divine"; if he or she does not meet a certain threshold of caring for the people or support their idealization of him,that ruler can be "deposed," like Louis XIV and Marie Antoinette or Richard Nixon.

President Obama had a vision, the audacity of hope, based on a dream of his Kenyan, revolutionary father, to equalize health care and redistribute wealth. In 2012 he faced an opponent who provided an alternative vision to let the market forces govern with fewer safeguards. Neither party has the power to change the international forces that shape world economy and unrest. The American president has limited, restricted power in reality, so he or she is bound to ultimately disappoint the people.

Arthur Miller's classic play *Death of a Salesman* brings us back to the nuclear family where this all starts. Biff idealizes his father, and both crash when Willy Loman's infidelity and moral weakness are revealed. It is only the mother who holds onto hope in the family. We do need two parents to give us a choice and with choice, resilience. States and societies will probably always oscillate between secular and theocratic forms of government as they try to forge a path to a better compromise between their own projected good and evil. The problem is that each side's hubris gets in the way, and tragedy results. The rise and fall of nations occurs as religion provides either a force of oppression against the people or a defensive resilience. As history tells us, our sociopolitical enterprises become devastingly dangerous and debased if they are imperialistic or so intolerant that they ride on the rubric of "death to the infidel."

REFERENCES

Curlin, F. (2007). *Psychiatric Services* 58: 1193–98.

Daftari, L. (2012) "Islamic Fundamentalism Pervades Once-Secular Turkey." *Newsmax*, August 12;55–57.

Freeman, Tzvi. (2004). "Is Psychoanalysis Kosher?" *BaisChabad.com*, March 8.

Freud, Sigmund. (1986). *"The complete letters of Sigmund Freud to Wilheim Fliess, 1887–1904."* Translated by Jeffrey Moussaiff Masson. SC-Harvard Press.

Freud, Sigmund. (1905) *Interpretation of Dreams.* In Vol. IV of *Collected Works*. Standard ed. Translated and edited by James Strachey. London-Hogarth Press.

Freud, Sigmund. (1913–1914/1968). *Totem and Taboo.* In Vol. XIII of *Collected Works*. Standard ed. Translated and edited by James Strachey. London: Hogarth Press.

Freud, Sigmund. (1925) *Autobiographical Study.* In Vol. 20 of *Collected Works*. Standard ed. Translated and edited by James Strachey. London-Hogarth Press

Freud, Sigmund. (1927). *Future of an Illusion.* In Vol. XXI of *Collected Works*. Standard ed. Translated and edited by James Strachey. London: Hogarth Press

Freud, Sigmund. (1927–1931). *A Religious Experience.* In Vol. XXI of *Collected Works*. Standard ed. Translated and edited by James Strachey. London: Hogarth Press.

Freud, Sigmund. (1930). *Civilization and Its Discontents.* In Vol. XXI of *Collected Works*. Standard ed. Translated and edited by James Strachey. London Hogarth Press.

Freud, Sigmund. (1939) *Moses and Monotheism.* In Vol. 23 of Collected Works. Standard ed. Translated and edited by James Strachey. London-Hogarth Press.

Frum, D. (2012). "It's Mormon in America." *Newsweek*, June 18,19.

Jelly-Schapiro, J. (2012). "'Shelf Life'"—A Review of Dubois' New Book *Haiti: The Aftershocks of History.*" *The Nation*, April 2, 19.

McFarland, M. J. J. (2010). Gerontology. *British Psychological Scientific Society.* 65: 621–30.

Miller, Arthur. (1949). *Death of a Salesman*. New York-Penguin Books

Saver, J., and J. J. Rabin. (1997). Neuropsychiatry Clin. *Neuroscience* 9: 498–510.

Theilman, S. (1998). *Handbook of Religion and Mental Health*. Waltham, MA: Academic Press.

CHAPTER 13

FUNDAMENTALIST REVOLUTIONARY IDEOLOGY AND ITS CONSEQUENCES

J. Harold Ellens

INTRODUCTION

Fundamentalism is more a state of mind than a form of religion, more a psychological than a spiritual matter. As a psychological state of mind, it is always pathological. Wherever it appears and in whatever form or context, it is psychopathology. It is destructive of the health and function of the fundamentalist and dangerous to those around him or her.[1]

The fundamentalist ideology appears with surprising frequency in every form of religion, profession, and facet of human society. It has been a prominent characteristic of Judaism, Christianity, Islam, Hinduism, Shintoism, and other types of religion throughout their history. Engineers can be fundamentalistic about engineering, attorneys about the interpretation and practice of law, and politicians about their views of statesmanship. It surfaces in every worldview and social system, every profession, and every human form of operational practice; in ethical, theological, political, and social systems; in scientific perspectives; and in the manner in which a significant percentage of people in every type of human community carry on their lives and crafts.

This psychological outlook involves rigid adherence to regulation, strict constructionist interpretation of principles and standards, and stringent methods for control of functions and behavior taking priority over freedom, flexibility, and creative imagination. Fundamentalism is therefore an inherently disruptive force for revolution in any society or culture that sees itself open to growth, exploration, experimentation, and liberation in humane or humanitarian ideas and values.

The emphasis in fundamentalism is on maintaining a static and orthodox system, rather than on growth and the risks of change. This approach to life may evidence itself in the practice of medicine, dentistry, surgery, or psychology. Philosophers may be fundamentalistic in their quest for truth and in their crafting of the formulae or constructs in which it must be expressed. There are physicists, astronomers, surgeons, and rhetoricians who are inflexible in theory and method, producing systems and procedures that ultimately prove counterproductive.

Fundamentalism is a mode of operation that is driven and shaped by obsessive-compulsive forces in the human psyche, insists upon predictable structures, and affords people who manifest it or adhere to it little capacity for coping with ambiguity. Because the ability to deal with ambiguity with a reasonable degree of comfort and efficiency is crucial to healthy life, the psychopathology of fundamentalism is particularly evident in this obsessive characteristic. Perhaps there is a certain degree of advantage in this obsessive-compulsive rigidity for brain surgeons, dentists, and certified public accountants, but I know of few other settings in which it is a virtue. It is still pathology.

This dysfunctional characteristic is further evidenced in the virtually inevitable tendency of any fundamentalism to produce an orthodoxy in whatever field it arises. Orthodoxies of any sort paint a static and ossified picture of reality, one that does not provide room for the dynamism of growth and change or critique and response, so the system inevitably becomes delusional. It manufactures an altered state of mind and sense of reality out of the rigid ideology of that particular form of fundamentalism at play in any given situation or system of thought or practice. Because it is, therefore, untrue to reality, fundamentalism is always and inherently a heresy.

Orthodoxy, which claims to be orthodox precisely because it dogmatically insists that it is the one and only possible formulation of the truth, is always therefore exactly the opposite of what it claims.[2] It is fundamentally unorthodox; that is, untrue! It is always an erroneous formulation of purported truth and can never be anything other than that, because it refuses to be open to any new insight that might be generated by the ongoing, open-ended human quest for understanding.

EXPOSITION

The pathology of orthodoxy-producing fundamentalisms arises from the wellspring of prejudice, an insidious part of the unconscious strategies for survival and meaning that are inherent in every human psyche. Prejudice has, and should have, a bad reputation. It is everywhere and always destructive. Prejudice prevents an objective and sympathetic view of, or address to, anything. It is uniformly and consistently uncongenial with the best interests and quality of human life. Most human beings, I am quite sure, find prejudice reprehensible, but all of us are afflicted by it. We disapprove of it, but we are guilty of it nonetheless. Pogo was right, "We have met the enemy, and it is us!"[3]

Prejudice afflicts us in two ways. We are all prejudiced about something, and that obstructs our ability to deal with that specific matter, or the persons to which it applies, in the best possible way. Moreover, we are all recipients of the damage other persons' prejudices inflict upon us. I am eighty years old. It was a shock to me to notice that as I passed the age of about sixty, at which time I suffered some heart trouble and aged rather more than I had before, the young clerks in the drugstore or hardware store clearly distanced themselves from me. Whereas the former attendants had been rather congenial, the new and younger ones now treated me as an object. Of course they had no way of knowing that I was a retired U.S. Army colonel, an internationally known scholar, a noted lecturer, and a rather nice guy. They could only see that I was an old man who had not had the good sense to die and stop cluttering up their lives.

I notice that whether it is a matter of courtesy in driving on the highway, caring for my interests at a department store, or responding to my requests at a restaurant, airline counter, or other service settings, I am no longer seen by young adults as a *person* unless they know me, need something from me, or are under my authority, as in the case of my students. Instead of being a person, I am now an object, often made to feel that I am an inconvenience to those folks. I notice that I am not alone. I watch this happening to my friends and colleagues also. It always makes me chuckle to see the reaction when I am with one of my elderly friends and we are treated like objects until I introduce him as the federal judge, or the U.S. senator whom they obviously have not recognized, or a general officer from my army days. Suddenly the prejudice that we are simply a couple of old guys who are a drag on the U.S. economy evaporates, and for a little while we are seen as persons, perhaps even larger than life.

If someone asked these young folks whether they were prejudiced against old people, I am sure they would be aghast at the suggestion. I am sure they are not at all aware of their internal image of gray-haired and wrinkled persons as irrelevant, burdensome, and undesirable. That is the nature of prejudice, theirs and mine. It usually operates quite destructively at the unconscious level, and for that very reason is very abusive and does much damage to the personhood and circumstances of real live human beings. Moreover, young folks have no special mortgage on prejudice or a special predilection for it. As I write these paragraphs, I am very much aware of my need to reflect upon my own temptation to tar all young adults with this same brush, when in fact my own adult children and young people I work with every day are ample evidence that most young adults are sensitive and generous, perhaps less dogmatic and judgmental than I.

The sensitivity of a senior scholar or an old soldier and the insensitivity of young people toward an old man are painful, of course, but they are relatively trivial forms of prejudice, if one compares them with the biases that have wreaked upon humanity the destruction of racism, genocide, exploitative warfare, economic manipulation, or class and caste distinctions and elitism. These forms of institutionalized prejudice have formed the underpinnings of the abuses of power and have written the subtext of human history since its earliest recording. Moreover, it is tragic that the pain and abuse of prejudicial behavior fall upon real, live, and lively human persons of flesh and blood, mind and spirit. This violence is tangible, not theoretical; palpable, not abstract. "If you prick us, do we not bleed? If you tickle us, do we not laugh? If you poison us, do we not die?" (Shakespeare, *The Merchant of Venice*, III, 1).

In "Notes on Prejudice," Henry Hardy quoted at length Isaiah Berlin's "hurried notes . . . for a friend" (2001). Hardy described Berlin's intense observations as "somewhat breathless and telegraphic," conveying "with great immediacy Berlin's opposition to intolerance and prejudice, especially . . . stereotypes, and aggressive nationalism." The wisdom of Hardy's selection of this material for the *New York Review of Books* is obvious when we note that its date was just one month after the World Trade Center tragedy. There venomous religious and cultural prejudice wreaked havoc on our entire nation—indeed upon the entire world. One might summarize Berlin's passionate expression in one paragraph: "Few things have done more harm than the belief on the part of individuals or groups (or tribes or states or nations or churches) that he or she or they are in the *sole* possession of the truth: especially about how to live, what to be and do—and that those who differ from them are not merely mistaken, but wicked or mad: and need restraining or suppressing. It is a terrible and dangerous arrogance to believe that you alone are right: have a magical eye which sees the truth: and that others cannot be right if they disagree."

Fundamentalisms have reared their ugly heads in every field of human endeavor throughout history and have been particularly noticeable in religion and ethics. One might cite the history of the Spanish monks who mounted the Inquisition of the late Middle Ages, some of the Gnostic forms of early Christianity that sought to suppress all other forms of Christianity, the Hassidim in Israelite religion, and the framers of the doctrines shaping al Qaeda today. In Christianity, the prominent forms of American fundamentalism arose out of the Great Awakening and the frontier revivals and their psychology, which characterized the eighteenth and nineteenth centuries in the United States. This mind-set has now been exported everywhere in the world. The late Henry Stob, a wise and very generative Christian philosopher and theologian of hallowed memory, who taught for an entire career on the faculty of Calvin College and Seminary, often referred to American fundamentalism as the most dangerous heresy extant in modern history. Today we would certainly be forced to include in that category of most dangerous movements both Islamic religious fundamentalism and fundamentalistic Israeli politics. All three of the great Western religions, which derive from the ancient Israelite religion of the Hebrew Bible, are plagued by the presence of this sick psychology and its prejudiced heretical products.

Moreover, no one in our world today, except apparently the fundamentalists, needs much persuasion to agree that the rigorist mind-sets of the orthodoxies that have taken the world by storm in our time are productive of immense real and potential violence. Whether they are the orthodoxies of the American Christian religious Right, which supports Zionism for the purpose of hurrying the cataclysm of Armageddon; or of the Islamic terrorists, whose dogmatism breeds suicide bombings and WTC assaults; or of the Israeli framers of preemptive defense, who do not desire to negotiate for peace, the sick psychology is in every case the same. The prejudices and delusions that substitute for truth are very much the same. All are caught up in the ridiculous apocalyptic notions of cosmic conflict and the fight against cosmic forces of evil, none of which are real.

The product of such worldviews is always violence. Whether it is violation of the truth or of persons, property, and appropriate procedures for social and juridical order, it is violence. Whether it destroys persons, the necessary conditions for healthy human existence, or useful understandings of the real world, it is violence. Whether it corrupts freedom, constrains legitimate liberty, or fouls the human nest with mayhem and bestiality, it is violence. Whether it oppresses persons or peoples with the force and power of empire building, represses hope and the resilience of the human spirit with the fear of mass casualties and intimidation, or terrorizes the tranquility of children with media reports of those kinds of mayhem, it is phenomenally destructive violence.

PSYCHOBIOLOGY AND FUNDAMENTALISM

Who generates these fundamentalisms and orthodoxies that are so destructive for the human spirit, the conditions of healthy human life, and the viability of truth and reality? John Medina published an article in the December 2002 issue of *Psychiatric Times* in which he presented some very enlightening data about violence. The article reported research on the nurture versus nature debate regarding the sources of aggressive human behavior. Acknowledging that genetic research has swung the pendulum from environmental models to biochemical models of the origins of human violence, Medina insisted that the real data show the importance of both. However, in discussing violent behavior in a specific set of human situations, he was forced to report the incredible influence of genetics.

The familiar enzyme monoamine oxidase is important to the "active concentration of neurotransmitters at the synapse" in the brain (Medina 2002, 10). That is what makes thinking and conscious feeling possible. Two types of genes produce the enzyme. They are very similar in structure and very near each other on the X chromosome, shared by males and females. Because of some interesting things that had been seen in animal behavior when one of these MAO genes, designated A, was knocked out, researchers interested in human aggression began to look for "mutations of this gene in human subjects to see if any correlation could be found between aggression and disrupted MAO A chemistry" (2002, 12).

Ten years ago a Dutch family was identified in which numerous generations of adult males were prone to extraordinary, sudden, explosive bouts of aggressive behavior. Examination of the data confirmed the inherited nature of the behavior. The cerebral-spinal fluid of all the subjects indicated a complete lack of MAO A. The mutation in this gene had neutralized its function in the neurotransmitter process. Only in early 2002 were new subjects identified so that the research could go forward. The New Zealand Dunedin Multi-disciplinary Health and Development research program studied the development of over 1,000 children from their births in 1972. "Tragically a specific subset of these children were found to be raised in severely abusive home environments" (Medina 2002, 12).

Four hundred and forty-two male children were selected for study, looking for a significant relationship between behavior and genetics. Fifty-five of those children who had grown up in violent households had both low MAO A levels and highly violent behavior themselves. Violent behavior in children from violent households but who had high MAO A levels was only about 25 percent of that of children with violent households and low MAO A levels. Children with high or low MAO A levels and stable structured homes all exhibited about 8 percent as much violent behavior as the children with abusive homes and low MAO A levels. The former were probably reflecting normal levels of aggression.

The import of this research for our concerns here is that genetic studies might prove to be very useful for a proper understanding of the kinds of people who are inclined toward fundamentalisms and orthodoxies. Fundamentalist psychology is known to produce not only rigid models of thought and worldviews, but also rigidity in other aspects of life, such as regulation of home life and views of professional and personal or family discipline. Fundamentalist Evangelical families commit a higher level of physical and sexual abuse of children than the general population. This phenomenon coincides with specific forms of prejudice among fundamentalists against ideologies and persons who differ discernibly from them and their thought systems. Moreover, fundamentalisms tend to run in families and in extended family communities. Orthodoxies tend to form specific discreet communities, and these tend to perpetuate themselves throughout generations. It would be of interest to know to what extent this reflects a genetic bias that produces at least a proclivity toward such rigid life and thought, an inclination to prejudicial attitudes, and a pathological lack of openness to more universalizing insights or perspectives on truth and life.

Most of all, it would be of interest to know whether such inflammatory leaders as Osama bin Laden, and many like him, who have created isolationistic groups of followers with the objective of wreaking violence upon the world at large or upon others within their own world, are persons with low MAO A genetics and highly abusive or rigid and oppressive developmental settings. This would be interesting information, because it would provide for a rational understanding of the horrid phenomena with which the world is faced in such persons as Joseph Stalin, Adolf Hitler, Osama bin Laden, Ariel Sharon, Yasser Arafat, and the like. These are people for whom early resort to massive violence as the ultimate solution to all major problems seems to have been an addiction. Arafat and Sharon may seem to have been men of different styles, but their methods were the same. Sharon was overtly aggressive in his promotion of massive violence, and Arafat was passive aggressive in his promotion of massive violence, but the outcome was the same. We ought to know why they resorted to radical violence as the ultimate solution to every major problem or sociopolitical impasse, so that we can see these kinds of characters coming on the world scene, but also so that we can anticipate the destructive forces of their fundamentalist orthodoxies in politics, ethics, or religion before they can wreak the havoc of slaughter in Palestinian refugee camps in Lebanon (Sharon), or exterminate an entire class of citizens in the farming communities of the Ukraine (Stalin), or commit genocide in concentration camps (Hitler), or wreak havoc on innocent groups of persons with suicide bombs. Psychobiology may be our hope for the future.

In 1996 Elizabeth Young-Bruehl published a superb analysis of this affliction of human psychology and society called *Anatomy of Prejudices*. Her superior work has not been superseded. Her focus is mainly on anti-Semitism, racism, sexism, and homophobia. However, her general assessment of the psychodynamics of this psychosocial malady leads us to an appreciation of the similarities that all forms of prejudice manifest, the distinctive characteristics of each type, and the subtle and blatant forms of their social expression. From the slightest slur to the stupid joke to the violent act, even war, prejudice functions like the sophisticated computer virus that adapts its own structure as it goes along, eating up all the resources available and using the wholesome qualities and energies of any system or community by turning them on their heads and redirecting their trajectories to create evil. What were growth-inducing insights are turned into malevolent analyses and defensive-aggressive reactions, filled with and generating paranoia and hate.

Young-Bruehl comments on the great difficulty we have in stepping outside our own prejudices, even in our efforts to speak or write wisely about prejudice. She wonders why "on this topic of prejudices, so much has been written on such shaky foundations, with such a recycling of clichés and unfounded conclusions. I became convinced that the way we have learned to speak in ... America about prejudices is a very large part of our prejudice problem, a part of which we are, daily, unaware" (1996, 2). She points out that when Gordon Allport wrote his valuable treatise *The Nature of Prejudice* (1958) and surveyed the total scope of the subject in mid-twentieth-century America, he announced his objective as seeking out the root of prejudice so as to understand its nature.

Although the course Allport set for the investigation of prejudice was a worthy one, his model was limited by the implied assumption that "prejudice is something singular with one nature and one root" (Young-Bruehl 1996, 16). However, Allport actually is at some pains to declare that "It is a serious error to ascribe prejudice and discrimination to any single taproot, reaching into economic exploitation, social structure, the mores, fear, aggression, sex conflict, or any other favored soil. Prejudice and discrimination ... may draw nourishment from all these conditions, and many others" (1958, xii). Allport wishes to teach plural causation, but he acknowledges that he is by professional habit disposed to emphasize the role of learning, cognitive processes, and personality formation. "It is true that I believe," says he, "it is only within the nexus of the personality that we find the effective operation of historical, cultural, and economic factors ... for it is only *individuals* who can feel antagonism and practice discrimination.... I place a heavy and convergent emphasis upon psychological factors" (1958, xii–xiii).

He drew out these psychodynamics of prejudice in a surprisingly creative way for a scholar working on this issue so early in our cultural awareness of the need to study it systematically. He put his finger on the central dynamic of prejudice. His words seem as wise and applicable a half century later as they must have seemed forward looking and wise when he published them a decade after the close of World War II:

> At the time when the world as a whole suffers from panic induced by the rival ideologies of east and west, each corner of the earth has its own special burdens of animosity. Moslems distrust non-Moslems. Jews who escaped extermination in Central Europe find themselves in the new State of Israel surrounded by Antisemitism. Refugees roam in inhospitable lands. Many of the colored people of the world suffer indignities at the hands of whites who

invent a fanciful racist doctrine to justify their condescension. The checkerboard of prejudice in the United States is perhaps the most intricate of all.... some of the endless antagonism seems based upon a realistic conflict of interests, most of it, we suspect, is a product of fears of the imagination. Yet imaginary fears can cause real suffering. Rivalries and hatreds between groups are nothing new. What is new is the fact that technology has brought these groups too close together for comfort. (1958, ix)

Allport did not develop his psychological perceptions very extensively because his approach was, in the end, primarily sociological. However, one realizes throughout his work that he kept his eyes open to the inner psychodynamics of the individual. He would, I think, have agreed with the perceptions that prejudice is primarily a defensive-aggressive psychological phenomenon; is rooted in ignorance or bad information about the person or community against which the prejudice is directed; is generated by the primal human urge for survival combined with the paranoia that lack of accurate information produces; and expresses itself as an intention to devalue, disarm, and extinguish the relevance of the object of the prejudice. This psychological process may take the form of slights and verbal disrespect, intimidations and social degrading, physical deprivations and assaults, catastrophic violence and war, or extermination of the object of the discrimination and hatred.

Fundamentalism and its orthodoxies, in whatever field they appear, focused as they are by prejudice, are inherently violent. The reasons are few, consistently the same in all fundamentalisms, and straightforward. Fundamentalism is a psychology that insists addictively that its view of reality and truth is the only authentic one and is the whole truth. Therefore, any other perspective is willfully false, ignorant, and dangerous to the truth. In this logic, it is for the good of the nonfundamentalists that the fundamentalist's truth be imposed upon them.

In religious fundamentalism it is thought to be the will of God and a favor to all humankind to bring humanity under the umbrella of fundamentalism. So it is the imperative of fundamentalists to impose their model of the truth upon all nonfundamentalists, by force if they have the predominating power, or by seduction that is usually called evangelism if they do not have the dominant power. Therefore, those who resist inclusion in fundamentalism or who threaten it with repression or opposition must be neutralized, either by isolating, demeaning, or destroying them. This pattern may readily be seen in the history of religions in the violent imposition of Nicene orthodoxy upon almost all Christian movements in the fourth century and following, with the great destruction of many of the persons and movements that represented Christian alternatives. It is also illustrated by the Inquisition, the Christian Crusades, the witch-trials of the American Puritans, the frequent

Islamic fundamentalist crusades against other Muslims throughout history, and now al Qaeda terrorism against Muslims who disagree with them and against the non-Muslim world.

Stirling and McGuire explicate René Girard's model for explaining how specific persons or groups become identified in or by a society as the object of prejudice and its social consequences (Stirling 2004; McGuire 2004). They develop Girard's essentially psychoanalytic understanding of these forms of isolation, alienation, devaluation, and extermination, pointing out particularly his metaphor of the scapegoat. This is, of course, an old metaphor, already prominent in ancient Israelite religion and in the Hebrew Bible, which that religion produced. It is carried over in formative ways into the Christian scriptures of the New Testament and into Islam's sacred scriptures, the Qur'an.

Girard's point comes down to the psychoanalytic insight that the scapegoat, whether it is an individual or another society, becomes a projection of the shadow side of the source or enactor of the prejudice. Prejudice always generates and is generated by an "us versus them" mind-set. The circumstances of life often produce realistic situations in which there arises a real-life "us and them" setting. My family and I live in North America. There are many other humans who do not, including a number of my relatives for whom I have great affection. They live in Germany. Whether we discuss the geography of Greenland or the current perspectives on American policy toward the Near Eastern nations and cultures, it is inevitable that their perspective will be that of those who must look westward toward Greenland and ours that of those who must look eastward. That may seem irrelevant, but psychoanalytic psychologists know that such simple differences make a discernible psychological difference in the way we and they think of Greenland.

On the infinitely more complex and serious matter of Near East policy, the differences in perspective will inevitably be much more remarkable. We may even have the same basic facts and principles in mind, but we will see the implications of them differently if our primary unconscious interest is American and theirs is German. With some significant conscious and rational thoughtfulness, we may be able to place ourselves in each other's shoes and gain more global views that might be almost identical, but even then certain flavors and tastes, so to speak, will still make our feelings about the matter distinctive to each of us.

We can, of course, have important differences without resorting to prejudice. We may take a gracious, thoughtful attitude that empowers us to understand a wide range of views on a matter, without feeling less passionate about the one we support. We may be able to allow others to have their point of view as a legitimate alternative way of looking at things. Or we may feel strongly that the facts are such that they really have no moral right or rational justification to hold to such an ill-informed outlook. However, even then, it is not necessary for us to resort to prejudice, which is a need to devalue or damage other persons or communities because of the positions they take, the attitudes they evince, or the behavior they act out.

Prejudice is the irrational, unconscious devaluation of another for no other reason than that the "other" is different. It increases with ignorance and the paranoia ignorance generates. Prejudice identifies, isolates, and alienates its object. The further this process progresses, the easier it is to project upon that "other" those things we hate in ourselves. We always hate most in others what we cannot stand in ourselves. Our own flaws, distortions, iniquities, self-defeating habits, and failures we see readily in others, or believe we do, and unconsciously we attack those in them that we know we should extinguish from ourselves. Therefore, those things that we cannot face in ourselves, for which we cannot forgive ourselves, we make into the reasons for devaluing or destroying them.

If those dysfunctions in ourselves that we cannot stand, cannot deal with, cannot correct, or cannot forgive, happen to be religiously and morally laden with some kind of divine censure, we will see our attack upon those very things in others as divinely sanctioned, justified by God, even the imperatives of his own will and mandate for us. We may feel called by God, in such instances, to wreak havoc upon those others who are the "legitimate" objects of our prejudice. This surely was the motive and mind-set of the terrorists of the 9/11 tragedy. It is the outlook of Christian pro-lifers, whose disgust with abortion on demand may be appropriate, but who are intent upon killing doctors and nurses who work in abortion clinics. The same motive seems to have been clearly that of the ancient biblical Israelites, who confused their own acquisitive prejudices with the divine will when it came to extermination of the Canaanites, "because the cup of their iniquity was filled." Few readers notice that the Canaanite cup was filled with exactly the idolatrous and abusive behavior to which the Israelites were forever inclined themselves, given half a chance to diverge from the "call of Yahweh" to be a distinctive people of grace. That prejudicial motive is surely also the disposition and dynamics of the modern Palestinians and Israeli, who seem forever ready to destroy their own world in order to save it.

Allport (1958) had an interesting way of getting at the underpinnings of these psychological dynamics of prejudice. He thought that our negative prejudices are the obverse of those things that we love and cherish, and that the most important categories we have in terms of which to think and feel about things are our personal values. We live by and for them, without consciously needing to think about them or evaluate them. We defend them in terms of the intensity of our feelings about them and compel our reason and assessment of evidence to fit in with them. "As partisans for our own way of life we cannot help thinking in a partisan manner. Only a small portion of our reasoning is . . . 'directed thinking' . . . controlled exclusively by outer evidence and focused upon the solution of objective problems. . . . Such partisan thinking is entirely natural, for our job in this world is to live in an integrated way as value-seekers. Prejudgments stemming from these values enable us to do so" (Allport 1958, 24).

Unfortunately, prejudgments can easily slide into prejudice. Allport was aware of the fact that affirming our way of life may lead to the "brink of prejudice." He cites Spinoza's notion of "love-prejudice," namely having more love feelings for someone or something than is appropriate to that object. We "overgeneralize" the virtues of such objects, whether a lover, a doctrine, a church, a nation, or a cause:

> This love-prejudice is far more basic to human life than is its opposite, hate-prejudice (which Spinoza says "consists in feeling about anyone through hate less than is right"). One must first overestimate the things one loves before one can underestimate their contraries. . . . Positive attachments are essential to life. . . . Why is it that we hear so little about love-prejudice—the tendency to over generalize our categories of attachment and affection? One reason is that prejudices of this sort create no social problem. . . . When a person is defending a categorical value of his own, he may do so at the expense of other people's interests or safety. If so, then we note his hate-prejudice, not realizing that it springs from a reciprocal love-prejudice underneath . . . negative prejudice is a reflex of one's own system of values. We prize our own mode of existence and correspondingly under prize (or actively attack) what seems to us to threaten it. The thought has been expressed by Sigmund Freud: "In the undisguised antipathies and aversions which people feel towards strangers with whom they have to do, we recognize the expression of self-love, of narcissism." (Allport 1958, 24–26)

Particularly relevant to our present moment in history and the international circumstances in the Western world is Allport's next paragraph:

> The process is especially clear in time of war. When an enemy threatens all or nearly all of our positive values we stiffen our resistance and exaggerate the merits of our cause. We feel—and this is an instance of overgeneralization—that we are wholly right. (If we did not believe this we could not marshal all our energies for our defense.) And if we are wholly right then the enemy must be wholly wrong. Since he is wholly wrong, we should not hesitate to exterminate him. But even in this wartime example it is clear that our basic love-prejudice is primary and that the hate-prejudice is a derivative phenomenon. (1958, 26)

Isaiah Berlin thought that under these circumstances of significant conflict of values, we tend to operate from the certainty that there is only one worthy goal for one's self, church, nation, or humanity, "only one true answer to the central questions which have agonized mankind," and that it is worth risking all for that final solution, no matter how costly. We tend to be particularly willing to accept exorbitant costs in loss and suffering, particularly if it is mainly the enemy's loss and suffering. Berlin cited Robespierre as saying, "through an ocean of blood to the Kingdom of Love."[4]

Berlin feared that if we have not learned from history the foolishness and self-defeat in this outlook, "we are incurable." That may be so. It is almost certainly so if we cannot rid ourselves of the West's endemic tendency to assume that human conflicts, like God's conflicts in the Hebrew Bible, are ultimately best resolved by precipitating catastrophe. This leads us to delay earlier, safer, and saner resolutions of misunderstandings and collision courses of policy or ambition, trusting that if all else fails, which it surely will in such an irresponsible model, we can always resort to the ultimate violence. We are inherently addicted to cataclysm, so we do not fear our prejudices as much as we fear the loss of what we "love more than is right."

During the last decade of the twentieth century Robert M. Baird and Stuart E. Rosenbaum edited a series of psychosocial studies entitled Contemporary Issues. These amounted to a series of handbooks on various topics related mainly to legal and ethical issues in social management. One useful monograph in the series was entitled *Bigotry, Prejudice, and Hatred: Definitions, Causes, and Solutions* (Baird and Rosenbaum 1992). Two chapters in this volume proved to be particularly helpful. Chapter 10, by Elliot Aronson, investigated causes of prejudice. Pierre L. van den Berghe contributed a chapter on the biology of nepotism. Both of these chapters relate directly to this particular phase of our discussion, in that they address the underside of our love-prejudice and paint a picture of a Girardian take on our hate-prejudice. Aronson led off with the following paragraph:

> One determinant of prejudice in a person is a need for self-justification . . . if we have done something cruel to a person or a group of people, we derogate that person or group in order to justify our cruelty. If we can convince ourselves that a group is unworthy, subhuman, stupid, or immoral, it helps us to keep from feeling immoral if we enslave members of that group, deprive them of a decent education, or murder them. We can then continue to go to church (or Synagogue or Mosque, I would add) and feel . . . good . . . because it isn't a fellow human we've hurt. Indeed, if we're skillful enough, we can even convince ourselves that the barbaric slaying of old men, women, and children is a . . . virtue—as the crusaders did when, on their way to the holy land, they butchered European Jews in the name of the Prince of Peace. . . . this form of self-justification serves to intensify subsequent brutality. (1992, 111)

Sociological studies tend to suggest that the more the security of one's status and power is jeopardized, the more prejudiced one tends to be and behave. Van den Berghe, who also published *The Ethnic Phenomenon* with Greenwood Press (1987), makes a cogent argument for finding the roots of prejudice in nepotism. His basic argument is that "ethnic and racial sentiments are extensions of kinship sentiments. Ethnocentrism and racism are thus extended forms of nepotism—the propensity to favor kin over non-kin. There exists a general behavioral predisposition, in our species as in many others, to react favorably toward other organisms to the extent that these organisms are biologically related to the actor. The closer the relationship is, the stronger the preferential behavior" (Van den Berghe 1992, 125). Blood is still thicker than water, apparently!

It is interesting, of course, that humans are seldom cannibals, and if they are it is generally with great revulsion and in extreme circumstances. Most humans are willing to consume other mammals, birds, and creatures lower on the evolutionary tree, such as fish. Even many of those who argue for being vegetarian on the grounds that one ought not to eat "meat" will nonetheless eat chicken and fish. Chicken is presumably from the dinosaur line and fish more closely related to reptiles, both a long way from our human branch of the evolutionary tree. Those vegetarians who also avoid chicken, fish, and dairy, vegans, who consume only a strictly vegetarian diet, are usually mystified when I ask them how they can tolerate killing the living things they do eat, the poor lettuce leaf, celery stalks, beautiful carrots, and the like. They tend to respond that these are short-lived forms of life anyway, are planted for harvesting, and have no consciousness or feelings. Well, that is a very relative and imperialistic statement. I doubt the lettuce leaf would agree, should he or she or it be honestly "inquired of."

Of course there is a significant debate about whether the implied claim is true, that is, that plants have no consciousness or feelings. There seems to be adequate evidence that plants respond to what seems comparable to our central nervous system stimulation. However, when all is said and done, the argument boils down to the fact that plants are so far down the evolutionary tree as to be not worth considering as a life-form in the sense that humans are life-forms. Van den Berghe's claim is vindicated by this rather simple human proclivity to argue for the privilege of those most like us and against the privileged status of those most unlike us. Thus blacks can more easily feel and act out prejudice against whites than against other blacks, and whites have demonstrated the same thing on their side of the equation, in monstrous ways, throughout history.

However, Young-Bruehl is less certain than Van den Berghe that the familial connections in the dynamics of prejudice are biological or grounded in kinship issues. She wonders, with Erich Fromm, whether the familial influence is not rather psychosocial, particularly the sociological side of that. She investigated (1996, 64–65) the extent to which it is the family power structure and the values related to it that set the course for prejudicial patterns and dispositions. Adorno and Horkheimer (1950) were sure that the patriarchal family is the nexus of prejudice by reason of its authoritarian socialization of the family members. This is basically the "frustration-aggression" model for explaining prejudice as rage displaced upon a scapegoat and forming the foundation for such models as Girard's.

In the end Young-Bruehl (1996) concludes in her study that the sources and dynamics of prejudice are so complex that one must avoid above all the temptation to make generalizations, normally the objective of all science. Instead, she urges, we must address the operational issues of prejudicial behavior in specific situations: specific categories such as racism, sexism, homophobia, and anti-Semitism, and specific incidences such as this lynching, that genocide, this caste system, that slavery, this riot, and that family feud. I agree, but it is clear that there are generalizing similarities at work in the tragedies of prejudice. They include the following factors. First is the difficulty humans have in living with the unknown and the very different. Second is the human tendency to make dogmatic claims that differences of values and styles mean the moral inferiority of the other. Third is the human inclination to fear the unknown or different and react to or act out that fear in defensive aggressive strategies. Fourth is the human need to justify those feelings and that behavior by demonizing the object of the prejudice. Fifth is the corollary behavior of isolating, alienating, devaluing, degrading, disempowering, and if necessary exterminating that object, whether a person or a community. Sixth is the human inclination to believe that there is a single and final solution to the impasse of difference and conflict. Seventh is the willingness to pay any price for the ultimate cataclysm, which will resolve the tension, stress, and burden of that impasse, particularly if that cost is mainly at the expense of the object of the prejudice, the enemy.

RELIGIOUS FUNDAMENTALISM WORLDWIDE

Christian fundamentalism is a uniquely American heresy. Unfortunately it has been exported worldwide by industrious mission efforts. Its central objective is the promotion of a strange kind of orthodoxy. Its components are mainly the following five. First, it holds to a theology of sacred scripture that claims the Bible is verbally inspired by God in such a way that it is totally inerrant in every word and detail of content and therefore is to be taken literally as the authoritative foundation of all truth. Second, fundamentalism subscribes to the apocalyptic worldview that a cosmic conflict between God and the devil, between cosmic forces of good and evil, rages everywhere and at all times on the battlefields of history and the human heart. Third, it claims that the communities of humans and of transcendental beings such as angels and demons are divided into two camps, namely the righteous and the unrighteous, and that the temporal blessing and the eternal destiny of each community, and the individuals within it, depend upon the degree to which those beings conform to the law of God. Fourth, fundamentalism professes that there is a mechanism for escape from the eternal judgment of God upon those who fail to keep his law, namely confession of sins and correction of behavior. In this case, the justice of God, which has been breached by misbehavior, is satisfied because the implorations of confession and reformation access the merits of Jesus's sacrifice for human sin in his crucifixion, and that merit balances the scales of divine justice. Fifth, fundamentalism expects that ultimately God will win the cosmic conflict and subdue what amounts to the evil god, the devil, and terminate history in a cataclysm that will damn the unrighteous to eternal hellfire and embrace the righteous in a blissful heaven.

Martin E. Marty and R. Scott Appleby have done us a great favor in helping us understand religious fundamentalism worldwide by publishing their immense and immensely important volume, *Fundamentalism Observed*, the first volume in *The Fundamentalism Project* (Marty and Appleby 1991). It offers a survey of fundamentalism in all major religious traditions. Sixteen scholars have joined them in trying to achieve both an appreciation and an assessment of fundamentalisms in North American Protestantism, the Roman Catholic tradition, Protestant fundamentalism in Latin America, the Jewish fundamentalism of the *Haredim*, Jewish Zionist fundamentalism, Sunni and Shiite Muslim fundamentalisms, Asian Islamic fundamentalism, Hindu fundamentalism, Sikh fundamentalism, Theravada Buddhist fundamentalism, Confucian fundamentalism in East Asia, and political and religious fundamentalism in Japan. Marty and Appleby call all this the hypothetical family of fundamentalism, implying the universal underlying psycho-spiritual commonality that reigns in all of these otherwise quite disparate movements:

> The premise . . . is that religious fundamentalism, a term historically associated with versions of American Protestantism and more recently employed to describe certain expressions of Islam, exhibits generic characteristics which apply to various religious settings. Hence, not only Christianity and Islam but also Hinduism, Buddhism, Judaism, and other religions may be found to have fundamentalist variants. Moreover, an understanding of each of these versions of fundamentalism, . . . will shed light on the phenomenon as a whole. (Marty and Appleby 1991, 197)

This encyclopedic work takes as its theme the proposition that fundamentalism of every kind is a dogmatically asserted and defended ideological system that is therefore not open to either review or critique. It is inflexibly closed to any continued acquisition of truth or insight, modification or expansion. North American Protestant fundamentalism expresses itself in a nonnegotiable creedal posture and has radicalized both ethics and politics in terms of that ideology. Its aggression has been channeled into an effort to shape national politics through infiltrating the historic system of American political process in efforts to elect fundamentalists to public office. It is also aggressively saturating the populace with mass media of all types and focusing on specific local sociopolitical and ethical battles such as assaults on abortion clinics. This strategy for getting fundamentalist ideology into the forefront of national life and significantly increasing its influence on the mind-set of the populace has been surprisingly successful. Moreover, no effective critique has been offered to counter it since the typical liberal approach has been, "The less said the better. Maybe it will go away." Of course, it will not. Only the open arena of dialogue, informed with good ideas founded in truth and reality, will maintain a decent balance and ward off the very real dangers that attend any significant rise of fundamentalism anywhere.

A fundamentalist fringe group of one sort or another has existed in Roman Catholicism since the beginning of its long history. Some of those groups became orders of monks or nuns within the church, eventually received papal consecration, and were domesticated into fairly mainline enterprises. Largely in response to the *aggiornamento* (updating) that Pope John XXIII brought into the Roman Catholic communion by convening the Second Vatican Council in 1962–1965 and shepherding it through its aggressively innovating agenda, a countermovement of fundamentalism resurged in the church. Archbishop Marcel Lefebvre claimed the church had lost its moorings in its creeds and traditions by the liberalizing openness of Vatican II, so he ordained three bishops into a new movement to reestablish the historical traditions of the church. This was an act that violated the order of the church, so he, his bishops, and their followers were excommunicated:

> The emergence of a "traditionalist" ... movement spearheaded by a "rebel" archbishop indicates the scope of the conflict that has divided Catholics ... of hierarchical leadership ... who claim the high ground of Catholic orthodoxy. The rise of the traditionalist movement also illustrates how Catholicism's troubled encounter with modernity has spawned movements and ideological orientations closely paralleling those associated with Protestantism's own fundamentalist reactions to the modern world. ... Lefebvre's brand of Roman Catholic traditionalism is a militant and organized reaction against the intellectual and cultural inroads of modernism ... to arrest and reverse religious change ... and to preserve the ideological, organizational, and cultic patterns altered, abandoned, or discredited ... ,

a protest against the blurring of Catholic identity and the loss of Catholic hegemony. (Marty and Appleby, 67)

This Catholic traditionalist movement is worldwide today and at least loosely organized as a fraternity. The church's response to this kind of dissent over the centuries has generally been surprisingly wise. It has tended to move with extreme patience, giving some room for the dissent to work itself out without enough pressure on it to produce overt violence or ruptured relationships, and then eventually co-opting the unconventional movement. Frequently this very process has energized the inner spiritual drivers of the whole church. Particularly in the United States, such an approach has worked rather well for the last forty years with regard to the absorption of this traditionalist movement back into the mainstream of the church.

In Latin America, on the other hand, the Roman Catholic Church, traditionally the dominant religious force in culture, politics, society, and liturgy, has lost a great deal of ground to Protestant fundamentalism, exported from North America by evangelical fundamentalist missions. This is thought by some to be the result of a rather arid formalism having permeated the Roman Catholic Church in Latin America from the sixteenth century to the mid-twentieth century, together with the rather unsuccessful strategies of liberation theologies in all of the mainline denominations in South America. With the demise of the USSR the Marxist liberation theologies have lost much of their impetus. The vacuum has been filled in Latin America by fundamentalism in the Christian traditions, but also fundamentalist mystery religions with quasi-African roots, instead of Christian foundations.

Within Judaism, worldwide an ultra-orthodox scion has grown up called the *Haredim*. Fundamentalist orthodoxy has always been a significant presence in Judaism, as well as in ancient Israelite religion. These Jews hold to the ideology that *their* religious truths, precepts, and formulations have been and must be an unbroken tradition from Abraham to the present moment and on through the future until the Messiah arrives. "To these Jews the past is the great teacher: today is never as great as yesterday, and the best that tomorrow can promise is a return to the great days of yesteryear" (Marty and Appleby, p. 197). The name by which they are called means "those who tremble at the word of the Lord." They are sure that they are the only ones to whom God pays attention.

Historically, the term *Heredim* referred to those who were scrupulous or obsessive about religious punctiliousness. It is interesting that one of the sins that the Roman Catholic Church named in the Middle Ages was scrupulosity. To call it a sin and require confession for it was a hedge against the psychological illness that is manifested in or incited by obsessive religiosity or self-discipline. In this is the typical rigidity of fundamentalism evident in the *Haredim*. It is true of their approach to theology, biblical study, ethics, social controls, and personal habits. Judaism worldwide has been radicalized to a significant degree by the forces of this movement. This is particularly true in Israel itself, where the ultra-orthodox have managed to achieve significant political power by manipulating the various coalition governments, made necessary by the increasingly divided society.

Historically, *Zionism* was a relatively general term referring to the Israelite longing for a homeland in Palestine. In the late 1960s it was radicalized by a small group of people who, armed with military weapons, militantly began to force the occupation of Palestinian territories by Jewish settlers, at the same time wreaking havoc upon the persons and property of Palestinians. The current memory is that this movement arose in response to a sermon by Rabbi Kook the Younger on the nineteenth anniversary of Israeli independence. In the sermon, given at a Jerusalem religious academy, Merkaz Harav Yeshiva, Kook passionately emphasized several messianic tenets of his mystical system, which he claimed would constitute the spiritual base of the revolutionary Jewish-Zionist movement.

Kook claimed that divine redemption of Israel was in process at that very moment, nationally and politically, since Israel had been established and successfully maintained as a nation for nearly two decades, but that what was lacking was a corollary religious and ethical redemption. Most Israeli were secular, and the moral and ethical codes of the society were not those of the Torah or Talmudim, but rather merely utilitarian ethics of secular Western society. This launched the course that the Israeli nation has come to follow into the tragic mayhem of perpetual violence and mutual destruction of Palestinians and itself. Moreover, this form of violent Jewish fundamentalism has produced the current general world crisis in and regarding the Near East.

According to the Jewish scholar Gideon Aran, at the outset few people in Israel took the Jewish-Zionist drive seriously, and most Israelis were greatly offended by its violence, injustice, and ideological dogmatism (1991, 265). This movement promoted the illegal establishment of Israeli settlements in the land properly belonging, by treaty and title, to the Palestinians. Moreover, it claimed that the territories from the Tigris to the Nile properly belonged to Israel, as in the golden age of David's and Solomon's kingdoms. This bizarre ideology became a driving undercurrent in Israeli politics and social ferment until an increasing number of Israelis began to endorse the vision. General Sharon and the Israeli Defense Force took advantage of this perspective to support the invasion of Lebanon, and progressively the movement gained political power, until it can now essentially manipulate the government. It was of some considerable help to the movement that General Ariel Sharon was for a few years Prime Minister Ariel Sharon. It is largely in response to this abusive form of Jewish fundamentalism that the Islamic fundamentalism of al

Qaeda and of the militant Palestinians has become increasingly focused, unified, and aggressive against the United States, the primary ally of Israel.

As a result of Anwar Sadat's rapprochement with Israel, Sunni Egyptian fundamentalists shot and killed their president on October 6, 1981. They were carrying out a jihad that they believed was mandated by God. That was, for many of us, the opening gun of the militancy of Islamic fundamentalism and its worldwide battle against all those who do not agree with their religious ideology. Their spirit is the same sick psychology as that of the Israeli Zionists who provoked the evil these evil fundamentalist Muslims oppose. The momentum of this violently destructive Islamic religious movement has increased weekly since that day three decades ago when Sadat fell victim to the supposed divine mandate. Its victims now number in the tens of thousands and are fast growing to the hundreds of thousands, in Europe, Asia, India, Africa, Israel, Kurdish Iraq, the Mediterranean basin, and the Americas. Their violent guerrilla-type warfare has been carried out on land, in the air, and on the sea. It has been targeted mainly against civilian noncombatants, demonstrating the inherently unethical barbarism and cowardly abusiveness of these psychopathic fundamentalists.

Their movement is referred to as Islamic fundamentalism because it is their attempt to reaffirm the foundational principles that they think shaped original Islam and should shape the structures and laws of Muslim society, religion, and ethics everywhere today. Just like the Jewish-Zionist movement, these Sunni Muslims wish to recall fellow Muslims to the correct path of their religion, which they, of course, feel divinely appointed to define. All Muslims adhere to the authority and life-shaping claims of their sacred scriptures, but the fundamentalists have an exclusivist and literalist interpretation of the message, mandates, and moral program of the Qur'an, from which they derive a rigorist pattern for social and political regulation of life in Islamic nations. "Islamic fundamentalism is . . . a distinctive mode of response to major social and cultural change introduced either by exogenous or indigenous forces and perceived as threatening to dilute or dissolve the clear lines of Islamic identity, or to overwhelm that identity in a synthesis of many different elements" (Marty and Appleby 346). Like their Jewish counterparts, these fundamentalists are eager to resort to armed violence and open assault upon civilian or military targets to gain their vicious and lawless objectives.

The Ayatollah Ruhollah Khomeini represented, in his lifetime and his days of power in Iran, the other branch of Islamic fundamentalism, that of the Shiites. He came to power on February 1, 1979, after being befriended and promoted by France for fifteen years, contrary to Western political policy and, as it turned out, contrary to the best interests of the people of Iran. Saddam Hussein, a secular Arab, and his fellow Iraqi leaders, described by Osama bin Laden as a nest of infidels, made war upon Khomeini and his fundamentalist regime in Iran. It was, as we remember, a phenomenally destructive war for both nations. Hundreds of thousands of citizens died on both sides. Hussein's opposition to Islamic fundamentalism was illustrated at that time by his execution of the noted Shiite leader in Iraq, Ayatollah Muhammad Baquir al-Sadr, on April 9, 1980. Subsequently, Hussein supported the Taliban and al Qaeda in Afghanistan against the USSR, as did the United States, and subsequently Hussein seemed to be willing to work with al Qaeda, if it paid off for him in his war with the United States.

One form of fundamentalism is difficult to distinguish from another, and fundamentalists' willingness to resort to unlawful and barbarous forms of violence to gain their short-term objectives, with little good vision for the long-term consequences, makes strange bedfellows out of a great variety of fundamentalists in specific ad hoc situations. One gets the distinct impression that American fundamentalists, who are bent upon attacking and violently closing abortion clinics, however constructive their objective of decreasing abortions on demand, would welcome an al Qaeda terrorist to assist them by bombing a few such clinics. None of us would be surprised if CNN *Headline News* reported tomorrow that American fundamentalists in Atlanta had hired a Palestinian suicide bomber to go into an abortionist clinic and set himself off, with the promise that the suicide bomber's family in Hebron would get a check for $25,000 US. They all smell the same, look the same, act the same, resort to the same abusive aggression, and invoke the same nonexistent god, namely the ridiculous barbarous god of fundamentalist dogmatic heresy.

Of course it must be remembered that from the inside of the system, for the religious fundamentalist personally, the intention is to establish a structured and secure society, blessed by the order and discipline that they believe God's will and law should impose upon all society, religion, ethical systems, intellectual models, and philosophical worldviews. The fundamentalist is sure that such a world is not only God's imperative but also the best arrangement for humanity, and therefore the means of attaining it are justified by the ends achieved. The vicious and barbarous violence is not the legal pattern for the lawful world order to come, but merely the expedient to which one must resort to achieve God's ends and purposes here and now. This is thought by the religious fundamentalist to be not only justified; but required by the rubrics of sacred scriptures, whether those are the examples of Jesus's violence in the New Testament, the model of Muhammad's military jihad in the Qur'an, or the narrative of the divinely ordered extermination of the Canaanites by the ancient Israelis in the Hebrew Bible.

The fundamentalist character of a special kind of Hinduism that has arisen with strength in the last quarter century is becoming increasingly obvious. This sect is particularly evident in northern India and Kashmir, where it arose in the early 1980s as a response to the Islamic fundamentalism progressively causing sociopolitical and religious turbulence in that region. Initially it was militant and has subsequently turned murderous. This barbarously violent Hinduism is now seeding itself throughout India, giving traditional Hinduism generally a new quality and a rigid, sharp edge. This could easily turn to generalized violence throughout India, particularly where it can be aimed at Islam. It has unified Hindus of a rigid, conservative mind-set and given a new and violent revolutionary tone to the religion and its culture throughout the country. The movement now dominates the leadership of the religion virtually everywhere in India, creating a tinderbox of volatility that could easily carry the entire nation into an irrational and destructive revolutionary mood.

The more rational and traditional forces of Hinduism have always been rather low key, disparate, and scattered in focus. It has tended to be a religion of the individual rather than of communities. This has begun to change under the instigation of what is now called the Arya Samaj, a movement that arose in Mumbai in 1875 as a religious reform and appealed largely to the educated classes. It supported the nationalism movements in the early twentieth century that led to the demise of the British Raj. Though quite different from the Arya Samaj, a second movement has had a similar effect upon Hindu India. It is the Rashtriya Svayamsevak Sangh or RSS, which styles itself as a movement for the reform and renewal of Hindu culture and society, secular in its identity and character. The effect of these two forces, particularly in northern India, where the clash with Islamic religion and culture is a prominent issue, has been to reinforce the destabilizing and frequently violent actions of local communities. Both of these Hindu organizations have worked unsuccessfully for caste reform in India. They were effective in creating a network of schools for raising the educational level of the citizenry, but the effort has proved to be vastly inadequate for the needs of the whole country.

These Hindu fundamentalisms continue to flourish in modern India and are "an increasingly growing force in cultural as well as political life" (Marty and Appleby, 575). An important question is what forces perpetuate fundamentalist religion among Hindus, particularly its frequent recent resort to mob violence. The original energy of these fundamentalisms was generated by their resistance to colonialism. Now the movements seem to be stimulated and energized by the combination of hostility toward Islam; the rise of a new tribalism within Hindu culture; and a reaction to the disillusionment of ineffective social, political, and economic structures in Indian society. These movements have acquired the use of contemporary weapons, which has enhanced the lethalness of their historical militancy. Daily reports of vicious and horrible abuse, exterminating human life, are increasingly the way of Indian life.

There are numerous other manifestations of fundamentalist psychology in the religions and politics of India. The most prominent is probably that of the Sikh religious tradition. Theravada Buddhism may be encountered on that subcontinent to a lesser degree. India is organized as a secular constitutional democracy, but the Sikh religion, while operating within that setting, does not concede any separation between politics and religion. Although its local worshipping groups are comparable to the Christian churches of the Western world, the faith communities consciously claim that no dualistic categories or idolatry of either images or creeds is tolerable. Life is a unity: a spiritual, social, religious, political, military, and economic unity.

Sikhism was founded upon the precepts of the Adi Granth, also referred to as the Granth Sahib, its sacred scriptures. The Golden Temple at the center of Sikh worship and consciousness was built by Guru Arjan, the fifth of ten Sikh leaders. He lived from 1563 to 1606. The temple is called Harmandir, the temple of god. Arjan's son, Guru Hargobind (1595–1644), built a second temple the year his father died. It is known as Akal Takht, the throne of the immortal god, and it faces Harmandir. The religious perspective of these gurus was universalistic. Harmandir has four doors, one toward each of the points of the compass. Guru Arjan said, "My faith is for the people of all castes and creeds from which ever direction they come and to which ever direction they bow" (Marty and Appleby, 595).[5] The Golden Temple was built for the singing of hymns of peace; reflections upon the sacred scriptures; and listening to the teaching of the gurus regarding life, god, and godliness. The Akal Takht, however, became the site for celebration, in song and lecture, of heroism, military exploits, conquest, and religious instruction that promoted those perspectives.

A persuasive guru named Bhindranwale led an armed militant movement beginning in the early 1980s to give concrete and operational expression to Sikh "assertion of the political and economic rights and religious prerogatives of the Sikhs," which were thought to be under threat (596). He is generally viewed in India as a fundamentalist, namely a leader who has selected a few militant aspects of Sikhism to motivate his fellow Sikhs to action. His intention was purportedly to protect the rights and interests of Sikhs and freely promote his notion of what Sikhism ought to be. He and his armed band are considered, even by most Sikhs, to be extremists. He created a bizarre orthodoxy that would be considered by most Sikhs to be unorthodox in terms of the historic principles of their faith. True Sikh orthodoxy, it is generally understood, would work against this fundamentalism, since historic Sikhism was oriented to peace, ecumenism, and universalistic openness to a great variety of people and ideas, and advocated "catholicity and not narrowness of the mind" (596).

In 1983 this band of fundamentalists barricaded themselves in the temple complex, increasingly reinforcing it militarily over time. They conducted a terrorist campaign during which they murdered and pillaged at will, killing hundreds of innocent Hindus. In 1984 the Indian armed forces, under the command of two Sikh generals and one Hindu general, directed an assault on the temple complex, killing Bhindranwale and many of his associates. This was a source of great sadness to Hindus and Sikhs alike throughout India, because such violence is contrary to the ethics of both communities, but particularly that of the Sikhs. Moreover, the temple complex was badly damaged by Operation Blue Star, as it was officially called. While these fundamentalists considered themselves to be the authentic Sikhs, "defenders of the 'basic teachings' of the Sikh gurus . . . and of the economic interests of the Sikh community," the government could only see them as terrorists, judged by their behavior and their publicly announced creeds and objectives (597).

The 1984 fundamentalist crisis took place against the background of numerous preceding violent sectarian clashes within the Sikh community and between Sikhs and Hindus. In 1978 a particularly bloody riot had killed members of two battling conservative sects fighting over political party issues. This conflict brought Bhindranwale into prominence as a religious and political leader and led to the later violence. The difference between the two sects was their view of their sacred scriptures. One held that nothing could be added to the sacred scriptures, and that they constitute the "written guru" from which all truth and authority is derived. The other claimed that only living gurus have authority, and each can add to the sacred scriptures as he is led to understand new insight or revelation. Each claimed, with a fundamentalist militant rigidity, that its orthodoxy was the true historical Sikh orthodoxy. They resorted readily to murderous terrorism, and that tradition continues. This has regularly resulted in destructive clashes between fundamentalist Sikhs and the Hindu majority of India.

Like all other fundamentalisms, the Sikh variety depends on a radical notion of the authority of their sacred scriptures, selective emphasis on elements of the historic faith that promote current militancy and terrorism, charismatic leaders who are willing to inflame the community with paranoia and violence, commemoration of past events that can be made to seem like abuse of Sikh fundamentalists by other groups, a cultivated and manipulated sense of isolation, and aggressive reaction to any perception of constraint upon Sikh fundamentalist rights by outside powers. Madan (1991) is quite sure that there is no good sign that Sikh fundamentalism will abate in the near future. The basic difference between the definition of the relationship between the state and religion in the secular Indian constitution, on the one hand, and in the mind of the Sikh fundamentalists, on the other, is so radical and persistent that it will continue to stoke the fires of dissent, isolation, hostility, paranoia, and aggressive behavior. This psychology, and the aggression it incites, is always just a hair's breadth from terrorism in India. It tends to bleed into other partisan conflicts present in that very complex society and inflame them further with Sikh fundamentalist energy.

Two additional fundamentalist movements complete this cursory survey of the phenomenon of fundamentalism in our modern world: Theravada Buddhism and Confucianism. Buddha died in 544 BCE, and his influence throughout the world has competed aggressively with that of Jesus of Nazareth for the last two millennia. Theravada Buddhism, a product of the original Hinayana Buddhism, is a fundamentalist form of conservative Buddhism. It arose early in the history of this faith tradition. It is not quite clear why one should call Buddhism a religion or faith tradition, because it is really a form of nontheistic ethical philosophy. However, it is regularly listed as one of the great religions of the world, probably because it takes the form of a humanist spirituality and has a transcendental dimension, the achievement of nirvana.

Buddhism sprang up quickly and spread widely from the moment of Gautama Buddha's original enlightenment. Nearly simultaneous with the rise of Theravada Buddhism, two other mainstreams of the tradition developed, Mahayana and Vajrayana Buddhism. These are complex philosophical systems, which have become widely syncretistic and eclectic and emphasize the importance of social responsibility and cultural development for the improvement of the quality of human life, as well as the encouragement of all humans to practice Buddhist philosophy and ethics. This is a type of Buddhism that has appealed rather intensely to the Western world. Theravada Buddhism tends to be oriented toward escape from mundane material desire, by meditation that enhances self-transcendence and access to nirvana. It functions in intense tension, therefore, with its social environment and earthly existence.

The fundamentalism of Theravada Buddhism is expressed in a claim that its roots are in the original true traditions of Hinayana Buddhism of Buddha himself, and that it has preserved the true form of these traditions. It is rigorist and rigid in its prescriptions for spiritual and social function, is militant in whichever culture it finds itself, and aggressively promotes itself worldwide. It has been very influential throughout history in providing the partisan energy for consolidating the sense of identity and hence the unification of nationalism in many countries, such as Thailand, Burma, Laos, Cambodia, and Sri Lanka.

In these processes, Theravada Buddhism has tended to be terroristic and violent to achieve its ends. It is difficult to discern how this comports with the transcendental orientation of Theravada Buddhism, but it is easy to see its sense of social tension reflected in this aggressive behavior. In Sri Lanka, for example, the Sinhalese are Theravada Buddhists for the most part, and the Tamils are Hindus. The violent and destructive repression of the Tamils by the Sinhalese has been a virtually uncritical process of the Buddhists for generations. It is quite surprising how terroristic these policies have been.

Only in recent years, as a result of the militant rise of the Tamils themselves, has any significant constraint been imposed upon these vicious practices of the Buddhist fundamentalists.

A great variety of Theravada Buddhism has developed in the numerous nations in which Buddhism has had significant presence and influence over the centuries. This was particularly true in the postcolonial and is now in the postmodern era. These variations have taken the form of rigorously disciplined, conservative ethical systems, focused on the eradication of social evils and the demeaning of human life and equality. In "Fundamentalistic Movements in Theravada Buddhism," Donald K. Swearer summarizes the entire matter crisply:

> Fundamentalistic movements ... [are] frequently led by strong, often militantly aggressive, charismatic leaders whose followers ..., perceive themselves to be variously threatened as individuals, communally, or as a nation. The ideologies embraced by such movements tend to rest upon simplistic, dualistic, and absolutistic worldviews. Often exclusivistic (although ... evangelistic), the movements reject competing groups ... as morally evil, spiritually confused, and/or intellectually misguided. Possessed of an almost obsessive sense of their unique role ... these movements may be quasi-messianic or explicitly millenarian in nature ... anti-rationalist, anti-intellectual, ... anti-ritualistic ... open to the criticism that it ... lacks the depth of its classical predecessors. (Marty and Appleby 1991, 678)

In China things took a slightly different turn, but with similar consequences. Confucius was certain when he died that he had thoroughly failed. Subsequently, and rather quickly after his fifth-century BCE pilgrimage, his philosophy spread throughout East Asia, permanently shaping China and heavily influencing Korea, Mongolia, Japan, and most of the rest of East Asia. Particularly in the last century, Confucianism experienced a vigorous revival. It is an ethical philosophy with neither a theistic nor a transcendental orientation. From its beginning in the life and teaching of Confucius, it was oriented toward the enhancement of the education, social order, economic development, and quality and equality of life for all humans.

The recent revival of Confucianism has taken the form of a quest for the roots and specific precepts of the teaching of Confucius. As a result it has tended toward a fundamentalist character and psychology. This has driven the quest back to the *Analects* of Confucius himself. In the nineteenth century Japan chose a Westernization process rather than a fundamentalist resurgence of Confucianism. In China and Korea, attempts to strengthen Confucianism largely failed to produce workable political and social structures. Thus it was largely in the pre-Maoist government in China, carried over in 1950 to Taiwan by the evacuation from mainland China of the Kuomintang forces under Chiang Kai-shek, that the resurgence of Confucianism was seeded. So it is in Taiwan that the fundamentalist revival has borne the most fruit.

The struggle between Maoist Marxism in China and Confucianism in Taiwan has been carried out primarily as an ideological contest. However, it has regularly degraded into actual military conflict. Mainly, it has persisted in the form of political barrages, regularly exchanged. Over the last half century, however, with the modernization and capitalization of China, Confucianism has resurged in China itself. Meanwhile, moderation of Taiwanese policies and political rhetoric has resulted in the fundamentalist Confucians in Taiwan being increasingly forced into a defensive posture, marginalized, and isolated in their own society. This has increased their militancy and their calls for radical opposition to any rapprochement with China.

Thus, the potential for violent conflict between the fundamentalist Confucians in Taiwan, and in a larger sense throughout industrialized East Asia, and the forces in power there is ideologically greater, while at the same time politically and militarily less likely of success. The Confucian resurgence has been in part a response to Westernizing influences everywhere in the world today, a quest for a more idealistic, homegrown ethical and social code. It is an attempt to hold in check the Western type of modernization in the hopes of preserving more traditional or historical ideologies and codes, indigenous to East Asia itself. Moreover, the appeal to the fundamentalist mind-set of this Confucian revival lies in the general dissatisfaction with Western moral and ethical values, as well as with what is perceived to be trivial and trivializing Western philosophy and cultural models. It is not surprising that this is so, considering that so much of what is purveyed to the world in general as Western culture has taken the form of rather risqué Hollywood movies, rather cacophonous American music, rather violent videos from many sources but most surprisingly even Disney productions, remarkably cynical Western philosophies, and weapons-oriented U.S. industrial products.

Tu Wei-ming reminds us of the 1958 manifesto that was prepared by a number of Chinese scholars as their proposal for Chinese understanding of how Confucian tradition might be made relevant to the future development of a holistic model of psychosocial idealism for their nation:

> A faith in the efficaciousness of the Confucian core curriculum and an assumption of the authentic transmission of the Confucian heritage throughout history are implicit in the manifesto, but the main thrust of the argument is to present a Confucian perspective on the human condition defined in terms of modern Western categories . . . a denunciation of the sterility of modern commercial culture and the New Confucians' reconstruction of the meaning of the human "life world." (1991, 773–74)

This Confucian revival is widespread and diverse in East Asia. It is a search for "cultural roots" as an "integral part of modern consciousness and ... persistent universal human concern." Confucian fundamentalism seems to have been the least violent form so far in history. That may be the result of a nonparanoid Chinese communal personality or the lack of need for violent aggression to achieve the goals of this conservative philosophical reawakening. It also may be a characteristic inherent to Confucian principles themselves.

CONCLUSION

Fundamentalism was once thought to be merely a special type of rather obsessive and rigorist Protestant Christian heresy, championed by people who had a psychological need for high levels of spiritual and socio-theological control, who tended to be rather esoteric in their belief systems, passionate in their certainty that they alone possessed God's truth, and aggressive in their compulsion to impose it and its implications on others. Now we understand that fundamentalism is a psychological pathology that can shape and take possession of the framework of thought and action in any arena of life, and particularly any ideology. This makes religion particularly vulnerable to the pathology of fundamentalism, a dangerous heresy almost anywhere we find it.

The danger in fundamentalism takes the shape of false orthodoxies. They are dangerous in many ways, but especially in how they corrupt the truth, disrupt community, violate personal and communal prerogatives, and promote sociopolitical and physico-material strategies of destruction. We have been made profoundly aware in recent years of the intimate links between religious fundamentalism and worldwide terrorism. This is associated in our minds at this time primarily with Islamic fundamentalism. However, what we need to discern is how and the degree to which every form of fundamentalism has the potential for terrorist tactics to achieve its "divinely appointed" ends. Most fundamentalisms have resorted to gross violence at some point.

It is imperative, therefore, that we identify fundamentalism wherever it may be found, define and name it as the psycho-pathology that it is, engage it, contain its violent potential, and reduce its influence as much as possible. As in countering all strategies of organized violence, the greatest challenge is to defeat it without resorting to its own tactics and thus being dragged down to its subhuman moral level. In America's leadership in the elimination of the fundamentalist violence of worldwide terrorism today, it is crucial that we find our way without triumphalism or resorting to the arrogance of power. Power properly and humanely applied is one thing. Arrogant power is quite another. Ignorant arrogance is the worst of all.

The incredibly grace-filled late medieval or early modern philosopher Baruch Spinoza, in his tract on politics, said that in his quest for understanding the facts, foibles, and fruits of human life and thought, he tried to be very careful not to laugh, cry, or denounce humans in their very human pilgrimage, but instead to simply and gently understand.[6] This reminds me of the noted acerbic cartoon editor of the *Kansas City Star*, who upon retirement was asked to say what he really thought of the human race, after his years of printing rather vicious caricatures of it. He rose and said, "I think we should be kind to it. It is the only one we've got." So in the spirit of Spinoza and the cartoonist, I hope we can learn something crucial from the pathological experiments of the fundamentalisms of the world and history, and shepherd ourselves to greater gracefulness and mutual goodwill.

It is clear that prejudice is a devastating force in our political and social order, and that it arises in a very sick psychology at the center of our souls and imposes a large toll on our spirituality. It is the shadow side of our inherent need to survive, grow, develop, and achieve freedom and stasis. It may be considered to have a positive side, in Spinoza's sense of "love-prejudice." Humans are capable of imagining a virtually perfect world and are able to create only a flawed one. The distance that our real world falls short of our idealized imagination we identify as failure and pain. We internalize that pain as guilt rather than simply being able to accept it as a function of our limited humanness. That guilt prompts us to self-justification and defensive aggressive behavior, setting in motion the strategies of prejudice discussed in this chapter.

The general claim here is that some of our ancient religious metaphors create the kind of negative psychological archetypes at the center of our selves that inflame our prejudices and the psychodynamics behind them. At the center this is a spiritual problem, and there is no fixing it except through a spiritual renewal framed and shaped and driven by a theology of grace, a religion of grace, a sociology of grace, and a self-psychology of grace. Divine grace! Human grace! Grace is unconditional positive regard for the other. Judaism hatched this idea of unconditional grace as the redemptive dynamic of true religion and healthy psychology. As I argued previously, all three Western religions, Judaism, Christianity, and Islam, have as their mainstream this notion of grace inherited from the precursors of Judaism, namely the ancient Israelite religion, the religion of the Hebrew Bible.

For 3,000 years, however, this mainstream has been muddied, distorted, and obscured by a completely erroneous religious metaphor also derived from ancient Israelite religion and the Hebrew Bible: the notion that this world is the arena of an apocalyptic cosmic conflict between good and evil. This useless and psychotic metaphor seems to justify our worst prejudices and our most destructive behavior. Yet it has no basis. There is no evidence for ontic evil. However, in all three of these major religions, our sacred scriptures lock us into this notion. That defines us. Unless we radically revise our theology of sacred scriptures in all three religions, we cannot escape this prison house of prejudice. We cannot transcend the built-in bigotry. We cannot become fully human. We cannot escape the tragedy of terroristic fundamentalisms, which lead to spiritual devolution, social violence, and war. We cannot achieve a communal life of grace.

NOTES

1. An earlier form of parts of this chapter appeared in J. Harold Ellens, ed., *The Destructive Power of Religion: Violence in Judaism, Christianity, and Islam*, Vols. I–IV (Westport, CT: Praeger, 2004). See, for example, the following chapters by J. Harold Ellens in that set: in chapter 4, "The Dynamics of Prejudice," in volume II, *Religion, Psychology, and Violence*; and chapter 7, "Fundamentalism, Orthodoxy, and Violence," in volume IV, *Contemporary Views of Spirituality and Violence*. This modification of that material is published here with permission. This chapter also appeared as "Fundamentalism, Violence, and War" in Mari Fitzduff and Chris E. Stout, eds., *The Psychology of Resolving Global Conflicts: From War to Peace*, Volume. 1, *Nature vs. Nurture* (Westport, CT; London: Praeger Security International, 2006), 109–36, and is used here by permission.

2. The use of the term *orthodox*, as it appears in the names of various Christian denominations, such as the Greek or Russian Orthodox churches, is different than its use here. That use of the term is in official historical names of communities of faith, which derive from specific historical origins. Fundamentalisms and pathological orthodoxies may exist in such denominations, but that is not inherently implied by their official names.

3. This is a quotation I cited in J. Harold Ellens, "Fundamentalism, Orthodoxy, and Violence," in *The Destructive Power of Religion, Violence in Judaism, Christianity and Islam* (Westport, CT: Praeger, 2004), 121.

4. Hardy thinks this may be a reference Berlin makes "off the top of his head," so to speak, to Robespierre's sentence, "*en scellant notre ouvrage de notre sang, nous puissons voir au moins briller l'aurore de la felicite universelle*" ("by sealing our work with our blood, we may see at least the bright dawn of universal happiness"), in *Rapport sur les principes de morale politique que doivent guider la Convention nationale dans l'administration interieure de la Republique* (Paris, 1794), 4.

5. T. N. Madan, "Fundamentalism and the Sikh Religious Tradition," in *Fundamentalism Observed*, ed. Martin E. Marty and R. Scott Appleby (Chicago: University of Chicago Press, 1991). He cites Gopal Singh, *A History of the Sikh People* (New Delhi: World Book Centre, 1988), 177, as the source of his information about this story. He adds that according "to Sikh tradition, unsupported by historical evidence, the foundation stone of the Golden Temple was laid by a Muslim Sufi, Mian Mir. It bears testimony to the traditional Sikh approach to religious differences that such a story should be believed" (623).

6. I was reminded of this wonderful sentiment of Spinoza by Martin E. Marty's observation upon it in "Fundamentals of Fundamentalism," in *Fundamentalism in Comparative Perspective*, ed. Lawrence Kaplan (Amherst: University of Massachusetts Press, 1992), 15.

REFERENCES

Adorno, Theodor, and Max Horkheimer. (1950). *The Authoritarian Personality.* New York: Harper.

Allport, Gordon. (1958). *The Nature of Prejudice.* Garden City, NY: Doubleday Anchor.

Aran, Gideon. (1991). "Jewish Zionist Fundamentalism: The Bloc of the Faithful in Israel." In *Fundamentalism Observed,* edited by Martin E. Marty and R. Scott Appleby, ch. 5, Vol. 1 of *The Fundamentalism Project.* Chicago: University of Chicago Press.

Aronson, Elliott. (1992). "Causes of Prejudice." In *Bigotry, Prejudice, and Hatred: Definitions, Causes, and Solutions,* edited by Robert M. Baird and Stuart E. Rosenbaum. New York: Prometheus.

Baird, Robert M., and Stuart E. Rosenbaum, eds. (1992). *Bigotry, Prejudice, and Hatred: Definitions, Causes, and Solutions.* Contemporary Issues. New York: Prometheus Books.

Berlin, Isaiah. (2001). "Notes on Prejudice." *New York Review of Books,* October 18.

Ellens, J. Harold. (2004). "Fundamentalism, Orthodoxy, and Violence." In *The Destructive Power of Religion, Violence in Judaism, Christianity and Islam,* edited by J. Harold Ellens. Vol. IV, *Contemporary Views on Spirituality and Violence.* Westport, CT: Praeger.

Hardy, Henry. (2001). "Notes on Prejudice." *New York Review of Books,* October 18, quoting Isaiah Berlin, "Hurried Notes [on Prejudice] for a Friend."

Madan, T. N. (1991). "Fundamentalism and the Sikh Religious Tradition." In *Fundamentalism Observed,* edited by Martin E. Marty and R. Scott Appleby. Vol. 1 of *The Fundamentalism Project.* Chicago: University of Chicago Press.

Marty, Martin E. (1992). "Fundamentals of Fundamentalism." In *Fundamentalism in Comparative Perspective,* edited by Lawrence Kaplan. Amherst: University of Massachusetts Press.

Marty, Martin E., and R. Scott Appleby, eds. (1991–). *The Fundamentalism Project.* Chicago: University of Chicago Press.

McGuire, Cheryl. (2004). "Judaism, Christianity, and Girard: The Violent Messiahs." In *The Destructive Power or Religion, Violence in Judaism, Christianity, and Islam,* edited by J. Harold Ellens. Vol. II, *Religion, Psychology, and Violence.* Westport, CT: Praeger.

Medina, John. (2002). "Entitled Molecules of the Mind: The MAO A Gene and Exposure to Violent Behavior in Childhood." *Psychiatric Times* (December) (10–14).

Singh, Gopal. (1988). *A History of the Sikh People.* New Delhi: World Book Centre.

Stirling, Mack. (2004). "Violent Religion: René Girard's Theory of Culture." In *The Destructive Power of Religion, Violence in Judaism, Christianity, and Islam,* edited by J. Harold Ellens. Vol. II of *Religion, Psychology, and Violence.* Westport, CT: Praeger.

Swearer, Donald K. (1994). "Fundamentalistic Movements in Theravada Buddhism." In *Fundamentalism Observed,* edited by Martin E. Marty and R. Scott Appleby. Vol. 1 of *The Fundamentalism Project.* Chicago: University of Chicago Press.

Tu Wei-ming. (1991). Chapter 13, The Search for Roots in Industrial East Asia: The Case of the Confucian Revival. 740–81. In *The Fundamentalism Project,* edited by Martin E. Marty and R. Scott Appleby. Chicago: University of Chicago Press.

Van den Berghe, Pierre L. (1987). *The Ethnic Phenomenon*. Westport, CT: Greenwood.
Van den Berghe, Pierre L. (1992). "The Biology of Nepotism." In *Bigotry, Prejudice, and Hatred: Definitions, Causes, and Solutions*, edited by Robert M. Baird and Stuart E. Rosenbaum. New York: Prometheus.
Young-Bruehl, Elizabeth. (1996). *Anatomy of Prejudices*. Cambridge, MA: Harvard University Press.

CHAPTER 14

Fundamentalism in the Methodist Church, 1890–1930: Did the Failed Revolution Ultimately Succeed?

Jack T. Hanford

George Marsden's (2006) *Fundamentalism and American Culture* is probably the most authoritative single volume on the subject. After reading the book, I wrote to him:

> Prof. Marsden, I have a very high respect for your work but I think you might have missed an important part of the fundamentalist or conservative movement in the Methodist Episcopal Church 1890–1930. You (2006, 178) do refer to Harold Paul Sloan, a District Superintendent in New Jersey. But, Sloan was a front man. The main source for Methodists was John Alfred Faulkner, a historian at Drew Seminary. He fed material to Sloan but remained in secret because he feared he would be removed from Drew if his fundamentalist-conservative leanings were known. I would appreciate your response.

Professor Marsden responded:

> Thank you for your message. You are correct that I did not say much about Methodist fundamentalism. It is covered in Cole as I recall, but I did not find much about it as part of an interdenominational coalition in the sources I was looking at and have assumed it was a more traditionalist conservative movement as one finds in many denominations and did not have the lasting impact that Baptist, Presbyterian, and Independent fundamentalism had. I am ready, though, to believe that there is more to the story. I will file it away as a good topic for a student to work on sometime. If I do that, I'll be sure to have the person consult you.

The literature on the fundamentalist movement within the Methodist Episcopal church is indeed very meager. What has been written is incomplete and in some cases even erroneous. Norman Furniss (1954/1963), in his chapter on Methodism, does not even mention or index John A. Faulkner, even though Faulkner was the major theologian of the Methodist conservative movement. This situation calls for research and reevaluation of the conservative emphasis in the Methodist Episcopal church.

The scope of this chapter is limited to one of the three main branches of Methodism, that is the Methodist Episcopal church. This branch existed before the unification of 1939, and this chapter is limited to the period 1890–1930. Within these boundaries, the focus is on the 1920s.

The scope of treatment is narrowed further by centering attention on the activity of Harold Paul Sloan. There were many facets of action by conservatives within the Methodist Episcopal church. I have chosen the main movement and its drama, which unfolded through the leading role of Sloan. This means that discussions of such broad topics as the course of study controversy, doctrinal purity in education, and other such concerns of conservatives are confined primarily to Sloan's participation in them. It means also that such major personalities as John Alfred Faulkner and Edwin Lewis are treated mainly within the shadow of Sloan.

This is not a development of the fundamentalist–modernist conflict. Only one side of the controversy in one denomination is dealt with in detail in this chapter. Of course, mention must be made of the liberals in order to understand the conservatives. However, there are important distinctions between liberalism and modernism and then further distinguishing features within each of the two. To limit the scope of this chapter, liberals are grouped together and treated simply as the opposition to Sloan's forces.

The word *fundamentalism* was loaded with emotion during the period 1890 to 1930. The label *fundamentalist* had a very distasteful connotation in some circles. For others it suggested honor. Because the term did not originate within Methodism, its meaning must be considered in the context of its origin in American Protestantism.

No one definition can describe fundamentalism adequately. H. Richard Niebuhr (1930) presents a good starting point:

> Fundamentalism is the name of an aggressive conservative movement in the Protestant churches of the United States which flourished after the [First] World War. It manifested itself chiefly in the Baptist, Disciple, and Presbyterian churches but received considerable support from other ecclesiastical groups. It was characterized not only by its conservatism with regard to traditional popular Christian beliefs but also by its aggressive efforts to impose its creed upon the churches and public and denominational schools of the country.

What creed did the fundamentalists try to impose? In 1910 The Fundamentals, a series of publications, presented five points that were the marks of the movement. The first and most important fundamental stressed an *inerrant* and *infallible* Bible. Historical study of the Bible and the theory of evolution became threats to the authority of *the* Book. Niebuhr thought that the conflict between the biblical account of creation and the scientific account of evolution was the crux of the controversy. The other four theological touchstones were Christ's virgin birth, his substitutionary atonement, physical resurrection of his body, and the Second Coming. Using these precepts, the fundamentalists sought to prove the incompatibility of modernism in Christianity. The rigid fundamentalist could be distinguished from the conservative by the former's emphasis on the infallible Book and the latter's acceptance of a theology shaped by the outline of the five points.

Though fundamentalists and conservatives affirmed some of the same doctrines, they differed in practice. The fundamentalists were organized into a definite fellowship forming a militant force. This group waged war on all who did not overtly accept certain doctrines. They gained strength by negation of others. Stewart Cole (1931) was on the right track in trying to discern the psychology and sociology of the fundamentalists in order to understand them fully. But we have no evidence that Cole succeeded.

Both fundamentalists and conservatives represented a particular frame of mind. Usually stereotyped as persons who were chained to the past and not able to adjust to new, modern ideas, they distrusted philosophy, reason, and modern science. They had a deep appreciation for "creedal definiteness," emotion, and the traditional faith. The supernatural was stressed over the natural. Ought such issues to be settled on the authority of the Bible or personal religious experience?

Norman Furniss (1954/1963) presented six characteristics of the fundamentalists. The first was a vaguely defined fear. This resulted from the First World War; in 1918 the fundamentalist movement became a major issue in American life. Second was a longing for certainty. Here, the issue of biblical authority played a role. The third characteristic was that sometimes people were attacked instead of issues. Fourth was an inevitable clash between laity and clergy over the meaning of the Bible. A favorite Bible quote of the fundamentalists was, "The Lord hath chosen the foolish things to confound the wise." The fifth characteristic was that some fundamentalists exaggerated reports of success and saw their struggle in terms of a great battle to save the world. The question "Are you saved?," with its implication that the questioner was already saved, reflected egotism. Finally, the sixth characteristic was great sentimentality. There were positive results from this in their concern for children, the faith of college students, and consideration for the uneducated. But on the negative side, in America anti-intellectualism arose from fundamentalism and from revivalism and popular religion (Noll 1994; Hofstadter 1962/1963).

Fundamentalist activity had a particular expression in each denomination. Interdenominational activity was weak among fundamentalists. One particular fundamentalist denomination is of interest here: the Methodist Episcopal church.

What was the relationship of Methodist conservatism to the sweeping movement of fundamentalism that stretched across America? At what points did the conservative movement within Northern Methodism differ from the fundamentalist movement that had a national thrust? Emphasis on the literal and infallible Bible was the most important mark of pure fundamentalism in America. This emphasis was strong only during the origins of unrest in Methodism, and the issue of an infallible Book was not the dominant concern of conservative Methodists. As definitions of fundamentalism and conservatism developed, it was obvious that the latter term described John Wesley's followers better than the former. Nevertheless, it should not be assumed that the flavor of mind or mood of the fundamentalists did not taint Methodism.

The second important factor that distinguished Methodist conservatism was the issue of evolution, which did not play a conspicuous role in the Methodist controversy. While the Scopes trial dramatized the climax of a fundamentalist movement across America, this was not the primary concern of conservative leaders in Methodism. They were debating issues that were more relevant to the denomination. The course of study for nonseminary ministers was one such issue. Furniss (1954/1963, 148) pointed out that the Methodists were spared debate over the two issues of the infallible Book and evolution because of John Wesley's teaching.

A third strong feature of the Methodist conservatives was their urge to return to American heritage. Methodists were not unique in stressing origins. Each denominational right wing wanted a return to the Bible and the old-time religion of salvation, which was often cradled in Calvinism, or in the case of Methodism, Wesley.

The following section traces the chronology of Methodist conservatism beginning in 1890 and relates this historical transition to biblical criticism. The next section then covers 1913 through 1928 and deals with the controversy about the course of study for the nonseminary minister.

BIBLICAL CRITICISM: 1890–1912

The conservative movement in Methodism developed gradually, so no one particular date marks its beginning. The limited discussion here begins with 1890 and the activity of conservatives. John Alfred Faulkner (1921, 28) claimed that the decade 1883–1893 was "seething" with controversy. James William Mendenhall became the editor of the *Methodist Review* in 1888 and carried on a defense of scripture against "higher criticism" until his death in 1892. So for convenience we begin with the approximate date of 1890.

The initial phase of the conservative–liberal controversy was characterized by sporadic conflicts in various sections of the United States. Within Methodism the conflict centered around its colleges and universities, such as Lawrence and Syracuse, and its seminaries, especially Garrett and Boston. The attack concentrated on specific professors, including Samuel Plantz of Lawrence, Charles Little and Milton Terry of Garrett, and H. G. Mitchell of Boston. These men were all interpreters of scripture and were involved in controversy over biblical criticism.

Representative of the character of early Methodist conservatism was James William Mendenhall. He advocated a strong doctrine of the inspiration of the Bible and conducted an uncompromising yet enlightening dialogue with the higher critics. A well-educated, gifted writer, and a man of deep, strong convictions, he traveled to Europe to meet his opponents face to face. He criticized American modernists for not being original, because most of their ammunition for higher criticism came from Europe. Unfortunately for the conservatives, Mendenhall died in 1892, just a few months after receiving an almost unanimous vote to continue as editor of one of the most important Methodist periodicals. Even the opposition respected Mendenhall as a keen thinker, who was orthodox to his innermost fiber. Mendenhall paid tribute to Franz Delitzsch at his death.

H. G. Mitchell of Boston, another representative of the early period, also did his doctoral dissertation under Delitzsch in Germany. Although there was this connection between Mendenhall and Mitchell, they did not agree on theology. Mitchell became the main target of the more extreme conservatives from the early 1890s to about 1910. He considered his celebrated instructor, Delitzsch, to be somewhat conservative, which indicates that the professor of the Old Testament in the oldest Methodist seminary knew the conservative position. He was not an extreme liberal, as was sometimes charged. Some conservatives were rather free in their charges of Unitarianism.

Central to Mitchell's conviction was the individual scholar's right to believe what research verified. He risked not receiving his doctoral degree by taking a position on the facts against his esteemed teacher. Mitchell was a self-educated man, influenced by Phillips Brooks. He was thorough in scholarship and had a sincere reverence for the Bible. His criticism of the Bible was intended to make God's word clear and meaningful. In interpreting scripture he tried "always to let the authors say what they will in their own way, without reference to my opinions, and never, for the sake of ecclesiastical favor, to tamper with their utterances" (Mitchell 1922, 92).

After a trip to the European Continent and England in 1892, Mitchell was completely convinced of the soundness of higher criticism as a method of studying scripture. He asserted that the critical method "was dangerous to the doctrines only in so far as they were based on incomplete or mistaken data" (1922, 116). From his seminary days at Boston, Mitchell was primarily interested in systematic theology. Thus he was not merely a literary critic, coldly dealing with manuscripts, but a man of faith seeking enlightenment.

Mitchell was in contact with O. A. Curtis while both were professors at Boston. Mitchell reported in his autobiography: "While I was discussing the Pentateuch, Professor Curtis was lecturing on the incarnation and the atonement, and some of the students repeated to him disjointed remarks which I had made. He being in a polemical mood, declared them heretical and the zeal of his hearers was kindled by his indignation" (1922, 116). Whether or not the disturbance at Boston resulted in personal animosity between the two professors is difficult to assess. Curtis left for Europe after the incident, and those at Boston were sorry, because he was a well-liked theologian. Mitchell tried to persuade his colleague to remain, but to no avail.

This conflict was in the background of the controversy over Mitchell that began about 1896 : "In 1896, thirty-eight students of Boston University sent to the Board of Trustees of the university a petition calling for disciplining of Professor Mitchell because his teachings leaned toward Unitarianism and naturalism" (Fletcher 1954, 3). In his autobiography, *For the Benefit of My Creditors* (1922), Mitchell never mentioned that there were as many as thirty-eight men in opposition to him. In fact, he mentioned only five or six agitators and suggested that there were reactionary troublemakers in the seminary spying on him. President William E. Warren of Boston tried to reconcile the professor and his students, but the charges of heresy did not abate.

Around 1900 the Board of Bishops warned Mitchell to be more conservative and less disruptive. This threat came at a time when the board had the power to appoint or discharge professors in Methodist seminaries. On May 26, 1900, Mitchell replied to the committee of overseers: "I accept the Old Testament as divinely authoritative, recognizing a supernatural element manifested in miracles and prophesy. I accept the Gospel statement respecting Jesus' advent into the world. I believe in the Trinity including the Deity of Christ and the Holy Spirit. . . . I have not, and never had, any sympathy with the doctrines of Universalism" (1922, 159).

Mitchell longed for peace and hoped this carefully worded response indicated sufficient faith. Although his statement was quite affirmative, it did not satisfy his assailants. "In March, 1901, H. W. Peck, the bitterest and most reckless of my former accusers, and others, residents in Sothern California, began a new campaign with the publication of a periodical called the Methodist Outlook" (1922, 199).

Ironically Mitchell, who yearned for the quiet of his study, was accused of renewing the agitation through his publication *The World Before Abraham* (1901). This book contained Mitchell's lectures, which had been used for some time. It was not an uncommon practice to have lectures printed at Boston. In addition, *The World Before Abraham* came out six months *after* the attack had begun. The assault was personal, extreme, and not a great challenge to the intellect or to basic academic questions.

In 1905 the Board of Bishops refused to approve Mitchell's reappointment, which had been confirmed and submitted by the Board of Trustees of Boston to the bishops. Part of the reason for his dismissal was Mitchell's denial of the Mosaic authorship of the Pentateuch, a technical question of biblical criticism. The decision to dismiss him was made by the bishops, who were not specifically trained in biblical criticism, and Mitchell was an unusually well-trained specialist. He was deposed not for false teaching, but primarily for the sake of conciliation and peace within the church and with the denomination's best-known school of theology.

When Mitchell received the news of his dismissal from the committee of bishops, he was heartbroken. For some time he walked past his former classroom in great despondency. He was ejected from a school where the president, board of trustees, faculty, and almost all of the students loved, respected, and accepted him.

Throughout the conflict Mitchell asked, By which standard of norm am I being judged? It was obvious to him that an evaluation depended most of all on the principle or standard on which one made the decision. If there was one harmonious Methodist view of theology, Mitchell wanted to know it. He knew of the Methodist authorities Professors Newhall and Clarke, yet these men differed on important issues while both were endorsed by the church. Mitchell further wondered what the normative interpretation of scripture for Wesley's followers was. After asking these questions and getting no answers, Mitchell was certain "that there is no consensus of Methodist teaching on the origin or interpretation of the Old Testament. . . . There is no law or precedent giving any Methodist a right to dictate to another what he shall, or shall not, think or teach on the Old Testament" (1922, 169). Mitchell was a student of Wesley and Methodist heritage. He thought the Article of Religion on the scripture freed the Bible to be interpreted for the sake of truth and not for any other standard. Since there was no authoritative interpretation of the early chapters of Genesis to direct Methodists, he was being judged arbitrarily.

Consequently, Mitchell made an appeal to the Central New York Conference for a trial. This was not granted, and the matter of his dismissal landed in the General Conference of 1908. Here he made two appeals: the first was that the Central New York Conference decision be reconsidered. In the reappraisal, the New York ruling was declared null and void. Second, he asked that the Board of Bishops' conclusion be reevaluated. Their two main charges pertained to Mitchell's Christology and his view of scripture. The charge of denying the deity of Christ was not upheld. The complaint about the historicity of the early chapters of Genesis was sustained.

Because there was no legitimate accusation against Mitchell's character, he was entitled to a trial. Yet he later reported that the bishops decided: "In view of the fact that Mitchell no longer holds a professorship, and in view of the *great disturbance* that a church trial would occasion, we [committee of bishops] recommend: That the Conference do not proceed to the extremity of a trial" (emphasis added) (1922, 268).

The desire to keep the peace prevented a man who was called a "saint" by F. J. McConnell (1924) from getting a fair trial. In essence, Mitchell was dealt with in the opposite manner of common justice. He was considered unorthodox until proven orthodox and was never given an opportunity to prove his orthodoxy.

R. L. Moore (1986) theorized that the fundamentalist–modernist controversy might have devolved into problems between insiders (bishops) and their decision, which made Mitchell carry the stigma of being an outsider simply because some students complained about him.

Mitchell died while he was writing his autobiography. His last energy was devoted to an effort to justify his right to stand for truth in spite of all denominational authority. After leaving Boston he wrote about Haggai and Zechariah for *International Critical Commentary*. Later he accepted a teaching position at Tufts, a Universalist college. Nevertheless, he remained a Methodist until his death. As the editor of the *Christian Century* expressed the case: "The Bishops found a way by which to eliminate Mitchell without forcing the denomination to face the doctrinal issues supposedly involved. . . . The incident is immensely revealing as indicating why, with Bishops about, there has been so little doctrinal uproar in Methodism" (1926). Though Mitchell was defeated, the cause he represented was eventually victorious.

Liberals remembered the injustice of their opponents. The conservative sentiment of the bishops changed within a few years to evangelical-liberalism. As liberals gained strength, the conservatives organized an opposition. In 1908 the General Conference ended trials of professors in response to appeals from Mitchell. Another major issue in the conservative–liberal conflict within the Methodist Episcopal church was about the course of study for nonseminary students and preachers. Harold Paul Sloan considered the course of study controversy of primary importance, probably because of his commitment to traditional theology, and he viewed contemporary modernism and naturalism as threats to orthodoxy. His powerful leadership led Methodism in the direction of neo-orthodoxy.

LEADERS

This chapter began with George Marsden (2006) identifying Harold Paul Sloan as the leader of fundamentalism in the Methodist church. I added John Alfred Faulkner. These two were the main leaders of the conservative movement.

Sloan

Sloan was a leader in the course of study controversy; in churchmanship, especially at the General Conference of 1928; in doctrine; in his relationships with American fundamentalists such as J. Gresham Machen and William B. Riley; in his relationships to Harry Emerson Fosdick and Methodist bishops; in his editorship; and in his significance in the Methodist Episcopal church.

Although Sloan must have aroused interest earlier than 1913, his known involvement began at this time in the early phase of the course of study controversy in New Jersey. Sloan gave himself completely to this issue. He spoke to persons who were responsible for selecting books and consulted John A. Faulkner of Drew Seminary, who carefully read each book in the course of study. Sloan was active on committees that studied the conflict. He won the support of his colleagues because of his competence and intense interest.

His work on pure doctrine within the course of study resulted in national prominence, as reported in the *Journal of the General Conference of the Methodist Episcopal Church* (1920, 426). His proposal was adopted 481 to 286. He rallied support to his cause by powerful speeches and political maneuvering. During the General Conference of 1920 the liberal leader, E. P. Robertson, admitted that Sloan had outsmarted and outmaneuvered his opponents.

He kept a list of influential men, talked with them face to face, and persuaded them to accept conservative ideals. The level of his personal ethical ideals dropped somewhat during the struggle between political forces within the church. Nevertheless, his determination and aggressive leadership won for him the number one spot as spokesman and organizer among conservatives from 1920 into the 1930s, especially for his work on the important course of study. By 1922 the course of study was the principal means for entering the Methodist ministry (Norwood 1982, 530).

Sloan's churchmanship came to a climax at the General Conference of 1928. He spent his energy, personal funds, and time on this stormiest quadrennial meeting. While he and his followers were exerting every effort to make the conference face controversial theological issues, the conference leaders were trying every means to steer clear of theological debate. Through the headquarters of the conservatives, which were set up at the General Conference, Sloan tried to force the delegates to debate theology. Sloan and his followers were successful in moving the adoption of the part of the Bishops Address that affirmed a strong doctrinal statement. However, this was stated in general terms, and the liberals held the positions where the specific application of doctrine would take place.

For example, conservatives were worried about the large number of teaching positions in Methodist colleges and universities that were held by modernists. This concern had legitimate grounds. Edwin Lewis, of Drew Seminary, complained that one had to be a graduate of Boston to get a teaching job in Methodism. This was called the "Boston Bloc." The evangelical conservatives were especially anxious about Bible teaching by liberals. Exacerbating the problem, conservatives charged that the Methodist Book Concern was producing only liberal books. Sloan compared the liberal Methodist schools with Moody, Asbury, Taylor, Wheaton, and others. He felt the latter were doing a better job of giving their students a meaningful theological foundation.

Methodist colleges were frequently charged with not maintaining Methodist doctrine. For example, Sloan felt that Allegheny College was teaching a spiritual resurrection rather than a physical resurrection. In his mind this teaching diluted the Christian faith. He was also concerned that the Allegheny chapel had the local Unitarian pastor as its preacher. Considering schools such as Connecticut Wesleyan and Syracuse, Sloan charged that the faith of loyal young Methodists was being damaged. Such accusations as these exemplified conservative anxiety about higher education. This involvement of conservatives was not all negative; some positive suggestions were also put forth.

During this time the greatest conservative theologian in America was J. G. Machen of Princeton Theological Seminary. Machen and Sloan had considerable contact both personally and through the mail. Machen (1923) sympathized with Sloan, writing, "I have followed with the deepest possible interest your contention for the truth. It is brave and wonderful." Machen was asked to speak at meetings of the major conservative organization, the Methodist for Faith and Life League, and he assured its members of his thorough endorsement. Since Machen was having difficulties in the Presbyterian church, Sloan sent materials on the League's plan of organization to his friend. They worked together on a common cause. Machen was one of the best biblical scholars in America and could interpret the Bible and "fundamentalism" as rational, which is a good description of conservativism as embodied by Sloan.

Bishop Francis J. McConnell was the most outstanding Methodist overseer of the 1920s. He led a vast network of social concern organizations.

Sloan (1960–1962) asserted that McConnell "was a firm evangelical, who had an over-towering impression of the social consequences of the Gospel. Bishop McConnell and I were in complete accord upon the Trinity, the person of Christ, the reality of Christian experience, and upon the necessity of that spiritual infilling we call the New Birth. He wrote the introduction to my *He Is Risen*, and fully endorsed its position." Sloan was a courageous editor. His position on editorial policy was unequivocal. He had a high regard for scholarship and endeavored honestly to be fair to a variety of views, yet unswerving in his personal commitment.

Sloan's active role in the conservative cause ended by 1930. His movement was strongest in the East around New Jersey, Philadelphia, and Baltimore. Yet even in there the League was weakest where modernism was strongest, for example in Boston. Efforts were made to vitalize and expand conservatism in the Midwest. To implement this movement, the League sent a hundred letters to ministers and laymen in important positions around Chicago and asked them to evangelize ten persons. But Chicago remained a strong modernist center. Though the movement declined, its leader rose in popularity.

In the early 1930s Sloan declared that the liberal–conservative controversy had ended. More than anyone else, he had been in the spotlight for the conservatives of the Methodist Episcopal church. He was their speaker, organizer, writer, and source of inspiration, aided and abetted by a great source of encouragement and a brilliant mind in the person of John A. Faulkner.

Faulkner

John Alfred Faulkner (1857–1931) was the second most important leader in the conservative evangelical movement of the Methodist Episcopal church. His leadership was different from Sloan's. Yet it is difficult to say whether either man played a more important role. Sloan has been presented in this chapter as the organizational genius, spokesman, and writer for the evangelical conservative cause. Faulkner is presented here as the greatest mind for the conservative cause. Although he was not on the front line of battle as was Sloan, Faulkner still exercised a decisive influence on Sloan's thought. Faulkner was significant as an unusual person and because of his ideas.

Faulkner was born in Nova Scotia on July 14, 1857, where he received his early education. His began graduate study in 1878. In 1881 he was granted the BD degree from Drew Theological Seminary.

In 1897 Faulkner was called to serve on the faculty of Drew. He succeeded his own teacher, George R. Crooks, who was also an editor of the *Hurst Book of Church History*. It was during his thirty-four years at Drew that Faulkner made his contributions to scholarship and the conservative cause.

Faulkner made a great impact on Drew and still lives on in legend. There are probably more stories about his character still extant on the campus of Drew than about any other faculty member, living or dead. Many of the stories about Faulkner were humorous. It was alleged that he once prayed in chapel: "Lord, as you no doubt know, if you saw the *New York Times* this morning, this world is in a terrible mess."

Faulkner kept his close and cooperative relationship with Sloan a secret because he feared removal from the faculty of Drew. He knew that his was a conservative voice in the wilderness at Drew. Thus even Faulkner's closest associates did not know of his involvement in the liberal–conservative conflict. From his book *Modernism and the Christian Faith* (1921), it was known that Faulkner was opposed to the major evangelical liberal thrust of Methodist theology. But no one knew of his dominant influence over Sloan. Faulkner insisted that his name not be officially listed with the Methodist League for Faith and Life. Nonetheless, he was associated closely with the League (Faulkner to Sloan 1925a).

He agreed that his writings could be used by the conservatives. But he did not want his name linked with the leadership of the conservative forces that fought bitterly with Drew. Through the grapevine, news came to him that his name had been mentioned at a Baltimore meeting by Sloan, who identified Faulkner as a leader of the conservative movement. Immediately Faulkner wrote to clear up this matter:

> My dear Sloan: I think after all I ought to send a part at least of that Baltimore letter.
>
> If the brother or any one else who heard you sent a similar letter say to Dr. Tipple, [president of Drew] it would be fearfully embarrassing both to him and to me, and might lead him to ask for my resignation. It would be an intolerable situation to a president to be told that one of his professors is fighting the school and the other professors. And it is an intolerable situation for me and my family to be living in daily dread lest some hearer of your address write a letter similar to that I enclose to our President.
>
> Remember:
>
> Practically all the professors (except me) here are "liberals."
>
> Practically *all* the trustees are "liberals".
>
> Practically *all* the alumni in the three nearest Conferences are "liberals."
>
> Practically *all* the colleges which send us students are "liberals."
>
> Lewis is one of the most popular—I think the most popular—professors we have. Besides he is the one the president most depends on for practical help.

During the President's absence in Europe last Summer, he was acting President.

Now think what chance I would have if the President were to receive a letter like that sent to me from Baltimore after your address! It would probably cost me my place here. Where could I go? *All* in theological seminaries are liberal. Even if they were not, they would not have a professor thrown out elsewhere for being divisive, etc. Back into the pastorate into my Conference, carting around 10,000 volumes of Church History every year or so.

Therefore for God's sake and my sake, in future speeches do not refer to me directly or indirectly in matters spoken of in that letter, consider what I say in letters marked "confidential" as being confidential and consider on what a fearfully delicate thread hangs my peaceful continuance in this chair. Remember also *all* my family have been bitterly opposed to my articles appearing in *The Call* and to my defending the faith in articles in any other paper, after I had written *Modernism and Christian Faith.*

I am awfully sorry to have to write thus, but you see where I would be if such a letter as the enclosed should reach our authorities here.

Cordially yours,

(Faulkner 1925b)

Sloan was not happy with the clandestine nature of his relationship with Faulkner. But he honored his covenant of secrecy with his friend. Though Sloan never betrayed Faulkner's trust, the letter never ceased to aid the spokesman of the conservative cause. During the course of study controversy Sloan passed judgment on certain books that he had not read. He could do this because Faulkner had gone over all the books in the course of study with care and supplied Sloan with extensive notes. Moreover, Faulkner guided Sloan in a study of theology and history. Specifically, Faulkner maintained that certain views could be held about the Second Coming, and he emphasized future judgment. However, he did not consider premillennialism to be an essential doctrine. This conclusion kept the Methodist conservatives free from fanaticism in American fundamentalism. This study and help on the course of study resulted in Sloan's *Historic Christianity and the New Theology*.

It must have been puzzling to Edwin Lewis that Sloan had such an abundance of personal information on or about him. This knowledge came from Faulkner and was used by Sloan in his attacks on Lewis. In a single letter from Sloan to Faulkner, six questions were raised about one of Lewis's books. The strident conflict that raged between Sloan and Lewis for ten years was touched off and continued by material from Faulkner to Sloan. During this time Faulkner and Lewis were considered good friends at Drew. Their families were closely related.

In conclusion, Faulkner's thought and personality inspired the evangelical conservatives. Through Sloan, Faulkner's ideas influenced the entire movement. While these events were unfolding with their clandestine source, another professor at Drew, Edwin Lewis, was undergoing a great struggle for faith. He was gradually coming to accept some of the basic convictions of his attackers. Did Faulkner's ideas live on through Lewis?

Lewis

Edwin Lewis was the cause of both heartaches and rejoicing within the evangelical conservative camp. During the heat of battle in the mid-1920s, Professor Lewis was the main target of the conservative attack. By the early 1930s he was the occasion for conservatives to claim victory.

Tension existed between Lewis and Sloan throughout the 1920s. While Sloan attacked, Lewis ignored his assailant. In spite or because of Sloan, Lewis made a major transformation in his theology. After this change he was completely endorsed by Sloan.

Lewis faced his own involvement in liberalism. He feared that modern theology had diluted the Christian faith, though the new fields of scholarship had made a positive contribution. With stress on the Bible in the words of men, the Word of God was lost. Too much concern with contemporary thought forfeited historic truth. On the whole the plight of the church was traced by Lewis to the vacuum of its dogmatic bases. The word "dogmatic" was used by Lewis in a positive manner. In a reversal of his earlier thought, he claimed that experience was derived from belief. His *A Christian Manifesto* (1934), written in just two months, presented the gospel with complete freedom. It came out of a great burst of deep conviction. Much of it was in finished form from the first draft. The ideas of Lewis climaxed in a profound experience of transformation. He was on fire with a new message.

His manifesto did not fully repudiate liberalism. Rather, the book urged Christendom to go beyond the new theology with the old message of Christ. Modernists made an unnecessary retreat when they were apologetic about the traditional Christian message of salvation. Lewis appealed for Christians to embrace the goodly heritage of scripture. Such a message of the supernatural eliminated naturalism in Lewis's thought.

Christianity as a religion of redemption was revived in Lewis. He viewed sin with quickened seriousness. Sin was not only a deed, but a precondition of man's nature or will. Atonement was possible as a work of grace, not necessity. Lewis complemented atonement with the incarnation. This was quite different from his earlier use of the category of progress to explain the incarnation.

CONCLUSION

The extent to which Lewis's manifesto suggests an insight or element of potential truth in the popular saying that neo-orthodoxy is "fundamentalism in Bermuda shorts" is an open question. There are varied views of neo-orthodoxy. There were many different groups of fundamentalists, and within the contemporary scene knowledge has increased about neo-orthodoxy and fundamentalism. This chapter has been simply an effort to understand and appraise one phase of the fundamentalist and mainly conservative movement.

The conservatives, despite being a small minority, made a considerable impact on the theological development of the Methodist Episcopal church. Although this study concentrated on New Jersey, the influence of conservatives—especially during the 1920s—extended beyond that state. But more important than geographical expansion were the significant movements in which the conservatives were involved.

One of these was the controversy over doctrinal truth versus church unity. Certain incidents during the period 1890–1930 indicated that the conservatives were more willing than the liberals to risk unity for truth. To illustrate, Mitchell was removed from his teaching post because of his liberal theology. His legitimate appeal to the bishops and the General Conference was ignored mainly because the case endangered the church's unity. From an entirely different theological point of view, Sloan's forces sought a change in the course of study. The conservatives were ignored by the General Conference of 1928 for the sake of peace and unity. The major charge leveled at conservatives was that they imperiled the oneness of the church. These two cases involving Mitchell and Sloan show that theological principles were sometimes sacrificed to the principle of unity.

Both Mitchell and Sloan were victorious in the end. Nevertheless, the treatment of Mitchell was probably the most tragic and most vicious or violent (in a subtle way) part of this story of a movement struggling for truth and unity in Methodism.

The major single force for unity in the church was the episcopacy, which held the connectional system together. This power of Episcopal authority, which distinguished Methodists from other denominations, was the obvious factor that mitigated the pressure of fundamentalists. However, other factors distinguished Wesleyan conservatives from Protestant fundamentalists. Though Methodists emphasized a strong doctrine of the inspiration of scripture, they did not accept the belief in a literal and infallible Book. And although Methodists were suspicious of modern scientific presuppositions, they did not reject evolution. Methodists did not endorse premillennialism as other Protestant fundamentalists did. The conservatives of Methodism sought reform within their church rather than participation in inter- or antidenominational fundamentalism. Thus the course of study conflict and the urgency to rediscover Wesley were central.

The main organization of the conservative cause within Methodism was the League for Faith and Life. This institution was an outgrowth of the course of study controversy. Its aim was to foster the true church within the church. It had both lay and clerical members, and its leaders were well educated and deeply dedicated. A small but orderly minority, they formulated clear-cut objectives and made considerable penetration into the thought of the church.

Harold Paul Sloan saw the course of study controversy as of major importance, probably because of his commitment to traditional theology, and he viewed contemporary modernism and naturalism as threats to orthodoxy. His powerful leadership led Methodism in the direction of neo-orthodoxy, Reformation theology following Martin Luther, John Calvin, and John Wesley, culminating in Karl Barth. Yet at the same time, he respected the authority and power of the Methodist episcopacy, which proved to be wise in terms of church politics. Consulting Sloan's letters shows that he apparently failed in 1928, but ultimately succeeded in anticipating the direction of the theological movement in future decades.

The reference to Methodist episcopacy suggests related issues and questions. Did Methodists want a professional ministry, and if so, what kind of professional identity? Would the course of study be adequate to produce satisfactory preparation for professional clergy? It appears doubtful that books alone would do the job. Consequently, there has been tension between clergy produced by the course of study and those who were seminary trained. These questions about the academic requirements for a professional ministry and whether the church is committed to rigorous professionalism are very important and still haunt the Methodist church.

Sloan did not focus on professional ministry, but rather on theology. He was the outstanding leader of the conservatives. His prominence reached its climax in 1936 when he became the editor of the New York *Christian Advocate*. The history of the conservatives was, in a manner of speaking, a biography of Sloan. He advocated a strong adherence to historic Christianity. His relationships with Machen and Riley were cordial, though they had no official connection.

Sloan's leadership would have been much less effective without the support of John Alfred Faulkner. His was the greatest mind in support of the conservative forces. His intellect and personality had a decisive influence on Sloan, though this fact was kept secret for fear that Faulkner might lose his teaching post at Drew. Faulkner was a first-rate scholar who held a peculiar theological position for his day. His chief concern was for classical Christianity, especially as expressed through Athanasius, Luther, and Wesley.

The decisive event for conservatives in Methodism was the 1928 General Conference. Here the bishops upheld peace at all costs. Their control and power through the connectional system were the main factors in subduing controversy. The bishops wielded tremendous authority through superintendents and a strong press. Superintendents held the loyalty of their ministers plus the economic power of the church.

A critical appraisal of the controversy shows that the conservatives of the Methodist Episcopal church had many legitimate and significant concerns. For example, the need for creedal decisiveness within Methodism was rightly asserted. Theological debate was a practical concern for the conservatives. Many in Methodism felt that the church was stagnant. These persons were distressed that their church appeared to be a large body without a spirit of life. For the church to witness, it must know its identity. Conservatives were convinced that this identity had been lost. Their hope for restitution rested in scripture, Reformation, and Wesleyan tradition.

This study has raised some of the significant problems that occupied the conservatives of Methodism. It is the writer's hope that direction has been given for further investigation into the conservative movement of the Methodist church. Further detail and documentation can be found in Hanford (1962) and Lewis (1963).

Note: Materials from the Harold Paul Sloan collection were used with permission from the Methodist Collection at the Drew University Library, Madison, New Jersey.

REFERENCES

Christian Century. (1926). May 20.
Cole, S. G. (1931). *History of Fundamentalism.* New York: R. R. Smith.
Faulkner, J. A. (1921). *Modernism and the Christian Faith.* New York: Methodist Book Concern.
Faulkner, J. A. (1925a). Letter to H. P. Sloan, March 14.
Faulkner, J. A. (1925b). Letter to H. P. Sloan, November 30.
Fletcher, B. (1954). "A Critical Re-evaluation of the Fundamentalist Controversy in the M.E. Church." Unpublished paper, University of Chicago, March, .
Furniss, N. G. (1954/1963). *The Fundamentalist Controversy, 1918–1931.* New Haven, CT: Yale University Press.
Hanford, J. T. (1962). "The Fundamentalist Movement in the Methodist Episcopal church, 1890–1930." Master's thesis, Northwestern University, Evanston, Illinois.
Hofstadter, R. (1962/1963). *Anti-Intellectualism in American Life.* New York: Alfred Knopf.
Journal of the General Conference of the Methodist Episcopal Church. (1920). New York: The Methodist Book Concern.

Lewis, E. (1934). *A Christian Manifesto*. New York: Abingdon.

Lewis, W. B. (1963). "The Role of Harold Paul Sloan and the Methodist League for Faith and Life in the Fundamentalist Modernist Controversy of the Methodist Episcopal Church." *ProQuest Dissertations and Theses*.

Machen, J. G. (1923). *Christianity and Liberalism*. New York: Macmillan.

Marsden, G. (2006). *Fundamentalism and American Culture*. New York: Oxford University Press.

McConnell, F. J. (1924). "The Methodist Church and Fundamentalism." *Homiletic Review*, 94–96.

Mitchell, H. G. (1890). *The Methodist Review* (September): 757.

Mitchell, H. G. (1901). *The World Before Abraham*. Boston; New York: Houghton Mifflin.

Mitchell, H. G. (1922). *For the Benefit of My Creditors*. Boston: Beacon Press.

Moore, R. L. (1986). *Religious Outsiders and the Making of Americans*. New York: Oxford University Press.

Niebuhr, H. R. (1930). "Fundamentalism." In *Encyclopedia of Social Sciences*, edited by E. R. Seligman, 526. New York: Macmillan.

Noll, M. A. (1994). *The Scandal of the Evangelical Mind*. Grand Rapids, MI: Eerdmans.

Norwood, Fredrick A., ed. (1982). *Sourcebook of American Methodism*. Nashville, TN: Abingdon.

Sloan, H. P. (1942). *He Is Risen*. New York: Abingdon.

Sloan, H. P. (1958). *Historic Christianity and the New Theology*. Kentucky: Herald Press.

Sloan, H. P. (1960–1962). Letters to author.

CHAPTER 15

DOUG HALL ON THE DEATH OF THE IMPERIAL CHURCH

J. Harold Ellens

INTRODUCTION

Doug Hall has written many popular and professional books on the Christian faith. In *The End of Christendom and the Future of Christianity* (1997) he proposes a profoundly revolutionary program for the survival of Christianity in the twenty-first century and the long future beyond. He is professor emeritus of Christian theology at McGill University of Montreal and is referred to frequently as the most widely read Christian theologian of our time. He bases his proposal on the claim that the Jesus movement described in the Bible was badly betrayed by the action of Constantine 300 years after Jesus's life. He made Christianity the official religion of the Roman Empire and invested both the political and spiritual power of Rome in the hierarchy of the church's bishops.

Of course most of us are aware that he did more than that. He shifted the course of Christendom away from its roots in the life and ministry of Jesus and in the documents that were to become the New Testament. He ordered the bishops to identify the source of authority for Christian faith, namely, an official canon of sacred scripture. He also required them to draw up a set of doctrinal statements to which all Christians should be required to adhere or be declared heretics and be exterminated (Drake 2000). The bishops therefore produced the Apostles' Creed, the Nicene Creed, the Athanasian Creed, and a number of other such summaries of dogma. Finally, Constantine required a unified political system for the empire and the church in which the metropolitans and archbishops of the official church enforced both spiritual and secular authority.

THE IMPERIAL CHURCH

Thus was born what Doug Hall calls the "Imperial Church," which held forth with vigor on both the ecclesiastical and political fronts from the early fourth century CE until the modern era. The mighty medieval Roman Catholic Church was the epitome of the imperial ecclesiastical model. Hall claims that the rise of the Enlightenment in the Western world in the eighteenth century killed that Imperial Church, and the only people who have not caught on to that revolutionary fact during the last three centuries have been the ecclesiastical survivors who are playing church in the ruins of dying Christendom.

Hall believes that the Christian movement can have a significant future that will be faithful to the original vision and impulse of the Jesus movement described in the New Testament. He thinks the church can be of immense service to our beleaguered world, but to have that revolutionary future Christians will have to stop trying to have the kind of future that sixteen centuries of official Christianity in the Western world have conditioned them to expect. Hall asserts that the Christian movement must recover in the twenty-first century the revolutionary character of the "witnessing" church of the first and second centuries CE. He sees that as differing widely from the Imperial Church, which became the power broker of the Roman Empire and persisted after the empire's demise as an institution of power and glory, developing from the persecuted church of the first three centuries into the role of the oppressive church of the Middle Ages and the authority-brokering church in Western culture ever since.

THE MODERN CRISIS

Hall launched his argument with the observation that modern culture and Christian mission are in crisis today. Although they are often considered antagonists, they are in large part responsible for each other's current perplexities. The modern mission movement, which achieved prominence in the nineteenth century, and the contemporaneous rise of the technological revolution, operated from those beginnings forward in a symbiotic relationship. A century and a half later, both the viability of the Christian traditions and general confidence in technology face an uncertain postmodern future. The role of religion in Western culture has been redefined. In the world of Christendom and the Imperial Church, religion played the authoritative role. Modern culture, with its empirical science orientation, severely criticized and devalued the authority of religious claims and values, sliding increasingly into secularism in its assumptions and ideals. Religion has been under siege to "banish it to the backwaters of our present culture" (Hall 1997, vii).

Religion continues to function in our postmodern era as the twenty-first century gains increasing sociopolitical and cultural momentum, but religious worldviews are still under aggressive siege by the secularization of our values and ideals. Technology is emerging as the new source of power and authority. The worldview of secular technology stands in contrast and confrontation to Christian faith and outlook. Hall proposes that nothing short of a revolution in the church that will produce a revolution in secular society will give the Christian faith a usable future.

Christianity is changing all over the world. That is true at the macrocosm level, in the comparison of Christian traditions to the current prominence of other religious traditions in the East and West. These other traditions are now successfully competing with the Christian faith. It is also true at the microcosm level of local denominations and regional judicatories and parishes. Church members and other members of society are increasingly moving toward a religionless Christianity, declaring that they are spiritual but not religious. Christendom is in relatively chaotic ferment everywhere in the world. The medieval preoccupation with questions of Christian philosophy and the Reformation's focus on lethal doctrinal conflict have both dissipated. In their place has arisen, on the one hand, the syndrome of pooled ignorance characterizing the burgeoning community of those who confess to being "spiritual but not religious." On the other hand, we now have the rationalistic literalism of Christian fundamentalist evangelicalism, which is bearing fruit in the independent mega-church movements.

THE STRATEGY OF EVANGELICAL FUNDAMENTALISM

Fundamentalism is inherently a psychological posture, not a theological or religious perspective. It can manifest its literalist rigidity in any philosophy, worldview, or profession. However, in response to the positivist empiricism of the Enlightenment, a religious form of this psychological disposition arose as American religious fundamentalism. It attempted to establish a set of authoritative assumptions, such as the verbal inspiration and inerrancy of the biblical text, and from it drew a system of rationalistic deductions that, under the tutelage of Carl F. H. Henry, Harold Ockenga, Charles E. Fuller, and others, came to form this new religion. It was rapidly exported to every continent on the planet during the nineteenth and twentieth centuries.

That struggle was and is merely the dying gasps and terminal energy surges of the dying Imperial Church and authoritative Christendom. "What is happening is nothing less than the winding down of a process that was inaugurated in the fourth century.... To the great shift that began to occur in the character of the Christian movement under the Roman emperors Constantine and Theodosius I, there now corresponds a shift of reverse proportions. . . . The Imperial Church now comes to an end. That beginning and this ending are the two great social transitions in the course of Christianity in the world" (Hall 1997, 1). Semblances of the Imperial Church may persist for a while in Africa, Asia, and Latin America, but the age of the dominant authoritative church is ending in the Western world.

A NEW POSSIBILITY

Christianity was once a great power in the world, and the Imperial Church can still be seen here and there, but the forms and institutions of this faith tradition are changing rapidly, as are those of all other major religions. Christianity has become a peripheral voice everywhere in the world. This positions the church and its worldwide movement in a potentially revolutionary stance if the community of believers recognizes its radically changed status. Its voice may shift from that of power and authority to the tones and tenor of prophetic expression. "From the edges of imperial societies, a disciple community possessing awareness of its changed relation to power can exercise a prophetic vigilance for God's beloved world that, as part of the world's power-elite, it never did and never could achieve" (Hall 1997, 2).

This would require a departure from the church's historic posture as a powerful force standing against the forces of power in societies and cultures worldwide. Failing to shift into the prophetic stance, the churches will "forfeit the opportunities for truth telling and justice that historical providence is affording them" (Hall 1997, 2). The Constantinian posture must be abandoned. The pronouncements of the World Council of Churches and their national counterparts still speak as though they are power centers of society, although such official utterances seem to have no consequences on the national or international systems. Those headquarters seem to be the only entities that do not realize that no one is hearing them any longer or listening to their message.

While the official church officiously assumes the right to speak to the authentic sources and centers of power, the latter are no longer listening to the church for wisdom or guidance. Its frame of reference appears to lack awareness of the real-world situation. Its proposals seem naive and trivial. The church appears unable to raise the essential questions, and its rationale for its claims and answers lacks sufficient suasion because of a paucity of theological cogency. Everyone seems to have caught on to the irrelevance of the historic institutional church except the church institutions themselves. "Presumption upon the past power and glory of Christendom is perhaps the greatest deterrent to faith's real confession in our present historical context" (Hall 1997, 3).

In Eastern Europe under Marxist regimes, Imperial Christianity was precipitously closed down or, as in the case of the Russian Orthodox church, coerced and co-opted into complicity with the government and essentially secularized. Such a sudden repression by an alien force prompted a certain persistent vitality in the believing community but eliminated the functional Constantinian institutional church. Now that the official oppression has been lifted in those former Soviet regions, it is interesting to note that the Orthodox churches are moving again into the service of the new regimes, particularly in Russia, and resuming the imperial posture. It remains to be seen if this will eventually lead to the suppression of the free churches in Russia, Byelorussia, Georgia, and similar locales.

In North America those churches that continue to function as Constantinian-type institutions are declining in membership and institutional prowess at an alarming rate. Only the free churches, operating as innovative witnessing communities, are flourishing. Because the latter tend also to be theologically rather conservative communities, it remains to be seen how much their theology is the driving force, and how much their prosperity is due to the shift away from a power stance to a prophetic posture.

However that may be, it is becoming increasingly clear that Christendom is passing through a watershed that will lead to a form of Christianity not recognizable today. This process of change has been moving forward for the last three centuries. "Whereas eighteenth-century rationalism was ameliorated by evangelical pietism—and nineteenth-century 'pagan' romanticism by the Christian romanticism of Schleiermacher, the Oxford Movement, and other groups—the process of secularization was well under way, and, despite religious revivals of various types, it has continued to be so" (Hall 1997, 4).

ALTERNATE VISIONS

Christians have generally cherished the expectation that the church as institution stood as a symbol of the certainty and blessedness of its members' access to the eternal world. This expectation was too often vested in the institution as symbol rather than in the believing community as a spiritual wellspring. The resistance to the demise of Christendom and the failure of the church to readily acknowledge its current crisis may lie mainly in that fact and in the vacuous unknown that believers face if they accept the end of the Imperial Church.

However, there have always been alternative visions in the history of Imperial Christendom. Kierkegaard's depressingly negative critique of historic Christianity in the nineteenth century, and the triumphalist idealization of this faith tradition in the early twentieth century (Jones, Latourette, and Mackay 1934; Griffith-Jones 1926), both seem to be rather wild-eyed exaggerations, as we look at the status of things Christian from the perspective of the twenty-first century, with the secular siege currently besetting Christendom in the West and the strident Muslim attack upon it and aggression against it in Africa.

Hall remarks that the triumphalistic other-worldliness of orthodox Christianity and evangelical fundamentalism, on the one hand, and of the this-worldly vision of the progress of the faith held by the liberal version on the other, were both quite obviously utopian (1997, 16) and out of touch with reality down on the ground in human lives. The former has continued to look for the apocalyptic denoument of history in some kind of second coming of the Messiah and a cataclysmic final judgment that will end history and favor the orthodox believers. This is especially epitomized in the ridiculous vision of Christian Zionism.

The liberal version of the Christian future envisioned that the modern world was becoming the pervasively Christianized new world order, in which "Man should at last rise to the fulfillment of his Providential function, and join his energies with the mighty power and wisdom of God, in loving obedience and joyful service. On the sunlit hills of time—the City of God, the Commonwealth of the Redeemed!" (Hall 1997, 16). Griffith-Jones (1926) envisioned the day when the entire world would be under the thrall of Christendom and the church's only task that of evangelizing the youth of each new generation to prevent the forces of evil from poisoning this virgin soil of the new humanity. Thus each generation can develop its knowledge of the Lord from the outset and spread its burgeoning spirituality into the fullness, fruit, and power of authentic Christian faith (Hall 1997, 15). The view of E. S. Jones and his colleagues (1934) was an arrogant and insensitive one from the ivory tower of the power and prosperity of the privileged clergy.

Karl Barth and Reinhold Niebuhr in the first half of the twentieth century, and more recently such theologians as Langdon Gilkey, Hans Kung, and Hendrikus Berkhof, looked at things very differently. Niebuhr was a thoughtful pastor in Detroit during the heyday of Henry Ford's labor policies and the rise of the trade unions. Only later did he become a professor at Union Theological Seminary. Langdon Gilkey honed the perspective of his ministry in a Chinese prisoner of war camp during World War II and came into his mature theological stride in the culture of conflict in Chicago. Hans Kung was forbidden to teach in the official institutions of the Roman Catholic Church because he spoke truth to ecclesiastical power that destabilized the illegitimate hegemony of the hierarchy in that community of faith. Hendrikus Berkhof hammered out his worldview in the radical secularizing process of post–World War II Europe and the particularly reprehensible loss of historic values in The Netherlands.

These theologians saw life from the urban streets of our world, not from the pinnacles of power. Consequently, they saw Christianity as a largely failed system. They realized that this faith tradition had accomplished good things here and there in the tragedy of human affairs, promoting orphanages, hospitals, educational institutions, local communities of faith and good will, and charity projects of some significance throughout its history. However, it hardly made a dent in the travail of the human beings down on the ground, suffering from neglect, insensitivity, trivialization, exploitation, and jeopardy to life and limb everywhere in our world.

Moreover, Christianity has a horrid record of abuse of women and children by priests, bishops, popes, clergymen, and patriarchal policies from its beginning to the modern-day pervasive pedophilia scandals in Catholic dioceses worldwide. This record is perhaps equaled only by the trivialization and exploitation of unempowered men throughout the ages as well. Moreover, these scandals are not new and modern tragedies. This pattern has been the criminal character of many persons of power in Christian communities for twenty centuries. Berkhof declares that, "To a great extent official church history is the story of the *defeats* of the Holy Spirit" (1979, 422, quoted in Hall 1997, 18).

Hall observes that Berkhof expresses a new realism that most thoughtful Christians share today:

> Many influences have brought about this historiographic change: the decline of Christianity in the West; the decline of the West itself; the failure of the modern vision; the new consciousness of their own worth on the part of the non-European peoples; a critical perception of the technological society on the part of many who have experienced its most advanced forms; the impact of religious and cultural pluralism, especially perhaps in North America; and (not least of all) the self-criticism of serious Christianity, its recognition of its own questionable triumphalism, of patriarchalism, of the equation of the Christian mission with Euro-American imperialism, and so forth. (1997, 18)

It is hardly a consolation that all other religious traditions have performed even more poorly in all regards. Religion has not significantly healed the world over time, except in the simple consolations it has afforded those rare, thoughtful people who have sensed in its symbols and signals the presence of the Divine Spirit here and there, and have downloaded that experience into their personal quests for authentic inner spirituality.

The net result of this state of affairs seems to be that most churches with historic traditions are trying to carry on as they did in their imperial age, but they are everywhere failing and depressed, struggling financially, losing members, pumping up failing projects intended to sustain the life of the church, cutting programs, and settling with decreasing quality in leadership because the first- and second-class brains are going into other professions than the historic three ideals of ministry, medicine, and law. The only exceptions are the innovative mega-churches, whose style is existential and pragmatic rather than idealistic and historic. There is no evidence that these, however, are more than a temporary whim, the dying gasp of a terminal movement. Most mega-churches seem to hit a membership level of about 5,000, with church attendance of 2,000, annual intake of members of 1,500, and annual exit of members of 1,500. These statistics seem to be consistent across the board, with few exceptions, in which the numbers are somewhat higher or somewhat lower, but the pattern is the same.

Increasingly what was formerly the Christian community is sliding into a society with the new confession, "I am not religious any more, but I am spiritual." Is the prophecy of an impending religion-less spirituality coming true? Is that the cult of the twenty-first century? Can that ever become a more profoundly informed quest than a pooling of mutual ignorance, detached from both the main questions and any knowledge of the past struggle for meaningful answers?

Moreover, the foreign cultures and world religions are no longer far from us, anonymous caricatures in distant lands. They are now our neighbors, significant segments of our cultures, opening their minds to understand Western religions and society and requiring that we see and understand them for who they really are. This stimulating pluralism is reinforcing the shift from historic cherished dogma to openness to the common elements of spirituality in all spiritual quests. This makes it seem easier and more imperative to most young people that they take a more open-minded approach toward spirituality than was customary in traditional religious communities of previous generations, most certainly than in the age of the Imperial Church.

Consequently the church's sense of mission is remarkably confused. Mainline churches, with their history of liberal theology and triumphalist ideology, have shifted from evangelizing unbelievers to projects of social justice and interfaith dialogue. It will soon be difficult to discern the difference between this style and mission of the church and that of the YMCA or many charitable fraternal organizations in our society. Hall declares persuasively: "The liberal temperament today can endorse foreign aid and global service, but not foreign missions and global evangelism; for the latter seems inseparable from the white Western imperialism that liberal Christians, among others, have learned to regret and suspect. . . . If it is not the vocation of Christians to convert everyone to Christian faith, to expand the church's sphere of influence and its territory, and so to grow and prosper in every way as the doorway to the divine Kingdom, then what is our vocation, and what sort of future can we expect and work for" (1997, 23).

What are churches for? Perhaps what was important was never the grand things of church politics and power. Is the church about fellowship, mutual consolations in the tragic adventure of life, worshipful times of meditation, contemplation, reflection, and personal prayer? Perhaps it is about that and telling each other the stories of life experience, the narratives of those moments when it is clear in our experience that we have encountered the illumining Divine Spirit that provides humans life-changing episodes of Aha! What if that is all the church was supposed to be about from the beginning: the simple, quiet process of recognizing and witnessing to each other about the way the Divine Spirit is moving and shaking in shaping life and history? If that is the mission and destiny of the authentic church, we will have to keep our eyes open for how the Divine Spirit shows up around the next corner, leading out the future. We will need to shift from our perpetually frenetic preoccupation with the projects of *Churchianity*. What a surprising new way of life that would be, personally and communally!

Hall believes that if we want "to preserve the faith and not just some of its moral and aesthetic spin-off," we need to articulate clearly and confidently our essential "beliefs and the manner in which these beliefs, when taken seriously" set us off from the values and pursuits of our secular Western society (1997, 32). The Christian community has been marginalized—"disestablished." Hall suggests that we take a page from the Anabaptist branch of the Protestant Reformation and see if we can find a way to disestablish ourselves so that we can move from the Imperial Church model, which has failed, to a prophetic church model of a witnessing community, as was the case in the minority and often persecuted church before it became the oppressing church of imperial power under Constantine.

THE ROAD TO A USABLE FUTURE

I recall that my father spoke frequently of this issue without realizing what a whale of a fish he had by the tail. It was his opinion that the church's main focus needed to be on the cultivation of members of congregations who were well informed theologically, lived out their theology as a consolation and hope and not as a weapon of power to coerce others' faith perspective, and thus were persons of character and Christian personality styles in society. He was sure that in this way the Christian community is called to be a salt that gives wholesome flavor to the tragic adventure of life, a yeast that empowers the loaf of human society to become a nurturing community, and a light on a hill signaling the high ground of human idealism and quality. I think he did not know how revolutionary and how urgently necessary was his perspective, as Doug Hall asserts (1997, 36).

Such a perspective is a positive disestablishing alternative to despair over the death of the Imperial Church. Hall believes, as do I, that despair is inappropriate and unnecessary. "Christians today can prepare themselves to see precisely in our disestablishment, not an impersonal and inglorious destiny such as may be the fate of any institution, but the will and providence of God . . . God is at work in history . . . the divine Spirit creates, recreates, judges, and renews the 'body of Christ'. . . . The hand of God is in it! . . . We are stewards of the mysteries of God" (1997, 41). John Calvin's enjoinder of *Reformans Reformanda*, "reformed and always reforming," defines the church as a community of believers that is always in the process of disestablishing its routines and traditional roles and creating new modes of being and functioning in society that are demanded by each new age of cultural evolution. This current era of the church's decline and transition is potentially a gift that awakens us and compels us to find the new modes for faith-filled folk in the new posture of society.

Conscious and intentional disestablishment of ourselves as the church means disengagement from the historic structures and styles of the Imperial Church and the cultural norms with which it conformed, such as Calvinistic Capitalism and engagement with our social order as a leaven, salt, and light. We might call this mode and model of being the believing community by the name of witnessing church, existentially being the believing community in the context of the general society and its dominant secular culture.

The difficulty in expecting this to become a reality lies mainly in the fact that members of the churches today do not know what they believe or do not understand the fundamental issues and questions of Christian faith. How can they know and critique the intellectually and spiritually demanding answers that have been hammered out for good or ill over the centuries of evolving Christian tradition? How can they be a salt, leaven, and light in society? "Profoundly altered moral attitudes and specific ethical decisions are consequences of the hearing of the gospel. When they are presented as if they were immediately accessible to everyone as categorical imperative, so to speak, gospel and law are being confused" (Hall 1997, 47).

It must, therefore be clear that the community of believers must return to profound theological inquiry. This will demand more thoroughly educated and biblically informed clergy than we have now, because first-line brains have not sought out the vocation of ministry since the 1970s in North America. The church will need a new surge of superior quality persons inspired to a divine calling. Only then can we expect to develop an informed community of believers equipped to be an existential Christian presence in the world at all levels of society's operation. Moreover, this requires inspired, superior leadership:

> If a revived public church is indeed on the horizon, moderate Protestantism will play a key role in bringing it into being. This will require forms and qualities of leadership that have seldom been forthcoming from the protestant middle, a revitalized ecumenicity and new, bold theological affirmation are critical . . . , especially a theology that resonates with and gives meaning to the experience of middle America. (Roof and McKinney 1987, 243, quoted in Hall 1997, 48)

Hall introduces his final chapter with the observation that the present state of the church is an opportunity for the renewed authenticity of the Christian believing community, in keeping with the disciple community of the Jesus movement in the first through the third centuries. It involves disengaging from our cultural structures as an official or dominant religion and reengaging our society at the level of truth, justice, and love.

THE REVOLUTIONARY CHURCH OF THE FUTURE

"If at the level of fundamental belief and lifestyle we disengage ourselves, as a Christian movement, from the dominant societies, classes, and institutions we have been for centuries trying to court, we may be able to serve those societies, classes, and institutions in ways far more faithful and more humanly needful than Christendom usually did" (Hall 1997, 51–52). Contrary to the model of the Imperial Church, particularly in the ancient world and the Middle Ages, the church is not the society, and the society is not the church. Each has its own modes, models, passions, and purposes. Each has its own objectives and responsibilities, values, and goals. For centuries the symbiosis between the two has blurred the identity of both. As the society became more secular under the influences of the Enlightenment and the scientific revolution, the identity of the church became less clear. The dominance of the general culture's values and influence increased. Only when the church, in its values and goals, achieves sufficient distance from the sociopolitical culture will it be able to realize its authentic identity. Only from such an independent stance will we be able to engage the society as a leaven, salt, and illumining energy. Only then will the church provide its own constituency and society with the voice of authentic theology, not as the fashionable or traditional crowd demands it, but as the clarion call of the essentials of the gospel of radical, unconditional, and universal grace for both the nice and nasty people of the world.

What Would That Revolutionary Stance Look Like?

Hall believes that this would require the church to express existentially the posture of moral authenticity, meaningful community, embrace of transcendence and mystery, and sturdy and earnest quest for meaning. In our moment in time, none of us needs much persuasion to be convinced of the utter immorality we encounter in the church as well as throughout society. The social revolution of the 1960s and 1970s has produced a world in which the guardrails are blown away, the lighthouses of ideals and values have been torn down, and the notion of a focused and worthy objective for life that transcends personal narcissism and greed has lost its meaning. The language of such an ideal focus is no longer comprehended. Moral chaos at the level of generalized life-endangering individualism is epidemic in the drug culture, AIDS, and other consequences. Can the church distance itself from that cultural flow, recover its distinctive moral compass, and be existentially present to such a society as a leaven, light, and savory salt (Lasch)? Lasch views the future church with the suggestive passion of a parent and the teasing compassion of a shepherd.

The church as meaningful community would be an existential illustration of the degree to which the narcissistic individualism in contemporary society is limited in its function and productivity for individuals and the community and rather quickly becomes counterproductive and therefore dysfunctional for both. In such a stance both church and society would hear again the echoes of that tough guy from Nazareth. Meaningful connection with other humans in this tragic adventure of life leads inevitably to closer connection with other creatures and with the majesty and mystery of the material and moral universes. This sense of mystery leads to an openness to the transcendent.

Can our *society* hear again the five reasons to believe in God: 1) the mindfulness of creation, 2) the benevolence of persistent providence that turns our pain into growth, 3) the universal urge in all things toward beauty, 4) the incredible way the notion of unconditional grace fits our deepest need, and 5) the continuing incarnation of the divine in illumined and illumining humans and in the universal human experiences of paranormal illuminations—moments of the Divine Spirit? Can the *human community* take seriously, in a fresh way, the mystery of the dynamic presence of the all-pervasive Divine Spirit as a force to be dealt with in everyday human experience? Can the *believing community* become a leaven and a light, reflecting those facts of life in its way of living the gospel? How utterly meaningful that could be for church and society. It could be life-saving for our society to rediscover in the life of the believing community the mysterious and the transcendent. It might even be interesting. Even compelling?

What kind of model of such a usable future for the Christian religion can we realistically derive from Hall's challenging perspective? Obviously it will be a revolutionary model. As suggested in the previous section, one can only imagine that it might not be revolutionary only for the shape of the church. It might possibly have a change-inducing influence in its interface with society wherever it is an interesting, wholesome presence, as well. What kinds of style would generate forms of Christianity that are authentic, meaningful, and constructive of genuine human community?

To be more specific, in what operational ways can the church as institution and the believing community as vital organism live out in daily life the new mode of being Christian? How can these two manifestations of Christianity be independent of societal values, styles, goals, methods, and objectives, yet be a constructive presence to the human societal organism? How can we be in the world but not of the world, as Jesus enjoined us to be?

Although that is a complex and somewhat mysterious question, it seems to me that at least the following can and must be said. First, for the Christian movement to express its own identity and inherent nature with any kind of authenticity, it must have the shape of a community that is focused in worship, the kind of worship that provides the meditation and illumination in which profound personal spirituality can be cultivated. I envision such meditation as the life of prayer in prose, poetry, and hymns. Surely it can be both deeply personal and gratifyingly communal.

It seems to me that the illumination worship can provide is to be found in the celebration of the historic spiritual modes and memories of the past, instruction in the ancient questions together with a struggle for honest contemporary answers, and scriptural exposition that reveals again the genius of the Jesus movement and of what Paul saw in it and made of it. None of that memory, history, or tradition should be resurrected dogmatically, but all of it should be the context and content of the preachers' proclamation. We need to know what in all of that worked, why it worked, and in what context it was constructive. We need to know what in the church's history and tradition did not work, why it was dysfunctional or pathological, and in what context it went wrong.

In any case, the authentic life of the Christian movement begins and ends in worship. Moreover, if that is all that it can achieve, that may well be enough. The church as consistently celebrative local communities of worship will ensure three essential things: 1) intensely informed and thoughtful members, 2) grace-filled member care for those within the worshipping community who have special challenges, and 3) a profound level of conscious and intentionally cultivated personal spirituality. Such a mode of life for the church will manifest the potential for humans, individually and in community, to experience life as joyful, peaceful, hopeful, and secure. This would show up readily as a remarkable, even desirable alternative to the frenetic, scattered, distracting, and distracted triviality of much of the life of our society.

In such a mode and model the church will be a different kind of existence, a different way of being, in which life will seem much more meaningful than that outside this unique community. Just being that kind of existential process of human life may adequately accomplish the entire mission of the church to be an inviting redemptive presence in our world today. That may be all the church can ever do constructively in society, all it could ever do constructively, and all it ever needs or needed to do. The presence of such a hopeful and wholesome community of free association will be the incarnate presence of the Divine Spirit in our world, in which society can see the face of God and healing godliness, if it cares to look.

A second thing that can and must be said is this. The witnessing and often persecuted church of the first three centuries was a mission movement that attracted many adherents spontaneously. Mission was not a project of the church. By the end of the apostolic age (120 CE) there were three million Christians in the Mediterranean Basin. By the time Constantine appeared on the scene (300 CE), there were ten million. The Romans were reported to have said, "Take notice of how the Christians love one another!" That seemed to have made the difference.

When Constantine made the church the queen of the Roman Empire, establishing the Imperial Church, everything in the church's life seems to have become a project. The bishops had the project of deciding what documents constituted authoritative scripture. They had the project of defining the content of the faith in the form of dogma and creeds. That gave them the project of ensuring that every member conformed to the creeds in faith and life. Out of that came the project of heresy hunting, which turned the church from a witnessing church into an oppressing and persecuting church. Nonconformists and free-thinking believers, most of whom were more correctly authentic to the essence of Christianity, were literally exterminated. Finally, shaping the government and authority structure of the church was a project designed to keep the empire orderly and to enforce conformity to the prescriptions of the bishops for the correct mode of faith and life.

Throughout the history of the Christian movement, even in the churches that arose from the Protestant revolution of the sixteenth century, the church's sense of its mission as a project forced it into an officious institution with the form of project Christianity. Such modes of thought and consciousness led inevitably to the church conceiving of itself superficially as a mere institution, preoccupied with material objectives of budgeting, funding, programming, managing, and planning for long-term goals and objectives. They moved the church into a kind of corporate mode.

The corporate mode drew the enterprise of the church into a business of the head and away from the heart. Christianity became an intellectualized enterprise of ideas, doctrines, mission policies, and sociocultural projects. Its teaching programs were increasingly designed to service this mechanistic corporate perspective. This led to political and social action projects, worthy in themselves, but not springing from profound spiritual motivation or informed theological imperative. The church lost its ability to simply *be* a worshipping community, as it became an institution whose identity shifted from *being* to *doing*. Its goals and achievements, hence its sense of self in the world, became trivialized as its programs shifted it from the quest for the personal spiritual and the transcendent divine. It lost its essence as Christian religion and its authentic spirituality.

Two-thirds of the church's members consequently noticed that it was difficult to tell the difference between the church and the YMCA or other charitable and fraternal organizations, so they left in droves from 1960 onward, declaring that they were spiritual but not religious. The religious institutions were not addressing their spiritual hunger. Those churches that were focused simply on meaningful worship and member care retained their membership, grew, and sustained a wholesome vitality.

This distraction, away from the hungry human hearts and away from the heart of the church's essence, away from faith and spirituality, produced *Project Churchianity* and failed as a model of being Christian in the world. Hall referred to the "Fellowship Model of the Church" (1997, 23ff) and pointed out its limitations, but in that context he asked the key question: What is our vocation as Christians and Christian community? I think the revolutionary answer is that the essence of the church being the church, of the Christian community being true to its own nature, and of a Christian being a Christian, lies in our being worshipful persons for whom our primary interest is the quest for our palpable experience of the presence of the Divine Spirit in our personal lives.

Community derived from that mode of life will rather automatically take on a wholesome and healthily disciplined focus that will readily manifest itself as ideal in our society. Such Christians will carry out on their own the social and political tasks that ring true to being Christian. The church does not need to program them as projects of *Churchianity* that distract the worshipping community from its main focus.

It was the loss of essential quality that led to the loss of quantity in the mainline churches over the last half century in North America and over the last three centuries elsewhere. A Christian who is not engaged with the needs of society in his or her personal life is not taking seriously the implications of his or her own deep spirituality. Likewise, a church whose preoccupation with sociopolitical projects that are not an automatic overflowing of its profound experiences of worshipful spirituality is trivialized and empty in its engagement with the needs of society.

CONCLUSION

Jesus's entire point, as depicted in Paul's Epistles and John's Gospel, the presentation of Jesus by the first and last New Testament writers, was to revitalize personal spirituality and an intimate sense of the presence of God in human lives. He was rather indifferent to just how that affected the social projects of the world, though he healed the sick and raised the dead. He had no special focus on the unempowered, nor on the powerful. He acted as though the spiritual problem of both categories was the same. He could be cavalier about the poor, as when he said, "You always have the poor with you," implying that one could always tend to them when there was time, but he emphasized that personal spirituality has a much higher priority. He often exploited the needy to make a political or theological point, as when he healed the blind man in John 9, a healing that had horrendous consequences for that man but was a strong theological score for Jesus against the legalistic Nomism of the Pharisees. This same effect can be seen in Jesus's encounter with the Syrophoenician woman.

Jesus seems to have been pressing the point that Israel needed to return to the unconditional, universal nature of God's radical grace as articulated in the arbitrary covenant promise to Abraham. He contended that this kind of renewal meant setting aside the Mosaic law and its covenant, or at least reinterpreting it, and returning to the Abrahamic Judaism of Micah 7:18–20. Paul apparently caught this genius in Jesus's perspective and elaborated it theologically in terms of the radical, uncalculating, and universal grace that it asserts, debunking Mosaic law, despite the fact that he was educated as a Pharisee (Rom. 8). Paul is not focused on social action. He lives in the social structure of his day and witnesses to it about spiritual renewal in that context. He does not oppose slavery, but insists on its being "humane." He almost never mentions the poor and needy, heals no sick persons, and takes a collection for the suffering persons in Jerusalem to demonstrate that Gentile Christianity is working better than James's Jerusalem church.

The focus of the Jesus movement, evident in Jesus, Paul, and John, was on personal and communal spiritual renewal from the inside out. The purpose of missions was to witness to the resurrection as evidence of God's presence in this world, fostering that kind of transcendent change within human nature. Their claim was that such experience was possible because of the evident presence of the Divine Spirit as the matrix of personal existence in this world. Paul spoke of it as living eternal life in the here and now, that is, living on that eternal transcendent plain on which God lives or the Divine

Spirit functions fully: human spirits attuned to the presence of that spirit within.

This contrasts with the nineteenth- and early twentieth-century church's projects of missions, which, however well intended as inspiration to spiritual renewal, tended to impose Western cultural values, ethics, and style upon societies that were viewed as inherently inferior, primitive, or heathen. From that came the social gospel movements that, however fruitful and productive of psycho-social and intellectual good, issued forth into the forms of project *Churchianity*, eclipsing the focus on worshipful spiritual vitality.

I was involved, albeit peripherally, with the National Council of Churches in New York and the World Council of Churches in Geneva during the 1970s and 1980s. I found it difficult to discern that the work, staff, and vision of those bodies reflected in any way the promotion of Christian spirituality. The focus on projects by the institutional church led to fashioning organizational structures to support the projects, which fostered the necessary power processes for managing the organizations. From that came a formulation of political goals, leading inevitably to external orientation rather than interior spirituality. That posture prompted a distancing from internal issues of growth and development of persons and communities and a decreasing focus on personal spirituality, accompanied by an increase in financial pressure on congregants to support the increasingly irrelevant church as institution.

The outcome was a decline in worship, a decrease in need for or interest in the church as a living organism of spiritual communion, discernment, and celebration. It did not take the laity long to recognize that this was a trivializing of their lives and more costly than the YMCA. Membership nose-dived, as well it should have.

Christianity is not a command to be obeyed. It is not a burden to be labored under or an obligation to be met. Authentic Christianity, hence the authentic life of the church, is an opportunity to be sought out and an invitation to be seized and celebrated. The Imperial Church has been busy for seventeen centuries making it more than that, indeed, making it something very different from that, and thus its project is no longer interesting; to many it no longer makes sense. The church as simple worshipping presence in the world, creating wholesome community for its members as a witness in our world regarding how life may be lived redemptively, might just work as the revolutionary new way for the church! The spirit-inspiring aesthetic of worship and sacred song, combined with engaging instructional oratory, is in itself the heart and soul of the true life of the church. Where that life is authentically and imaginatively present, Christian members will be busy with the work of the reign of God in the world: doing justice, loving to be merciful, and walking humbly in the Divine Spirit. That may give us a long, usable future: subtle, resilient, but significant and operationally relevant in our chaotic world.

REFERENCES

Barth, Karl. (1992). "Theologian of Freedom." In *The Making of Modern Theology*, Minneapolis, MN: Fortress Press

Berkhof, Hendrikus. (1979). *Christian Faith: An Introduction to the Study of the Faith.* Translated by Sierd Woudstra. Grand Rapids, MI: Eerdmans.

Berkhof, Hendrikus. (1989). *Two Hundred Years of Theology: A Report of a Personal Journey.* Translated by John Vriend. Grand Rapids, MI: Eerdmans.

Drake, H. A. (2000). *Constantine and the Bishops: The Politics of Intolerance.* Baltimore; London: Johns Hopkins University Press.

Gilkey, Langdon. (1970). *Naming the Whirlwind: A Renewal of God Language.* Indianapolis, IN: Bobbs Merrill.

Gilkey, Langdon. (1976). *Reaping the Whirlwind: A Christian Interpretation of History.* Eugene, OR: Wipf and Stock Publishers.

Gilkey, Langdon. (1991). *Through the Tempest.* Minneapolis, MN: Fortress.

Griffith-Jones, E. (1926). *The Dominion of Man,* London: Hodder and Stoughton.

Hall, Douglas John. (1997). *The End of Christendom and the Future of Christianity.* Harrisburg, PA: Trinity Press International.

Jones, E. Stanley, Kenneth Scott Latourette, and John A. Mackay. (1934). *The Christian Message for Today.* New York: Round Table Press.

Kierkegaard, Søren. (1854–1855/1968). *Attack Upon Christendom.* English ed. Translated by Walter Lowrie. Princeton, NJ: Princeton University Press.

Kung, Hans. (1986). *The Freedom of Religions, in Attitudes Towards Other Religions.* Lanham, MD: University Press of America.

Kung, Hans. (1988). *Theology for the Third Millennium.* Translated by Peter Heinegg. New York: Doubleday Anchor Books.

Kung, Hans. (2003). *The Catholic Church: A Short History.* New York: Modern Library.

Kung, Hans. (2005). *Why I Am Still a Christian.* Edinburgh; London; New York: T&T Clark.

Lasch, Christopher. (1983). *The Culture of Narcissism.* New York: Warner Books.

Lasch, Christopher. (1991). *The True and Only Heaven: Progress and Its Critics.* New York; London: W. W. Norton.

Niebuhr, Reinhold. (2002). *Moral Man and Immoral Society: A Study in Ethics and Politics.* Library of Theological Ethics. Louisville, KY: Presbyterian Publishing Corporation.

Niebuhr, Reinhold. (2008). *The Irony of History.* Chicago: Chicago University Press.

Roof, Wade Clark, and William McKinney. (1987). *American Mainline Religion: Its Changing Shape and Future.* New Brunswick; London: Rutgers University Press.

CHAPTER 16

MALCOLM X AND AMERICAN SELF-UNDERSTANDING: ON THE LEGACY OF ISLAMIC LEADERSHIP

Joseph M. Kramp

INTRODUCTION

In Crispin Sartwell's important *Act Like You Know: African American Autobiography and White Identity* (1998), he makes a compelling case for what he calls the structure of knowledge as power in the West. In the following excerpt, Sartwell describes how modern epistemology has been inflated with an unacknowledged taxonomy of power, in which race guides the classification of both ideas and their value as well as persons and their value:

> Knowledge as power in the West is a structure of comprehension, in which particular facts are ranged under general facts, formulated as generalizations. The particular facts are gathered, categorized, and then presented as freed from their particularity, as released into the general. In the case of sociology, the particular is abstracted into the statisticial. . . . No fact is recalcitrant to comprehension. . . . Notice that this shows that modern science is raced. (1998, 56)

For Sartwell, the scientist or researcher who controls the modes of interpretation and surveillance is able to hide behind a safe wall of objectivity, explaining movement and behavior, and classifying value by the particularities of experiences, attitudes, movements, and behaviors. What Sartwell then shows is that these taxonomies of power that unwittingly enter the cultural, interpretive mind-sets of Western peoples play a significant role in forming the self-understanding of various groups and individuals. He is mostly interested in studying individuals, because it is through the exposure of particular lives and their uniqueness that a critique of knowledge as power in the West can be built.

The first individual Sartwell examines is W. E. B. Du Bois, the first black PhD graduate from Harvard and a highly regarded sociologist both in his time and today. What Sartwell finds so interesting about Du Bois is his interest in the personal dimension of experience—an odd, awkward concern for a sociologist. Sartwell describes a "white Du Bois" (1998, 64) who was concerned with scientific objectivity, and a "black Du Bois" (64) who focused on particularized narratives of personal experience. He concludes that "Du Bois engaged in both modes of authorship [scientific, objective prose and revealing, personal testimony] with the utmost devotion" (64). He later argues that this split in thinking was "not addressed very elaborately by Du Bois; it would have been achievement enough for Du Bois to have identified the self-division, and to issue a call to racial pride, a call to the invisible to make themselves seen" (88). Sartwell describes this self-division as accompanied by a powerful self-loathing and -contempt, a diminished interest in the outside world reflected in one's ambivalence toward racial integration, and often a hope for an apocalyptic end to present pain and suffering accompanied by a spiritual revolution that would wipe away those feelings of self-contempt.

This description of self-division mirrors Sigmund Freud's understanding of melancholia. In Freud's famous essay "Mourning and Melancholia" (1917), he describes the differences between the two concepts. In mourning or grief, the world becomes deprived of joy and can feel hollow. In melancholia, it is the ego or self-identity of the individual person that becomes joyless and empty, spurring personal attacks on oneself from an unconscious motive. This motive remains unconscious because it is much easier for the psyche to bear it unconsciously, berating itself in the process, rather than face the pain of making the motive conscious and attempting to unburden itself.

The self-loathing in Du Bois's scholarship that Sartwell describes is therefore best characterized as a kind of melancholia of race. He shows that the precise reason such self-loathing was extremely difficult for even a reflective person such as Du Bois to identify was the incredible pain that such a thought would cause in conscious, waking life: "When you become visible [and make your melancholia of race conscious] . . . you make yourself vulnerable to our [white] power in certain ways that you were not before" (1998, 88). Here Sartwell describes socially what Freud interprets psychologically—namely the "pain" of making one's unconscious self conscious of that hate. In other words, it is ostensibly less painful to the psyche to inflict the self-hate of melancholia rather than to make such self-hatred conscious and face the social and institutional oppressions on which it rests.

The melancholia of race was and is undergirded by a vast system of racial oppression, reflected in scholarly methods as well as cultural norms; to face such social codes consciously and aggressively would have had serious consequences in waking life. Perhaps one of the reasons melancholia of race was consciously inaccessible to Du Bois was connected with his quest to earn a PhD and the public recognition that he craved. His melancholia of race could be viewed as a mere secondary "benefit" that accrued in the midst of a brave and courageous personal quest by a black man in a (literally) white man's world at Harvard University in the 1890s.

Although Du Bois's melancholia of race remained unconscious throughout his lifetime, Sartwell argues that "[i]n the works of Malcolm X, these themes are explored with single-minded ferocity" (1998, 88). In other words, X was a Freud of his time, taking what was id and making it ego or making conscious what was unconscious so as to confront it and seize power over it. X identified the systemic nature of the melancholia of race, consciously accepted it in his waking life, and embraced the vulnerabilities this would inevitably place him in. He therefore caused a systemic interruption of the cultural, political, and economic status quos with a conscious force undergirded by what was ostensibly his Islamic faith.

Nevertheless, X's own particular brand of Islam evolved over the course of his life, and I argue that this development was guided by his own management of his melancholia. As his religious self-understanding changed, so did his political agenda and his means of handling his own melancholia of race. X's legacy of Islamic leadership has been embraced by many influential leaders—both black and white—and he has led a revolution founded on the infallibility of individual dignity in spite of the social forces designed to thwart it. The substance of such a revolution may be largely qualitative and difficult to measure; however, its intangible influence has had measurable impact on contemporary American leaders such as Barack Obama, who is also examined in this chapter. In summary, my thesis is that Malcolm X's management of his melancholia of race guided his conversion process and religious leadership, making his legacy relevant and meaningful to millions of people regardless of their race or religion. He led a revolution in self-understanding that remains critical today, when our present American leaders are informed by his legacy.

THE MELANCHOLIA OF RACE AND MALCOLM X'S CONVERSION

Malcolm X's famous autobiography, written in the same format as any classic religious autobiography in Western history, such as Augustine's *Confessions* or Thomas Merton's *The Seven Storey Mountain*, traces the life of an individual lost but slowly progressing toward some kind of salvific ideology or way of life. Such autobiographies also have their own unique guiding themes. Whereas Merton's may appear to be his recovery from the sudden death of his mother and his struggle with his sexuality, X's topic of obsession is personal dignity or merit. He voices concerns about pride or dignity early in his life: "'In late 1934, I would guess, something began to happen. Some kind of psychological deterioration hit our family circle and began to eat away our pride'" (quoted in Capps and Capps 1970, 235). At this point X blames the family's financial hardships for his feelings of low self-worth, but he later reveals his moment of enlightenment while "conking" his hair to look as though he were white.

As the acid burned into his scalp to straighten his hair, X managed to ease the burning by dunking his head in the toilet bowl water in a nearby bathroom. After this incident, his physical pain forcefully reveals the depths of his shame over his race and the degree of his own self-revulsion. He is able to reflect on his family history as well, as marked by the stripping of dignity and pride from the family's identity. With the brutal murder of his father by white racists and the slow progression of his mother into severe mental illness, X began to take on a kind of black nationalist viewpoint well before his conversion to Islam. Nevertheless, his black nationalism did not have any kind of supporting ideology that would incorporate him into mainstream society, and as a result he made his living as a social deviant, engaging in drug and prostitution deals in Harlem and Boston.

Malcolm X's conversion to the Nation of Islam occurred while he was in prison. More than anything else, his conversion experience provided a necessary means for framing his personal past, which up to that point he appears to have had little control over. His descent into the identity of a social deviant had ostensibly more to do with his mistrust of society in general and a general suspicion of authority. Readers of X's autobiography never get the sense that hustling was a profession he aspired to; in fact, his earliest professional aspirations were in the direction of the law. This ambition was squelched by X's white grammar school instructors.

The Nation of Islam provided a means to quickly frame X's personal past, so as to provide prospects for a future under his control and freed from his melancholia of race. As X reflects in his autobiographical writings: "'Why am I as I am? To understand that of any person, his whole life, from birth, must be reviewed. All of our experiences fuse into our personality'" (quoted in Capps and Capps 1970, 242). The Nation's demonizing of white Christianity and overall framework designed to provide dignity and self-esteem to blacks such as X provided him with a powerful mechanism through which to confront and control his own self-revulsion or melancholia of race. In summary, the Nation of Islam provided X with the framework through which he could build his self-understanding free from any form of self-revulsion; in the process it allowed him to find a form of work through which to lead his black brothers out of the bondage of the melancholia of race. This was the beginning of X's leadership legacy in the quest for self-understanding:

> I walked, "fishing" for converts [to the Nation of Islam] in the Detroit black ghetto. I saw the African features of my black brothers and sisters whom the devilish white man had brainwashed. I saw the hair as mine had been for years, conked by cooking it with lye until it lay limp, looking straight like the white man's hair. Time and again Mr. Muhammad's teachings were rebuffed and even ridiculed.... My head would reel sometimes, with mingled anger and pity for my poor blind black brothers. (quoted in Capps and Capps 1970, 245–46)

Most important, the religious truths X preached never acquired any meaning apart from his own articulation of the black American experience of the melancholia of race. X's poetic descriptions of overcoming self-revulsion through spiritual awakening made him a popular minister in the Nation of Islam, not because he was reciting religious dogma like any old clerical drone, but because he wedded the Nation's religious ideology with the lived self-understanding of black Americans.

MALCOLM X'S BIRACIAL LEADERSHIP: THE ADAPTIVE QUALITY OF A FRATERNAL SELF

In *The Religious Personality* (1970), Capps and Capps construct a four-part typology of religious personalities: the fraternal self, the chastised self, the aesthetic self, and the resigned self. They classify Malcolm X as a fraternal self. The fraternal self "identifies his own spiritual pilgrimage or religious ventures with that of a larger group of individuals" (6). X's anger and pity toward his black brothers exemplify this personality trait in the fraternal self.

For the fraternal self, "the problem of the relation of personal and group identity is fundamental" (Capps and Capps 1970, 6). The fraternal self is willing to undergo suffering for the sake of the betterment or "growth of the community with which he has identified" (6), indicating the act of sublimation at work within the fraternal self's personality. Volney Gay (1982) argues that the Capps and Capps typology can be improved by locating each personality type along a spectrum from repressed (maladaptive) to sublimated (adaptive). In other words, Gay constructs a hierarchy of personality functioning, and he concludes by locating the fraternal self at the top as most adaptive and exemplary of the sublimatory ideal (1982, 164).[1] Perhaps most important, fraternal selves contribute to a new understanding of ethics in their communities and forge new possibilities for understanding divinity, government, and the individual:

> Fraternal/sublimated selves become vehicles for their communities' new self-understanding. They serve others by example and through their role as confessors summon others to participate in exercising their "true nature." Thus, fraternal/sublimated individuals become community workers and cultural workers; their interaction with both the smaller group and its encompassing culture manifests what Erikson has called mutual regulation. Thus, Malcolm X needs the others to confirm and stabilize his new achievement, and the others need him to secure the possibility of and to bear witness to their own eventual liberation. (Gay 1982, 166)

Fraternal selves are therefore culture makers who experience a profound crisis of meaning relative to both their own personal experiences and the combined experiences of those they identify as their brethren. Therefore, in the case of X, it is critical to account for the significance of his disillusionment with the Nation of Islam and his pilgrimage to Mecca. Upon his return to the United States, X indicated that cooperation between whites and blacks was critical to recovering black identity and communal unity. He believed and hoped that once such a project was completed, cooperative racial integration in America would be possible: a complete reversal of the racial tension and violence in his historical context. This change in his leadership agenda had a number of immediate consequences. He became a target for assassination by the Nation of Islam and a racist American government; his sense of community and those whom he identified with as brethren expanded; and his community's understanding of divinity, ethics, and self-identity was transformed.

Although the pre-Mecca-experience X is still revered among black nationalists today, the post-Mecca X has arguably affected a much larger and diverse constituency. Both of X's conversion experiences, the first in prison and the second in Mecca, reveal a changing attitude toward handling his melancholia of race. In the first conversion experience, X made his melancholic self-degradation conscious. This became the guiding theme of his ministry up until his disillusionment with the Nation of Islam.

The conversion experience in Mecca, however, revealed X's fatigue with merely fighting off his own self-loathing and fighting for respect from the American government. This onset of fatigue coincided with what X identified as the moral failures within his own ministerial ranks in the Nation of Islam. In his disillusionment he was forced into a position of greater autonomy of judgment and self-reflection. While the post-Mecca X reasserted his own goals for black dignity and communal fidelity, he acknowledged the wounds inflicted on all Americans by the melancholia of race—including whites. An increased capacity for empathy and vulnerability are obvious in the post-Mecca X, sustained by his study of the origins of Islamic faith and the totality of his experience with different races.

In the next two sections I profile two representative Americans, one white and one black, who were heavily influenced by the pre- and post-Mecca X. In both cases, X's attempt to work through his melancholia of race, not his particular Islamic beliefs, became the basis upon which these Americans felt a connection with him. As such, these individuals are representative of X's continued influence in forging American self-understanding, even beyond his physical death, and his legacy of leading a revolution in American self-understanding.

CRISPIN SARTWELL: MELANCHOLIA OF WHITE IDENTITY

Sartwell's (2003) hagiographic work, in which he identifies and describes the ethics of five notable Americans, concludes with a chapter on X. The book begins with an ostensibly simple point: to show how the discipline of ethics is founded on learning "what is admirable by observing people I admire, and I also learn who is admirable by exploring the question of what is admirable. Such a rough methodology perhaps would not be satisfactory in a philosophical system of ethics, but it mirrors the process by which . . . we actually do come to learn moral concepts" (2003, 3). Sartwell describes his approach as "pluralist" (7). In other words, he concedes a great deal of autonomy to his readership—he understands that others may not admire what he does. However, his central concern is with what he describes as "virtue." For him, virtue is not living in accord with any particular moral principle per se, but rather living with a kind of intangible personal authenticity, so as to elicit both praise and opprobrium, even simultaneously. "The idea that one's admirable qualities also are destructive is a fundamental point in this book" (2003, 2). Sartwell's understanding of ethics is therefore unburdened by the idea of moral probity or righteousness; in this respect, his approach reveals psychoanalytic influences, though these remain largely concealed from the reader.

Such ostensibly simple goals make for complicated chapters, especially the concluding chapter on X. One example will suffice: the issue of X's embrace of traditional modes of masculinity. This issue was extremely complicated, because even though X believed women to be subservient to men, he was so comfortable within his own skin that he was able to give the women he interacted with a great degree of autonomy and respect (2003, 126).[2] Sartwell argues that X's commitments must be contextualized in his world, where traditional masculinity was "simultaneously valued and feared, encouraged and made impossible" (127). In such a context, X's disciplined fury would be received with "deep spiritual and political power" (127). Sartwell closes this section on X with an important "defense of traditional masculinity":

> If traditional masculinity entails self-possession, autonomy, courage, and defiance, then to some extent it is extremely desirable in a leader. When contemporary politicians seem to have no real commitments and to focus-group their every phrase, then one reason they are despicable whether they are men or women is that they have no balls; they have far too little capacity for defiance, self-reliance, and self-assertion. It is impossible to conceive of Malcolm apart from both the positive and negative aspects of masculinity. (2003, 127)

This point is important for assessing X's legacy, because it reveals that even in the larger revolutionary ideology he preached, dangerous (if also beneficial) and seemingly antiquated (if also important) values were also reinscribed. Such a point illustrates the difficulty of determining when precisely a revolution has been "won," even if it also clearly and undeniably illustrates that a systemic interruption of cultural norms has taken place through conscious action.

Sartwell ends his chapter on X in his 2003 work by pointing to the goals of the third chapter in his 1998 work: namely, to show that X's influence and power were consolidated on the basis of his ability to work through the melancholia of race. "Malcolm's was indeed a call to action, but it was first of all addressed to each person one by one, and it called for a conversion experience in which that person could unify and become herself" (2003, 132). The obstacles to this self-unity are sufficiently described for black Americans in the previous sections of this chapter. In Sartwell's earlier chapter (1998), he describes the experience of self-estrangement for white Americans or, in other words, the white American experience of the melancholia of race.

Sartwell describes the white melancholia of race as an internal struggle between mind and body, consciousness and experience—a hierarchy of demands that make self-understanding exceedingly difficult, although also intensely pleasurable. Sartwell writes of himself, a white man:

> I am the slavemaster of myself. My consciousness takes itself to have been made for mastery; it arrogates to itself the undoubted right of mastery, without reflection. And above all, it feels *detached* in its empowerment from my body and from my environment; it *separates* itself from the physical situation. My self is dual: word of power, recalcitrant physical material.

I can oppress you because I *am* oppression, because my *self* is hallucinated as a pure will. (1998, 98)

In the case of the black American, X indicated that the melancholia of race is difficult to make conscious because it would force one into courageous confrontation with the outer, social mechanisms that instill such self-hatred. To do so would make one extremely vulnerable to exterior forces. It is ostensibly less painful, in other words, to accept the conditions of self-degradation than to refuse them and confront the system that imposes those conditions. In the case of the white American, Sartwell indicates that X has shown that the melancholia of race is difficult to make conscious because of the pleasure unwittingly received when one is relieved of responsibility for one's actions. In both cases, to rid oneself of the melancholia of race requires accepting greater vulnerability, increased autonomy, and full personal and social responsibility. In both cases, courage and risk taking are required.

Malcolm X's legacy and influence therefore transcend the category of race and religion, in this case Islam. Although religion and race were the prominent topics through which he explained his vision of self-understanding, he used them for the sake of fusing his own attempts at self-unification with those of his ever-expanding community, which ultimately became humankind. X's legacy of preserving and advocating for self-understanding is crystallized in the present leadership of Barack Obama, also a fraternal self. In Obama's election to the presidency, X's systemic interruption of social and political norms contributed to paving the way for a black individual to assume America's most powerful office. As I demonstrate in the next section, Obama's own adoption of the psychological traits of the fraternal self can potentially be attributed in part to X's influence on his own life, and this has significant consequences for the future of American self-understanding.

OBAMA'S FRATERNAL SELF AND LEADERSHIP IN THE SHADOW OF MALCOLM X'S LEGACY

The autobiography of Barack Obama, *Dreams from My Father* (1995), is the story of a boy becoming a man through the process of grappling with his biracial heritage and the fatherless past that he has inherited. His engagement with black nationalism in his youth and his struggles with his beloved white mother and grandparents, combined with his eventual vocational path in community organizing and politics, are deeply revealing of a man who "senses that his own personal conflicts are already inherent in the identity of the group" (Capps and Capps 1970, 6). This is a quintessential trait of the fraternal self. Obama thus has always viewed himself as occupying a "formative place in the destiny of his people" (6); the only decision he had to make was *who* would be *his* people.

Obama's decision to ultimately self-identify as black has, I think, something to do with tracing his development back to his mythic father's roots in Africa. While the mystery of his father's paternal presence is psychologically oppressive and ostensibly disabling because of the loss young Obama experienced in not having known his father, his father's mysteriousness also gave him the opportunity to view himself as significant in the destiny of his people. Obama's probing autobiographical narrative is further evidence of his awareness of his melancholia of race and his linking of this experience with that of black Americans in general.[3]

He also acutely understands the effects of the melancholia of race on whites. He demonstrates this in numerous places in his autobiography, but perhaps most notably in his commentary on black nationalism. For all the psychological health that Obama believes black nationalism brings about for blacks, he is ultimately deeply suspicious of it: "Notions of purity—of race or of culture—could no more serve as the basis for the typical black American's self-esteem than it could for mine. Our sense of wholeness would have to arise from something more fine than the bloodlines we'd inherited" (1995, 204). Nevertheless, Obama also praises his friends and relatives who have adopted a black nationalist ideology: "I came to see how the blanket indictment of everything white served a central function in their message of uplift; how, psychologically, at least, one depended upon the other" (198). Obama is therefore ultimately ambivalent toward black nationalist ideology, and this ambivalence reflects a profound and sincere empathy for both the white and black races who, together with others, make up the American nation. The post-Mecca-experience X, who also grew ambivalent toward black nationalist ideology, undoubtedly influenced Obama's views on this issue. In many ways, Obama has taken up where X left off—never excusing any form of racial degradation, whether of the outwardly violent kind or of the melancholic variety, and at the same time recognizing that the purity codes that function to psychologically protect the races carry with them the seeds of their own (and possibly others') destruction.

Malcolm X's religious self-understanding changed in conjunction with his handling of the melancholia of race, and the same process occurred in Barack Obama. Both men ultimately did not exalt in the power of God, but rather the power of the idea of God. Both exhibit a considerable degree of skepticism about religious belief that is not consciously wedded to practical social issues. Such individuals have the potential to inspire willingness to endure and suffer for the sake of some kind of larger goal. In addition, they have the potential to assist others in their disenchantment with the power of one leader to magically fix life's problems. Therefore, they are able to assist others in taking on a greater degree of personal responsibility for both their own and others' destinies.

CONCLUSION

Malcolm X's legacy of religious leadership continues in the life and work of Barack Obama. The style of such leadership will undoubtedly elicit wide-ranging criticism, much of which the fraternal self (who, it has been shown, has an expansive capacity for empathy) will want to be aware of. A good deal of the work of fraternal selves such as X and Obama is difficult to measure in quantitative terms. Nevertheless, the fraternal self's generally noncoercive style of leadership is grounded in a relentless struggle to bring about a kind of individual and communal self-understanding marked by mutuality, reciprocity, and acceptance of individual uniqueness. In the process of developing such leadership, the historic values and symbols of American society can be continually revived, in spite of a vast amount of suffering and acknowledged imperfection on the part of that leadership.

NOTES

1. I have challenged Gay's hierarchy relatively recently (Kramp 2007), even as I argue in both that article and this chapter that his hierarchy has a great deal of merit.

2. Sartwell (2003) rightly questions whether one could say the same of Martin Luther King Jr. or other liberals advocating women's rights while treating them as "sexual objects" (126).

3. Describing one telling interaction with a black nationalist college friend, Obama writes: "I wondered whether, for now at least, [the friend] wasn't also right in preferring that that [melancholic] anger be redirected; whether a black politics that suppressed rage toward whites generally, or one that failed to elevate race loyalty above all else, was a politics inadequate to the task" (Obama 1995, 199).

REFERENCES

Capps, D., and W. Capps, eds. (1970). *The Religious Personality*. Belmont, CA: Wadsworth Publishing.
Freud, S. (1917). "Mourning and Melancholia." In *A General Selection from the Works of Sigmund Freud*, edited by John Rickman, 124–140. New York: Doubleday Anchor Books, 1957.
Gay, V. P. (1982). "Repression and Sublimation in Religious Personalities." *Journal of Religion and Health* 21 (2): 152–70.
Kramp, J. M. (2007). "Ritual and Heroism: A Study in Cross Cultural Religious Practices and Religious Personalities." *Pastoral Psychology* 55 (3): 321–39.

Obama, B. (1995). *Dreams from My Father: A Story of Race and Inheritance.* New York: Three Rivers Press.

Sartwell, C. (1998). *Act Like You Know: African American Autobiography and White Identity.* Chicago; London: University of Chicago Press.

Sartwell, C. (2003). *Extreme Virtue: Truth and Leadership in Five Great American Lives.* Albany: State University of New York Press.

CHAPTER 17

THE RELIGIOUS IDEOLOGY OF REFORM IN IRAN

Avideh Mayville

Religious dissent in Iran has taken many different forms. This chapter analyzes the role of religious dissent before, during, and after the Iranian revolution. The role of the dissident in each period was unique. Prior to the revolution, Iran's government was a secular monarchy. Clerical dissidents were often shunned outright. Not all agreed on how or even if religion should be incorporated into a state system. However, it is clear that the monarchy's treatment of religious dissidents and complete disregard for the clerical establishment in Iran contributed to its downfall. This tug-of-war first between the state and the clerical establishment, and then, following the revolution, among the clerical establishment, shows the political manifestation of Iranians' struggles with the role of religion in their society.

PREREVOLUTIONARY YEARS

Before the revolution, the clerical establishment had no official political role. For the most part, the monarchy and the clergy existed independently of one another, with some instances of placid coexistence or friction (mostly leading up to the revolution). Although there were a number of political parties in Iran, it was not until the latter half of the twentieth century that religion came to the forefront in most parties' political agendas.

During the 1950s there were several political organizations with religious factions. The major opposition group to the government was Mohammad Mossadeq's National Front party. The National Front was comprised of a variety of groups that wanted to nationalize Iran's oil industry and reduce the influence of the West in Iran's internal politics. The pervasiveness of Western influence in Iran is one of the major recurring themes among the religio-political groups in Iran throughout the twentieth century and continuing to the present. Arguably, the country still grapples with what qualifies as "Western influence"; the effects it has had on Iranian society; and the extent of the "damage" it has caused to the country, and on a broader scale, to the Islamic world.

The more religious among National Front members eventually split off because of differences in ideology and formed the Movement for the Liberation of Iran, founded by Mehdi Bazargan (Abrahamian 1979). Bazargan was instrumental in nationalizing the Iranian oil industry and even served as the first Iranian head of the National Iranian Oil Company under Mohammad Mossadegh. Following the revolution, Khomeini appointed Bazargan as the first postrevolution prime minister of Iran, a post he eventually resigned because of disputes with Khomeini's brethren during the hostage crisis. However, Bazargan was influential in formally introducing the concept of a religio-political nexus into the mainstream with the establishment of the Movement for the Liberation of Iran, the organization from which the Islamic movement that led to the revolution got its start. The organization's philosophy was a unique combination of Iranian Shiism and European socialism and appealed not only to religiously inclined nationalists and intellectuals, but also to lower-ranking clergy members (Abrahamian 1979, 6).

Although the group eventually splintered into smaller organizations, some espousing more radical ideologies, the seed of the religious political reform in Iran was planted with the establishment of the Movement for the Liberation of Iran. One of the leaders of the movement was Dr. Ali Shariati, who came from a clerical family and was actively involved in the efforts to nationalize Iran's oil industry. Eventually he joined the Movement for the Liberation of Iran (Abrahamian 1979, 6). Shariati was internationally educated; he had studied at the Sorbonne and then returned to Iran to open a religious school that became famous for his sermons espousing his beliefs on Shiism (6). Shariati viewed Iranian Shiism as a national identity that would eventually free Iranians from the confines of imperialism and bring down the ruling class and with it, by extension, the monarchy (Matin-Asgari 1997, 104). Although some of the religio-political movement overlapped with the Marxists, Shariati included Marxism under the banner of imperialist ideas that were causing the deterioration of his country (98). Ironically, Shariati and his father at one point joined a group called the Movement of the Theist Socialists, a group of Muslim socialists who respected private property (Javadzadeh 2007, 151).

There is another important distinction to make in the major themes of religious dissent in Iran: discerning who qualifies as an imperialist. Broadly speaking, there was, and still is to an extent, a general anti-Western sentiment among religious dissidents. However, some of the clergy viewed all foreign influences, including those associated with the Far Left—the Marxists, socialists, etc.—as falling under the same destructive umbrella as the West. One such organization was the People's Mujahidin of Iran, which viewed Iran's problems as a religio-nationalistic struggle against imperialistic forces, including Marxism. The People's Mujahidin of Iran was another offshoot of the National Front; it splintered off because its members felt Mossadegh was un-Islamic and had quite a following in Iran at the time (Abrahamian 1982, 276).

Although the Iranian Left was generally anti-Western, its members diverged from many of the religious conservatives about who qualifies as an imperialist power. In addition, the constituency of the Iranian Left was not limited to the religiously minded. It may seem contradictory that Marxists could also be religious; however, this is just another example of the philosophical fusion of ideas that has occurred in Iran. In fact, many Marxist groups used Islamic political ideology to organize and mobilize masses of Iranians (Javadzadeh 2007, 91).

Shariati believed that the best government would be a dictatorship run by the *roshanfekrane dini*, or religious-minded intellectuals (Razavi 2006, 1227). He felt that clerics should proclaim their political stance and stand up for their beliefs, and he harshly criticized the clergy members who were passively cooperating with the government (Javadzadeh 2007, 154). Shariati's ideas were instrumental in inspiring discontented Iranians, especially university students, lower-ranking clergy, and the lower middle class (Abrahamian 1979, 5). Unfortunately he would not live to see the revolution his ideas inspired. He was imprisoned numerous times under the Shah's reign and died in 1977 under mysterious circumstances (Rahnema 2000, 368).

The Movement for the Liberation of Iran continued to gain strength, although some more extreme members split from the group and created new factions. There were many different political groups active at the time of the revolution, but most fell under the following five categories: religious conservatives, religious radicals, religious reactionaries, secular reformers, and secular radicals (Abrahamian 1979, 7–8) (see table 17.1).

Among the religious factions, several major figures influenced the Islamic ideology that permeated the opposition groups. It is very important to note that although the Revolution of 1979 was an "Islamic" revolution, there never was a uniform interpretation of Islam among the opposition, or by extension, among the Iranian population. This is partially why Shariati's version of Islam was so appealing to the masses. He envisioned a "true" Islamic society as one that did not incorporate the clergy as state leadership, "a utopia . . . a classless community of Moslems ruled by enlightened

Table 17.1.

Opposition Category	Description
Religious Conservatives	Led by Ayatollahs Shirazi and Shariatmadari; aimed to eliminate the monarchy, but not to overthrow the government; supported primarily by senior clergy and the well-off bazaaris.
Religious Radicals	Led by the Movement for the Liberation of Iran, inspired by Bazargan and Shariati; they are interested in a complete political and social revolution. They were unable become an organized political party with a formal structure and guiding principles.
Religious Reactionaries	Similar to the religious radicals, but without a social agenda. Comprised primarily of mullahs.
Secular Reformers	Led by the National Front, comprised mostly of the professional and upper middle class. The Secular Reformers called for a modern constitution and, "prefer a secular republic or even a democratic Islamic republic rather than a purely Islamic Republic . . . some . . . favor socialism . . . through parliamentary democracy."
Secular Radicals	Comprised of a number of different political groups, the most organized of which were the *Fedayi*, the Tudeh Party (Marxist), the Revolutionary Tudeh, and the Marxist-Leninist Organization. These organizations mostly consist of some university students, white collar associations, and trade associations.

thinkers, a dictatorship of secular intellectuals with no room for the ulama" (Ashraf 1990, 132). In direct contrast to that view was Khomeini's vision of "an Islamic state ruled by the ulama as vicegerents of the hidden Imam" (132). Both Shariati and Khomeini developed revolutionary interpretations of the relationship between Islam and the state, supporting a very Machiavellian, "ends justifies the means" philosophy that espoused violence as a justification in the transformation of "society into an Islamic utopia" (Ashraf and Banuazizi 2001, 238).

On the nonviolent front, there were those, such as the Grand Ayatollah Shariatmadari, who sought peaceful means to incorporate Islam into modern life (Ashraf 1990, 118). This ideology was best expressed by Bazargan's organization, the Iran Liberation Movement (Zonis 1985, 89). The differences and conflicts on politicized Islam in Iran between competing factions are best summed up as follows:

Broadly speaking, there are four major sets of internal and external questions with respect to which the different ideological and political factions can be distinguished. The two internal issues are (1) the degree to which the state should intervene in economic life of the society; and (2) the degree to which the Islamic modes of behavior should be imposed on Westernized middle classes—particularly women, music, films, sports, and even chess. The two external questions relate to (1) the degree to which Iran should normalize its relations with the United States, the West, and the Soviet Union; and (2) the mode of exporting the Islamic revolution in the Near East and North Africa. (Ashraf 1990, 134)

These major sets of internal and external questions still apply today, but with some minor modifications, because the Soviet Union no longer exists. These four questions dominate the political discourse among clerical dissidents in Iran.

THE ISLAMIC REVOLUTION OF 1979

In the years leading up to the Revolution of 1979, there were many different opposition groups, operating with often conflicting agendas. The religiously oriented groups were more successful in gaining a following, because regardless of social and political leanings, religion was a common ground for many of the opposition groups. Aside from the influence of commonality in identity working as a factor for the religious-leaning opposition groups, other circumstances helped to create an environment conducive to their rise to power.

First, the monarchy did not target the religious opposition groups as openly as it targeted the nationalistic and left-leaning organizations. Although the secular grassroots organizations were quashed, the bazaar guilds, clergy, seminaries, local mosques, and general religious institutions were permitted to operate without interference (Abrahamian 1979, 8). In fact, "by 1977, the religious institutions were the only organizations left in the country free of state domination. Not surprisingly, public opposition to the state tended to converge into the mosques" (8).

Furthermore, many of the leftist organizations had a hard time gaining credibility with the masses because the Soviet Union and China had openly supported the Shah, at least for a brief period (Garver 2006, 33). Many of the subjugated poor and lower middle class in Iran found a valuable sense of community through their faith that they did not have before, united under the would-be leader of the revolution, Ayatollah Ruhollah Khomeini (Roy 1999, 210).

To comprehend Khomeini's ideology, it is necessary to understand his background and the context in which he rose to power. Prior to the revolution, the tone of the official relationship between the religious establishment and the monarchy was for the most part set by the religious leaders of the day. Iran is a Shiite Muslim state. In Shia Islam, religious authority is institutionalized through marja-iyat, in which a leading religious scholar, known as a *marja*, is supposed to be a model for his followers (Akhavi 1992, 100). The marja is the scholarly and administrative authority within the seminary community and has the right to silence critics, also acting as a model for other seminarians (Kurzman 2001, 342).

The peak of marja'iyat authority occurred during the 1950s with Ayatollah Hossein Borujerdi, the marja of his era. Borujerdi did not have any serious disputes with the monarchy, nor did his predecessor, Ayatollah Ha'eri (Zonis 1985, 89). The clerical establishment and the state coexisted relatively peacefully. In the 1960s and 1970s a more collaborative relationship developed between the state and the Pahlavi regime, with some members of the ulama directly appointed establishment by the shah to lead Friday prayers in major cities and to maintain influential roles within the clergy, which inspired much criticism (Ashraf 1990, 119).

Ayatollah Khomeini and Borujerdi disagreed on many issues, and given Borujerdi's status as marja, he had the right to silence Khomeini. Khomeini believed that religious scholars should be increasingly engaged in politics and was very critical of the Iranian monarchy, eventually resulting in Borujerdi virtually placing him under house arrest in the seminary community (Moin 1999, 73). Ironically, even after Borujerdi's death, Khomeini supported the idea of the unquestioned authority of the marja. This system of authority was one of the primary causes of dispute between the theological reformers and the regime.

When Borujerdi died in the early 1960s, many members of the clergy became dismayed by the passive and/or collaborative approaches taken by their fellow clergymen, including Ayatollah Khomeini. Khomeini was so dismayed at the relationship that had developed between the monarchy and the clerical establishment that in 1963 he led antigovernment riots with a small group of students (Moin 1999, 104). He eventually was exiled from Iran for his opposition to the government, returning on the eve of the revolution.

The period immediately following the revolution was characterized by uncertainty and instability, and the need for unity in Iran in the face of the Iraq War solidified Khomeini's power (Brumberg 2001, 65). The country either had to come together or it would fall apart. Khomeini was best able to consolidate the structure of what is now the Islamic Republic.

To truly understand the Islamic Republic today, it is important to review Khomeini's personal Islamic philosophy. His understanding of Islam had a significant effect on the current governing structure of Iran. Throughout the twentieth century, there were four periods in which the Iranian monarchy seemingly attacked the religious establishment in Iran:

- the Constitutional Revolution of 1905–1911,
- the drive for modernization during the 1920s and 1930s under Reza Shah,
- the rise of Marxism in the 1940s and early 1950s, and
- the White Revolution of the 1960s and 1970s.

These eras had a profound effect on Khomeini's philosophy. During each the religious authority of the clergy was systemically undermined in favor of the state. The Constitutional Revolution resulted in many powers traditionally controlled by the clergy being reassigned to the state, such as judicial functions and the provision of education. In direct defiance of the clerical system, in which a minority of clergy members publicly held jurisdiction over political and economic matters, the new system embraced liberal ideas espousing humanism and majority rule, effectively eroding the very power structure upon which the clergy was based (Ashraf 1990).

Reza Shah's drive for modernization also introduced such measures as the defamation of Islamic dress, best exemplified by the forced de-veiling of women in public (Rostami Povey 2004, 258). Consequently, the rise of Marxist ideas among Iran's intellectual elite also involved the rejection of tradition and the condemning of religion as mere superstitious thought (Boroujerdi 1996, 65). This erosion of the religious establishment in Iran by the state was perceived by some conservative theologians, such as Khomeini, as a clear indication that the monarchy was moving Iran in the wrong direction.

Later, during the White Revolution of the 1960s and 1970s, the shah implemented a number of educational and agricultural reforms in hopes of "modernizing" Iran (Watson 1976, 27). Many of these initiatives were viewed as Western-imported attempts to restructure Iranian society and establish an increasingly centralized state. In many parts of the country, religious schools were the only option for students. Following the shah's reforms, secular schools with a focus on the liberal arts were opened, and educational requirements included meeting a standardized curriculum (Sobhe 1982, 275, 279).

Consequentially, many young clerics who previously would have gone only to religious schools now also had an educational background in the liberal arts upon entering the seminary (Ashraf 1990, 118). Though this resulted in a new generation of clerics who were educated in both the liberal arts and religion, Khomeini viewed these reforms as yet another way the monarchy was infringing upon a jurisdiction previously held by the religious establishment in many parts of the country (Ashraf 1990, 118).

Khomeini remained in exile in Iraq for 14 years and only returned to Iran when the shah left in 1979, which was his one condition for going back. Following the revolution, Khomeini incorporated the concept of *velayat-eh faqih* (guardianship of the jurisprudent) into his Islamic Republic, with himself as the representative of the Mahdi (the Muslim equivalent to a messiah) to what he considered to be the "first government of God" (Ashraf and Banuazizi 2001, 239; Ahdiyyih 2008, 27).

POSTREVOLUTION

Since the revolution and Khomeini's death, many political dissidents have spoken out against the regime in Iran. Most call themselves reformers; they do not want a revolution. The reform movement in Iran is anything but homogenous. Some reformers are secular humanists who call for a state based on the rule of law and completely reject any recourse to religion; others are activists who would like to reform the current legal system from an Islamic standpoint. In the Islamic Republic of Iran, the only reformers who have gained political power or status are those who belong to the latter group, such as former president Mohammad Khatami.

This section provides a brief overview of the role of religious dissidents in Iran both before and after the revolution. Furthermore, this chapter aims to shed light on the role of religious dissidents in Iranian political society by examining the religious ideology and the regime's response to several of the more influential Iranian dissidents.

Among the religious reformers in Iran, Mohammad Khatami and other leaders of Iran's main reform parties admit that they have been heavily influenced by the ideas of key contemporary Iranian intellectuals (Adib-Moghaddam 2006, 667). Though generally excluded from official political discourse, these men have had a profound influence on the reform movement in Iran and represent a religious alternative to the Islamic Republic of Iran. And even though they are unable to hold political positions of authority, religious dissenters have effectively questioned the legitimacy of the regime's authority.

One such dissenter is Mohammad Shabestari. He is mostly known for espousing the idea that religion is perfect, but not all encompassing (Schirazi 1997). He argues that what is essential and eternal are the general values of Islam, not necessarily the particular forms of how Islam has been represented throughout history, including during the time of the prophet (Sadri 2002). Shabestari has been quoted as saying: "The meaning of perfection of religion is not that it contains everything under the sun, so that if we were unable to find a specific item in it, we could go off calling it imperfect. It is not perfection for religion to function as a substitute for science, technology, and human deliberation" (Sadri 2001).

In his book *A Critique of the Official Reading of Religion* (2000), Shabestari criticizes religious absolutism as naïve and supports the modern concepts of individualism, democracy, and human rights, asserting that by nature, religious knowledge and religious jurisprudence are insufficient for modern governance (Schirazi 1997). According to the current government of Iran, these concepts of individualism, democracy, and human rights are products of Western influence and undermine Islam.

Another famous religious dissenter is Abdol-Karim Soroush. Whereas Shabestari focuses on the limited nature of religious knowledge, Soroush perceives religious knowledge as varying. He asserts that religion itself is different from religious knowledge. Religion is beyond human reach, "eternal and divine," while religious knowledge is "a sincere and authentic but finite, limited, and fallible form of human knowledge" (Sadri 2002). Soroush has challenged the legitimacy of the clerical elite in Iran and of the clergy within the Islamic tradition, because they do not perform sacraments and have no role in the relationship between man and God (Sadri 2002). He believes that human beings, though innately good, are weak and susceptible to temptation, even predation, and they need a vigilant and transparent form of government with checks and balances (Wright 1996). The government did not take legal action against Soroush, but underground militant groups in Iran attacked him and his supporters in the 1990s (Wright 2000).

Mohsen Kadivar believes that Islam has a pluralistic nature. In his writings he presents nine possible forms of governance, all based on sacred sources and revered religious scholarly work (Macleod and Siamdoust 2004). Kadivar determined that the concept of velayat e Faqih (the concept of governance of the Iranian regime, literally translated as the rule of the supreme jurist) is "neither intuitively obvious, nor rationally necessary . . . neither a requirement of religion nor a necessity for domination . . . neither a part of Shi'ite general principles (osoul), nor a component of detailed observances (forou) . . . it is, by near consensus of the Shiite Ulama, nothing more than jurisprudential minor hypothesis" (Sadri 2002). He was arrested, tried, and sentenced to eighteen months' imprisonment in 1999 because of a sermon he made lambasting the Islamic Republic for the murder of Iranian intellectuals (Sadri 2002; Kurzman 2001, 349–50). He is currently teaching at Duke University in the United States. In spite of the actions taken against Kadivar, generally speaking, dissension is more legitimate if one is a religious scholar in Iran than if one is not. The difference between the religious reformers and the regime comes down to the issue of religious authority, a recurring theme that is ever present in the squabbles within the religious establishment.

Many other religious dissenters have suffered for their beliefs at the hands of the regime. Hossein-Ali Montazeri, a longtime supporter, student, and initial successor of Khomeini, began to doubt the direction of the Islamic

Republic. Following his disagreements with Khomeini over such concepts as the velayat e Faqih, which he only supported as a popularly elected position, Khomeini removed Montazeri as his successor, replacing him with Khamenei (whom Montazeri unabashedly criticized for his lack of qualifications to fill the role of marja) (Kurzman 2001, 347). Eventually, as a result of Montazeri's disturbances, he was arrested and jailed for a brief period in 1993 and eventually placed under house arrest (Kurzman 2001, 347–48).

There are countless other religious dissidents whose differences in interpretation of scholarly texts have resulted in house arrest, landed them in jail, or worse. Some of the more notable dissidents are Mohsen Saidzadeh, Abdollah Nuri, and Hasan Yusef-Eshkevari. Their cases are only a few examples of how the current regime has dealt with religious opposition. Furthermore, the struggle between the regime and religious dissidents is more heated than that with the secular opposition, which is generally disregarded in the political discourse. However, those who attempt to use their interpretation of Islam to challenge the regime are accused of being not only against the state, but against Islam itself and of contributing to the destruction of society as a whole. "Conservatives have branded the critics as relativists . . . [arguing] that 'right and wrong are relative' and that 'even the Imams and the prophets were not absolute.' Ayatollah Mesbah-Yazdi argued, 'the culture of tolerance and indulgence means the disarming of society of its defense mechanisms'" (Kurzman 2001, 354). The danger of dismissing such discourse as outright treason is that it justifies absolute political authority as a method for addressing dissent. There will never be room for open political discussion, because there can only be one valid interpretation.

AHMADINEJAD'S IDEOLOGY

Between 2005 and 2013, Mahmoud Ahmadinejad has been the president of Iran. To understand how the government of Iran has recently addressed religious dissidents, it is necessary to examine (1) Ahmadinejad's personal religious philosophy and (2) his relationship with the current supreme leader, Ayatollah Khamenei. Table 17.2 outlines the division of power between the supreme leader and the president of Iran ("Structure of Power" 2012).

As shown in the table, the supreme leader clearly holds more authority than the president of Iran. However, each president has made his own mark on how their relationship has affected the supreme leader's policies. From the beginning, Ahmadinejad has had a tumultuous relationship with the supreme leader. He purportedly was part of a now-underground radical anti-Bahai group, the Hojjatieh Society. The organization was founded by clerics in 1953 and played an important role in radicalizing Iranian Muslim youth prior to the revolution (Abedi and Fischer 1990, 50, 230). The group became too powerful, however,

Table 17.2.

Position	Function and capabilities
Supreme Leader	- Guides domestic and foreign policy - Commander in chief of the armed forces, intelligence, and security operations; Supreme Commander of the Islamic Revolutionary Guard Corps (IRGC) - Appoint and dismiss leaders of judiciary, state radio, and television networks - Appoints half of the twelve members of the Council of Guardians (oversees Parliament, determines political candidate qualifications)
President	- Second highest ranking official in Iran - Sets economic policy - Nominal rule over Supreme National Security Council, Ministry of Intelligence and Security - Manages 8 vice presidents and a cabinet of 22 ministers, confirmed by Parliament

causing Khomeini to drive it underground to prevent it from gaining too much power (Ahdiyyih 2008, 29). There are rumors that underground members of the organization are now active within Ahmadinejad's government (29).

For the most part, Ahmadinejad's relationship with the current supreme leader, Khamenei, is strained, largely because of his personal religious philosophy. Ahmadinejad was influenced by the likes of philosopher leaders such as Nayyab Safavi, Jalal Al-e Ahmad, and Ahmad Fardid. Safavi, a religious radical who during his short life in the early twentieth century founded a group known as Fadayan-e Islam, which assassinated numerous Iranian liberals (Ahdiyyih 2008, 28). Al-e Ahmad and Fardid were both very anti-Western and espoused very strong criticism of what they perceived to be the profound influence of the West in Iran (Mottahedeh 1985/2000, 289). They even coined a term, *gharbzadeghi* or "westoxification," alluding to the transformation of Iran's cultural identity to accommodate Western ideas on society, education, and culture (Boroujerdi 1996, 65). In many of Ahmadinejad's speeches, he names the West as the source of most problems in the world.

This perception of Western infringement on culture is still very real and tangible and ties into major thematic differences between East and West, most notably in different interpretations of religious, social, political, and economic structures. These differences are felt in Iran through the country's continuous struggle to reconcile traditional religious beliefs with modern Iranian society, which, many in the current religio-political establishment believe, is far too influenced by the West. The disagreements that occur between religious dissidents and the government of the Islamic Republic are broader than differences over interpretations of religious texts; rather, they are symptomatic of the nation's struggle with defining its identity in a world that is largely submissive to liberal Western political thought and tradition. Unsurprisingly, Ahmadinejad and many other Iranian intellectuals have been drawn to the writings of German philosopher Martin Heidegger, primarily for his criticism of the pervasiveness of Western thought (Ahdiyyih 2008, 28):

> Ahmadinejad seeks an Islamic government in Iran that is free from democratic pretenses and devoid of modern concepts of human rights and equality of the sexes. . . . The achievement of these preconditions, Ahmadinejad believes, will enable Shi'I domination and the establishment of a world government. When Ahmadinejad declares frequently that his government represents a return to Khomeini's revolutionary ideals from which previous governments have allegedly deviated, he is suggesting that he believes it is time to return Mahdisim—and the achievement of its precursor steps—to its rightful place among the Islamic Republic's priorities. (Ahdiyyih 2008: 30)

Arguably, this was the goal at the foundation of the Islamic Republic. However, under Ahmadinejad's tenure dissident clerics have been targeted and publicly decried as corrupt and against Mahdism (Ahdiyyih 2008, 32). It is Ahmadinejad's very fervent support for Mahdism that has, ironically, put him at odds with Ayatollah Khamenei. Nominally, the supreme leader is the Mahdi's representative in his absence, but Ahmadinejad claims to also have links to the Mahdi (Sahimi 2011).

This uneasiness between Ahmadinejad and Khamenei has been manifested in political battles—over the ousting of Majlis speaker of the house Ali Larijani and over the appointment and dismissal of numerous cabinet members (Sahimi 2011). This shows that though more liberal religious dissidents are being silenced from participating in the political discussion, differences in religious interpretation are already playing a serious role in the struggle for power within the government of Iran.

CONCLUSION

The role of religious dissent in Iran has taken a surprising turn. During the last decades of the monarchy, the state and the religious establishment performed an awkward dance, pushing and pulling each other in different directions as the music played and time passed. Though the monarchy was undoubtedly influenced by the West in its policies espousing the precondition of economic development on the road to modernization, the Shah did so undemocratically. By selectively including monarchy-friendly clergy members, the state marginalized the lower-ranking clergy members, leftists, and other forgotten-about members of society who seemed to be slowing down the modernization process. Religious dissenters during the monarchy, though diverse and most definitely not the only discontented political dissidents, had the advantage of encompassing divided factions through a common denominator: Islam. Ironically, the man who seized authority had a vision for an Islamic society that marginalized many of the nominal supporters who helped him rise to power.

Following the revolution, the major bone of contention between the religious reformers and the state has been religious authority and the right to govern. The inherent assumption on the part of the current regime is that those who hold the highest religious authority are most fit to interpret religion and effectively govern society based on those interpretations. Arguments that the dissidents use for reform, such as granting further rights for Iranian women, always come from the same sacred sources and scholarly texts that the regime uses to legitimate itself. The Islamic reasoning behind these positions follows the logic, "Islam is *this* and therefore *that*." The reformers are split into two camps: those who argue that Sharia (revealed law) requires Muslims to adopt liberal positions, and those who argue that Sharia allows Muslims to devise their own solutions to the issues on which revelation is silent (Kurzman 2001, 345).

Allowing this sort of discourse is very much a challenge to the theocratic administration in Iran, because it requires an admission that if Islam can be interpreted in many different ways, then it is not necessarily Islam that is x or y, but *person x* who claims that Islam is x or y. *Truth* becomes a personal interpretation, rather than a commonly held belief regarded as fact. This would acknowledge the assertion that religious knowledge is human and therefore fallible and completely undermines the legitimacy of the marj'iyat and the regime. Thus a debate between the reformers and the state is played out as a seminary debate between authority and originality: Does scholarly authority include the right to end a debate, or do qualified scholars have the right to continue debate?

The Islamic Republic has chosen authority, even when the authority is not qualified. An example is the case of Ayatollah Kazem Shariatmadari, who was largely considered Khomeini's senior in terms of religious scholarship (Fischer 2003). When the revolution took place, Shariatmadari reluctantly consented to the new establishment, but was explicit about his preference for a constitutional monarchy, such as that created in Iran's 1906 constitution, over an Islamic Republic (Fischer 2003). Following the revolution, he joined a movement in his home province that challenged Khomeini's legitimacy, which resulted in Khomeini putting Shariatmadari under house arrest until his death in 1985 (Fischer 2003).

In a sense, the treatment of religious scholars calling for reform in Iran by the regime has crushed the hope for a legitimate reform movement there. Individuals such as Soroush, Shabestari, and Kadivar are well versed in Islamic theology and have been vocal critics of the regime and the idea of an Islamic state, yet the regime continues to either ignore or punish them. This does not bode well for reform and is rather a recipe for producing more radical reformers who will be willing to use any means necessary to bring about change. The Islamic Republic's resistance to a pluralistic discussion of religion and its right to rule has resulted in it being considered illegitimate by not only the secular humanist reformers, but also the Islamic religious scholars. However, political struggles within the administrations of the past two decades suggest that there will be continuous conflict over religious interpretation—if not over ideas, at least over who has the right to authority—with the role of religious dissenters relegated to the political periphery.

REFERENCES

Abedi, M., and M. Fischer. (1990). *Debating Muslims*. Madison: University of Wisconsin Press.

Abrahamian, E. (1979). "Iran in Revolution: The Opposition Forces." *MERIP Reports* (March/April): 5–8.

Abrahamian, E. (1982). *Iran Between Two Revolutions*. Princeton, NJ: Princeton University Press.

Adib-Moghaddam, A. (2006). "The Pluralistic Momentum in Iran and the Future of the Reform Movement." *Third World Quarterly*, 27(4), 667.

Ahdiyyih, Mohebat. (2008). "Ahmadinejad and the Mahdi." *Middle East Quarterly* (Fall), 27–32.

Akhavi, S. (1988). "Islam, Politics and Society in the Thought of Ayatollah Khomeini, Ayatullah Taliqani and Ali Shariati." *Middle Eastern Studies*.

Akhavi, S. (1992). "The Clergy's Concepts of Rule in Egypt and Iran." *Annals of the American Academy of Political and Social Science*, (524), 100.

Ashraf, A. (1990). "Theocracy and Charisma: Men of Power in Iran." *International Journal of Politics, Culture, and Society* (Autumn), 118–134.

Ashraf, A., and A. Banuazizi. (2001). "Iran's Tortuous Path Toward 'Islamic Liberalism'." *International Journal of Politics, Culture, and Society* (Winter), 238–239.

Boroujerdi, Mehrzad. (1996). *Iranian Intellectuals and the West: The Tormented Triumph of Nativism*. Syracuse: Syracuse University Press.

Brumberg, D. (2001). *Reinventing Khomeini: The Struggle for Reform in Iran*. Chicago: University of Chicago Press.

Fischer, M. (2003). *Iran: From Religious Dispute to Revolution*. Wisconsin: University of Wisconsin Press.

Garver, J. (2006). *China and Iran: Ancient Partners in a Post-Imperial World*. Seattle: University of Washington Press.

Javadzadeh, A. (2007). "Marxists into Muslims: The Iranian Irony." *FIU Electronic Theses and Dissertations,* Paper 36. Retrieved March 12, 2010 from http://digitalcommons.fiu.edu/cgi/viewcontent.cgi?article=1051&context=etd.

Kraft, J. (1978). "Letter from Iran." *New Yorker,* December 18.

Kurzman, C. (2001). "Islamic Scholars' Protests against the Islamic State in Iran." *International Journal of Politics, Culture, and Society* (Winter), 342–354.

Macleod, S., and N. Siamdoust. (2004, May 5). The Critical Cleric: Reclaiming Islam for a New World." *Time Magazine.* Retrieved March 12, 2010 from http://www.time.com/time/2004/innovators/200405/kadivar.html.

Matin-Asgari, A. (1997). "Abdolkarim Sorush and the Secularization of Islamic Thought in Iran." *Iranian Studies* (Winter/Spring), 104.

Moin, B. (1999). *Khomeini: Life of the Ayatollah.* London: I.B. Taurus.

Mottahedeh, Roy. (1985/2000). *The Mantle of the Prophet: Religion and Politics in Iran.* Oxford: One World.

Rahnema, A. (2000). *An Islamic Utopia: A Political Biography of Ali Shariati.* London: I.B. Taurus.

Razavi, Shahra. (2006). "Islamic Politics, Human Rights and Women's Claims for Equality in Iran." *Third World Quarterly,* 27(7), 1227.

Rostami Povey, E. (2004). "Trade Unions and Women's NGOs: Diverse Civil Society Organisations in Iran." *Development in Practice,* 14(1), 258.

Roy, O. (1999). "The Crisis of Religious Legitimacy in Iran." *Middle East Journal.* (Spring), 210.

Sadri, M. (2001). "Sacral Defense of Secularism: The Political Theologies of Soroush, Shabestari, and Kadivar." *International Journal of Politics, Culture, and Society.*

Sadri, M. (2002, February 13). "Attack from Within: Dissident Political Theology in Contemporary Iran." *The Iranian.* Retrieved March 12, 2010 from

Sahimi, M. (2011, May 7). "Ahmadinejad-Khamenei Rift Deepens into Abyss." PBS *Frontline,* Retrieved March 12, 2010 from http://www.pbs.org/wgbh/pages/frontline/tehranbureau/2011/05/opinion-ahmadinejad-khamenei-rift-deepens-to-an-abyss.html.

Schirazi, A. (1997). *The Constitution of Iran: Politics and the State in the Islamic Republic.* London: I.B. Tauris.

Sobhe, K. (1982). "Education in Revolution: Is Iran Duplicating the Chinese Cultural Revolution?" *Comparative Education,* 18(3), 275–279.

"The Structure of Power in Iran." (2012). PBS *Frontline.* Retrieved March 12, 2010 from http://www.pbs.org/wgbh/pages/frontline/shows/tehran/inside/govt.html.

Watson, K. (1976). "The Shah's White Revolution-Education and Reform in Iran." *Comparative Education,* 12(1), 27.

Wright, R. (2000). *The Last Great Revolution.* New York: Random House.

Wright, R. (1996). "Islam and Liberal Democracy: Two Visions of Reformation." *Journal of Democracy.* (May), 64–75.

Zonis, M. (1985). "The Rule of the Clerics in the Islamic Republic of Iran." *Annals of the American Academy of Political and Social Science,* 482, 89.

Conclusion

J. Harold Ellens

History demonstrates vividly that religion, on the one hand, is often a revolutionary force, sometimes for good and sometimes for evil. On the other hand, it is equally apparent that religion has frequently been a stultifying presence that imprisons the mind and represses the human spirit. This volume has focused more on the former concept than on the latter. However, both the inspiring creativity and imprisoning control for which religion has been responsible are addressed or implied in the imaginative and analytical chapters presented in this volume, *Religious Revolts*. This sets the stage for volume II, *Political Revolts*. This work is completed by volume III, *Economic Revolts*. I am grateful to the scholars who have joined me in making this project a work of great scope and quality.

Index

Abelard, Peter, 152
Abishag, 148
Abramski, S., 123
Abuya, Elisha b., 129
acceptance, 167–168
action, 18–20, 24, 27–28
Adams, Samuel, 174
African Americans: civil rights movement and, 22–25; Malcolm X, 289–300; melancholia and, 290–293
Ahmadinejad, Mahmoud, 310–312
Albrecht of Brandenberg, 26
Allport, Gordon, 228–229, 231–232
Alon, G., 123
al Qaeda, 12, 187, 230, 239–240, 241
altruism, 170
American colonies, 173, 174–175
American fundamentalism, 224–225, 237, 241
American Revolution, 174–175, 176, 199–200
Amit, David, 69

Anglican Church, 27
anti-intellectualism, 255
anti-Semitism, 149–150
Apocalypse of Peter, 121–123
apocalyptic expectations, 129–138
apostasy, 130–131
Appleby, R. Scott, 236–237
Aqiva, Rabbi, 56–58, 66, 111–112, 129
Arab Spring, 8
Arafat, Yasser, 227
Aran, Gideon, 239
Arendt, Hannah, 7, 8–9
Aristobolus II, 36
asceticism, 211
Ataturk, Mustafa Kemal, 218
Augustine, St., 152, 291
Aune, David, 91
authoritative discourse, 11–12
Azzai, Ben, 129

Baird, Robert M., 233
Bar-Cocheba, Sim(e)on, 56, 60–62, 65, 66, 75, 82, 86–87. *See also*

Bar Kochba revolt; messianic status of, 111–113
Bar-Giora(s), Simon, 71, 73
Bar Kochba revolt, 53–87, 109, 110; apocalyptic expectations and, 129–138; archaeological evidence, 65; cave usage during, 66–79, 85; coins from, 74–79, 84; Jerusalem, 54–55; Jewish followers of Jesus and, 109–128; leading personalities of, 55–62; literary evidence, 62–66, 84–85, 113–123; numismatic evidence, 76–79; strategic outline, 79–84; suffering following, 130
Barth, Karl, 276
Battir, 83
Bauckham, Richard, 121–122
Baumgaertner, Jerome, 153–154
Bazargan, Mehdi, 302
Behind the Sun (film), 1–13; life as revolution in, 9–11; metaphorical meaning of, 7; story of, 4–6; theology in, 7–9
Benedict, Philip, 159
Bergson, Henri, 196
Berkhof, Hendrikus, 276, 277
Berlin, Isaiah, 233
Bethar, 83
Bethsaida-Julias, 35, 36, 40–42, 45–47, 50–51
Bhindranwale, 243–244
Bible, 148, 149, 150, 255, 256, 271
biblical criticism, 256–261
bin Laden, Osama, 12, 210, 227
black church, 23
Borujerdi, Ayatollah Hossein, 306
Brooks, Phillips, 257
Brown, John, 202

Brown v. Board of Education, 23
Brueggemann, Walter, 13n1
Buddhism, 245–246
Bush, George W., 207

Caesarea, Bishop of, 64–65
Calvin, John, 28, 147, 156–160
Calvinism, 159–160
Campaign for Forgiveness Research, 176
Carroll, James, 149
Catholic Church, 25–29, 145, 152, 156, 157, 237–238, 272. *See also* Imperial Church
Catholicism, 155–156, 237–238
causal relationships, 199
"Cave of Letters," 65, 67, 76
cave usage, in ancient Israel, 66–79, 85
celibacy, 150, 153, 155, 156–157
change, 1; action stage of, 18–19, 20, 24, 27–28; contemplation stage of, 17–18, 20, 23, 26; maintenance stage of, 19, 20, 24–25, 28–29; nonvolitional, 30–31; organizational, 21–22; precontemplation stage of, 16–17, 20, 22–23, 25–26; preparation stage of, 18, 23–24, 27; process of, 16–33
charisma, 197
Charles II, 207
China, 246–248
Chorazim, 51
Christianity, 211; emergence of, 120, 142; fish symbol and, 150–151; forgiveness and, 168; fundamentalism in, 224–225, 229–230, 235–238, 248; Imperial Church and, 271–288; Pauline Revolution and, 139–145; separation of, from

Judaism, 110–111, 124;
  sexuality and, 147–160
churches, 271–288. *See also specific churches*
Church of England, 27
Cicero, Marcus Tullius, 36
circumcision, 149
Civilization and Its Discontents (Freud), 212
Civil Rights Act, 24
civil rights movement, TTM model applied to, 22–25
Civil War, 202
Cocceianus, Dion Cassius. *See* Dio Cassius
cognitive mechanisms, 166–168
Cohen, Shaye J. D., 39
coins, Bar Kochba, 74–79, 84
Cole, Stewart, 255
collectivistic self-construal, 167
Collins, J.J., 62–63
Columbus, Christopher, 173
community formation, 1
compassion, 170, 195, 196
conformity, 3–4, 15
Confucianism, 245, 246–248
consciousness-raising, 17, 22, 23, 26, 30, 32
Constantine, 271, 273–274, 284
contemplation, 17–18, 20, 23, 26
contingency management, 19, 29
Copper Scroll, 72–73
cost-benefit analysis, 17
Coulanges, Fustel de, 8
Council of Nicea, 26
Council of Trent, 28
counterconditioning, 19, 20
criminal justice system, 167
Crooks, George R., 263
Crossan, John Dominic, 93
crucufixion, 105, 208
Curtis, O. A., 258

Dali Lama, 205
Daniel, 134–135
Darwin, Charles, 210
David, King, 148
dead, touching of the, 208
death, 191, 201
Death of a Salesman (Miller), 219
de Burre, Idelette, 159
decisional forgiveness, 170
de la Cruz, Juan, 152
Del Banco, Andrew, 200–201, 202
deterrence theory, 167
The Dialogue with Trypho (Martyr), 115–117
Diaspora Revolt, 132
dictators, 9
Dio Cassius, 62–64, 66, 74–75
disobedience, 206–207
Divine Spirit, 282, 284, 286–287
divorce, 154–155
dogma, 12
Donatists, 151
dramatic relief, 18, 22, 23, 26, 30, 32
Dreams from My Father (Obama), 297–298
Du Bois, W. E. B., 290, 291
Dunn, J. D. G., 110

Ebionites, 119
Egypt, 194, 217
Emmaus, 82
emotional forgiveness, 170
empathy, 170
Emperor Cult, 141, 142
Enright, R. D., 174, 176
Enright's Process Model, 174
environmental reevaluation, 17–18, 20, 22, 23, 26, 29
Epicureans, 131
Epistle of Barnabas, 122–123
Eshel, Hanan, 69

Eusebius, 117–120
evangelical fundamentalism, 273–274, 276
evolution, 165–166
exogamy, 209
exploitation, 171

family values, 8
Farel, William, 158, 159
Faulkner, John A., 254
Faulkner, John Alfred, 256, 263–266, 268
Fetzer Institute, 176
First Apology (Martyr), 114–117
First Diet of Spyer, 27
First Jewish revolt. *See* Great Jewish revolt (66–73 CE)
First Temple, 110, 132
fish symbol, 150–151
Flavius, Josephus, 35, 36, 38–41, 48–50, 62–63, 69–74, 84–85, 134–135
Florus, Gessius, 40
forbearance, 167
forgiveness, 163–181; cognitive mechanisms in practice of, 166–168; communication of, 177; communities that practice, 172; decisional, 170; emotional, 170; forces that spread, 171–173; minirevolution, 173–178; religion and, 175; religious component of, 168; vs. revenge, 164–168; as social and societal good, 168–173; social evolution and, 169–171; study of, 176–178
fraternal self, 293–295, 297–299
Frazer, James G., 207, 208
French Revolution, 199
Freud, Sigmund, 8, 205–219, 290
Fromm, Erich, 234–235

fundamentalism, 12, 218, 221–252; American, 224–225, 237, 241; Buddhist, 245–246; Christian, 224–225, 229–230, 235–238, 248; Confucianism, 246–248; danger of, 248; definition of, 254; evangelical, 273–274, 276; Hindu, 241–242; Islamic, 225, 230, 239–241, 248; Jewish, 238–240; in Methodist Church, 253–269; pathology of, 222–223; prejudice and, 222–224, 227–235, 249–250; psychobiology and, 225–235; Sikh, 243–245; violence and, 225; worldwide, 235–248
Furniss, Norman, 254, 255

Galilee, 39, 50, 69–70
Gallus, Cestius, 40, 54
Gamala, 39
Gamla, 35, 36, 40–47, 50–51, 70
Geneva, 28
Geneva Academy, 28
Geneva Consistory, 157–158
Gilkey, Langdon, 276
Girard, René, 230
Gitman, Shemarya, 46
Gnosticism, 131
God, 7–9. *See also* Jesus Christ; concept of, 210; grace of, 143–145; kingdom of, 91–106
goddesses, 210–211
Golan, 69–70
Golan Archaeological Museum, 47
The Golden Bough (Frazer), 207
Golden Temple, 243
Goren, David, 46
grace, 143–145, 249
Grant, Michael, 59
Gray, John, 71–72
Great Jewish revolt (66–73 CE), 35–52, 54–55, 62–63, 84;

apocalyptic expectations and, 129–138; archaeological evidence, 46–48; Bethsaida-Julias, 41–42, 45–47, 50–51; Gamla, 41–47, 50–51; literary evidence, 48–50; major developments, 37–38; research sources, 38–41; suffering following, 130
group behavior, 15

Hadrianus, Publius Aelius, 58–59, 65–66, 84
Haiti, 218
Halakic Midrashim, 135
Hall, Doug, 271–288
Hamas, 187
Hardy, Henry, 224
Haredim, 238–239
Hasmon, Mattathias, 72
healing touch, 207
Heidegger, Martin, 312
Heloise, 152
helplessness, 8–9
Herod, 69–70
Herod Agrippa II, 40, 42, 47, 50
Hilsum, Lindsey, 184–185
Hindu fundamentalism, 241–242
historical Jesus, 92, 93–101, 103
Hitler, Adolf, 227
Holocaust, 196
homeostasis, 15
homosexuality, 147, 159
hopelessness, 8–9
human condition, 11
The Human Condition (Arendt), 7
human discourse, 2–4
human nature, 1–2
Hunt, Lynn, 194
Hussein, Saddam, 210, 240–241

icons, 184
Imperial Church, 271–288

incest, 206, 210
India, fundamentalism in, 241–245
indulgences, selling of, 25–26, 28, 152
in-groups, 176–177
internal revolutions, 16–33
Iran, 217, 240–241, 301–314; Ahmadinejad and, 310–312; Islamic revolution in, 303–314; postrevolution, 308–310; prerevolutionary, 301–305; religious dissidents in, 308–310; White Revolution, 307
Iraq, 188, 207, 240–241
Islam, 12, 148, 187
Islamic fundamentalism, 218, 225, 230, 239–241, 248
Islamic leadership, 289–900
Islamic revolution, in Iran, 303–314
Israel, 199, 217–218, 225, 231, 239; cave usage in ancient, 66–79

Jebus's caves, 71
Jefferson, Thomas, 200–201
Jerusalem, 40, 42, 50, 54–55, 71–72, 84, 133–134
Jesus Christ, 197, 207, 286–287; artistic portrayals of, 153; celibacy of, 150; Jewish followers of, 109–128; kingdom of God and, 91–106; patriarchy and, 148–149; sacrifice by, 211; Second Coming of, 144, 145; St. Paul and, 139–141
Jesus Database project, 92, 93–101
Jesus Seminar, 92, 93, 97; postresurrection appearances of, 140–141
Jewish-Christian engagement, 110
Jewish followers of Jesus, 109–128

Jewish identity, 130–131
Jewish revolts. *See* Bar Kochba revolt; Great Jewish revolt (66–73 CE)
Jews, apocalyptic expectations of, 129–138
jihad, 188
Jim Crow laws, 22, 23, 24
John, gospel of, 144–145
John Hyrcanus II, 36
John Templeton Foundation (JTF), 176
Jonah, 101, 105
Jordan, 218
Jossa, Giorgio, 39–40
Judaism, 141; fundamentalism in, 238–240; schism between Christianity and, 110–111, 124; sexuality and, 149–150
Judgment Day, 144, 145
justice, 164–167, 170, 172

Kadare, Ismail, 6
Kadivar, Mohsen, 309
Ketef Yericho, 76
Khamenei, Ayatollah, 310–311
Khatami, Mohammad, 308
Khomeini, Ayatollah, 240–241, 302, 304, 305–308, 311, 313
King, Martin Luther, Jr., 23, 24
kingdom of God, 91–106
kingship, 207–208
Kohlberg, L., 174
Kook, Rabbu, 239
Kung, Hans, 276

laws, 165–166
leadership, 171–172
Lefebvre, Marcel, 237
Lewis, Edwin, 254, 265, 266–267
lex rex, 165–166, 170
liberal theology, 278

life and death, 191, 201
life as revolution, 9–11
Lincoln, Abraham, 202
Locke, John, 174
Lord's Prayer, 100, 102
loss, 1
love-prejudice, 232–233, 249
Luke, 133–134
Luther, Katharina, 153–154
Luther, Martin, 26–27, 28, 147, 152–157, 160
Lutherism, 27
lynchings, 23

Maccabaeus, Judas, 72
Maccabean Revolution, 84
magical thinking, 198
maintenance, 19, 20, 24–25, 28–29
Malcolm X, 24, 289–900
Mali, 184–185, 187
Mandela, Nelson, 171
Manilian Law, 36
marriage, 153–155, 157–158, 197–198, 209–210
Marsden, George, 253, 261
Marty, Martin E., 236–237
Martyr, Justin, 113–117, 123, 124
Masada, 73–74
McConnell. F. J., 260, 262–263
McCullough,, 164, 171, 174, 176
Medina, John, 225–226
mega-churches, 278
melancholia, 290–293, 295–297, 298
Melanchthon, Philipp, 154
Memorial Day, 200
Mendenhall, James William, 256–257
mental health treatment, 173–174
mercy, 170
Merton, Thomas, 291–292
Methodist Church, 253–269

Micah, 143
Middle Ages, 185
Middle East, 217–218
Middlekauff, Robert, 199–200
Miller, Arthur, 219
Mishnah, 135
missionaries, 238
Mitchell, H. G., 257–261, 267
Mithraism, 141–143
Mithridates VI, 37
Mithridatic Wars, 37
monoamine oxidase, 226
monogamy, 150
Montazeri, Hossein-Ali, 309–310
Moore, R. L., 260
moral imperatives, 206
Mosaic Code, 13n1
Mossadeq, Mohammad, 301
mother-goddesses, 210–211
Movement for the Liberation of Iran, 302–303
Muslims, 240

Nahmani, Samuel b., 135
National Association for the Advancement of Colored People, 22–23
National Front party, 301–302
Nation of Islam, 292–298
Nazi Party, 203
Neoplatonism, 142
nepotism, 234
neurotransmitters, 226
New Testament, 91–92, 149, 271, 286
Nicene Creed, 159
Niebuhr, H. Richard, 254, 255
Niebuhr, Reinhold, 276
Nietzsche, Friedrich, 155
Ninety-Five Theses (Luther), 26
Northern Ireland, 176
numismatic, 76

numismatic evidence, of Bar Kochba, 76–79
Nuremberg trials, 163, 171

Obama, Barack, 218, 297–299
Oberman, Heiko, 158
Oedipus complex, 205–206
Oedipus Rex (Sophocles), 205–206
Old Testament, cave usage in ancient, 68–69
Oppenheimer, Aharon, 112, 124n1
order, 3–4, 11
organizational change, 21–22
orthodoxies, 222, 225, 227, 248
out-groups, 176–177

Palestine, 231, 239
Pamphili, Eusebius, 64–65
patriarchy, 148–149, 234–235
patricide, 210
Paul, St., 139–145, 150, 286–287
Pauline Revolution, 139–145
Peace of Augsburg, 28
pity, 196
Pliny the Elder, 35
polygamy, 149–150, 154
Pompey, 36, 37
Pontus, 37
power, 171; knowledge as, 289–290
precontemplation, 16–17, 20, 22–23, 25–26
prejudgments, 232
prejudice, 222–224, 227–235, 249–250
preparation, 18, 23–24, 27
primal sin, 211
pro-lifer movement, 231
Protestant Reformation, 145, 147–161; TTM model applied to, 25–29
psychiatrists, 209

psychobiology, 225–235
psychology, 15–33
Puritanism, 158
Pussy Riot band, 187–191, 195, 202
Putin, Vladimir, 187–191

Qumran, 72–73, 74

race, melancholia of, 290–293, 295–297, 298
racial segregation, 22, 23
Rashbi, 57
Rasmussen, Susan, 186–187
REACH Forgiveness Model, 174
reconciliation strategies, 165
Reed, Jonathan, 101
relapse, 19
relational offenses, responses to, 168
relationship-rending acts, 169
relationship-restorative acts, 169
relationship value, 171
relics, 184
religion, 7–9. *See also specific religions*; forgiveness and, 168, 175; Freud on, 205–219; sacred and, 185; therapeutic value of, 213–217; totems and, 209
religious fundamentalism, 221–252
religiosity, 208, 209
Renaissance art, 153
restorative justice, 172
Revelation of John, 132
revenge, evolution of, 164–168
revolution(s): life as, 9–11; roots of, 1–13; sacred and, 182–304; stages of change model applied to, 15–33
rex lex, 165, 170
rituals, 209

Rivkin, Ellis, 56
Roman Catholicism, 237–238
Roman Empire: Christianity and, 271, 272, 284; competing religions of, 141–143
Romans, 54–55
Rome, 36, 37, 53, 101, 133–134, 151
Rosenbaum, Stuart E., 233
Rufus, Tinneius, 80–81, 84, 86
Russia, 187, 188–190, 191, 195
Russian Orthodox Church, 275
Rwanda, 176

sacred, 182–304; difference and, 194–196; formations of the, 184–185; moments, 196–203; religion and, 185; revolution and, 183–204; secular and, 185–187; secularity of the, 191–194
sacrifice, 200, 201, 211
Sadat, Anwar, 240
Salles, Walter, 1, 2, 7, 8, 12
Sartwell, Crispin, 289–290, 295–297
Saudi Arabia, 12
scapegoats, 230
Schäfer, Peter, 112, 121
Schussler-Fiorenza, Elizabeth, 149
Schwartz, Seth, 41
Scott, James C., 100–101
Second Coming, 144, 145
Second Jewish Revolt. *See* Bar Kochba revolt
Second Temple Judaism, 87, 98, 105–106
secular, sacred and, 185–187, 191–194
segregation, 22, 23
Seleucids, 72

self-construal, 167
self-division, 290
self-liberation, 18–19, 20
self-perception, 2
self-reevaluation, 18, 20, 27, 32
self-sacrifice, 211
Sepphoris, 50
Severus, Julius, 59–60, 82–83, 84, 86
Severus, Sulpicius, 120–121
sexuality, 147–160
sexual pleasure, 147–148, 150–152, 154, 159, 160
sexual revolution, 147
Shabestari, Mohammad, 308–309
Shah, Reza, 303, 307
Shariati, Ali, 302, 303–304
Shariatmadari, Grand Ayatollah, 304, 313
Sharon, Ariel, 227, 239
Sierra Leone, 208
Sikh fundamentalism, 243–245
Simeon, Prince of Israel, 53–54, 67. *See* Bar-Cocheba, Sim(e)on
Sinhalese, 245–246
sit-ins, 23–24
slaves, 202
Sloan, Harold Paul, 254, 260–269
Smedes, Lewis, 174, 175, 178
Smith, Morton, 45–46
social conformity, 3–4, 15
social context, 2
social discourse, 2–4, 11–12
social evolution, 169–171
social order, 3–4, 11, 199
social trust, 202–203
society, 1, 8
Sophocles, 205–206
Soroush, Abdol-Karim, 309
South Africa, 163–164, 171, 176
Soviet Union, 175
Spalatin, Georg, 155

Spinoza, Baruch, 248–249
Sri Lanka, 245–246
Stalin, Joseph, 227
state autonomy, 169
Steinberg, Leo, 153
stimulus control, 19, 20–21, 29
Stob, Henry, 224–225
Strickert, Fred, 76, 85–86
sublimation, 212
Swearer, Donald K., 246
symbols, 184
sympathy, 170
Syria, 187, 192, 193, 196, 199

taboos, 206–208
Taiwan, 247
Taliban, 185, 241
Tamils, 245–246
Tannaim, 135
telos, 169
Templeton, John, Jr., 176
terrorism, 8, 225, 230, 231, 241, 244–245, 248
Tetradrachm Cave, 76
Tetradrachm of Bar Kokhba, 76, 77
Tetzel, Johan, 26
Theissen, Gerd, 103
Theodore of Mopsuestia, 151
theology, 7–9
theory of mind, 166–167
Theravada Buddhism, 245–246
Theresa of Avila, 152
Till, Emmitt, 23
Tolokonnikova, Nadezhda, 190
Tosefta, 135
totemism, 206, 209, 210
Track I diplomacy, 172, 176
Track II diplomacy, 172, 176
Track III diplomacy, 177
tradition, 3, 4, 8, 13n1, 197
Trajan, 129

transtheoretical model (TTM), **16–33**; application to revolts and revolutions, 21–29; change process in, 16–19; clinical example, 19–21; implications of, 29–32
Treaty of Versailles, 172
trust, 202–203
Truth and Reconciliation Commission (TRC), 163–164, 171
Tudor, Mary, 27
Tutu, Desmond, 163, 171

Van den Berghe, 234
Vasa, Gustavas, 27
vegetarians, 234
vengeance, 164–167
Vespasianus, Titus Flavius, 83
violence, 201; fundamentalism and, 225, 244–245, 248; strategies that limit, 165
Voting Rights Act, 24

war crimes trials, 163
Warren, William E., 258
wars, 165
Washington, George, 199–200
Weber, Max, 197
Wei-ming, Tu, 247
Wesley, John, 256
West Bank, 199
What Would Jesus Do (WWJD) paradigm, 92
white identity, 295–297
work, 7
Worthington, Everett, 174, 176

Yazbek, Samar, 193
Young-Bruehl, Elizabeth, 227–228, 234–235

Zionism, 225, 239
Zoma, Ben, 129
Zwingli, Ulrich, 27

About the Series Editor and Advisors

SERIES EDITOR

J. Harold Ellens is a retired Professor of Philosophy, Psychology, and Classical Studies, a research scholar, a retired Presbyterian Theologian and ordained minister, and a retired U.S. Army colonel. He has published 227 books and 176 professional journal articles as well as 276 reviews. He served for fifteen years as Executive Director of the Christian Association for Psychological Studies, and as Founding Editor and Editor-in-chief of the *Journal of Psychology and Christianity*. He has a PhD from Wayne State University in the Psychology of Human Communication, a PhD from the University of Michigan in Biblical and Near Eastern Studies, and Master's Degrees from Calvin Theological Seminary, Princeton Theological Seminary, and the University of Michigan. He was born in Michigan, grew up in a Dutch-German immigrant community, and determined at age seven to enter the Christian ministry as a means to help his people with the great amount of suffering he perceived all around him during the Great Depression and World War II.

His large number of publications is focused on the interface of psychology, social processes, and religion/spirituality. His recent publications include *The Destructive Power of Religion* (4 vols., 2004), *Psychology and the Bible* (4 vols., with Wayne Rollins, 2004), *God's Word for our World* (2 vols., 2004), *Sex in the Bible* (2006), *Text and Community* (2 vols., 2007), *Radical Grace* (2007), *Understanding Religious Experience* (2007), *Miracles: God, Science, and Psychology in the Paranormal* (3 vols., 2008), *The Spirituality of Sex* (2009), *Probing the Frontiers of Biblical Studies* (2009), *The Son of Man in The Gospel of John* (2010),

The Healing Power of Spirituality (3 vols., 2010), *Honest Faith for Our Time: Truth-telling about the Bible, the Creed, and the Church* (2010), *Light from the Other Side: The Paranormal as Friend and Familiar* (2010), *Explaining Evil* (3 vols., 2011), *Psychological Hermeneutics of Biblical Themes and Texts* (2012), *A Dangerous Report: Challenging Sermons for Advent and Easter* (2012), *God's Radical Grace: Challenging Sermons for Ordinary Time(s)* (2013), *Heaven, Hell, and Afterlife: Eternity in Judaism, Christianity, and Islam* (3 vols., 2013), *By Grace Alone: Forgiveness for Everyone, for Everything, for Evermore* (2013). He is a psychotherapist in private practice.

ADVISORY BOARD

Donald Capps, psychologist of religion, is Emeritus William Hart Felmeth Professor of Pastoral Theology at Princeton Theological Seminary. In 1989 he was awarded an honorary doctorate by the University of Uppsala, Sweden, in recognition of the importance of his publications. He served as president of the Society for the Scientific Study of Religion from 1990 to 1992. Among his many significant books are *Men, Religion and Melancholia: James, Otto, Jung and Erikson and Freud*; *The Freudians on Religion: A Reader*; *Social Phobia: Alleviating Anxiety in an Age of Self-Promotion*; and *Jesus: A Psychological Biography*. He also authored *The Child's Song: The Religious Abuse of Children* and *Jesus, the Village Psychiatrist*.

Zenon Lotufo Jr. is a Presbyterian minister (Independent Presbyterian Church of Brazil), a philosopher, and a psychotherapist, specializing in transactional analysis. He has lectured both to undergraduate and graduate courses in universities in São Paulo, Brazil. He coordinates the specialization in pastoral psychology of the Christian Psychologists and Psychiatrists Association. He is the author of *Relações Humanas (Human Relations)*, *Cruel God, Kind God*; and *Disfunções no Comportamento Organizacional (Dysfunctions in Organizational Behavior)*, and coauthor of *O Potencial Humano (Human Potential)*. He has also authored numerous journal articles.

Dirk Odendaal is South African, born in what is now called the Province of the Eastern Cape. He spent much of his youth in the Transkei in the town of Umtata, where his parents were teachers at a seminary. He trained as a minister at the Stellenbosch Seminary for the Dutch Reformed Church and was ordained in 1983 in the Dutch Reformed Church in Southern Africa. He transferred to East London in 1988 to minister to members of the Uniting Reformed Church in Southern Africa in one of the huge suburbs for Xhosa-speaking people. He received his doctorate (DLitt) in 1992 at the University of Port Elizabeth in Semitic languages and a master's degree in counseling psychology at Rhodes University.

Wayne G. Rollins is professor emeritus of biblical studies at Assumption College, Worcester, Massachusetts, and adjunct professor of scripture at Hartford Seminary, Hartford, Connecticut. His writings include *The Gospels: Portraits of Christ* (1964), *Jung and the Bible* (1983), and *Soul and Psyche, The Bible in Psychological Perspective* (1999). He received his PhD in New Testament studies from Yale University and is the founder and chairman (1990–2000) of the Society of Biblical Literature Section on Psychology and Biblical Studies.

About the Editor and Contributors

EDITOR

J. Harold Ellens is a retired Professor of Philosophy, Psychology, and Classical Studies, a research scholar, a retired Presbyterian Theologian and ordained minister, and a retired U.S. Army colonel. He has published 227 books and 176 professional journal articles as well as 276 reviews. He served for fifteen years as Executive Director of the Christian Association for Psychological Studies, and as Founding Editor and Editor-in-chief of the *Journal of Psychology and Christianity*. He has a PhD from Wayne State University in the Psychology of Human Communication, a PhD from the University of Michigan in Biblical and Near Eastern Studies, and Master's Degrees from Calvin Theological Seminary, Princeton Theological Seminary, and the University of Michigan. He was born in Michigan, grew up in a Dutch-German immigrant community, and determined at age seven to enter the Christian ministry as a means to help his people with the great amount of suffering he perceived all around him during the Great Depression and World War II.

His large number of publications is focused on the interface of psychology, social processes, and religion/spirituality. His recent publications include *The Destructive Power of Religion* (4 vols., 2004), *Psychology and the Bible* (4 vols., with Wayne Rollins, 2004), *God's Word for our World* (2 vols., 2004), *Sex in the Bible* (2006), *Text and Community* (2 vols., 2007), *Radical Grace* (2007), *Understanding Religious Experience* (2007), *Miracles: God, Science, and Psychology in the Paranormal*, (3 vols., 2008), *The Spirituality of Sex* (2009), *Probing the Frontiers of Biblical Studies* (2009), *The Son of Man in The Gospel of John* (2010), *The Healing Power of Spirituality* (3 vols., 2010), *Honest Faith for Our Time:*

Truth-telling about the Bible, the Creed, and the Church (2010), *Light from the Other Side: The Paranormal as Friend and Familiar* (2010), *Explaining Evil* (3 vols., 2011), *Psychological Hermeneutics of Biblical Themes and Texts* (2012), *A Dangerous Report: Challenging Sermons for Advent and Easter* (2012), *God's Radical Grace: Challenging Sermons for Ordinary Time(s)* (2013), *Heaven, Hell, and Afterlife: Eternity in Judaism, Christianity, and Islam* (3 vols., 2013), *By Grace Alone: Forgiveness for Everyone, for Everything, for Evermore* (2013). He is a psychotherapist in private practice.

CONTRIBUTORS

Jeni L. Burnette, PhD, is an assistant professor of psychology at the University of Richmond. She received her undergraduate degree at the University of North Carolina and completed her PhD in psychology at Virginia Commonwealth University. Jeni's research applies basic social psychological theories to understanding fundamental social issues such as obesity and healthy relationship functioning. She primarily focuses on how mind-sets matter for self-regulation and goal achievement. Her work has been published in journals including *Psychological Bulletin, Journal of Personality and Social Psychology, Journal of Experimental Social Psychology*, and *Personality and Social Psychological Bulletin*.

Hector F. De Los Santos is a recent graduate of Westmont College, where he completed his bachelor's degree in psychology. He will be attending Purdue University's doctoral program in clinical psychology in fall 2013. His research interests include how social relationships impact coping and resilience after trauma and grief, as well as better understanding ethic and cultural differences to improve the efficacy of clinical interventions. He also works as a residential counselor at Noah's Anchorage Youth Crisis Shelter in Santa Barbara, California.

Richard Fenn, PhD, is professor emeritus of Christianity and society at Princeton Theological Seminary. His work has concentrated on three closely related themes: secularization, time, and the sacred. His most recent work is *Key Thinkers in the Sociology of Religion* (Continuum Ltd., 2007). He has two works currently in press, one on the sacred, the other on the crisis of secularity in the United States from the 1960s to the present.

John T. Greene, PhD, is emeritus professor of religious studies at Michigan State University. He has lectured on the history of religions, scriptural and historical studies, Hebrew language and literature, and archaeology. From 1983 through 2006, he directed MSU's Archaeology, History of Religions and Hebrew Language Summer Program in Israel (Haifa University) at Et-Tell/Bethsaida, where he is the excavations codirector. He is the author of *The Role* *of the Messenger and Message in the Ancient Near East and Balaam and His Interpreters* (Brown Judaic Studies Series) and *What Did The Apostle Paul Really Mean? The Case of Christ in Paul's Thought* (Mellen); coauthor with Mishael Caspi of *Parables and Fables as Distinctive Jewish Literary Genres* and *The Rebellion of Korah* (Mellen); coeditor of five anthologies with Mishael Caspi: 1) *Unbinding the Binding of Isaac,* 2) *"And God Said: 'You're Fired!'": Elijah and Elisha* (Bibal), 3) *How Jonah Is Interpreted in Judaism, Christianity and Islam,* 4) *Problems in Translating Texts About Jesus* (Mellen), and 5) *Eve: The Unbearable Flaming Fire* (Gorgias); an anniversary volume coedited with J. Harold Ellens, *Probing the Frontiers of Biblical Studies* (Wipf & Stock); as well as numerous chapters and journal articles. Contributions related to his work in the archaeology of ancient Israel can be found in *Bethsaida: A City by the North Shore of the Sea of Galilee,* Volumes I, II, and III (Thomas Jefferson University Press) and *Cities Through the Looking Glass,* a study of urbanization in the Galilee (Eisenbrauns). Professor Greene has participated in excavation projects at Tell Gezer, Tel Halif, Gamla, and Et-Tell/Bethsaida. He is an active member of the Society of Biblical Literature and is co-convener of the Seminar in Biblical Characters in Three Traditions (Judaism, Christianity, Islam).

Jack T. Hanford, ThD, is professor emeritus of biomedical ethics at Ferris State University in Michigan. He is a member of the American Philosophical Association, American Academy of Religion, Christian Association for Psychological Studies, and Association of Moral Education. He is also an associate of the Hastings Center, the foremost center for biomedical ethics; The Center for Bioethics and Human Dignity; the Kennedy Institute of Ethics; and several other societies. He has published *Bioethics from a Faith Perspective: Ethics in Health Care for the Twenty-First Century* and many professional articles, including in *Religious Education, Journal for the Scientific Study of Religion, Journal of Psychology and Christianity,* and *Journal of Pastoral Psychology, Ethics and Medicine.*

Gregory C. Jenks, PhD, is an Australian religion scholar and Anglican priest. He is academic dean at St Francis Theological College, Brisbane, and a senior lecturer in the School of Theology at Charles Sturt University. His PhD was awarded by the University of Queensland for his research into the origins and early development of the Antichrist myth. Dr. Jenks has a long-standing interest in Christian origins and is the lead researcher for the Jesus Database project. He has been visiting professor and scholar-in-residence at St George's College, Jerusalem, on several occasions, and is a codirector of the Bethsaida Archaeological Excavation. He is a fellow of the Westar Institute and served as its associate director from 1999 to 2001. His recent publications include *The Once and Future Bible* (Wipf & Stock, 2011), *The Once and Future Scriptures* (Polebridge Press, 2013) and *The Once and Future Jesus* (Polebridge Press, forthcoming).

Kayla Jordan is a graduating senior serving as a research fellow in the Department of Psychology at Evangel University, Springfield, Missouri. Her research interests focus on conflict and religion.

Cassandra M. Klyman, MD, received her MD from the University of Michigan Medical School and her psychoanalytic training from the Michigan Psychoanalytic Institute. She has lectured and published in peer-reviewed journals nationally and internationally. As Assistant Clinical Professor of Psychiatry at Wayne State University School of Medicine she has taught, supervised, and mentored medical students, resident and analytic candidates; and endowed scholarships at her *alma mater*. Serving as President of the Michigan Psychiatric Society allowed her to have a voice in local and national medical politics. She is a Distinguished Life Fellow of the American Psychiatric Association, Fellow of the American Academy of Psychoanalysis and Dynamic Psychotherapy and Fellow of the College of Forensic Examiners. Previous collaborations at the interface of psychology and religion with Dr. Ellens can be found in *The Destructive Power of Religion* (2004, v2, ch.11) and *Explaining Evil* (2011, v2, ch.4). Dr. Klyman maintains a private practice of psychiatry, psychoanalysis, and forensic consulting in Bloomfield Hill, Michigan.

Joseph M. Kramp, PhD, is a Research Scholar at The Ronin Institute. He also teaches as an Adjunct Professor at numerous institutions, such as Chicago Theological Seminary, Edison State College, Florida Gulf Coast University, and Barry University, among others.

Caroline Lavelock, BS, is a doctoral student in the Counseling Psychology program at Virginia Commonwealth University (accredited by the American Psychological Association). She conducts research in basic positive psychology and interventions to promote the virtues of forgiveness, humility, patience, and self-control. With her collaborators, she has also developed workbook interventions to promote positivity and self-forgiveness.

Raymond J. Lawrence, DMin, is a pastoral clinician and general secretary for the College of Pastoral Supervision and Psychotherapy. He is the author of *The Poisoning of Eros: Sexual Values in Conflict* (1989), *Sexual Liberation: The Scandal of Christendom* (2007), and its German translation, *Sexualitat und Christendum: Geschichte der Irrwege und Ansatze zur Befreiung*. He has published articles in medical and theological journals, including the *Journal of the American Medical Association, The Annals of Behavioral Medicine, The Christian Century, Christianity and Crisis*, and *Journal of Religion and Health*. His opinion pieces on social ethics have appeared in almost every major newspaper in the United States. He is an authority on the infamous Bubble Boy case.

About the Editor and Contributors

Avideh Mayville, MA, is a program associate at HasNa, Inc., a Washington, DC nonprofit engaged in peacebuilding and development programs with groups from Cyprus, Turkey, and Armenia. Her work involves developing and coordinating projects and publications. Avideh received her BA in political economy of development from St. Mary's College of Maryland and obtained her master's in international peace and conflict resolution from The American University's School of International Service (SIS). She has published in the University of Michigan's *Journal of Public Affairs* on governance issues in Pakistan; worked as a research assistant to WWICS-USIP Distinguished Scholar Robin Wright on her book *Rock the Casbah: Rage and Rebellion in the Islamic World*; and presented her work on Pashtunwali as the basis for peacebuilding in Afghanistan and Pakistan at Kennesaw State University's International Conference on Indigenous Conflict Management Strategies in April 2012.

Patricia Nobre da Silva is a graduate of the Catholic University of Sao Paulo, Brazil, and is matriculating for her PhD in social-psychology and religion. She is a published essayist and a medical social worker in the Senior Care Facilities of Sao Paulo. She is the proud mother of two very accomplished children who are following in her professional footsteps.

Isaac W. Oliver earned his PhD in Near Eastern studies at the University of Michigan in 2012. He has studied at the Hebrew University of Jerusalem as well as in France, Argentina, and Austria. He also lived for several years in French Guiana and is a citizen of the United States and Brazil. In the fall of 2012 he was a fellow for the Frankel Institute for Advanced Judaic Studies. In January 2013 he became an assistant professor in religious studies at Bradley University in Illinois. He has written articles for *New Testament Studies*, *The Journal of Ancient Judaism*, and *Henoch*. His forthcoming book, *Torah Praxis after 70 CE: Reading Matthew and Luke-Acts as Jewish Texts*, focuses on the question of Sabbath keeping, kashrut, and circumcision in the gospels of Matthew and Luke as well as the Acts of the Apostles. He is the associate editor of *Reviews of the Enoch Seminar*, a digital book review service of the Enoch Seminar Online.

Steven A. Rogers, PhD, is an associate professor of clinical psychology at Westmont College. He is the co-author of *The Estrogen-Depression Connection*, and he has written over 35 book chapters and professional articles. He has also given over 100 professional presentations. His research focuses on the interaction between spirituality and psychotherapy, the relationship between neuropsychology and religion, and the neuropsychology of aging. In addition, he maintains a private psychotherapy practice in Santa Barbara, CA and serves as the lead neuropsychologist at the Pacific Neuroscience Medical Group in Oxnard, CA.

Daryl R. Van Tongeren, PhD, is an assistant professor of psychology at Hope College. He is a social psychologist who primarily studies the social motivation for meaning and its effects on moral behavior. Specifically, his research interests include meaning, religion, morality, and virtues, such as forgiveness and humility, as well as the function of such virtues in close relationships.

Everett L. Worthington Jr., PhD, is a professor of psychology at Virginia Commonwealth University. He is a counseling psychologist, with additional interests in health psychology, social and personality psychologies, developmental psychology, and positive psychology. His research interests include forgiveness and other virtues, religious and spiritual values, beliefs, and practices, and the hope-focused couple approach to helping couples.